The Fateful Year

The Fateful Year

England 1914

MARK BOSTRIDGE

VIKING

an imprint of

PENGUIN BOOKS

VIKING

Published by the Penguin Group

Penguin Books Ltd, 80 Strand, London WC2R ORL, England
Penguin Group (USA) Inc., 375 Hudson Street, New York, New York 10014, USA
Penguin Group (Canada), 90 Eglinton Avenue East, Suite 700, Toronto, Ontario, Canada M4P 2Y3
(a division of Pearson Penguin Canada Inc.)
Penguin Ireland, 25 St Stephen's Green, Dublin 2, Ireland (a division of Penguin Books Ltd)
Penguin Group (Australia), 707 Collins Street, Melbourne, Victoria 3008, Australia
(a division of Pearson Australia Group Pty Ltd)
Penguin Books India Pvt Ltd, 11 Community Centre, Panchsheel Park, New Delhi – 110 017, India
Penguin Group (NZ), 67 Apollo Drive, Rosedale, Auckland 0632, New Zealand
(a division of Pearson New Zealand Ltd)
Penguin Books (South Africa) (Pty) Ltd, Block D, Rosebank Office Park,
181 Jan Smuts Avenue, Parktown North, Gauteng 2193, South Africa

Penguin Books Ltd, Registered Offices: 80 Strand, London WC2R ORL, England

www.penguin.com

First published 2014
001

Copyright © Mark Bostridge, 2014

Set in in 12/14.75pt Bembo Book MT Std
Typeset by Jouve (UK), Milton Keynes
Printed in Great Britain by Clays Ltd, St Ives plc

A CIP catalogue record for this book is available from the British Library

ISBN: 978-0-670-91921-5

www.greenpenguin.co.uk

For My Mother
and in Memory of My Mother's Mother
N. W. C. (1889–1989)

Contents

We are like a steamship running at full speed,
through a fog, towards an unknown shore.

Leslie Stephen, 'War' (1878)

So true it is – according to my favourite axiom . . .
that the Expected does not Happen.

H. H. Asquith to Venetia Stanley, 25 March 1914

'How's the weather, Jeeves?'
'Exceptionally clement, sir.'
'Anything in the papers?'
'Some slight friction threatening in the
Balkans, sir. Otherwise, nothing.'

P. G. Wodehouse, 'Jeeves in the Springtime' (1921)

List of Illustrations

Text Images

Plates

First Inset

Second Inset

Preface

The photograph (overleaf) captures a moment in what was in many ways a typical August Bank Holiday Monday. The staff of the Curzon Laundry, from Acton, the laundry capital of West London, were on their annual outing, a trip on a steam-powered boat up the Thames to Windsor. The weather, as so often in England, had been difficult to forecast. In many parts of the country over the past couple of weeks, there had been a mixture of heavy showers and high winds. But on the afternoon of this river excursion the sun came out and the skies were as blue and cloudless as they ought to have been.

No doubt there were high spirits among the laundry workers, washers, ironers and delivery men, encouraged by the good weather and the consumption of alcohol. The young women wear their prettiest white summer dresses, with miniature floral bouquets pinned to their waists. Many of the young men sport straw-boaters, once the prerogative of gentlemen, but now ubiquitous across the classes. The taking of this photograph – whether it was on the outward or return trip isn't known, but one guesses that it was probably on the latter – completed their sense of occasion.

Only this was a holiday with a difference. The date was Bank Holiday Monday, 3 August 1914, and it was destined to be a day of final, irrevocable and fateful decision. Even as the camera shutter fell, preserving this carefree scene, the larger issues of peace and war continued to hang in the balance. The imminent threat to Belgium by Germany's army weighed heavily on the nation's consciousness. That afternoon, the British Parliament would move decisively closer to entering a European war to defend Belgian neutrality. Nearly thirty-six hours later, Britain would declare war on Germany. Life for many of the men and women on this river excursion would never be the same again, as the country was overwhelmed by a conflict that was to become the first total war in modern history.

Staff from the Curzon Laundry in Acton, West London, enjoying a Bank Holiday outing, 3 August 1914

It seems only natural for us, a hundred years on, to scrutinize the faces in this group for some trace of foreboding, or presentiment about the tornado of change and destruction that was about to hit them. Yet, even if we were able to discern such thoughts or emotions, we would be unlikely to find any sign of them here. War with Germany, frequently imagined and predicted, had none the less managed to creep up on the British people, catching them unawares. 'It has all come as by the leap of some awful monster out of his lair,' the novelist Henry James wrote on the eve of war, 'he is upon us, he is upon all of us here, before we have had time to turn round.'

That shocking transition from peace to war has always been one of the terrible attractions for anyone writing about the English experience of 1914. Philip Larkin's popular and much anthologized poem 'MCMXIV', with its famous lines 'Never such innocence, / Never before or since', ingeniously dramatizes the way in which the year took an unexpected turn by employing one long sentence without a main verb. Larkin's use of multiple present participles evokes the onward flow of time, but the poet's voice in the final stanza hints at the violent break that is about to occur, unsuspected by the men and women of 1914. (Larkin used Roman numerals for the title of his '1914', rather than Arabic ones, both in order to suggest the inscription on a war memorial and because he felt that the 'emotional impact of 1914 was too great for anything I could possibly write myself'.)

Larkin's poem also mythologizes a vanished English way of life, destroyed by the war, and suggests a world of prelapsarian innocence. In the most obvious sense, of course, England in 1914 was no more or less innocent than any other time or place. Moreover, the first half of the year had seen violent challenges to the established order from three broad areas.

The labour movement's acceptance of class-war doctrines had contributed to a wave of strikes, and there were widespread predictions that the country would soon find itself paralysed by continuous outbreaks of industrial action. Secondly, the publicity-seeking stunts of the suffragettes, demanding 'Votes for Women', had turned increasingly from symbolic gestures of protest to actions which posed serious threats to life as well as property. Finally, the direst portents of all were reserved for the situation in Ireland, where the prospect of a new Home Rule Bill was provoking resistance in Ulster, increasing fears that Ireland would soon be on the brink of a civil war.

A hundred years on, we should easily be able to dispense with a more trivial, but none the less indelible part of the myth of a lost Eden: the image of 1914's magical English summer, which has etched itself on the collective imagination as marking an abrupt end to a golden age. In fact, the weather during the summer of 1914 was by no means as remarkable as it's so often made out to have been. A quick glance at the meteorological records indicates that June was sunny and hot, but also rather wet; July was dull and rather dry with temperatures near normal; and August was fairly cool, and unsettled, at first.

It's not difficult to understand why the generation of 1914, after four years of bloody conflict, might have enshrined that last summer before the war in romantic memory as a perfect idyll. And yet, in another, much less clearly definable way, the myth of a lost Eden does highlight an element of truth. There is indeed something of a poignant lost innocence about the men and women of 1914, if only because they were so imaginatively unprepared for the brutalities of the war that finally broke out on 4 August.

This is not a formal history of England in 1914. Rather, it is an attempt to capture the character, spirit and shape of this momentous year through stories and episodes that illustrate significant events and different aspects of English life at that time. These encompass a wide variety of themes and characters, many of them familiar, others comparatively forgotten, or almost completely unknown. They also differ in tone, ranging from the quirky to the more serious.

Some of these stories have been part of my intellectual baggage for much of my life. At the age of fourteen I wrote a play about the first night, in April 1914, of Shaw's *Pygmalion*, and it's been interesting to return to the subject of this memorable display of theatrical fireworks from the vantage point of several decades on.

I've known about the diary of the Reverend Andrew Clark, with its portrait of an Essex parish in wartime, since edited selections from it were published in the 1980s; and I've found it fascinating, in researching the chapter on Clark's diary, to examine the original volumes for 1914 in the Bodleian Library in Oxford, and to consider in passing another of Clark's preoccupations: his interest in the effects of the war on the expansion of the English language.

Others among the stories told here, such as the popularity of aviation as a spectator and participatory sport in the months leading up to the war, ignited new interests for me; and I hope that readers, who may be familiar with the general outline of the period, will also find something in the plethora of characters and incidents that have a novel appeal to them.

This isn't a book about Britain either, though inevitably there is a degree of overlap between England and other parts of the British Isles (the elision of 'England' with 'Britain', a marked development of the late Victorian era and a product of its obsession with 'Englishness', is unavoidable at times, too). Scotland, Wales and Ireland have their own separate histories. In the case of Scotland, for example, not the least interesting aspect of its experience of 1914 is that the country produced a disproportionately high number of volunteers for Kitchener's New Army in the early phases of the war.

I have given *The Fateful Year* the structure of a three-act drama. The first act covers the period of January to April 1914; the second, the summer of that year, leading to the outbreak of war; while the final section covers the first five months of the conflict, August 1914 to the end of the year. A book that opens with the mysterious murder of a young boy on a London train nears its conclusion with the multiple deaths of children in the German naval attacks on the East Coast in December 1914. The curtain falls on the year as England is raided from the air for the first time by a German biplane, which drops a small bomb in a Kent garden on Christmas Eve.

When I was a child of no more than six or seven, I held a 1914 penny in my hands and wondered for the first time about the year's place in history. Some of the lettering had rubbed away, but the numerals, and the head of the King, George V, were still clearly visible. It seems extraordinary now that in those days, pre-decimalization, one could be brought into everyday contact with such a relic from the relatively distant past.

But my first consciousness of the significance of 1914 began to develop soon afterwards when I learned of its impact on my own family. In the tiny sitting-room where my maternal grandmother lived out the final decades of her long life, up to her death in 1989 in her hundredth year, there hung a photograph of a young man in a First World War private's uniform. He had a 'moustached archaic' face, like the ones described in the Larkin poem. He wore a benign expression: beneath the thick, brush-like moustache a smile played on a pair of full lips, while the eyes were alive with merriment.

Thomas Arthur Rose was not my grandfather – not my mother's father – but my grandmother's first husband, killed in the 1914–18 War. 'Blown to pieces', as my father once told me, a blunt, even brutal phrase, made all the more brutal by the fact that my grandmother was within earshot when he said it.

I remember it dawning on me instantly that 1914 had precipitated some abrupt, violent break in my mother's family, followed by the slower realization that had it not been for the events of 1914, I wouldn't have existed at all.

On the other side of my family, my father's relations, hostilities with Germany had started early. John Joyce, my father's maternal grandfather, was a well-known footballer of the period. Just how well-known I'd never really appreciated until I started to read newspapers for 1914 as part of my research for this book. There he was, time and again, in photographs, and singled out in match reports. Admittedly, he would have been difficult to overlook. John 'Tiny' Joyce was a great hulking bear of a man, over six foot in height and sixteen stone in weight, a forbidding figure on the field. He played in goal for Tottenham Hotspur, and in April 1914 – the month when professional football received its royal seal of approval, with George V's visit to the final of the FA Cup – achieved his finest hour when he became the first goalkeeper in the history of his club to score a goal from the penalty spot. 'Joyce had a joy-day in goal', the *Daily Chronicle* reported with a facile pun. 'His terrific ball punching and his big kicking caused vast amusement in the crowd, and they cheered wildly when he scored from a penalty.'

Towards the end of April 1914, Joyce accompanied the other Spurs players on an educational tour of Switzerland and Germany. During a match at Pforzheim, in south-western Germany, they were met with ugly scenes. The German team made running kicks at the English players. When the German goalkeeper deliberately kicked one of Joyce's team-mates on the way to the dressing-room, Joyce leaned over the stairway to prevent further injury being inflicted, only to be hit by a spectator who brought his umbrella down heavily on Joyce's head, cutting it open. The English players escaped from the field in a shower of stones. 'We went for football, not war,' one of them protested.

It was to my grandmother's experience, however, that my thoughts often turned while writing this book, and of how her quietly contented domestic existence was shattered by the events of 1914. This was especially true when it came to recounting, in the chapter 'Dim Fading Hope', the attempts of Violet, Lady Edward Cecil, to discover the fate of her son George in the weeks following the Battle of

John Joyce, Tottenham Hotspur's goalkeeper, playing in a cup-tie against Leicester Fosse in January 1914

Mons; and her efforts, after his body was found in a mass grave, to notify working-class mothers and wives from his battalion of the final resting place of their loved ones.

My grandmother's husband, Thomas Arthur Rose, a gas-fitter in civilian life, and the father of her three children, one born not long before his death, was twenty-eight when he enlisted in May 1915. In February of the following year he was sent out to France with the Royal Engineers. He was declared missing, presumed killed, on 1 July 1916, the first day of the Battle of the Somme.

A year later – by which time my grandmother had suffered the further loss on the Somme of her younger brother William – her husband's property was sent home to her: his wristwatch (broken) and strap; ring (9 carat); pack of cards; lighter; shaving brush; pipe; pair of shoes; postcards; razor in case; swimming drawers; photo frames; fishing tackle; handkerchiefs.

In a letter to the War Office, which astonished me when I first read it in the National Archives, as much for what it left unsaid as for its tone of controlled deference, my grandmother wrote: 'Dear Sir, could you be so kind as to try and let me know if you have found my husband's body. As you have sent his things to me, I thought perhaps you had. Yours sincerely, Mrs Rose.'

The Fateful Year is dedicated to the memory of my grandmother, and to my mother, who formed part of my grandmother's new life built up after the First World War.

Mark Bostridge

NOTE: £1 in 1914, according to the Bank of England's inflation calculator, was worth £97.71 in today's money (20 shillings in a 1914 pound, 12 pennies in a shilling). For further background information about England in 1914, see p. 359.

Prologue
Welcoming 1914

It may well be that [1914] will prove a very fateful year in the history of our land.

Cosmo Gordon Lang, Archbishop of York, 31 December 1913

In parts of Central London, 1914 was ushered in to the suggestive rhythms of a controversial new dance craze. At the Savoy Hotel, where 2,000 guests had assembled to see in the New Year, the Coldstream Guards sounded a fanfare of trumpets just before midnight. As the last note died away, the Savoy's great ballroom was plunged into darkness. Exactly on the hour, a dazzling beam of light illuminated a dais on which a pair of dancers, representing 1914, 'tangoed gracefully into the festive scene'.

At the Piccadilly Hotel, not far away, 1914 was welcomed more conventionally with flashing lights of many colours and a cracker fight among partygoers involving 10,000 crackers. At the Ritz, an enormous illuminated cracker, in red and green, bearing the inscription '1914', exploded on the stroke of twelve.

Meanwhile, at Hendon Aerodrome in North London, the birth of the New Year was celebrated in an even more dramatic fashion as Reginald Carr, piloting a 50 h.p. Grahame-White biplane, circled over various enclosures to the unrestrained excitement of a vast crowd. The course of the airman was followed by a powerful searchlight attached to his machine as he flew into 1914 before finally descending at 12.15 p.m.

For days afterwards, it was the prevalence of Tango displays and competitions as part of New Year celebrations at various principal London hotels and restaurants, in addition to the Savoy, that attracted most attention in the British press. 'Everybody's crazy about this Tango game/in a Spanish way learning how to sway,' Ethel Levey had sung recently in *Hullo, Tango!*, her hit show at the London

Hippodrome. The sensuous, erotically charged movements of this imported dance – 'passionate and often primitive', according to one commentator – were suddenly all the rage, though to some they seemed derisively at variance with the statelier traditions of the English character and English ballrooms.

In Germany, the Kaiser had already banned his officers from dancing the Tango, while the Vatican was shortly to denounce it as 'an outrageous, indecent, heathen dance, which is an assassination of family and social life'. In England, the views of leading society hostesses were canvassed. The Duchess of Norfolk declared that 'Such dances are not desirable; for the tango in itself and in the comments that it leads to is surely foreign to our English nature and ideals, of which I hope we are still proud.' Lady Layland-Barratt considered the dance altogether too immodest for any girl of refinement. Lady Beatrice Wilkinson was more damning. The Tango was corrupt and immoral, she said, and sad evidence of the moral decay that faced England in 1914.

In other parts of the country, the New Year had been marked noisily and jubilantly, though less controversially, with only bad weather hampering the celebrations. There was ice everywhere and widespread snow, giving parts of West Yorkshire the opportunity to show off its new motorized snow-shifters for the first time. In one New Year's scene worthy of a Thomas Hardy novel, a flock of sixty sheep, at Sandwich in Kent, was drowned in a ditch during a severe snowstorm. In the docklands of the North-West, the deafening roar of ships' sirens and fog horns proclaimed 1914. In Manchester's Albert Square, 10,000 people sang ragtime songs and blew on tooters. In Liverpool's cotton market, fireworks were exploded and employees swung around the exchange hall on a huge rope. Across the country, in private homes, an age-old tradition was observed. On the stroke of midnight, people opened the back door of their houses to let the old year out. For luck, the first person they welcomed through the front door was a dark-haired man, carrying bread, salt and coal to ensure that everyone in the house would have sufficient to eat, enough money and be protected from the cold in the year ahead.

And 1914 appeared to be in need of a more than usual share of good fortune. As the Archbishop of York commented in his New Year's message, 'It may well be that it will prove a very fateful year in the history of our land.' Not only was 'Ireland in all our thoughts', with the imminent possibility of civil war between Ulstermen and Irish nationalists, but the continuing wave of strikes threatened to paralyse the country. There was a stark reminder of this within the Archbishop's own diocese. A strike of Leeds corporation workmen, starting a fortnight before Christmas, had brought out 3,000 men employed in the sanitary, water, gas and electricity departments, and these had soon been joined in strike action by 1,000 tramway men. The strike had still to be resolved. In the meantime, the streets of Leeds at New Year were shrouded in darkness, the cotton mills were running on short time, and, in churches, evensong was being conducted by the light of lanterns.

In opposition to the doomsayers stood those, like another church leader, the Bishop of Rochester, who foresaw 'wonderful possibilities for 1914'. And some sections of the population were indeed able to look to the future with confidence. For the rich, of course, things had rarely appeared so prosperous and buoyant, not least because the national income had risen by one fifth since the beginning of the century. Suffering and deprivation, however, remained a constant feature of the lives of the poor, with as much as 10 per cent of the British population unable to feed themselves adequately to maintain their health. But the advent, since 1909, of a raft of improvements in social welfare, including old-age pensions ranging from five shillings to a shilling a week, and national insurance schemes, offered at least the promise of an easier and more secure future, and in 1914 average real wages, so long the bane of the ordinary worker, would at last catch up with the cost of living, while unemployment fell to just over 2 per cent.

Perhaps inevitably, there were some who saw one natural concomitant of material prosperity as the growth of decadence in society – exemplified in a small way by the moral laxity of innovative dance forms. Others believed that the dark forces of unrest in England 1914 – the striking workers and 'the war of the women' being fought by the suffragettes – presaged the decline of the British Empire

itself. It was primarily to this group that an anonymous correspondent in *The Times* addressed his remarks on the first day of the New
Year. 'Too few eyes nowadays care to see either the fairness or the
greatness of England,' the article began. 'Too many tongues are prat-
tling of England's decadence.' Instead, the writer continued, they
should forget the 'national habit of self-deprecation' and instead
'rejoice in the greatness of England in the past, and rejoice still more
in the conviction that England and the Empire were never greater
than they are today'.

If proof were needed of the unparalleled 'virility' of the British
Empire in 1914, the article concluded, one had only to turn to the
moral fibre displayed by Englishmen during the sinking of the *Titanic*,
twenty months earlier; or still more to the recent example of heroism provided by Scott, Wilson, Bowers and Oates in the final stages
of their ill-fated British Antarctic expedition to the South Pole.

News of the deaths of Captain Scott and his party as they struggled against insuperable odds on their homeward journey, and of the
subsequent discovery of their frozen corpses, had badly shaken England in the early months of 1913. In January 1914 the trustees of the
British Museum in London accepted the loan of the original manuscript of Scott's journals from his widow, with their tale of 'hardihood,
endurance and courage', and placed them on display to enormous
public interest. The museum's Director, Sir Frederic Kenyon, wrote
of the trustees' belief that the journals would 'do much to enforce
the lesson which was often in Captain Scott's mind during the latter
days of his great march, the lesson that men of English race can face
death without flinching for the honour of their nation'.

Plans were afoot at the beginning of 1914 for the commemoration
of two significant anniversaries. The first, falling at the end of the
year, would mark the centenary of the Treaty of Ghent, and a hundred years of peace between the two great branches of the
English-speaking peoples, Britain and the United States. The second
anniversary was still more than a year off, but was already causing a
headache for the British government. The centenary of the Battle of
Waterloo would fall on 18 June 1915, a hundred years since a British
army had drawn blood in Western Europe. Commemorating Water-

loo, it was feared, might offend France, once Britain's traditional enemy but now her cherished entente partner; it would also entail grudging recognition of the decisive part played in Wellington's victory by Blücher's Prussian army. As the Kaiser himself had pointed out, in a public speech a year or so earlier, without Blücher's crushing intervention at Waterloo, Britain would almost certainly have faced defeat on the battlefield.

However, in 1914 Germany no longer posed a serious threat to Britain. That, at any rate, was the widely reported view of the Liberal government's Chancellor of the Exchequer, David Lloyd George. In an interview with the *Daily Chronicle* on 1 January, Lloyd George attacked the extravagance of Britain's new Naval Estimates, and immediately set tongues wagging. Was he allying himself with his party's radical peace wing; attempting to compensate for his own profligate spending as Chancellor; or were more personal motives involved, such as his need to bring in a slimmed-down budget to rescue his reputation from the sleaze of 1912's Marconi Scandal, which had undermined people's faith in his financial judgement?

Whatever the truth of the matter, Lloyd George's reasoning behind the need to reduce defence estimates must certainly have made many newspaper readers sit up and pay attention. 'Our relations with Germany are infinitely more friendly than they have been for years,' the Chancellor told his interviewer. '[Britain and Germany] seem to have realized what ought to have been fairly obvious long ago ... that there is nothing to gain and everything to lose by a quarrel and that they have everything to gain and nothing to lose by reverting to the old policy of friendliness which had been maintained, until recent years, for centuries between Germany and this country.'

Several days after Lloyd George's remarks were spread across the press, the marriage in Berlin of the Honourable John Mitford, younger son of Lord Redesdale, to 'Baby' Marie-Anne von Friedländer-Fuld, only child of the Prussian 'coal king' and one of Germany's richest heiresses, was eagerly seized upon as a notable new Anglo-German alliance, and as further evidence, admittedly on the flimsiest of bases, of a definite thawing of relations between the two countries. A civil marriage on 5 January was followed, two days later, by a religious ceremony and a dazzling reception at which the couple and their society guests danced the Tango. A magnificent Berlin mansion was presented to the couple as a wedding gift by Herr von Friedländer-Fuld, and, shortly afterwards, John Mitford started work in his father-in-law's business.

Ten weeks later, though, the newlyweds separated and Marie-Anne Mitford entered a sanatorium in Baden-Baden to consider her future. 'Incompatibility' was initially offered as the reason for their separation. This was subsequently amended 'to grounds of a more serious character' as rumours began to spread that John Mitford had done something unspeakable in the bedroom.

As an inspiring symbol of Anglo-German relations, it did not, in retrospect, present the most favourable of omens.

ONE

January to April

Murder on the 4.14 from Chalk Farm

The light was fading fast as a train pulled out of Chalk Farm Station at 4.14 on the bitterly cold afternoon of Thursday, 8 January. Visibility had been poor all day as a result of the dense fog still clinging to the atmosphere, distorting shapes and muffling sounds. Earlier in the week, foggy conditions had caused a tragedy on this section of the line, when a platelayer, working on the track, ignored the fog signals and was knocked down by an approaching train, which sliced off his legs and killed him instantly.

The 4.14 train was part of the North London Railway, which ran a shuttle service every quarter of an hour between Chalk Farm and Broad Street. Passing through the wintry grey townscape of Camden Town, Caledonian Road and Highbury, the train reached Mildmay Park at precisely 4.33. Here three passengers stepped from the platform on to the train. One of them, a sixteen-year-old apprentice cabinet-maker named George Tillman, got into a third-class compartment near the engine. He was the sole occupant of the carriage.

A minute or so later, Tillman saw that his bootlace was undone and stooped down to tie it. He immediately noticed 'something white' under the seat opposite. He looked more closely and recognized it as a small bare knee, 'which was rather dirty'. Then he saw a pair of hands resting on the knee.

Stiff with fright, he was for a moment unable to move. At Dalston Junction, however, Tillman climbed out of the carriage and tried to attract the attention of the guard at the other end of the train. But by the time the guard saw him the train was already on its way, and it was only at the next stop, Shoreditch, after officials there had been hurriedly notified of a problem by telephone from Dalston, that action was taken. The guard, Charles Pett, called out to the station porter, Edward Cook, 'There is something under the seat of 3rd class coach 129.' Opening the door of the carriage, Cook found the dead body of

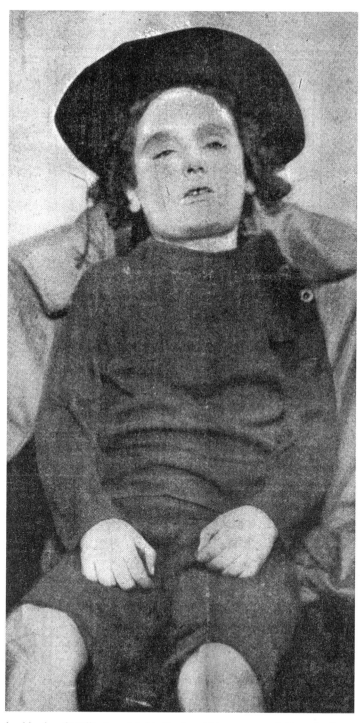

The dead body of Willie Starchfield, displayed like a waxen doll on the front page of the *Daily Sketch*

a young curly-haired boy, dressed in a dark blue jersey, grey knicker-bockers and a soft felt hat, lying in the dust under the seat. 'I then called to the boy, "Come on, sonny!"' Cook recounted later. 'I took the cap from off his face and got hold of him . . . I pulled him from under the seat . . . I took the body out of the carriage. I found nothing loose: no ticket; no bleeding, or vomit; no sign of any struggle.'

The child's name was Willie Starchfield. He was five years old, and his death had been caused by strangulation.

Two murders, one real, one fictional, already held a firm grip on the public's imagination in the early days of 1914. The real-life murder was that of Christina Bradfield, which had taken place a fortnight before Christmas. Soon to become notorious in the annals of crime as 'The Liverpool Sack Murder', it was the kind of English murder that followed along classic lines, sufficiently macabre, but with a none too taxing solution as to the identity of the murderer. Miss Bradfield was a forty-year-old spinster who managed her brother's tarpaulin shop in Old Hall Street, Liverpool. She was an unsympathetic employer with a sharp tongue, and nothing that her 22-year-old clerk George Ball did was ever right in her eyes.

On 10 December 1913, Ball took his frenzied revenge against her. While Bradfield was counting the day's takings, he grabbed her, raped her, and then battered her to death with a blunt instrument before sewing her body into a sack. Enlisting the help of Samuel Ell-toft, a young man of extremely low intelligence who also worked in the shop, Ball wrapped the sack containing the body in a tarpaulin, loaded it into a handcart, and pushed it into the local Leeds and Liv-erpool Canal. Unfortunately for Ball and Elltoft, the sack, despite being weighed down with iron bars, didn't sink, but was discovered the next day, along with its grisly contents, obstructing one of the lock gates.

It was bad luck, too, for the murderer and his accomplice that a ship steward waiting for his girlfriend outside the shop had witnessed the two men wheeling away the handcart with the suspiciously shaped sack. On reading the newspaper reports of the murder, the steward went straight to the police, and a manhunt was launched for the pair. The police quickly arrested Elltoft at home in bed, but it was ten days before Ball was apprehended. To evade arrest Ball had adopted a bizarre disguise: he'd shaved his eyebrows and covered one of his eyes with a pirate's eye-patch.

On 8 January, the day that Willie Starchfield's body was discovered on the North London Railway, the jury at the inquest into Christina Bradfield's death returned a verdict of 'wilful murder' against Ball and Elltoft. The case was sent for trial at the Liverpool Assizes. Elltoft was found guilty as an accessory after the fact and sentenced to four years' penal servitude. Ball was hanged at Walton Prison on 26 February.

Meanwhile, the mock trial of the fictional character of John Jasper, choirmaster and opium addict, for the 'wilful murder' of his nephew Edwin Drood, had been attracting almost as much attention as 'The Liverpool Sack Murder'. Charles Dickens's final novel, *The Mystery of Edwin Drood*, unfinished at his death in 1870, had left unexplained the disappearance of Drood during a violent thunderstorm one Christmas Eve. Was Drood really dead, and, if so, was Jasper the murderer? This was the puzzle that the proceedings at the King's Hall, King Street, in Covent Garden, on the evening of 7 January, aimed at resolving.

The 'trial' was organized by the Dickens Fellowship, and was a charity event in aid of some of the novelist's grandchildren, who had fallen on hard times. The presiding judge was G. K. Chesterton, a champion of Dickens's writing, whose tall, corpulent figure had led some to compare him to Shakespeare's Falstaff. Chesterton's fictional detective Father Brown, the stumpy, nondescript Catholic priest with the large umbrella who solves crime through his intimate knowledge of the human heart, rather than by the kind of close attention to scientific detail championed by Conan Doyle's Sherlock Holmes, was about to make his appearance in a second volume of stories, *The Wisdom of Father Brown*.

The counsel for the defence was Chesterton's brother, Cecil (prosecuting counsel was J. Cuming Walters, an expert on the Dickens novel). The twelve-man jury included W. W. Jacobs, author of the horror story 'The Monkey's Paw', in which a couple's mutilated son returns from the dead, Hilaire Belloc, William Archer, Oscar Browning, with George Bernard Shaw as the foreman. The actor Frederick T. Harry, playing Jasper, listened to the evidence with 'callous indifference', and special applause was reserved for the performance of the publisher Arthur Waugh as the unassuming clergyman Canon Crisparkle.

The evening, which ran from 6.30 to nearly midnight, had excited such intense public interest that it had had to be moved to a larger space at the King's Hall. Even so there was standing room only, with people offering as much as a guinea for a seat on the stairs. Shaw, who objected to second-guessing Dickens, punctuated the proceedings with facetious remarks, much to the irritation of fervent Dickensians in the audience, who denounced Shaw's behaviour as an outrage.

Shortly before midnight, Shaw gave the jury's verdict. He admitted that, in the absence of a body, the jury had initially been inclined to return a verdict of 'Not Guilty'. But the 'more judicious' elements of the panel had felt that to allow a man who had committed 'a cold-blooded murder' of a close relative to leave the dock 'absolutely unpunished' was to run the risk 'of our all being murdered in our beds'. The jury therefore found Jasper guilty of manslaughter. Amid laughter from the audience, Chesterton then committed everyone but himself to prison for contempt of court.

Several nitpickers in the press argued that the case against Jasper was much more clear-cut than the mock trial allowed. Hadn't Dickens confided to his friend and biographer John Forster the plot of *Drood*, in which an uncle murders his nephew, a plot denouement later confirmed by Dickens's son Charles? And hadn't Luke Fildes, who illustrated the magazine instalments of the story, been told by Dickens that he needed a double necktie in one illustration so that Jasper could strangle Edwin Drood with it?

However, unlike the murders of Christina Bradfield and Edwin Drood, the mystery surrounding the death of the strangled boy on the 4.14 train from Chalk Farm permitted no such straightforward solution. Within days of the discovery of the boy's body, detectives were privately admitting they were utterly in the dark as to the circumstances of Willie Starchfield's murder, or any motive for it;

meanwhile, large swathes of the British public had turned amateur sleuth in the hope of solving the crime.

———

Agnes Starchfield, Willie's mother, had last seen her son alive at about 11.15 in the morning on the day of his murder, 8 January. She had given him his breakfast, a large helping of bread pudding with currants and raisins – a staple of the diet of the very poor – which he consumed hungrily, only refusing the crust because his teeth were bad. She then left the house, entrusting the boy to the charge of her landlady, Mrs Longstaff, saying as she went that Willie could run any errands for her.

An attractive child with long, dark brown curly hair, Willie Starchfield was approaching his sixth birthday. He was a delicate boy with a history of ill-health, characteristic of many young children from poorer working-class backgrounds. At age two and a half, Willie attended a charity school in Endell Street, Covent Garden, and had remained there until he was taken into King's College Hospital suffering from pneumonia. Subsequently admitted to two further schools, Willie left the first after contracting scarlet fever, and the second, in the summer of 1913, after being infected with ringworm. In November of that year, he was knocked down by a car, breaking his collar bone, an injury for which he was still receiving treatment at the Temperance Hospital, a hundred yards or so from his home in Hampstead Road. Willie hadn't been back to school since.

Mother and son occupied one room on the first floor at the front of 191 Hampstead Road, a busy, major thoroughfare leading from Camden Town to Euston. The room had been sublet unfurnished to them, the previous October, by Emily Longstaff, a gunsmith's wife. Agnes Starchfield, aged about thirty, was separated from her husband, John, Willie's father, a 35-year-old newspaper vendor whose pitch was near the Oxford Music Hall, on the corner of Tottenham Court Road and Oxford Street. 'She is not a quarrelsome woman,' Emily Longstaff testified later, 'and lives a moral life. She has no man to visit her.'

John Starchfield was at best an erratic provider for his estranged wife and son. Since living apart from them, he was meant to give

Agnes £1 a week, from which she paid her weekly rent of 5s.6d. But he was not always dependable, and that morning Agnes had been out looking for work. She was a plain tailoress by trade. Pay was meagre – and Agnes probably had to fund the hire of her sewing machine from her wages – the working hours long, but at least it was possible to work from home. She could also save on household expenses by making her son's clothes as well as her own.

However, as Agnes trudged the streets of Covent Garden on 8 January, it became clear that there was no available work. She went first to Fortescue's Registry Office in Cleveland Street, and then, with diminishing hope of finding anything, to various paper shops, in Pulteney Street, Fouberts Place, and Berwick and Brewer Streets, where bills advertising tailoring work were usually posted. At about 2 o'clock, after visiting a friend at Bateman's Buildings in Soho Square, Agnes Starchfield passed along Oxford Street to look for her husband, as she had not seen him at his stand that morning. But he wasn't there, and she returned home by bus, arriving at Hampstead Road at 3 p.m.

She called for Willie, but, receiving no reply, went up to her room, where she was met by Mrs Longstaff, who immediately exclaimed, 'I have lost Willie.' 'I thought she was joking,' Agnes remembered, 'but, as she started crying, I realised she was not and suggested going out to look for him. I picked up his overcoat and muffler and we both went out to search.'

At about 12.45, Mrs Longstaff had sent Willie to a newsagent, a little way up the street from where he lived. He was given written instructions to hand to the shopkeeper, asking for an 'Unfurnished Apartment' card. The shopkeeper recalled afterwards that Willie had played with the toys on the counter and knocked one of them down. Willie came back with two cards for Mrs Longstaff to choose from. She kept one and told Willie to take the other back to the shop. When, an hour later, he hadn't returned, Mrs Longstaff went to the shop and learned that Willie had never made a second visit.

The landlady and Agnes Starchfield scoured the neighbourhood in search of the boy, but found no sign of him, nor any news of his whereabouts. At 4.30 that afternoon, they passed the spot in Oxford

Street where John Starchfield sold papers to see if Willie had gone to meet his father. This time Starchfield was there, but there was no sign of his son.

After further inquiries at hospitals and police stations, Agnes Starchfield, by now thoroughly distressed and distracted, returned home. Descriptions of the boy had been circulated throughout the entire Metropolitan Police area, and at 9.30 that evening a police constable called at Hampstead Road and asked Mrs Starchfield to accompany him to Shoreditch Mortuary to see if she could identify the child found on the train from Chalk Farm.

'Her identification of the body was as immediate as it was harrowing,' wrote Chief Inspector Gough of Scotland Yard, who had been put in charge of the murder investigation, 'and it was only by the utmost persuasion that, in a state of pitiable collapse, she consented to return home.'

Gough, in his early fifties with a thick brush moustache, had joined the Metropolitan Constabulary at twenty after a brief period as a junior assistant at the Meteorological Office at Kew. He had risen steadily through the ranks, and was promoted to Chief Inspector at a comparatively early age after successfully bringing Herbert Bennett to trial for the murder of his wife, found strangled on Yarmouth Beach, in one of the more celebrated murder cases from the beginning of the century. Less gloriously, Gough had once attempted to arrest a suffragette presenting a petition at Downing Street, only to find himself at the mercy of her friends, who sprang 'from all sorts of odd corners and doorways where they had been hidden', and began stripping off his clothes. Down to his shirt-sleeves, his face 'one crimson blush', Gough was forced to release his prisoner when they began to unfasten his braces.

In addition to interviewing witnesses from the train and station, and visiting Chalk Farm with Basil Thomson, Assistant Commissioner of Police, Gough went to see John Starchfield, the boy's father, at his lodgings at 12 Hanover Court, in Long Acre, Covent Garden, before bringing him in for questioning at Old Street Police Station.

Common lodging houses, of the type occupied by John Starchfield, offered shelter for the lowest level of society at a cost of anything from 4*d.* to a shilling a night. In 1914 there were around 27,000 common lodging house beds in London, catering to two main types of clientele: the settled boarder, like Starchfield, who had his bed in a shared dormitory or matchboard cubicle, and the temporary lodger, who was just passing through.

Starchfield's cross-examination yielded little definite information. He had felt unwell on the day of the murder and stayed in bed until 3.30 that afternoon, after which he had left his lodgings to visit a coffee shop in nearby Endell Street. From there he had walked to his pitch and sold newspapers outside Tottenham Court Road Underground Station until 6.30 p.m. Of Willie, he merely divulged that his son 'was a bit of a rover and had been lost several times'.

However Starchfield's alibi could not be confirmed by Jules Labarbe, the Frenchman who kept the lodging house. Labarbe had allowed Starchfield to stay in bed on the morning of 8 January – normally the rooms were cleaned and locked and not reopened until 5 p.m. – but he couldn't swear that Starchfield had been on his premises after 12.30 p.m. Labarbe had gone to the pub and had returned not long before 2 o'clock. In a statement hedged about with prevarication, Labarbe was reported as saying: 'When I returned I did not find him in the house . . . There are 28 rooms in the house. I won't swear I looked in his bedroom . . . Starchfield sleeps on the 1st floor in No. 57 bed and it would be impossible to miss seeing him if I had looked in as his bed is just inside the door.'

Within twelve hours of the discovery of Willie Starchfield's body, the possibilities relating to the time and place of his murder were already beginning to expand and multiply. An initial examination by Dr Henry Garnett, the police divisional surgeon, had revealed a number of details about the killing. The scratches and marks about the child's neck indicated that there had been a struggle, while slight haemorrhages in the abdominal region suggested that Willie had been kneeling between a person's knees when he was strangled. In Garnett's view, it was entirely conceivable that a woman had committed the crime. 'The average loose skirt could have been taken up between the knees sufficiently to enable a woman to do it,' though if a female assailant had been wearing a hobble skirt, a current fashion, it would have been much more difficult.

As for the act of strangulation itself, a narrow band, like a blind cord, had been pulled tight, producing a groove in the soft tissue around the neck. There was nothing to suggest that anaesthetic had been used upon the boy, nor were there any signs of sexual assault. An examination of the body, two days after the murder, by Dr Bernard Spilsbury – the forensic pathologist who had become famous at Dr Crippen's trial three years earlier, when he had identified the supposed remains of Belle Elmore, Crippen's wife and victim – would add another telling detail. Willie Starchfield had been suffering from a condition known as *Status lymphaticus*, the enlargement of the thymus and lymph nodes, then believed to cause sudden death in infants and young children. From this discovery it was assumed that it would have taken a slighter shock to kill Willie than it would have a healthy boy.

What had Gough and his detectives really scratching their heads, though, was the information Garnett provided about the time of death. All the medical evidence pointed to this having taken place between 2 and 3 p.m., which accorded with Willie's disappearance shortly before 1, but left a gaping hole in the assumption that he had been killed on the 4.14 train, at one of the stops between Chalk Farm and Mildmay Park.

Had the body been placed on the train after Willie was dead? Or had he been strangled on an earlier service on the Chalk Farm–Broad Street shuttle, the body hidden under the seat and missed by the cleaners, who were supposed to sweep the trains before they set off again after reaching the end of the line? And would it have been possible for the killer to have strangled a child and hidden the body when the time elapsing between stations on the route from Chalk Farm to Broad Street was never more than three minutes?

When Chief Inspector Gough came to write his memoirs at the end of the twenties – a common enough practice among senior police officers eager to augment their retirement income, supplemented in Gough's case by money earned as a private investigator – he looked back on the Starchfield Case, and recalled that John Starchfield had been a kind-hearted man, who was fond of children and animals.

The evidence of witness depositions amassed during the investigation suggests something rather different and more complicated.

To state, as one of the witnesses in the case did, that Agnes Starchfield had led 'a most unhappy life' with her husband was putting it mildly. They had married in 1903, and she had given birth to their first child, John, in June the following year. Starchfield's cruel treatment of her began soon afterwards, and by the time the baby was fifteen months old, his cruelty was so severe that, according to Agnes's later account, 'I took salts of lemon with the idea of destroying my life.' Agnes was charged with attempted suicide, but discharged after being remanded to hospital for a week. The magistrate merely cautioned her husband to treat his wife better in the future.

Starchfield, though, continued his abuse, frequently getting drunk, breaking up their home and using physical violence against his wife. In desperation she sought help from the Society for the Protection of Women and Children, a mid-Victorian foundation. They took up her case, obtained a separation order for her under which Starchfield was instructed to pay Agnes maintenance of 5s. a week. He failed to do so and was sentenced to twenty-one days' imprisonment, boasting afterwards 'that he would rather do 21 days than pay . . . as he did not mind being a prisoner as he was allowed to wear his own clothes'. The next time Starchfield saw his wife, he physically assaulted her.

In February 1906, by which time the Starchfields were living apart, Agnes gave birth to their second child, a boy named Christopher, who survived only two months before dying from 'wasting' disease. At the end of that year, their elder son died from pneumonia after a bout of measles.

The next few years of the Starchfields' marriage followed a depressing cycle. He wrote to her, promising to change and begging her to take him back. They would resume cohabiting, and, after a while, he would start drinking and behaving violently again. This pattern repeated itself on several occasions. By the beginning of 1909, Starchfield, following another prison sentence, had deserted Agnes. She was 'destitute', forced to depend on parish relief, while Willie, her new baby, had bronchitis.

At this point Agnes Starchfield's life became increasingly peripatetic. To give Starchfield the slip – and, one suspects, to escape a mounting backlog of unpaid rent – she moved lodgings frequently: from Bloomsbury to King's Cross and from there to Oxford Street and Covent Garden, and latterly to Camden.

Then the Starchfields got as near as they ever would to a stroke of luck. In September 1912, John Starchfield was drinking at the Horseshoe Hotel in Tottenham Court Road when an Armenian called Stephen Titus ran amok with a revolver, shooting a barmaid dead and injuring three other people, one of whom died several weeks later from his wounds. Starchfield tackled Titus and captured him, receiving a bullet wound in the process, which penetrated his bowel five times. For this undoubted act of heroism Starchfield received an award from the Carnegie Hero Fund, established in 1908 to provide financial assistance to individuals injured in attempting to save another human life. A lump sum of £50 was accompanied by an allowance of £1 a week.

Starchfield, who had served in the South African War with the 4th Battalion King's Royal Rifles (and remained on the Army Reserve), had shown remarkable bravery. But the money from the Fund quickly became a matter of contention between Starchfield and his estranged wife. Agnes threatened to write to the Carnegie Fund to expose him if Starchfield didn't make the payments over to her, to compensate for his shortfall in providing maintenance for his wife and child, and for the ongoing cost of raising young Willie.

Starchfield had little alternative but to transfer the money to his wife if he wanted to avoid another spell in prison. But it remained a heavy source of resentment to him. Agnes told her landlady Emily Longstaff that she believed her husband to have been jealous of Willie. Later, in her testimony to the police, she stated that Starchfield 'had no love' for his son, and that the boy 'loathed going to his father with a message'. It may be that Starchfield was more indifferent to his son than actively unloving. This is certainly borne out by his comments to Chief Inspector Gough about his two older children, now dead. He admitted that he took no interest in 'it', as he referred to his firstborn, John; while he was 'not quite sure' of his second boy's name, hadn't attended his burial, and was unable to say what he'd died from.

A few days after the murder, John Starchfield attempted to call on Agnes at Hampstead Road. Reporters keeping a close eye on the movements of husband and wife noted that he was sent away without being admitted to her lodgings.

James Starchfield, the dead boy's uncle, was the first to suggest that his nephew's killing might not be a conventional English murder. An employee on the Metropolitan Railway at King's Cross, James Starchfield claimed that Willie had been murdered by a group of unidentified Armenians out of revenge for his father's part in Stephen Titus's arrest at the Horseshoe Hotel.

This theory was quickly superseded by one which appeared to stand on firmer foundations. Angelo Portinari, the son of an Italian coffee house keeper in Hampstead Road, who knew Willie Starchfield by sight, told police that he'd seen him at 1.10 on the afternoon of 8 January, within half an hour of his disappearance, in the company of an older boy who wore a dark suit and peaked cap. This youth, 'a big boy' according to Portinari, had barked 'come along' to the child, before dragging him off by the hand.

This appeared to be the lead detectives had been hoping for, but on closer examination it completely evaporated. Twenty-four hours later, following further cross-examination, Portinari withdrew his statement. He was no longer certain he'd seen Willie on the day of the murder, and thought on reflection that he'd probably come across him on the day before his disappearance. But already a large number of newspaper column inches were being devoted to the embellishment of a new solution to the crime: Willie's murder could have been the act of a mentally defective boy, who had got the idea of committing a horrific killing by reading a penny dreadful, or through attending 'a pictorial representation' of a similar crime at that relatively new emporium of dangerous pleasure, the cinema. Or perhaps the older boy had merely been 'pretending' to strangle Willie in the empty carriage, and had accidentally killed him.

With newspapers proclaiming the Starchfield Murder 'one of the greatest mysteries of these days', Gough and his detectives returned to Chalk Farm Station to try to solve a particularly puzzling aspect of the case. If Willie hadn't been killed on the train – and ticket office receipts from the station for 8 January showed that no child's ticket had been issued for the 4.14, nor for the service three minutes later from Camden Town – could he have been killed elsewhere, the station lavatory for instance, and the dead body carried on to the train in a sack? An experiment carried out, of a man carrying a live boy in a sack through the station barrier and on to a train, showed that nothing was simpler. However, the discovery, days before, of a possible murder 'weapon' – a yard-length of cord tied in a bow, picked up on the railway track near Broad Street at the other end of the shuttle run – once more highlighted the possibility that the boy had been killed on an earlier train and his body overlooked.

'The police find themselves brought up against a dead wall of seemingly impenetrable negatives,' the *Daily Mail* reported six days into the investigation, adding that 'one might almost as well . . . seek to trace the fate of some particular snowflake in a week-old snowstorm.' Fifty officers had now been assigned to the case, and over 1,000 people questioned, but Chief Inspector Gough was reportedly at the end of his tether, with no answer in sight. The police contacted Sherlock Holmes's creator, Sir Arthur Conan Doyle, to see if he would be able to throw any light on the case, but he was working on his final long Holmes story, *The Valley of Fear*, and declined to be involved.

Newspaper offices were being flooded, meanwhile, with letters from armchair detectives offering help. One, influenced by a familiar plot device from the world of Jules Verne's science fiction, wondered whether the murdered boy's retina had been photographed to discover if the last object he'd seen had been retained there. Another inquiry, of a more orthodox scientific nature, asked if the microscopic examination of Willie's jersey had revealed evidence of other human hairs or particles.

Exploiting the Metropolitan Police's close relationship with sections of the mass press, Gough arranged for an edition of the tabloid *Daily Sketch* to carry a front-page photograph of the dead boy's body.

This showed him fully clothed and resembling a little waxen doll, his lips parted in a disturbing grimace, and was accompanied by the offer of a £500 reward for information leading to the conviction of his murderer. The photo produced an outcry among some of the paper's readers, who wrote in to protest at the *Sketch*'s 'ghastly' lapse in judgement and good taste.

Unable to ignore the fact that the police were being criticized for marking time, Gough also resorted to enlisting the powers of the paranormal. In a strange episode, reported by the *Sketch*, the cord found on the railway line was given to Madame Roma, a clairvoyant of Regent Street. Sitting at a small table and gazing into her black Indian mirror while fingering the cord, Madame Roma offered insights of dazzling perspicacity: 'I feel this has been in a train. There is something dreadful about it.' Pausing to place her hands on her temples, she continued, 'I get the distinct influence of a foreigner . . . You can only get this kind of cord in the north of England or abroad.'

It wasn't much to go on, but the mere suggestion of a foreign identity for the killer had an instantaneous effect, as if a touch paper had been lit across London. Dozens of witnesses suddenly stepped forward claiming to have seen suspicious-looking foreign men speaking broken English to children on the day of Willie's disappearance. This time it wasn't just Armenians being incriminated, but any number of nationalities: Greek, Dutch, French and Italian – and, in a proportion of two to one over all the others, German. Suddenly the two-mile radius surrounding Willie Starchfield's home in Hampstead Road seemed to have been transformed into one of the most cosmopolitan areas of the capital.

The inquest into Willie Starchfield's death opened at Shoreditch on 15 January, and was suspended for a day at the beginning of the following week so that Willie's funeral, attended by a crowd of up to 4,000 people, could take place at Kensal Green. Dr Wynn Westcott, co-founder of the Hermetic Order of the Golden Dawn, whose authority had been compromised in the past by his association with Freemasonry and ceremonial magic, was the presiding coroner.

Agnes Starchfield walked through an immense crowd to the court-room, with her husband following directly behind her. Dressed in black and wearing a black hat with black feathers, she was shrouded from public view by two police officers who held large umbrellas in front of her face. The evidence that she and others present were about to hear, concerning the curly-haired boy who went on an errand never to return, would have more in common with a scene 'from one of the old Lyceum dramas', Chief Inspector Gough wrote later, 'than an actual occurrence in real life'.

One of the first witnesses to be called was a Mrs Clara Wood, of Kentish Town. At 1.15 p.m., on 8 January, she was shopping in Kentish Town Road when, by the corner of Angler's Lane, she noticed a thickset man with dark hair and a heavy, dark moustache, walking hand in hand with a curly-haired boy of about five. What particularly attracted her attention was that the boy was eating a piece of cake. 'As I am rather fond of children,' Mrs Wood told the court, 'I said as I passed him: "Oh bless it", meaning I was pleased to see the little boy enjoying his food so much.'

From photographs published in *Lloyd's Weekly Newspaper* on 11 January, Mrs Wood had recognized Willie Starchfield as the boy she'd seen. On reading that Bernard Spilsbury's analysis of the contents of the dead boy's stomach included the remnants of cake, Mrs Wood had decided to turn detective. She had purchased a coconut cake in a shop near where she had seen the man and child, as this was 'the size, colour and shape of the cake I saw in the little boy's hand'. She took it to Scotland Yard, where it was examined by Spilsbury, who confirmed it was similar in composition to the cake found in Willie's stomach. It seemed a startling corroboration of Clara Wood's testimony.

The court didn't have to wait long for an even more sensational development. Asked by the foreman of the jury if she had seen the man with the child since, Mrs Wood responded by pointing across the courtroom to John Starchfield with the words, 'Yes. There.'

Starchfield leaped to his feet, crying, 'Me, lady?'

Unshaken, Mrs Wood continued, 'I am sorry, but it is you . . . Yes it is you.' Turning to the jury she was more resolute: 'It is the man I saw that day. I saw him outside [the court]. I have seen him now and I saw him that day. Immediately I saw him I knew him.'

'It's a lie!' Starchfield shouted in a voice that resounded throughout the entire room.

Electrified, every head in the courtroom turned to study Willie Starchfield's father. He had a rather Italianate appearance, with dark complexion and eyes, and a dark, overhanging moustache.

The tension in the Coroner's Court increased when the next witness took the stand. John Morcher was an engine driver, working at Camden Coal Yard, which adjoined Chalk Farm Station. Between 2.30 and 3 p.m. on the afternoon of the murder, he had seen a man in the fourth compartment of the second third-class carriage – where Willie's body had been found – stooping over a seat as if he were trying to tie up a parcel. 'I did not see his face, but I judged from his broad shoulders that he was a powerfully built man.'

The testimony of George Jackson, a signalman at St Pancras, appeared at first to confirm Morcher's evidence. From his box between Maiden Lane and Camden Town stations, he too had seen a man bending over a little boy, whom he recognized as Willie Starchfield, in the third-class compartment of a train from Chalk Farm. However, under cross-examination Jackson qualified his statement with the comment that at the time he had thought that the stooping person might have been a woman.

Under questioning, Jules Labarbe, keeper of John Starchfield's lodgings in Long Acre, withdrew his earlier statement that Starchfield might not have been in the house after 12.30 on the afternoon of the murder. Now he admitted the strong possibility of having missed Starchfield's bedroom during his tour of inspection. This, together with Jackson's evidence, was a point in Starchfield's favour. But the strength of Clara Wood's testimony led the jury to bring in a verdict of 'Wilful Murder' against John Starchfield.

Willie Starchfield's father was arrested for his son's murder and remanded in custody pending trial. 'You no [*sic*] it is hard on me being in here all this time for nothing,' Starchfield told his brother in a letter written from his cell in Brixton Prison after his confinement

there for two months, 'as you no I am Innocent of this and you no I
should never have a heart to do a thing like that . . .'

There was evidently a growing and, to some, lamentable practice of
'fashionable' women attending murder trials to watch a man in the
dock fighting for his life, wrote the *Daily Sketch*'s reporter on 1 April,
the day after the Starchfield trial opened at the Old Bailey. The queue
for a place in the courtroom, which stretched around the block, had
included a number of expensively attired ladies wearing heavy veils
to hide their faces, though whether these were worn from a sense of
shame, or simply a desire to remain incognito, only the women in
question could tell.

It was almost exactly half a century since England's first train murder had taken place, also on the North London Railway, a coincidence
that newspapers were quick to pick up. In July 1864 the body of a
man, Thomas Briggs, had been discovered on a stretch of the line
between Hackney Wick and Bow stations, his feet lying towards
London, his head in the direction of Hackney. He had been bludg-
eoned to death in a train carriage and thrown on to the line. The
main clue to his assailant, a young German tailor called Franz Müller,
who was eventually hanged for the murder, was Mr Briggs's hat,
which his killer had mistakenly taken from the carriage, leaving his
own behind. Questions surrounding John Starchfield's headgear,
which was to form a major plank in his defence, would be another
coincidence tying the 1914 train murder to its Victorian predecessor.

Archibald Bodkin appeared for the Crown and Henry Margetts for
Starchfield. Mr Justice Atkin was the presiding judge. Much of the
ground covered at the Coroner's Court was retrodden. Clara Wood
repeated her testimony almost verbatim, with only the additional
detail that at the time she saw him Starchfield had been wearing a soft
felt cap which came down about his eyebrows. Richard White, a commercial traveller, was a witness who had come forward only latterly
after reading of the case in reports of the inquest. He, too, positively
identified John Starchfield as the man he had seen, with a slightly built
young boy, in the booking office at Camden Town Station, just before
the 2.02 train left for Broad Street. Only, in White's recollection,

Starchfield had been wearing a dark trilby hat and dark overcoat. Another witness, admittedly a blatantly unreliable one, who had been regaling his drinking mates in pubs around North London with variations on his story, maintained that he had met Starchfield outside Camden Town Underground Station on the day of the murder. He knew Starchfield well by sight, having partnered him at dominoes, though until that chance meeting they hadn't seen each other for about four years. He had nodded at Starchfield, who returned the greeting by twitching his cap, as if uneasy at the greeting.

Other witnesses described the man they identified as Starchfield as wearing a bowler on that day. But serious doubt about the circumstantial nature of the evidence against the prisoner in the dock only arose with the defence counsel's first real counter-attack: a man who swore that shortly before 1 o'clock on 8 January he had seen a woman with a small boy near the Princess Beatrice pub in Camden Town, only minutes from Willie's home in Hampstead Road. The woman had pulled the boy roughly towards her, hurrying him forwards. This witness went on to say that, although he had not seen the woman since the day of the murder, he had noticed her a dozen times in the neighbourhood before that, and would have no trouble recognizing her again. To a large extent, this evidence was confirmed by the conductor and driver of a bus passing Mornington Crescent Underground Station at lunchtime on 8 January, who both swore that they had picked up a woman and a boy, whom they identified as the murdered child.

Amid a buzz of excitement around the court, Judge Atkin asked the prosecuting counsel, 'Can the case possibly go on?', in a voice so quiet that people stood up in their places in order to hear more clearly what was being said. In the dock, John Starchfield leaned forward eagerly, straining to catch every word.

'I feel that under the circumstances, Mr Bodkin,' the judge continued, 'you will be exercising the proper discretion if . . . you say that the prosecution shall not continue.' Then, turning to the jury, Mr Atkin summarized the doubts regarding the identification of the killer before instructing them to return a formal verdict of 'Not Guilty'.

Outside the Old Bailey, John Starchfield was literally chased along the street by crowds of well-wishers before being forced to take shelter in a shop doorway. Here he was kept prisoner by the crush for several minutes until he was bundled into a passing taxi to repeated cheers and shouts of 'Good old Jack!' In a short period Starchfield had gone from being a Carnegie hero to the villain of a sensational murder trial. Now he was a hero once more. But the circumstances of his son's death, and the identity of his killer, remained as much a mystery as ever.

Nearly three months later, in the early hours of a Sunday morning in the third week of June, Police Constable Mundy was on his Camden beat when he came across a pathetic spectacle on the corner of Albert Road. Agnes Starchfield, wearing a thin nightdress, with a coat thrown over it, was sitting in the street, crying bitterly and threatening suicide with the words, 'I want to go to the angels.'

She was taken to the police station, where a bottle of hydrochloric acid was found in her possession. A suicide note was also discovered among her belongings. 'Everyone is against me because I am married to him,' it read. 'It is impossible to live without my baby . . . He has left me to bear my trouble and sorrow and alone. Don't let him [presumably 'him' was Starchfield] follow me.' Later, after being charged with threatening suicide, Agnes was released into the care of her brother. At this point she disappears from the historical record.

The murder of Willie Starchfield, which had briefly enthralled the British public in the early months of 1914, was quickly forgotten. The police file on the case stayed open until the beginning of the 1920s. Officially the murder remained unsolved. Was the culprit a mysterious man of German, or some other foreign extraction, who might have persuaded Willie to go along with him on the promise of a slice of cake? Was the murderer the unidentified woman seen roughly pulling a young boy resembling Willie through the streets of Camden Town? Or was John Starchfield really his son's killer after all? This was what Chief Inspector Gough privately believed. Gough's theory was that Starchfield had only intended to abduct the little boy, in order to distress his wife. Having met Willie and bought him a cake, he had boarded the train with him at about two o'clock. There had been an argument, and Starchfield had struck the boy. Alarmed at his cries, he had put a piece of the cord he used to tie up his newspapers around his son's throat in an attempt to quieten him.

Following his acquittal, the issue of compensation for John Starchfield was raised in Parliament, but the Home Secretary, Reginald McKenna, ruled that his case did not come into the category of miscarriage of justice, and that no payment therefore was to be made from public funds. For a brief period, Starchfield capitalized on the public's interest in him by earning his living as a film actor. In the provocatively titled *Was It He?*, a short feature released in September 1914, Starchfield played a variation on himself, a news vendor who is wounded while stopping a killer, becomes a gardener and saves his employer's child from kidnappers. Starchfield lived for just two years after the trial, dying at St Pancras Infirmary in April 1916, as a delayed result of his old bullet wound.

Not long after his death, a bottle was found floating in the Thames off Northfleet. Inside the bottle was a piece of paper with these words written in pencil: 'I J. S. hereby confess that I murdered my son William in 1914. God forgive me.' The handwriting was never positively identified as Starchfield's, but the message added one last tantalizing detail to the question of the identity of Willie Starchfield's murderer.

A Prime Minister in Love

She was twenty-six years old, a close friend and confidante of one of his daughters. He was sixty-one, nearly old enough to be her grandfather. The time they spent together was 'divine' and 'delicious'. He regarded her as 'a life-giver' and longed to see her more often, consoling himself with thoughts of their regular Friday afternoon drives out to Richmond or Hampstead, when they would hold hands under the travel rug, and he would surreptitiously snatch a kiss, as they sat in the back of his chauffeur-driven Napier.

He longed for the touch of her hand when they were apart, and, as his feelings for her grew more obsessive, admitted that he suffered depression at the thought of 'absence & separation' from her. He deliberately held himself in check, though, whenever they were together, 'more, I dare say, than you suspect'.

One vital outlet for his feelings was the letters he wrote to her. He had started by writing two or three times a week, as a form of relaxation and recreation from the cares of state. However, in the course of 1914, he began to write every day, sometimes several times a day. The postal system aided the intensifying of this epistolary relationship. If he posted a letter in Whitehall at 6 p.m., it could be delivered to her, if she was in London, that same evening. If she was staying at either of her parents' homes, at the family seat in Cheshire, or near Holyhead on the Anglesey coast, the letter would be with her first thing the next morning.

Initially his letters were filled with gossip about mutual friends or acquaintances, or recommendations of books she might read. But before long he had taken her into his confidence about current politics and the progress of his own political intrigues. She responded intelligently and sympathetically. As a mark of his love, he assured her that there was nothing he would not tell her, so 'great & deep' was his trust. Writing to her provided him with solace at times when

H. H. Asquith and Venetia Stanley, with one of Venetia's pet penguins, at Penrhos, Whitsun 1914

pressure from his work was at its most extreme. It made him feel 'happier and more hopeful', though occasionally he expressed slight concern that she might be careless and leave his letters lying around for others to read, or misplace them in an envelope addressed to someone else.

She was his 'darling'. He wrote constantly of his feelings for her, but somehow she would remain always out of reach, dearer to him than words could ever tell.

———

Herbert Henry Asquith – Herbert to his intimates, Henry to his wife Margot – was Britain's most successful peacetime prime minister. By 1914 he had won three successive general election victories, spearheading the Liberal government's programme of progressive social reform and introducing significant curbs on the constitutional powers of the House of Lords. Yet, at the height of his power, he was also lonely and disillusioned. In 1912 the negotiations to end a national coal strike had left him emotionally and physically drained. At the same time, Asquith's home life provided a quite different kind of friction. Margot Asquith, the curl of her upper lip, the result of an early hunting accident, giving an impression of haughty disdain, was critical and highly demanding. Nervous and depressive illness, as well as painful pregnancies and the deaths of three children at birth, had exacerbated these character traits. She had a habit of antagonizing Asquith's colleagues with her flamboyant, outspoken style, and was locked into fraught relationships with her husband's children by his first marriage, especially with his daughter Violet, who vied jealously with Margot for Asquith's attention. As Cynthia Asquith, Asquith's daughter-in-law, once remarked, 'Margot came away from a visit, leaving a wake of weeping, injured people.'

Venetia Stanley, the young woman who was the recipient of the prime minister's love letters, had pulled Asquith back from the brink of despair. Other British prime ministers have had their mistresses and lovers, of course. But no other prime minister has left such a revealing record of himself, his government and his leadership at a defining point in his country's history; at a time, moreover, when formal minutes of cabinet meetings had still to be introduced.

Asquith had been aware of Venetia Stanley for much of her life, as a childhood friend of Violet. She was the youngest child of Lord and Lady Stanley of Alderley and of Sheffield, a family of impeccable Liberal credentials (Bertrand Russell was numbered among her cousins). Venetia's upbringing and education had emphasized free-thinking and voracious reading in her father's library. She was irreverent with a strong intelligence, fond of practical jokes, and maintained a menagerie of animals at Alderley Park: a monkey, dogs, a fox, a penguin and, for a brief time, a bear. No one described her as beautiful, but she was undoubtedly attractive and striking, with 'dark-eyed aquiline good looks', and exuded a rather forbidding quality to her young male contemporaries. One of them, Lawrence Jones, later recalled Venetia's tomboyishness. She permitted herself, he wrote, 'in the morning of her youth, no recourse to her femininity. She carried the Anthologies in her head, but rode like an Amazon, and walked the high garden walls of Alderley with the casual strides of a boy. She was a splendid, virginal, comradely creature, reserving herself for we knew not what use of her fine brain and hidden heart.' Other contemporaries later remembered that when it came to politics, talking to Venetia was like talking to a man.

In 1907, when Venetia was just twenty, Margot Asquith observed that she had become part of her husband's 'little harem', the small group of young women whose company Asquith, then Chancellor of the Exchequer, sought for flirtation and recreation. However, it was only in January 1912, when Venetia accompanied Asquith, his daughter Violet and Edwin Montagu, the Prime Minister's former parliamentary private secretary, now the Undersecretary of State for India, on holiday to Sicily, that Asquith began to see Venetia in a different light. It was the first stage of their intimacy, 'one of the most interesting and delightful fortnights in all our lives'.

At Downing Street, after seeing Asquith off, Margot wept, jealous of those who had gone with him and realizing, perhaps for the first time, the seriousness of his infatuation with Venetia, whom she had dubbed 'Violet's squaw'. A few weeks after their return, Venetia was the Prime Minister's guest at a weekend house party on the edge of the New Forest, near Lymington. Here, Asquith told her later, the scales had dropped from his eyes. In an instant, 'the familiar features and smile and gestures and words assumed an absolutely new perspective', and he recognized that he had reached a turning-point in his life.

Asquith and Venetia met in London, or on her parents' estates at Alderley or Penrhos. She stayed, too, at The Wharf at Sutton Courtenay, on the Thames near Oxford, the Asquith family's country home. Venetia's letters to Asquith, with one exception, appear not to have survived. One imagines that, like much of the rest of her correspondence, these letters were terse and matter of fact. Asquith's letters, on the other hand, were generally expansive, designed to keep Venetia amused – they shared nicknames for members of the government and opposition, among them 'Bonar Lisa' for the leader of the Conservatives, Andrew Bonar Law – and to feed her appetite for current affairs. Asquith was donnish (and habitually scruffy) in appearance and inclined to be so in his behaviour. Possessing what he called the 'effortless superiority' of the Balliol man, he took a supercilious delight in supervising Venetia's reading, or quizzing her general knowledge (to his disappointment she could only name two of the twelve apostles, but then Venetia was scornful of all religion).

He needed her support, and increasingly he respected her opinion. As Asquith's dependence on Venetia grew, his alcohol consumption seemed to lessen. Known as 'the aged squiff' by some Conservative members, accused by others of being fuddled three or four evenings a week, Asquith and his drinking had become something of a talking point in Parliament, especially after he slumped on the Treasury bench, apparently tipsy, during the committee stage of the Parliament Bill in 1911. Now there was a new sobriety about him, accompanied by a renewed determination and commitment in his attitude to government.

Were Asquith and Venetia lovers? This is a question that has tantalized biographers and historians ever since Asquith's letters to Venetia were first published in the early 1980s. Did the passionate declarations and tender endearments of the letters translate to sexual consummation in the flesh? Or were the love and passion committed to paper merely an inviting, transitory romantic escape from the political problems of the moment?

Certainly contemporaries were well aware that Asquith was partial to a pretty girl. Winston Churchill's wife Clementine, a cousin of Venetia Stanley, disliked Asquith's predilection for peering down 'Pennsylvania Avenue' (an expression for a woman's cleavage) whenever he was seated next to an attractive young woman. In February 1914 the composer and suffragette Ethel Smyth expressed her disgust to the Archbishop of Canterbury, Randall Davidson, at Asquith's opposition to women's suffrage by commenting that it was disgraceful 'that millions of women shall be trampled underfoot because of the "convictions" of an old man who notoriously can't be left alone in a room with a young girl after dinner'. (Seven years later, Aldous Huxley would outrage Asquith's adherents when his novel *Crome Yellow* portrayed the former Prime Minister as 'an old man, feebly toddling across the lawn after any pretty girl'.)

On balance, though, the likeliest scenario appears to be that the physical relationship between Asquith and Venetia Stanley went no further than sexual foreplay. Venetia herself appears to have given different versions of the seriousness of the relationship to different people at different times, though perhaps due weight should be given to one unidentified source who maintained that Venetia, while flattered by the Prime Minister's attentions, was also repelled by the advances of a man more than three decades her senior. What cannot be in doubt is that Venetia offered Asquith important emotional comfort at a crucial stage in his premiership.

But there was a further complicating factor. Venetia Stanley was playing a double game. At the same time that she was being pursued by Asquith, she was also the main object of affection of another member of his inner circle, Edwin Montagu, their companion on that memorable trip to Sicily. At the beginning of August 1912 Montagu had proposed marriage to Venetia. She had turned him down, but continued to give him hope that she might change her mind. In September 1913 he tried again and received another rejection. Even this failed to dampen his ardent pursuit of her and he remained undeterred. 'Oh how I pant for you,' he wrote to Venetia as she continued to vacillate about her future. Her refusal to accept Montagu was in large part due to her reluctance to have a sexual relationship with him. Eight years her senior, Montagu was physically unprepossessing, with a pockmarked complexion and thick black moustache, his fearsome appearance somewhat accentuated by the large gleaming monocle he wore in one eye.

The realization that he had a serious rival for Venetia's affections only slowly dawned on Asquith. He reacted in his letters to Venetia by emphasizing Montagu's gloomy personality and brooding ugliness, as if this was a tactic that might succeed in putting her off him. Then, much more questionably, he began to make unpleasant and increasingly distasteful gibes against Montagu's Jewish origins. Asquith referred to Montagu as 'the Assyrian', an allusion to Byron's poem in which 'the wolf' is described as coming down 'on the fold', or as 'Mr Wu'. When Montagu bought a new house in Westminster's Queen Anne's Gate, Asquith sent Venetia some lines of verse portraying her as 'a Christian child' frequenting 'The silken tents of Shem'. The intent behind the thinly veiled anti-Semitism of these remarks was clear. Venetia was to understand that Edwin Montagu was a man set apart by his religion, an alien who could not possibly be considered a true Englishman (the irony was that Montagu possessed no strong religious beliefs and had been penalized financially by his father, a millionaire banker, for failing to keep Orthodox observance).

Asquith's growing jealousy, however, did not stand in the way of the advancement of Montagu's career. In February 1914 Montagu was promoted to the post of Financial Secretary to the Treasury. But Asquith couldn't resist making yet another anti-Semitic dig to Venetia, writing that 'every sum in Treasury arithmetic is irradiated in his eyes.'

By early 1914 the love triangle between Asquith, Venetia Stanley and Edwin Montagu was set firmly in place. Margot Asquith, only dimly able to perceive the triangle from the outside, was beginning to be acutely distressed by her husband's relationship with Venetia. She was too devoted to Asquith 'to show him how ill and miserable it makes me', but she poured out her heart to Montagu, unaware that he still had hopes of marrying Venetia, a woman Margot contemptuously dismissed as lacking in refinement or imagination. Margot suspected her step-family, especially her horse-faced stepdaughter Violet, of delighting in her discomfort and of laughing at her behind her back. One Friday evening she suffered '*tortures*', struggling to eat her dinner in bed, while knowing 'in my bones [that] Henry was with Venetia'.

If only Venetia would marry, Margot complained in a letter to Montagu. She loathed girls who couldn't love 'but claim and collect alike a cuckoo for their own vanity'. Venetia's head, she wrote damningly, 'is completely turned'.

According to one piece of oral testimony, handed down to later generations, Margot once came across Venetia while the young woman was staying at The Wharf, and told her with characteristic abrasiveness that 'It's a great bore having you here all the time, darling, but don't tell anyone I said so.' But, beneath her jealousy, even Margot must have recognized what Venetia meant to Asquith: she was someone with whom he could talk easily about matters of state. And nothing would more clearly demonstrate Asquith's growing need for Venetia Stanley than the crisis over the great issue of the day, Irish Home Rule. This was to overwhelm and destabilize the government in the first months of 1914, leaving the Prime Minister himself badly shaken.

In 1912 the Liberal government led by Asquith, partly dependent for its survival in the House of Commons on votes from Irish Nationalist members, had committed itself in principle to Home Rule for Ireland. This was seen as a unique opportunity to settle the question that had hung for decades like a millstone around the Liberal Party's neck, with the Conservative peers unable to vote the legislation down thanks to the Parliament Act of 1911, which had curtailed the powers of the Lords.

In the summer of 1914 the Home Rule Bill was due to become law after its third reading in the Commons. But Asquith had made a fateful miscalculation. Together with other members of his cabinet, he had underestimated the opposition that Home Rule, through the creation of a Dublin Parliament, would face from Protestant-dominated Ulster. Socially, economically and culturally, the north-east province saw itself as wholly distinct from the rest of Ireland. Under Sir Edward Carson, leader of the Irish Unionist MPs at Westminster, the Ulster Unionists had shown themselves prepared to resort, if necessary, to armed revolt.

Carson, once the scourge of Oscar Wilde in the Queensberry trial, was a bluff, melodramatic figure. In a brilliant propaganda coup at Belfast Town Hall in the autumn of 1912, he had been the first signatory of 'Ulster's Solemn League and Covenant', pledging himself to resist Home Rule. The tide of support for this pledge led, later that year, to the formation of the Ulster Volunteers, and subsequently to its establishment as the armed Ulster Volunteer Force. At the end of January 1914 it had a membership of 80,000, while, just a few months later, the

UVF's cache of arms of all descriptions, including modern rifles, amounted to almost 25,000. In response, the Nationalists had begun to raise their own private army. Only 10,000 had been enrolled in the Irish National Volunteers by the end of 1913, but by the spring of 1914 their strength equalled that of the UVF.

Realistically, Carson knew that his chances of wrecking the government's Home Rule plans were slight. Gradually it would become apparent to his opponents that Carson had forsaken his broader aim to concentrate on achieving the best possible settlement he could for Ulster. At Westminster, Carson had the resolute backing of the Conservative Party, which saw the defence of the 1801 Act of Union – which had integrated Ireland within the United Kingdom – as a sacrosanct part of its political creed, and which regarded any assault on the integrity of the Union as a challenge to the British Empire itself (the Union was so central to the identity of the Conservatives that, in 1886, they had incorporated the term 'Unionist' into the party's title). Bonar Law, the Conservatives' uncharismatic leader, himself of Ulster Protestant descent, had already publicly declared that he could imagine 'no length of resistance to which Ulster will go, which I shall not be ready to support'.

Yet, in spite of Ireland's atmosphere of menace and extremism, and the mounting threat of civil war, Asquith continued to believe that a workable parliamentary solution could be found. Remaining calm and unfazed, he adopted his customary approach of 'Wait and See'.

At first he procrastinated over a plan for 'Home Rule within Home Rule', whereby Ulster would be given special powers of veto in the Dublin Parliament. Recognizing, by the winter of 1913–14, that this would never come close to satisfying Carson and the Unionists, Asquith inched nearer to the compromise solution of excluding Ulster from the Home Rule settlement for a limited number of years.

But still the government appeared to drift. Playing for time, Asquith embarked on a sequence of private conversations with Bonar Law, with Carson, and with John Redmond, the leader of the Nationalists in the Commons, whose cooperation, if Ulster was to be excluded from the Home Rule settlement for any period, was vital.

In order to foil reporters, Asquith's meeting with Carson took place at Edwin Montagu's house. Venetia would 'have been amazed at the frankness' expressed 'on both sides', Asquith told her, if she 'had been ensconced behind one of the silken curtains', and he wrote that he hoped to give her details of the conversation in person before dinner the following day.

One piece of gossip he had been prepared to divulge in writing was that Carson, a recent widower, had fallen 'desperately' in love with Ruby Frewen, a young woman thirty years his junior. She was moved by Carson's speeches and by his 'noble & commanding demeanour . . . but apparently she is prepared to yield her homage but not her heart – not to speak of her hand.' It would be curious, Asquith wrote, to see 'what effect, if any, this little tragic-comedy' had upon political events. Reading this, Venetia may well have found herself wondering at its parallels with her own situation.

Contention surrounding another area of policy had briefly distracted Asquith's cabinet colleagues from the Ulster crisis in the first weeks of the New Year. The Naval Estimates produced by the 39-year-old First Lord of the Admiralty, Winston Churchill, had provoked widespread dissension in both the government and the Liberal Party, as well as controversy in the national press, and had resulted in predictions that Churchill would be forced to resign from the cabinet.

Churchill was a maverick. He was also widely viewed as a spoilt and bumptious child. He had already crossed the floor of the House of Commons, deserting the Conservatives ten years earlier to take a seat on the Liberal benches, and there was suspicion that this erstwhile renegade might soon repeat the process, only in the reverse direction.

On this occasion Churchill's demand for the construction of another four Dreadnoughts – maintaining a target of 60 per cent superiority over Germany in the building of these revolutionary battleships – and for the naval budget to be increased to nearly £52 million had immediately been met with serious opposition. Accusations were thrown at Churchill: that he was too warlike at a time when many Liberals were sceptical of claims about German aggression, and furthermore that he was completely out of step with the prevailing feeling in the Liberal Party that the steep rise in the level of armament spending must be halted.

Margot Asquith, making plain her opinions, as so often, wrote to David Lloyd George, the Chancellor of the Exchequer, to express this mood. 'Don't let Winston have too much money – it will hurt our party in every way . . . If one can't be a little economical when all foreign countries are peaceful I don't know *when* we can.' Budgetary economy and the prospect of a general election in 1915 were naturally very much on Lloyd George's mind. Increases in naval expenditure would hamper the production of a successful budget in the spring, to say nothing of plans for future welfare reform.

Lloyd George had been one of Churchill's closest political friends and allies, but now it was in the Chancellor's interest to clarify the extent to which he differed from the First Lord of the Admiralty. In his interview with the *Daily Chronicle* on 1 January, as we have seen, he had protested against 'the overwhelming extravagance of our expenditure on armaments' and argued that the Naval Estimates should be reduced because Anglo-German relations were more cordial at present than they had been for many years.

The majority of the cabinet, Asquith reported to Venetia, including the Foreign Secretary, Sir Edward Grey, regarded Lloyd George's interview as 'heedless folly . . . which has set all Europe by the ears'. The ship had very nearly foundered as she entered port, Asquith admitted to Venetia. 'By extra-careful steering, however, the calamity was averted.' Through his astute management of the cabinet split, Asquith had managed to manoeuvre Lloyd George back into the fold, and at the last moment the Chancellor had deserted his allies, who had hoped to gain his assistance in bringing Churchill down, ensuring that the Naval Estimates were carried.

At the opening of Parliament, on the afternoon of 10 February, full attention was once more focused on Ireland. Margot Asquith, who had been in Cannes for six weeks, nursing a chest infection, arrived back at Downing Street two days before to attend the official party that preceded the beginning of the new session. She had been so incensed by 'the dog's trick' that Lloyd George had played on Asquith over the Naval Estimates that she had had to be dissuaded from returning home earlier.

She was in good spirits, 'delighted to be alone' with Asquith, as the children were all away, and experiencing what she described in her diary as 'a honeymoon' in his company. But she knew that 1914 was going to be a decisive year for him. If he couldn't carry the Home Rule Bill, his career would be over and the fate of the Liberal Party sealed for many years. 'We are bound to be in for a strenuous & rather turbulent time,' Asquith warned her, shortly before she left Cannes for London.

Fashion conscious to a degree – she had once held a 'dress show' at 10 Downing Street, to the consternation of officials there – Margot prided herself on the black-and-steel dress with rose-pink velvet apron and collar that she wore to the official reception. It was so different from 'the confused and grotesque' prevailing women's fashions, like the hobble skirt (Asquith joked with Venetia about the sight of women dressed in these skirts, attempting to curtsey at court presentations, 'legs tied & manacled'), or the new trouser-skirt recently introduced from Paris.

Amid the pageantry of the state opening, the atmosphere in both Houses of Parliament was anxious and tense. In his speech from the throne, George V delivered a statement about Home Rule, regretting that the efforts which had been made to reach a solution had, so far, not succeeded, and emphasizing that it was his 'most earnest wish that the goodwill and cooperation of men of all parties and creeds may . . . lay the foundations of a lasting settlement'. The King was rumoured to be frightened of his Prime Minister, Asquith had told Venetia, though they had had a friendly discussion during a visit to Buckingham Palace several days earlier, when he'd been seated next to Queen Mary at dinner, who promptly informed him of how much she loathed music. But George V's concern about Ireland was uppermost in his conversation with Asquith, and the King directly warned him that if negotiations failed and civil war resulted, many army officers stationed in Ireland would refuse to fight.

As if heeding the King's heartfelt wish for goodwill and cooperation, Carson's contribution to the Commons debate later that afternoon included an appeal to the Irish Nationalists, sitting opposite, as his 'Fellow Countrymen', with a plea for sympathetic understanding rather than the use of force in deciding the fate of Ireland. Watching from the Speaker's Gallery, Margot felt choked with emotion as she listened to Carson's words. Entering into the spirit of conciliation, Asquith wrote to Carson, congratulating him on his speech. Carson was 'really very impressive', Asquith told Venetia, enclosing Carson's brief reply to his letter in order to keep her informed about the progress of events.

For the first time Carson had made a public statement on behalf of the Unionists which appeared to signal the end of their resistance to Home Rule for the rest of Ireland, on condition that Ulster was excluded. Throughout February, Asquith and Lloyd George seized the initiative by reopening negotiations with the Nationalist leaders to exclude loyalist areas from the scope of the Home Rule Bill. Redmond reluctantly agreed to this concession – though, as Margot learned, he 'all but wept' when he heard about it – but a major stumbling block remained. How long was the period of exclusion to be? Three years was initially proposed, only to be rejected and replaced by a term of six years after George V intervened to express fears that a three-year limit would make Carson's position impossible.

As for the area of exclusion, this was left deliberately undefined. Carson had always demanded the exclusion of at least six, and preferably all nine counties, but in practice it was thought that Ulster's four north-east counties, Antrim, Armagh, Down and Londonderry, together with the cities of Belfast and Londonderry, would opt to be left out of the Home Rule settlement.

The Amending Bill, introduced by Asquith, would confirm these details, granting Ulster's counties the right of opting out of Home Rule for six years, during which period there must be at least two general elections in the United Kingdom, offering the electorate two chances of confirming the exclusion. Otherwise, at the end of the period, the counties in question would automatically come under Home Rule, like the rest of Ireland.

On 9 March, Asquith presented his bill to the House. Margot was once again in the Speaker's Gallery, exchanging indignant looks with her old adversary, Lady Londonderry, a celebrated Conservative hostess and tireless campaigner against Irish self-government, who was carrying on a disparaging commentary about the proceedings. Violet Asquith, travelling in the Sudan since before Christmas, made a hurried return to London to hear her father's speech, reaching Charing Cross at 3.25 that afternoon, and arriving at the Commons just in time to find standing room only in the Gallery.

As Asquith rose to speak, his eyes scanned the rows of women, looking for Venetia, bitterly disappointed not to find her present. 'Why didn't you disguise yourself as a pressman?' he wrote to her, making an arrangement to see her as soon as possible after the debate was over. 'There was a huge crowd, but I did not count to excite them: so I adopted rather a funereal tone. Bonar Law was at his worst.'

It was Carson, though, who decisively threw the offer back in the government's face. He saw the concession as yet another example of Asquith's delaying tactics, arguing that the proposals would simply make Ulster a pawn in the British political game for a further six years. 'Ulster wants this question settled now and for ever,' he declared. 'We do not want sentence of death with a stay of execution for six years.'

The stakes on all sides were about to be raised higher. On 11 March, two days after the rejection of the offer to the Unionists, police reports from Dublin Castle were circulated among the cabinet. These provided evidence of a growth in the strength of the Ulster Volunteer Force – to more than 110,000 men and 80,000 rifles – and, even more alarmingly, of the UVF's plan of action for assuming military control of Ulster, including the severance of all railway lines and telephone and telegraph communications, and the seizure of arms and ammunition depots.

There was no indication of whether the UVF was planning an immediate coup, or a longer-term action, looking ahead to later in the year when Home Rule became law. But it would clearly have been unwise and irresponsible in the circumstances for the government to remain inactive any longer, with tensions on both sides running high, and exchanges in the Commons becoming more acrimonious.

At question time on 16 March, Carson denounced the government's concessions as a 'hypocritical sham', while Bonar Law proposed a vote of censure. After this, Asquith, who, up to this point, had remained optimistic 'of a real chance of *rapprochement*', had to admit to Venetia that it looked as if hopes for a compromise had broken down. Two days earlier, Winston Churchill, seeking to restore his standing in the Liberal Party after the storm over Naval Estimates, had made a provocative speech at Bradford, which, Asquith said, 'was quite opportune'. In a typical piece of Churchillian rhetoric, Churchill warned that the government would not surrender to threats from Ulster, and that there 'were worse things than bloodshed, even on an extended scale'. If the government's concessions were rejected and it was exposed 'to menace and brutality', then 'let us go forward together and put these grave matters to the proof!'

In the wake of intelligence about the likelihood of UVF action, the cabinet now made a decisive move to safeguard arms depots throughout the province. Instructions were given to the Commander-in-Chief of the troops in Ireland, Lieutenant-General Sir Arthur Paget, altering the disposition of some of the 23,000 soldiers stationed in Ireland to ensure the safety of government property. As a further precautionary measure, orders were given by Churchill for the 3rd Battle Squadron to steam from the north-west coast of Spain to Lamlash on the Isle of Arran, seventy miles from Belfast. Churchill claimed later that the squadron was intended as a reserve support for the army. However, as it turned out, on 21 March these orders were countermanded, by which time the battleships had only got as far as the Scilly Isles.

This spurt of action, after so many months of prevarication on the government's part, appeared to come just in time. On 19 March there were dramatic scenes in the House of Commons. When Carson declared threateningly, after listening to the Prime Minister, that he felt he ought not to be at Westminster but in Belfast at the head of his movement, someone shouted 'With your sword drawn?' Refuting as 'an infamous lie' the accusation from the Irish Nationalist MP Joseph Devlin that he had deserted Home Rule when he saw a chance of bettering his fortunes by supporting the opposite side, Carson left the chamber by the door behind the Speaker's Chair. As he reached the Chair, to rowdy Conservative and Unionist cheers, Carson raised his hand in a gesture of farewell. A hush fell over the House. 'I am off to Belfast,' he said before turning on his heel.

It was 5.15 p.m. At 5.55 Carson boarded the boat-train at Euston after telling a *Daily Express* reporter, 'I go to my people.' Rumours abounded that Carson had gone to Ulster to declare a provisional government, or even to light the touch paper for civil war.

Travelling aboard the same train from London as Carson was General Sir Arthur Paget, returning to Dublin after two days of consultations with the War Office about troop movements into Ulster. Paget was reportedly in a highly excitable and overwrought state. Once back in Ireland, he would precipitate a new level of crisis for Asquith's beleaguered Home Rule policy.

Asquith had made the excuse of a lingering cold to stay in London and avoid joining Margot for a weekend in the country. Instead, on the evening of Saturday, 20 March, he was the guest of Venetia and her parents, Lord and Lady Sheffield, at their house in Mansfield Street. At some time between 11 o'clock and midnight, a telephone call summoned Asquith from the bridge table back to Downing Street. There the Prime Minister was shown a telegram from General Paget. This, to his alarm, informed him that fifty-eight of the seventy officers of the Third Cavalry Brigade at the Curragh camp, thirty-five miles outside Dublin, had said that they would rather be dismissed from the army than take part in the coercion of Ulster.

The extent to which Paget's own bungling lay at the root of the incident soon became apparent. His behaviour was very much of a piece with his reputation, dating back to the days of his command during the South African War, for being rambling and irascible. Paget's temperament, combined with a fatal lack of clarity in the instructions given him by Secretary of State John Seely, had produced muddle and confusion, with disastrous consequences.

At their meetings at the War Office, Seely and Paget had agreed, at the latter's urging, that, in the event of precautionary troop movements in Ulster, officers domiciled in the province should be allowed to remain behind. They would be permitted to resume their places without their careers being affected once any action had been taken. All other officers, threatening to resign or disobey orders by refusing to march north, would be dismissed forthwith from the army, sacrificing their pensions.

Unfortunately these instructions, rather mysteriously, were never written down. Even more unfortunately, Seely failed utterly to make it clear that these principles were given to Paget for guidance only in the gravest of emergencies, should an individual officer fail to obey orders (this could be said to bear out one assessment of Seely that 'if he had just a little more brains, he'd be half-witted'). They were never intended to be put as hypothetical questions to the whole body of officers in the Irish Command, which is precisely what Paget had done next.

Arriving in Dublin early on the Saturday morning, Paget immediately called a meeting of his seven senior officers. He created the impression – despite the fact that the most that had been ordered was the movement of two battalions and some infantry companies – that plans were afoot 'of an offensive and aggressive character, and on an extensive scale', which would 'create intense excitement' and leave Ulster ablaze the next day. He then put before them the two options – exemption from operations for domiciled officers and immediate dismissal for the rest – as if he were holding a gun to their heads.

One of the officers listening to Paget was the commander of the Third Cavalry Brigade, Brigadier-General Hubert Gough, described by Asquith in a letter to Venetia as 'a distinguished Cavalry Officer, an Irishman, & the hottest of Ulsterians'. Gough wasn't domiciled in Ulster, though he had grown up there as a fervent anti-Home-Ruler, so he couldn't be exempted himself. But after returning to the Curragh he reported that five officers under his command would be claiming Ulster domicile. Of the rest, twelve were prepared to obey whatever the orders given, but fifty-eight, including himself, preferred to accept dismissal rather than be involved in the so-called 'initiation of active military operations against Ulster'.

'From what one hears to-day it seems likely there was a misunderstanding,' Asquith wrote calmly to Venetia, as details of what newspaper headlines were already declaring a 'Grave National Crisis' continued to filter through to Downing Street. 'They [the seven senior officers] seem to have thought, from what Paget said, that they were about to be ordered off at once to shed the blood of the Covenanters, and they say they never meant to object to do duty like the other troops in protecting depots . . . & keeping order.' It would all, he predicted, 'be cleared up in a few hours'.

Meanwhile, a procession of long faces kept turning up at 10 Downing Street. One of them belonged to the King's private secretary, Lord Stamfordham. George V had known nothing of events at the Curragh until he opened his copy of *The Times* that morning. He was 'grieved beyond words at this disastrous and irreparable catastrophe which has befallen my Army'.

But the full extent of the catastrophe had yet to unfold. Gough, and the officers of three of his regiments, were called to London for interview at the War Office on 22 and 23 March by members of the Army Council, including Seely, Sir John Spencer Ewart, the Adjutant-General, and Sir John French, Chief of the Imperial General Staff. French, who had been warned by Sir Douglas Haig that, if Gough was penalized, the resignation of every officer in the Aldershot Command could be expected, sought to persuade Gough and his subordinates to return to duty as if nothing had happened. Seething with self-righteous anger, Gough refused unless he was given a written assurance that the army would never be used to impose Home Rule on Ulster. A draft memorandum was prepared along these lines and submitted to the cabinet on 23 March. It was returned, amended by Asquith, in a new and uncontroversial guise. This merely stated that the Army Council was satisfied that the resignations derived from a misunderstanding, and that the intention behind Paget's questions had been an entirely legitimate one: to ensure that the lawful orders for the protection of lives and property would be obeyed.

Exactly what happened next has never been definitely established. There can be no doubt, though, of Hubert Gough's aptitude for out-manoeuvring the Army Council, in particular Seely, at every stage. Seely had returned to Downing Street just as the cabinet meeting which produced the revised memorandum was breaking up. He stuffed the document in his pocket and was chatting to John Morley, the aged Lord Privy Seal, when a message arrived from Gough requesting further reassurance that the army would never be used to quell opposition in Ulster to the Home Rule Bill. Seely together with Morley – too deaf, according to Margot Asquith, to have much idea of what was going on – then took the initiative by adding two further paragraphs to the document.

These 'peccant paragraphs', as they became known, stated that the government retained the right to employ the army to maintain law and order, but that the government had 'no intention whatever of taking advantage of the right to crush political opposition to the policy and principles of the Home Rule Bill'. The document was sent to French and Ewart, who signed it on behalf of the Army Council, under the impression that its terms had been sanctioned by the Prime Minister and cabinet.

Emboldened, Gough held out for more. He demanded a further pledge that the correct interpretation of the second 'peccant paragraph' meant that under no circumstances would troops 'be called upon to enforce the present Home Rule Bill on Ulster and that we can so assure our Officers'. French scribbled in the margin 'That is how I read it.' Asquith subsequently tried to recall the document. But it was too late. With the piece of paper in his possession, Gough had returned in triumph to the Curragh, to find himself cheered by the whole brigade.

'The immediate difficulty in the Curragh can, I think, be arranged,' Asquith wrote to Venetia on 22 March, while conceding that 'the permanent situation . . . is not a pleasant one.' Within forty-eight hours his words had taken on an added prescience. The prospects for the relationship between civilian politicians and senior officers were now indeed far from pleasant. General Gough had been given assurances which, at a stroke, meant the government no longer had the authority to impose Home Rule on Ulster by force – effectively paralysing government policy in the process. Before 20 March, the idea that the army might be ordered against Ulster, if political compromise failed, still retained some credibility. After 'Paget's tactless blundering and Seely's clumsy phrases', this was lost.

Parts of the press were by now proclaiming what it called the Curragh 'Mutiny' as 'The biggest story since the Boer War'. The Unionist papers, led by the *Morning Post*, boasted that 'The Army has killed the Home Rule Bill', while the *Nation*, representing the Liberal opinion, observed with mounting incredulity that 'A soldier has defied the Parliament from which he and his comrades draw their military existence and pay, and has gone back . . . in triumph, the most popular figure in the Army.'

In the Commons, the government faced accusations that it had plotted to use the army to provoke the Ulster Volunteers into violence, thereby providing it with an excuse to crush the movement. Asquith admitted to Venetia that he had 'rather a tough job to handle' explaining why the protection of arms depots in Ulster had required not only a cavalry brigade, but the dispatch of eight battleships. The only respite for the government was offered by the evident disquiet in the country about the notion of the army intervening in politics, and by the exposure of the weakness of the Opposition, who were attacked in Parliament for fostering discontent and mutiny among army officers.

The effect on Asquith personally of 'the stupid misadventure', as he referred to it, was severe. He was visibly shaken. The civil servant Almeric Fitzroy reported that Asquith had never been 'so overcome', adding that 'The folly of having created such a situation, without the power to handle it successfully, is incalculable.'

On Friday, 27 March, at the end of his most difficult week as Prime Minister, Asquith went for a drive with Venetia to steady his nerve before making a statement to the Commons. Afterwards he drove away 'in solitude' and missing her 'so much'. He had never wanted her more.

A month later, on the night of 24 April, the steamer *Mountjoy* sailed into the brightly lit harbour at Larne, on the east coast of County Antrim. Here the ship discharged its cargo of more than 30,000 rifles and millions of rounds of ammunition. These were driven away by the hundreds of motor-cars that had been waiting, headlights ablaze, on the quayside. When the operation was over, three cheers went up for 'the King' and for 'the Volunteers'.

This brilliantly conceived and executed plan by the Ulster Unionist Council to arm the Ulster Volunteer Force was met with no effective resistance. Coming so soon after the Curragh crisis, the illegal gun-running at Larne underscored the government's damaging loss of face and its inability to enforce a Home Rule policy in Ulster. 'It was no longer a question of our coercing Ulster,' Churchill wrote ominously; 'it was a question of our preventing Ulster from coercing us.'

The Slashing of the *Rokeby Venus*

On the morning of Tuesday, 10 March, a woman wearing a tight-fitting grey jacket and skirt left 48 Doughty Street in Holborn, once home to Charles Dickens but now a dilapidated boarding house, and walked in the direction of Soho towards Leicester Square. According to a recent report by New Scotland Yard, the woman was thirty-one years old, a little above five feet five inches tall, with brown hair and eyes. She was also described as anaemic-looking and of poor physique.

Secreted in the left sleeve of her jacket was a small axe, purchased the previous day at an ironmonger's in Theobald's Road. The axe was held in position by a chain of safety-pins, the last pin requiring only a touch to release it.

In Trafalgar Square, soon after 10 o'clock, the woman entered the National Gallery. It was one of the gallery's 'free days', so the stairways and rooms were heaving with crowds. On the first landing, where the stairs separate on the left and right, she stopped and glimpsed, through the maze of people, Velázquez's *The Toilet of Venus*, or the *Rokeby Venus*, as it was commonly known, hanging to the right on the north wall of Room XVII. In the painting, the naked figure of the goddess of love reclines languidly, her back to the viewer, and gazes at her reflection in a mirror held by her son Cupid. The face in the mirror is blurred, but her eyes stare into those of the beholder with a disconcerting intimacy.

The woman turned into an adjoining room and passed through several others, studying landscapes and portraits as she went. Finding herself back at the doorway of the room where the *Venus* was hanging, she took out a sketch book from her bag and started to make a drawing. Two attendants sat on a red plush seat in front of the painting.

At midday one of the men rose from his seat and left the room. The other, realizing that it was lunchtime, visibly relaxed, sat back,

Velázquez's *Rokeby Venus*, showing damage by the axe-wielding suffragette Mary Richardson

crossed his legs and opened a newspaper. Quickly grasping her axe, and letting her bag drop to the floor, the woman dashed up to the painting. Her first blow with the axe merely broke its protective layer of glass. With the sound of the glass breaking, the attendant rose from his seat, newspaper in hand, and walked round to look up at the skylight, which had recently been repaired. The other attendant, returning to the room, saw the woman and made a frantic attempt to reach her, slipping on the polished floor as he did so. This allowed the woman the time to get in further blows with her axe, driving its blade into the canvas, before she in turn was attacked.

Two *Baedeker* guidebooks aimed by German tourists came cracking across the back of her neck. By this time, the attendant, who had dimly realized that the breaking glass had no connection with the skylight, had reached the woman and was dragging the axe from her hand. Other passing visitors, attracted by the noise, aimed blows at her head, and in the ensuing commotion an angry scrum of people, fists flying, feet kicking, ended in a heap on the broad staircase outside the room.

Policemen, attendants and detectives were waiting at the foot of the stairs to march the attacker off along a corridor, down some more stairs and into a large basement. 'Are any more of your women in the gallery?' demanded a police constable, who was purple in the face and out of breath.

'Oh, I expect so,' the woman said.

'My God!' he exclaimed, turning to run from the room, pushing everybody else out of his way, and shouting the order as he went, 'Clear the gallery!'

At Vine Street Police Station the woman was named as Mary Raleigh Richardson, a militant suffragette. Richardson was immediately charged for 'malicious damage' to Velázquez's *Toilet of Venus*. Later that afternoon she was brought before the magistrate at Bow Street Police Court and committed for trial without bail. By now, a statement, written and signed by Richardson, had been released from the suffragette headquarters of the Women's Social and Political Union (WSPU) in Kingsway. This made it clear that the attack on the painting was retribution for the rearrest in Glasgow, the previous day, of the WSPU's leader Emmeline Pankhurst. A pale and fragile-looking Mrs Pankhurst had been sent back to Holloway, where she would resume her hunger strike, serving just four more days of her three-year sentence before being discharged again on licence, suffering from pains over her heart. In explanation Richardson wrote that she had set out to destroy 'the picture of the most beautiful woman in mythological history' in 'protest against the government who are destroying Mrs Pankhurst, who is the most beautiful character in modern history. Justice is an element of beauty as much as are colour and outline to womanhood, and for this she is being slowly murdered by a government of Iscariot politicians.' That evening Mary Richardson joined Mrs Pankhurst in Holloway, having been given a six-month sentence.

Mary Richardson was well known to the police as one of the most committed of militant suffragettes. Indeed, as she had pointed out to Mr Hopkins, the Bow Street magistrate, this was the tenth time she had been brought before the court in the space of a year for a variety of charges, including arson, assault and flinging an inkpot through a police station window. Unlike many of her co-conspirators, she had not been rearrested under the 'Cat and Mouse Act', presumably because poor health, including incipient appendicitis, presented the authorities with the strong likelihood that prison, and her resulting hunger strike, would kill her – though, as Richardson had told the packed court, she was not afraid of dying.★

Like other persistent militant offenders, however, Richardson was kept under regular surveillance. Plainclothes detectives shadowed her movements and photographed her unawares. The recent purchase by New Scotland Yard of a motorcycle was designed to make it easier to keep track of women like Mary Richardson, though in this case the experiment with motorized surveillance had evidently turned out to be a spectacular failure.

Mary Richardson possessed two qualities that immediately made her prime material as a militant foot soldier in the army of women dedicated to Mrs Pankhurst's strategy to win the vote through 'deeds not words'. One was her rootlessness. She was born in Britain, probably in 1883, but raised by her Canadian mother and grandfather in Ontario. At the age of sixteen, apparently orphaned and having shrugged off any remaining family responsibilities, she returned to Europe, studying art and travelling to Paris and Italy. In her twenties she settled in London, scraping a meagre living as a journalist for newspapers back in Toronto.

Richardson's other important prerequisite was her unmarried state. A high proportion of suffragettes who were arrested and imprisoned were single, and by 1914 over 60 per cent of the WSPU's subscribers were listed as 'Miss'. Richardson never married. There was no risk that she would share the fate of one middle-class Manchester wife and supporter of the WSPU, Eva Keller, who had been locked in the larder by her disapproving husband to prevent her from

★The 'Cat and Mouse Act', officially the Prisoners' Temporary Discharge for Ill-Health Act, had been introduced in April 1913. It allowed 'mice', suffragettes in a poor state of health, to be released back into the community until they were sufficiently recovered to be clawed back by the 'cat' to complete their sentence.

going on a window-smashing raid. 'In the fullest sense,' Mary Richardson later admitted, 'I was free to do what I was asked.'

In place of marriage, or any other form of lifelong partnership, Richardson devoted herself to the cause. Nothing else in her life – and she lived for almost half a century after her attack on the Velázquez painting – matched the 'wild emotions' and all-embracing sense of purpose of her involvement in the suffragette movement. In her autobiography, entitled *Laugh a Defiance* (after the line in the final verse of Ethel Smyth's rousing battle hymn of the suffragettes, 'The March of the Women') and published in 1953, Richardson makes scant reference to her life after 1914, choosing to dwell on the 'hectic excitements' of the campaign for the vote.

But one would no more look to Richardson's autobiography for a precise, chronologically accurate account of her years as a militant suffragette than one would expect the New Testament gospel writers to provide an objective history of the life and works of Jesus Christ. Her book is an article of faith in which dates and factual detail are constantly massaged and elided in order to provide a narrative which is strong on atmosphere, full of dramatic effects, and successfully captures the psychology of its main protagonist.

Richardson is present at significant events in the suffragette calendar. She says she was a witness to the attack at the House of Commons, on 18 November 1910 (henceforth known as 'Black Friday'), on the deputation of suffragettes attempting to reach Asquith to protest about his neglect of female suffrage, when police violently assaulted the women protesters. She claims to have been present at Epsom on Derby Day, in June 1913, when Emily Wilding Davison suffered fatal injuries after throwing herself on to the track in front of the King's horse, and to have been chased by an angry mob to the railway station, where she was forced to hide in the lavatory to escape them. She describes leaping on to the step of George V's carriage to present him with a petition as he passed through Bristol, and to have been struck by the incredible blueness of the King's eyes.

On less exalted occasions, Richardson debated the forcible feeding of suffragettes in Holloway with Arthur Winnington-Ingram, the Bishop of London, and suffered the indignity of being pelted with crusty bread rolls in a Holborn restaurant after she interrupted diners with a peroration about the vote.

Some of her accounts stand up to critical scrutiny. Others simply do not. My description, at the beginning of this chapter, of the turbulent crowd in the National Gallery, just moments after the *Venus* had been attacked, is taken from Richardson's autobiography, in which she makes much of being able to remember distinctly every detail of what happened. Contemporary newspaper reports, however, make no mention of any commotion and state that 'Slasher Mary', as she was soon to become known, allowed herself to be led away quietly from the gallery.

Mary Richardson had been converted from uncertainty about the suffragette movement to full-blooded enlistment 'in a holy crusade' by seeing Mrs Pankhurst at a rally at the Albert Hall. Mrs Pankhurst's dignity and eloquence on that day had left her spellbound. Later she would think herself 'greatly privileged' when she was granted an interview with the WSPU leader to receive Mrs Pankhurst's personal instructions about blowing up a railway station in the Birmingham area.

In most other ways, though, as Richardson attests, the life of a militant was a lonely, isolated and, at times, terrifying one, relieved only by brief respites in safe houses owned by suffragette sympathizers. There was the militant's fear of verbal, as well as physical, abuse, particularly from elderly men, who seemed to delight in whispering 'sex filth' into the ears of women selling suffragette newspapers on street corners; the terror in her Holloway cell of listening out for the rattle of the steel trolley, transporting the tubes and metal gags that formed the apparatus for forcible feeding; most of all, perhaps, there was her sense of a loss of individuality and her transformation into a complete automaton as she unquestioningly carried out orders from above.

And then there was the sick feeling in the pit of the stomach as she prepared, without triumphalism, to perpetrate her act of militancy – and the palpable relief once the job was done.

———

Outside the National Gallery on the afternoon of Mary Richardson's attack, a band of irate visitors hammered at the door, unable to understand why they couldn't gain admittance. Inside, an emergency meeting of the trustees, headed by the gallery's Director, Sir Charles Holroyd, was taking place.

The possibility of a militant attack on museums or art galleries had been entertained by the authorities for months. Warnings from New Scotland Yard about the likelihood of a suffragette 'outrage' had been circulating since the summer of 1913, when it was reported that 'a bomb' – which turned out to be no more than a box of cartridges – had been discovered in a room of the National Gallery. The plainclothes police presence at the gallery had then been increased, but, faced now with an actual attack, the trustees, including Lords Lansdowne and Curzon, were unable to agree on a course of action for the long-term future in a meeting that lasted two hours. In the end they confirmed the closure of the gallery for a fortnight, the protection of more important pictures by thicker glass, and the introduction of a new policy of the surrender on arrival of visitors' coats, bags and muffs.

The Keeper and Secretary of the collection, Hawes Turner, his voice, as someone once unkindly said, like a cat's miaow, had examined the Velázquez closely and now gave a report on the damage. He said that the glass was shattered, and that the canvas was damaged in seven places. There were six distinct cuts 'and a ragged bruise'. He thought it likely that this bruise was caused by the flat side of the axe – or, as he called it, 'chopper' – used by Richardson. Fortunately, he said, the chopper in question had possessed a keen edge, which was less destructive than an old and blunt weapon would have been.

Next day the press took up the theme of the 'wounding' of a great masterpiece with enthusiasm. In more popular papers, the shocking attack on a perfect female nude by the deranged 'Slasher Mary' was reported exactly as though it were a sensational murder. Only the figure of the pathological male assailant was missing. Even the stentorian tones of the report in *The Times* could not resist dwelling on the details of the attack as if it were describing the bludgeoning of soft flesh rather than stiff canvas. The most serious blow had caused 'a cruel wound in the neck'. There was 'a broad laceration' starting near the left shoulder and roughly forming, with two other cuts, a letter *N*; a 'gash' extending beyond the body and into the drapery below it; and other cuts cleanly made 'in the region of the waist'.

But the collective shock, as well as anguish, at this 'deplorable act of vandalism', as the *Morning Post* called it, stemmed from the fact that the *Rokeby Venus* was no ordinary masterpiece. Of course, the painting was unique in itself as the only surviving nude by Diego Velázquez. But, more than that, the *Rokeby Venus* had been accorded special status in the nation's affections as both a national icon and a truly national possession. Painted some time towards the end of the 1640s, the *Venus* was first recorded in 1651 in the collection of the son of the First Minister of Spain, who presumably displayed it privately to avoid the censure of the Inquisition. In 1813 the *Venus* was brought to England by the art importer and entrepreneur William James Buchanan, and purchased for £500 by J. B. S. Morritt, of Rokeby Hall, County Durham, on the advice of the artist Sir Thomas Lawrence. For almost a hundred years the Morritt family refused many offers to buy the painting. Then, in 1905, the current owner, H. E. Morritt, obtained the permission of the Court of Chancery to sell his heirloom, and the *Venus* came on the market, priced at a staggering £45,000.

The National Arts Collection Fund, newly founded to assist acquisitions for Britain's national collections, launched a public appeal. Although ultimately successful, the appeal, across all classes of society, was met with widespread suspicion and controversy. There were fears that the price of the picture had been artificially inflated by the art dealers to increase their own share of the proceeds, and even insinuations that members of the fund's committee were profiting from the sale. Public questions were raised about the morality of spending so large a sum on a representation of something as inherently impure as the human form (in Manchester, where, in a rare public exhibition, the *Venus* had been briefly displayed in the mid nineteenth century, local sensitivities had insisted that the nude be 'hung high up'). Finally, however, in January 1906, the fund was able to present the *Venus* to the National Gallery. From the King downwards, including 'An Englishman' who contributed £10,000 and 'A Young Student' who sent in two shillings, all classes and incomes had supported the appeal through their donations.

There can be no doubt, therefore, that Mary Richardson had chosen to attack the *Venus* because of public perception of the painting as a national asset of great financial value. What she may not have realized – though it would have been unlikely to give her much pause – was that the prime mover behind the purchase for the National Gallery had been Christiana Herringham, a supporter of the militant suffragette campaign as well as the only woman on the committee of the National Arts Collection Fund.

The impact of the attack on museums around the country was soon felt. A rule of 'No muffs, wrist-bags or sticks' was widely enforced. In London the effect was particularly significant. In addition to the National Gallery, there were short-term closures of the National Portrait Gallery, the Wallace Collection, the Guildhall Art Gallery and the collections at Windsor Castle, while measures were taken to protect works of art in public buildings like St Paul's Cathedral. At the British Museum, women could be admitted only if they were accompanied by a man or, if unaccompanied, could produce a letter of recommendation from a gentleman. In future the public were going to have to 'strip to nudity' to gain access to the great collections, joked Lord Wemyss, a Conservative peer.

Members of the public were understandably annoyed at the inconvenience of finding themselves barred from visiting museums and art galleries. Annabel Jackson wrote to D. S. MacColl, Keeper of the Wallace Collection, about the 'despair' of a Dutch friend, visiting London for a few days, who especially wanted to see the collection but found it closed 'because of these horrible suffragettes'. Would there be a chance of gaining entry if her friend submitted to a search by the authorities? As discontented American tourists were turned away from the National Gallery, the *Evening News* printed a story under the headline 'The Great Lock-Out of Art-Lovers': 'The visitors had to make the best of Nelson and the lions, who cannot be "locked up".' Meanwhile, outside the National Gallery's padlocked gates, a postcard vendor did a busy trade in reproductions of the slashed *Venus*.

For the non-militant suffragists of the National Union of Women's Suffrage Societies, led by Millicent Fawcett, the attack only confirmed the wisdom of their decision to diverge from the dangerous 'violent' militancy of the WSPU, which appeared to be precisely a product of the 'brute force' they were working against. A spokeswoman on behalf of the NUWSS commented on Richardson's ignorance of the true value of the *Venus* and deplored 'the spirit of revenge which has so poisoned the minds of a few of the supporters of the noblest and purest of all causes'.

Richardson's act also provoked fury among members of the public who had hitherto been sympathetic to the cause. One member resigned from the Suffrage Club, saying she considered 'that the destruction of works of art should be punishable by death'. Vera Brittain was a young woman, from Buxton in Derbyshire, who had been converted to the idea of women's suffrage by Olive Schreiner's feminist classic of 1911, *Woman and Labour*. On the day of the attack, she wrote angrily in her diary of the 'barbarity . . . of the Suffragette who . . . slashed & cut with a hatchet Velazquez's famous *Venus*! . . . Poor artist & genius! What has he done that the rancour & spite of a political maniac should be vented upon his creation! It shames the glorious cause for which the best women are fighting that *one* should act like this under cover of their standard.'

Christabel Pankhurst, Emmeline's eldest daughter, attempting, not always successfully, to direct WSPU policy from her exile in Paris, was quick to endorse Richardson's 'magnificent' speech in court. She contrasted the 'crocodile tears' and 'new-found love of art' of the 'Iscariot politicians' with their 'dry-eyed' acceptance of a male-only franchise and the industrial and sexual exploitation of women. In an article in the *Suffragette* at the beginning of May, Ethel Smyth advanced a slightly more conciliatory argument. The destruction of great works of art, she admitted, was disturbing. Nevertheless, she was interested in the present and future as well as the past, and did not believe 'in great art flourishing in unclean soil'. There was something 'hateful, sinister, sickening' in the heaping up of art treasures while the 'desecration' of women's bodies was going on. 'There is not an "old master",' she concluded, 'be it ever so dubious a specimen, whose disappearance I would not sincerely mourn more than that of most of the gentlemen now sitting in high places.'

Cartoonists, meanwhile, were having a field day. In one of a series of Donald McGill postcards lampooning the suffragettes, a smartly dressed couple gazed at the armless Venus de Milo with the caption, 'Now ain't that a shame, I bet it's them suffragettes done it!!' *Punch* seized the opportunity to make the connection, often used in suffragette propaganda, between Ulster militants and militants of the suffrage variety, depicting Asquith as Cupid protecting his Home Rule Bill from the threat of Bonar Law's axe.

The painting itself was being repaired by the National Gallery's Mr Battery at a cost of £100. There were fears that the *Venus* might have fallen in value by as much as £10,000 to £15,000, from its original asking price of £45,000. The cleanness of the cuts, though, made the relining of the picture and repair of its 'injuries' relatively easy to carry out.

There was a brief lull before a further storm. On 4 May an elderly, white-haired woman in a loose purple cloak walked into the Royal Academy in London's Piccadilly. In Room III, where John Singer Sargent's new portrait of the novelist Henry James was hanging, there was the sudden sound of shattering glass. The woman, afterwards named as Mary Ward, had made three gashes in the portrait with a meat cleaver. She was immediately attacked by a 'red-faced howling mob' of other visitors, and a man who went to her defence also had to defend himself from blows, his spectacles being broken over his nose. At Marlborough Street Magistrates Court, Walter Lamb, the Secretary of the Royal Academy, gave evidence that the picture, which had been admired by the King on his visit to the Academy a few days before, was worth about £700. Ward was heard to remark that if the picture had been painted by a woman it would never have fetched such a sum.

Later, at a local branch meeting of the WSPU at Knightsbridge Hall, a statement purporting to be from Mrs Ward was read out in which she said that she had tried to destroy a valuable picture 'because I wish to show the public that they have no security for their property nor for their art treasures until women are given political freedom'. This time it was the *Suffragette* that made the inevitable connection, contrasting the damage to a picture of a man with the potential killing of thousands of 'real' men by Carson's Ulster militants. In the same paper, an 'Eye-Witness' to Mary Ward's attack described the 'mob' in the Academy who did not realize that there might be something 'more valuable than the finely-wrought picture of a fine writer' and asked what James's 'subtle writings conveyed to these cruel obvious minds'.

Mary Ward, it was said, had never heard of Henry James, nor read any of his books, so she could hardly have been aware of James's sensitive portrayals of women, nor of his broad sympathy with 'the Woman Question'. Perhaps she had chosen the Sargent portrait as the object of her attack because James's bald pate and protruding expanse of waist-coated chest made him resemble so closely the archetypal figure of overbearing patriarchal authority. James reported receiving '390 kind notes of condolence'. Ward had got at him 'thrice over before the tomahawk was stayed', he wrote to a concerned friend. 'I naturally feel very scalped and disfigured, but you will be glad to know that I seem to be pronounced curable.'

A week later, another painting was slashed at the Royal Academy. On 12 May, Mary Ansell, a prominent militant, made two cuts in Hubert von Herkomer's portrait of the Duke of Wellington before being seized by an attendant. She 'made the usual protests', noted *The Times*, clearly having become jaded by the subject. At the Academy, ten days later, a Clausen nude was hacked in two with a cleaver.

The small axe or hatchet was fast becoming that season's weapon of choice for suffragettes. On the same day as the latest Royal Academy attack, Freda Graham managed to damage five paintings by Bellini in the National Gallery, despite the presence in the room of three plainclothes officers and two gallery attendants as she did so. There was a disturbing development at the Doré Gallery in New Bond Street on 3 June, when Ivy Bonn attacked an engraving by Bartolozzi, *Love Wounded*, and Shapland's *The Grand Canal, Venice*. She was just raising her arm to attack a third picture, when an attendant intervened. Bonn immediately turned on him and began to threaten him with her hatchet before she was overpowered by other attendants rushing to his rescue. Five days later, the new militant campaign moved out of the capital to Birmingham, where Bertha Ryland slashed Romney's *Master John Bensley Thornhill* at the City Art Gallery.

On 16 July, Millais's portrait of Thomas Carlyle in the National Portrait Gallery was attacked 'with very great force' by a woman who gave her name as Annie Hunt (her real name was Margaret Gibb). Carlyle's head was slashed 'through the left eye as far as the cheek', reported the *Morning Post*, while the suffragette's hands were left cut and bleeding from the smashed glass.

For almost three decades in London, women of every class had been asserting their presence in the public domain, challenging the traditional privileges of the male elite. By the spring and summer of 1914, however, women – especially women of refined appearance and respectable dress like Annie Hunt – were viewed more than ever as figures of suspicion and possible proponents of violent action against public property. Even the Prime Minister's younger daughter Elizabeth, visiting her father for the first time at the War Office – where Asquith had taken over the responsibilities of the Secretary of State for War as a steadying, morale-boosting measure following Colonel Seely's resignation after the Curragh incident – was initially 'repulsed' as a suspected suffragette.

In the meantime, the National Gallery, embarrassed that its security had been found seriously wanting on two occasions in less than three months, closed its doors indefinitely.

Back in March, Mary Richardson had occupied her usual cell at Holloway, overlooking the prison store. She was not there for long before she resumed the seemingly endless cycle of hunger strike, forcible feeding, release and rearrest.

Released with appendicitis on 6 April, three weeks after her *Rokeby Venus* attack, she was rearrested on 20 May, the operation on her appendix having been postponed because of complications. This time she was in Holloway for just five days before being released, suffering again from appendicitis. On 6 June she returned to prison and was released on 28 July, more seriously ill than ever with acute appendicitis.

Richardson had stated that the government's 'slow murdering' of Mrs Pankhurst had been the reason behind her slashing of the painting. Much later she would add that she had chosen that particular work of art to be the victim of her axe because she disliked its 'sensuousness' and the way in which men drooled over the figure of the naked Venus. But, while she never said so explicitly, her attack, on what *The Times* had described as the embodiment 'of the Goddess of Youth and Health . . . of the perfection of Womanhood at the moment when it passes from the bud into the flower', must also have been an attempt, however unconsciously, to draw attention to the violation of her own body through the brutality of forcible feeding.

The commonest form of forcible feeding was by means of a tube through the nostril, though other methods were sometimes used, including simultaneous feeding through nose and throat, and the excruciatingly painful practice of feeding a tube through the stomach. In two extreme cases in the summer of 1914, a militant prisoner had tubes forced into her bowels, while another was fed by the rectum and then through the vagina, a variation on usual practice carried out, it would seem, for no purpose other than pure sadism.

Forcible feeding was often accompanied by considerable violence. Richardson recalled being pinned down by as many as three wardresses at a time, while two doctors were present, one to manipulate the gags, one to force down the tube. When she could muster the strength, she would offer resistance, breaking two beds in her Holloway cell, so that a bed with a specially reinforced frame had to be purchased for her. One of the wardresses who wrestled with Richardson declared that she must have learned ju-jitsu. Once, the rubber came off one of the gags, causing Richardson almost to choke as two inches of thick rubber became stuck in her throat. In spite of this, they went on feeding her, continuing to push tubes down her nose and throat even when the pain from her appendix made her beg them not to force so much food down her.

'The worst fight on record is now raging in Holloway Infirmary, that Inferno of an Infirmary,' Mary Richardson wrote in an open letter published soon after her release in July, under the emotive heading 'TORTURED WOMEN. What Forcible Feeding Means'. She went on to give harrowing details of her own recent experience:

They fed me through the nose for 5 weeks, then my nose what they called 'bit' the tube, that was their expression. Instead of passing through into the throat, the tube went up into the top of my nose and injured the right eye, the nerves of my right eye . . . They then began feeding me through the mouth, one doctor used to put her finger through the extreme end of the left side of my jaw, and cut me; and the wardress put her finger through the right side of my jaw at the same time – so that between the two my lips were nearly torn.

In April, a statement from Dr Flora Murray, who acted as physician to the militants, accused the authorities at Holloway of having administered bromide to Mary Richardson to reduce her resistance to forcible feeding. The charge was strenuously denied. Two months later the Home Office issued a counter-accusation that, during her latest term of imprisonment, Richardson had been found in possession of tablets which, after analysis, proved to be Emetine Hydrochloride. These, when taken, would have caused severe vomiting. Neither charge was ever proved. The result, in effect, was a stalemate.

The first seven months of 1914 set a new record of 141 acts of destruction committed by suffragette militants throughout Britain. Works of art were far from being the only objects of attack. Railway stations, piers, sports pavilions and haystacks were set on fire. The Carnegie Library at Northfield, in Worcestershire, was burned by an 'arson squad' that destroyed all the books and left only the shell of the building standing. Parts of Redlynch House, in Somerset, were damaged by fire, while the destruction of church property became more frequent and extensive. The churches of Breadsall near Derby, with its Norman doorway and thirteenth-century chancel, and of Wargrave in Berkshire were burned down. Bombs exploded in St George's, Hanover Square, St John's, Westminster and St Martin-in-the-Fields. At Westminster Abbey, on 11 June, an explosion did a small amount of damage to the Coronation Chair in the chapel of St Edward the Confessor. A deafening noise, like a peal of thunder, and a huge column of smoke, which shot right up to the roof, sent visitors rushing for the exits.

Militants were becoming more daring, and their bombs and other incendiary devices more professional and effective, than during the early period of militancy. The barbarity of the indiscriminate assaults, sometimes of a sexual nature, inflicted on them at public meetings, together with their forcible feeding in prison, was tempting suffragettes into the kind of violent act that they would once have regarded as inconceivable.

The Home Secretary, Reginald McKenna, had opposed the idea during the passage of the Cat and Mouse Act of leaving suffragettes to die without forcible feeding by arguing that they were 'fanatical and hysterical women, who no more fear death in fighting what they believe to be the cause of women, than the natives of the Sudan feared death when fighting the battle of the Mahdi'. McKenna believed, probably correctly, that the public remained largely indifferent to the forcible feeding of suffragettes. The Church had made some disquieted noises, while George Bernard Shaw had protested about the illegality of the practice, which he described as 'a medieval abomination'. But the medical profession, including the presidents of the Royal Colleges and the editors of the key medical journals, had, with few exceptions, either remained silent or offered outright support to the Home Office. The moral implications of compulsory feeding bothered McKenna less than the practical necessity of keeping militants alive, and ensuring that there was no escalation of militancy – to the point of 'a life for a life' – which might ensue should one of these hunger strikers be allowed to die.

The leadership of the WSPU had always publicly declared their commitment to the sanctity of human life. Even the stones used for window-breaking had to be wrapped in paper, or attached to a string to avoid accidental injury to anyone. As new and more aggressive forms of militancy were adopted, the rule nevertheless remained firm: no life was to be taken. The only lives that could be lost were the militants' own.

However, militancy itself could not stand still. By its very nature it had either to develop in more extreme directions or to retrace its steps with a consequent loss of face. For the WSPU, the abandonment of militant tactics would not simply result in the appearance of indecision and defeat; it would also deprive it, in the struggle for the vote, of any reason for its continued existence, independent of the non-militant body of constitutional suffragists.

There were clear signs, though, that by 1914 the suffragette leadership was finding it increasingly difficult to regulate and restrain the pace of militancy among the more fanatical of its followers. Mary Richardson's attack upon a nationally owned work of art, carried out, as she always insisted, on her own initiative, was just one more moderate example of new acts of daring that had spawned a rash of imitators.

But there were also more extreme acts of militancy thrusting up from below, which revealed a disturbing escalation in violence over which the WSPU leaders appeared to have no control, and for which they were unprepared to accept responsibility. Some of these undermined the suffragettes' principled stand against damage to life and limb. In June 1914, for instance, two suffragettes, protesting against forcible feeding, set upon Dr Francis Forward, the deputy governor and medical officer of Holloway Prison, and attacked him with horsewhips. A month later, an explosion among mail bags being transported by train from Blackpool, caused by a suffragette-designed device of a glass tube containing sulphuric acid and 'flashlight powder', badly burned a train guard about the hands and arms.

With violence intensifying, and no likelihood of the concession of the vote to women, there remained the distinct possibility that some suffragette firebrand might leap forward with the ultimate nightmare scenario: political assassination. At London's Euston Station in February, while waiting along with two hundred other guests for a train to take him to a society wedding, Lord Weardale had been savagely attacked with a dog whip by Mary Lindsay, a suffragette who mistook him for the Prime Minister. Rumours already abounded of suffragettes practising with revolvers on shooting-ranges around London. As 1914 wore on, it must have occurred to many in authority that if Mrs Pankhurst were allowed to die on hunger strike, that distinct possibility might soon become a certainty.

Pupil Power

The village of Burston is a scattered hamlet, lying a few miles to the north of the neighbouring town of Diss, on the Norfolk–Suffolk border, and some eighteen miles south of the city of Norwich. It has a windmill and a village green. Its church, St Mary the Virgin, parts of which date back to the fourteenth century, sadly lacks a tower, because the villagers were too poor to replace the original structure when it collapsed in the mid eighteenth century.

In 1914 Burston comprised somewhere between 500 and 600 inhabitants. Families, consisting of as many as seven or eight members, were housed in cramped and unsanitary conditions in the two-up, two-down, pink-washed cottages that lined the main road. Some male villagers were employed on the railway, which provided a direct line to London, but most were agricultural labourers, scraping together a living on an income of as little as 12s.6d. a week. Burston had no resident squire. The main landowner, Sir Edward Mann of Mann's Breweries, lived at Thelveton, several miles away, never interfered in village matters, and rented out land and housing to tenant farmers, who, together with the Rector of St Mary's, made up the parish hierarchy.

As dusk fell on the evening of 31 March, a large crowd of villagers flocked on to Burston Green. They were there in response to a printed bill that had been posted in the village, 'To consider the School question and the steps that shall be taken'. The chairman of the proceedings was local parent, fish hawker and poacher, George Durbidge, a bulky man, over six feet tall, with a reputation for drunken violence. Every Wednesday, after spending his illicit earnings at Burston's Crown Inn, he would return home to beat his wife. The Green was lit by two giant flares from Durbidge's cockle-stall as a resolution was read out, protesting against the dismissal that day of Tom and Kitty Higdon after three and a half years as teachers at Burston Council School. 'Under

BURSTON STRIKE 1914.   MALI

Burston's striking children with parents, friends, and Kitty and Tom Higdon (*centre*) on Burston Green, 1914

the unjust circumstances, we protest against the introduction of new teachers to the school, and we urgently request the County Education Authorities to reconsider the whole matter with a view to our retention of the teachers whose services are so generally appreciated amongst us.' The resolution was carried with deafening cheers. Men and women stepped forward to make brief, angry speeches, full of indignation at what they saw as the victimization of the Higdons at the hands of the Rector, the Reverend Charles Tucker Eland, upholder of the status quo, whose name was greeted with hoots and jeers.

It must have been an extraordinary spectacle, and for its participants, most of whom had never made any kind of public statement before, both a forbidding and a completely exhilarating experience. George Durbidge's closing words entreated the villagers to maintain their newfound solidarity. 'Stick, stick, stick, like bloody shit to a blanket!' he told them. The children of the village, meanwhile, had begun to set in motion plans of their own. With their parents' approval they intended to go on strike, rather than be taught by new teachers introduced by the Education Committee.

A plucky and determined fourteen-year-old, Violet Potter, one of the Higdons' senior pupils, made a list of all the schoolchildren who were prepared to stay away from school. Out of the seventy-two boys and girls attending the council school, only six were unwilling to take part. On the evening of the meeting on the Green, Violet helped the Higdons to remove their personal possessions, including Kitty Higdon's camera, her sewing machine and typewriter, from the school into the schoolhouse. Then, slipping back into the classroom, Violet chalked some words on the blackboard, which would be clearly visible the next day when the board was put up on the easel by the replacement teachers. Her words, replicated in similar signs in the school-porch and on the village signpost, read: 'We are going on strike tomorrow'.

'The clouds are . . . hovering . . . over the peace of our industrial life,' the Archbishop of York, Cosmo Gordon Lang, had warned in his predictions of the 'Perils of 1914' at the start of the year. The dramatic levels of industrial unrest, dating from the large-scale, sometimes violent disputes of 1910–12, which had encompassed the eruption of a dock strike, a nationwide strike on the railways and a vast coal strike, remained high. Indeed, the first seven months of 1914 appeared to threaten an increase in strike action even greater than that of the previous year. Close to a thousand British strikes would be recorded up to the end of July, with the loss of a total 9.9 million working man-days.

In London, in the third week of January, as temperatures rapidly dropped to freezing point, 7,000 workers in the coal trade came out on strike for increased pay, followed two days later by a strike of 3,000 carmen, responsible for distributing coal to different parts of the capital. For one bitterly cold week, Londoners struggled to maintain their fires. Newspaper photographers pictured them trying to alleviate their frozen plight: students loading and transporting coal from St Pancras to supply Middlesex Hospital; officials at the Colonial Office forced to unload their own coal; and middle-class women, begrimed with dust, hiring a cab to bring their coal home.

Each week brought some new outbreak of conflict in the workplace.

At times it seemed like the unchecked spread of a contagious fever, or of a fire that was dangerously out of control. There was a five-month lockout in the London building trade, affecting 150,000 workers; a municipal employees' strike in Leeds and Blackburn; a dispute on the Yorkshire coalfields; a demand for an eight-hour working day among shipbuilders in Liverpool. In the cotton trade, the expiry of the Brooklands Agreement, which had stipulated that wages could be varied only annually and by no more than 5 per cent, meant that a strike or lockout was likely.

Nor was action limited to big industry. A prolonged strike of chair-workers in High Wycombe, which had begun in 1913 and trickled on to the end of February 1914, led to local rioting and an escalation of violence on the picket lines. In more dignified fashion, a mass walkout of members of the Amalgamated Musicians' Union, early in the year, brought down the curtain at Oswald Stoll's music halls in Chiswick, Shepherds Bush and Wood Green, while at the Manchester Hippodrome, twenty-three members of the orchestra quietly laid down their instruments and left the theatre at the beginning of a performance. That summer, strawberry pickers would strike in Kent, and in North Essex hay would be gathered under police protection following a walkout of farm labourers. Even professional football faced disruption when Warrington refused to play Hull Kingston Rovers after the team was denied a bonus.

Undoubtedly some of these strikes were simply imitative, or sprang from a wish to express solidarity, or to flex industrial muscle at a time when the national rate of unemployment was remarkably low, and average real wages had at last caught up with the rising cost of living. (In 1913, a year that witnessed the highest level of strikes to date, unemployment was 2.1 per cent, its lowest level since 1899. In 1914 it rose slightly to 3.3 per cent.) Trade union membership in Britain had jumped from 2.5 million in 1910 to just over 4 million in 1914 – almost a quarter of the workforce – and it can hardly have escaped the attention of either management or workers that the outcome of most strikes was successful, with only one strike in seven ending in outright defeat for unions between 1910 and 1914.

Much more disturbing, from the point of view of government,

Establishment and more conservative elements in society, were the negotiations, ongoing in the spring and summer of 1914, for the formation of a 'Triple Alliance', linking the unions representing railwaymen, transport workers and miners. This 'Triple Alliance' appeared to threaten the prospect of a nationwide general strike later in the year, even raising in some fevered minds the ugly spectre of revolution.

'Socialist and syndicalist agitation is interfering with sane, honest trade unionism,' commented the *Daily Express*. Yet, although there was widespread and genuine concern about the spread of industrial militancy, fanned by syndicalist ideas of class warfare and an apocalyptic general strike, in reality the notion of a giant formation of unions holding the government to ransom was something of a bluff. In practice the alliance was intended as a coordinating measure to spread the pain should one of the individual unions go out on strike. Behind the scenes, it was also an attempt by union leaders to control the militant rank and file, thereby averting industrial chaos.

There remained, however, an abiding sense of fear of an impending clash between capital and labour, based on the alarming experience of industrial relations in recent years. As H. G. Wells had observed at the height of the upsurge of rebellion in the summer of 1911, the new-fangled strike was less a haggle, 'far more a display of temper'.

Perhaps the most remarkable manifestation of working-class discontent was the incidence of children coming out on strike in elementary schools. There were historical precedents for this. In 1889 school strikes for fewer lessons and shorter hours, originating in the Scottish Borders, had quickly spread to Tyneside and as far south as Bristol and London. In September 1911 a strike which started at a school in Llanelli, on the coast of West Wales, had within two weeks spread to schools in sixty-two towns and cities around Britain.

These strikes centred on issues such as corporal punishment (six of the best on the hand was a standard punishment at the time, but there were plenty of more brutal canings), regulations concerning school hours, holidays, the school-leaving age, and the appointment and dismissal of teachers. In essence, action of this kind was a protest by working-class children, often in concert with their parents, against the authoritarian and centralized system of schooling which was removing control of education from the local community. School strikes employed practices and methods, like pupil pickets and street marches and demonstrations, picked up from the example of the children's parents, and these strikes generally took place at times when industrial conflict in the wider community was at its most intense.

The early months of 1914 had seen the outbreak of a number of school strikes in England, on a limited as well as larger scale. At Gaskell Street School in Bolton, the caning of an older boy brought a dozen of his schoolmates out on strike. Their brief absence from the classroom brought no concessions from the teachers, merely 'four raps apiece' when they returned to school. At St Jude's School in Bristol, there was a strike by monitors demanding payment for the instruction and disciplining of younger children in their charge. It was put down with some brutality, with the aid of the local curate.

A more organized and publicly backed strike action, over the contentious issue of a rise in the school-leaving age, took place among children and parents at Bedworth in Exhall, and the surrounding villages in north-east Warwickshire. The local authority's decision to raise the school-leaving age from thirteen to fourteen was seen as having decisive consequences for families dependent on income from seasonal child labour, for which there was great demand in the area. A petition against the proposal was signed by 6,000 local people. The strike lasted for several weeks that spring, and ended only when the education authority made various minor concessions, including an assurance that no children aged over thirteen from larger families would be immediately prosecuted for non-attendance. Meanwhile, at Harringay, in North London, pupils went on strike when the reorganization of local schools meant that they had to travel greater distances to school.

Attracting most publicity was the strike by Herefordshire schoolchildren, at the beginning of February 1914, in support of their teachers, among the worst paid in the country, who had come out en masse, demanding increased wages and a revised pay scale. When the local authority appointed new teachers, not all of them qualified, to replace the strikers, pupils in towns and villages through-out the county expressed their sympathy by refusing to be taught by them.

At Ledbury Girls' School, a riot broke out. After marching into town at morning break, chanting 'We want a strike', pupils returned to the classroom, where they upturned desks, smashed inkpots and 'amused themselves on the piano'. Similar scenes erupted at Ross Boys' School, where 200 students stood outside the school-gates chanting strike songs, and scrawling 'Strike boys, strike' on walls, pavements and even passing vehicles. Seventy schools had to close, rewarding 4,000 children with an unofficial holiday, before the strikers were successful, forcing Herefordshire Education Authority to reinstate their original teachers with increases in salary.

Some public commentators on these outbreaks of school action feared that they presented clear evidence of a decline in children's morals and their standards of deference. Others perceived in them something more dangerous: nothing less than a left-wing conspiracy to subvert the social order.

Running simultaneously with the Herefordshire school strikes was a case at Dronfield Elementary School, in Derbyshire, which revealed the reverse side of the coin in the relationship between the local authority, and parents and children of school age. There, par-ents, backed by a local petition with 1,200 signatures, were unable to persuade the county Education Committee to dismiss Miss Sarah Outram, head of the girls' school and a schoolmistress of twenty-six years' standing, who had been accused of giving 'sex teaching' to twelve-year-old girls. Miss Outram's pupils didn't go on strike, but their parents kept them away from school while a protracted investi-gation took place.

Miss Outram's defence was that her remarks to the girls about the 'mystery of birth' had initially arisen when she was asked by one of them to explain a scriptural reference to the birth of a child. But the sworn depositions of Miss Outram's pupils suggested that she had strayed beyond this. She had, for example, talked on one occasion about circumcision. On another, she had referred to the suffragettes in the context of a discussion about the relationship between a woman and a man, and said how wrong it was that women were being forcibly fed.

Parents were outraged, and protested that the headmistress's behaviour was a 'most disgusting and abominable' assault on the innocence of childhood. They in turn were threatened with prosecution for refusing to send their children to school. The Education Authority, for its part, hid behind a clause in the 1870 Education Act which stated that their inspectors had no right of direction in the content of religious education. The Dronfield affair drifted on into the summer of 1914, without ever reaching a resolution.

———

Tom and Kitty Higdon, the couple at the centre of 1914's Burston School Strike, had arrived in the village, to take up their positions as teachers, on the last day of January 1911. Kitty, at forty-six, was to be the headmistress, her husband, five years her junior, her assistant.

Kitty had been born Annie Catherine Schollick, the daughter of a foreman shipwright from near Wallasey in Cheshire, whose ancestors had fled to England from Austria sometime in the nineteenth century. Tom Higdon, whom she had married in 1896, was of Somersetshire stock, the son of a farm labourer. Their different social backgrounds were reflected in their status as teachers. Whereas Kitty had received a good education and been fully trained as a professional schoolmistress, Tom had received his training as a certificated teacher through the pupil–teacher system. This permitted brighter pupils to stay on at school at a low rate of remuneration, receiving practical training as a teacher, while continuing with their own education.

After their marriage the Higdons moved to London, where Tom was engaged as an 'energetic and conscientious' assistant master at St James's and St Peter's School, a Church of England establishment for children from the poorest quarter of Soho. In the spring of 1902, the couple moved to Norfolk to joint teaching positions as a husband-and-wife team at Wood Dalling Council School, some forty miles from Burston.

Kitty was small, bright-eyed and kindly, a born teacher, with an unbending sense of her own rectitude. Tom was a tall, burly figure, who spoke slowly and deliberately while pulling on his braces with one hand and tugging at his moustache with the other. His florid, slightly ornate speaking-style is captured in several books and pamphlets he wrote, including *Bodies without Abodes*, a fictional account of labouring life and the tied cottage system. Both Higdons were Christian socialists with rock-solid egalitarian principles. Tom was a Primitive Methodist, a chapel-going sect that encouraged the dissemination of trade union ideas alongside the gospel. Kitty had been brought up in the Church of England, but was also a chapel-goer, though there were those at Burston who later recalled her operating the magic lantern for the Rector's talks in the church during her early years in the village. Kitty called herself a pacifist. Tom, on the other hand, was altogether more hot-headed, switching in an instant from a calm, easygoing and playful demeanour to aggressive and even threatening behaviour (pupils remembered him as being 'very severe with the cane'). Neither husband nor wife had wasted any time in acquiring diplomatic skills.

This had quickly become apparent during the Higdons' time at Wood Dalling. Kitty was successful in agitating for better conditions in the school itself, which was ill-lit, damp and unsanitary, and £400 was contributed by the Education Committee towards improvements. The Higdons were also intent on widening the curriculum beyond religious instruction and conventional drilling in the three *R*'s (reading, writing and arithmetic). They took the children on nature rambles, gave them some grounding in foreign languages like French and Russian, taught singing and drawing, and offered social gatherings and entertainments outside school hours; Kitty also provided cookery lessons in her own kitchen. The couple's generosity extended to providing food, clothing and footwear for their pupils, most of them the children of farm labourers, out of their own pockets (Kitty, it appears, had a small private income of her own).

But the Higdons' efforts to prevent farmers in the area from illegally employing children in school hours inevitably led to friction – and on one occasion to Tom Higdon's being brought before Norfolk Magistrates on a charge of assault. In the autumn of 1902 Tom had caught one of his schoolboys, in the pay of Farmer Gamble, leading a drill horse through a field across from the schoolroom. This was the third such instance of the farmer poaching boys from the school in the past six months. 'After a few . . . words,' according to the report in the *Norwich Mercury*, Tom Higdon hit Gamble 'with his fist and knocked him down, and then hit him when on the ground.' Gamble's eye was blackened and his face cut, and there were several bruises on his head and back. Tom was severely reprimanded for his 'fit of violent temper', found guilty and fined.

In a further bout of misfortune for the Higdons, eighteen months later, Farmer Gamble became one of the managers of Wood Dalling School. By this time, it was already being noted, in a confidential report prepared by the school managers for the Education Committee, that the Higdons were becoming something of a liability. Both were scarcely on speaking terms with the managers. Kitty continued to demand improvements to the school buildings, while Tom's involvement in union politics, campaigning for wage increases for agricultural labourers, brought him increasingly into conflict with farmers.

Tom's formative years had coincided with the movement to establish rights for agricultural labourers founded in 1872 by Joseph Arch. Although Arch's National Agricultural Labourers' Union had fallen prey to internal division and the agricultural depression, a second union for farm workers emerged in 1906 following the Liberal landslide victory, which also saw the returning to Parliament, for the two-member Norfolk constituency, of one out of the twenty-nine successful Labour Party candidates in the country.

From 1907 Tom Higdon spent much of the time he wasn't teaching cycling miles around the Norfolk countryside, speaking and organizing on behalf of the rural workforce, and achieving small wage increases for the labourers, much to the fury of the farmers. In 1910 he persuaded labourers to vote each other on to the parish council in place of the farmers. Tom himself was voted in as Chairman, ousting J. J. Bussens, a farmer, pub landlord and one of the managers of the council school.

The resulting sequence of events for the Higdons at Wood Dalling was now almost inevitable. The farmers took their revenge, bringing trumped-up charges against the couple, including the accusation, vehemently denied by Kitty Higdon, that she had called two of the School Managers 'liars'.

An inquiry was held, which concluded with the Norfolk Education Committee offering 'these troublesome teachers' a choice between dismissal or a transfer to another school. However, on taking up their posts at Burston, the Higdons were to find that conditions there were even worse than those at Wood Dalling. Agricultural labourers' wages were lower, as there were no union branches in the area, housing conditions were atrocious, and the school was ill-lit, badly heated and poorly ventilated.

Worst of all, as events were to prove, the new incumbent of Burston, the Reverend Charles Tucker Eland, was 'a little man with big consequences', who was to rule parish and school with a sense of paternalistic authority, and of the deference due to him, that verged on the despotic.

In a variety of ways, the social prestige of the Church of England in the countryside had come under dramatic attack in the course of the past quarter of a century. Under the Local Government Act of 1894, parish councils had been established in rural villages and towns, thereby transferring the civil powers that had formerly belonged to the Church to representatives of the state, in the interests of greater democracy. At the same time, the growth of unionization in rural areas was widely seen as undermining the respect conventionally shown to the local parson. The Norwich Diocesan Conference had been addressed in 1902 on the subject of the clergy's loss of influence over the farm labourer. Ten years later, the Reverend Alban Baverstock, in his study of *The Failure of the Church in the Villages*, commented on the 'revolt of the labourer', defining his idea of 'revolt' as 'the expression by every means in his power of [the labourer's] independence of the classes to whom he has hitherto been in submission'.

By contrast, the new Education Act of 1902 – with its abolition of school boards, run by representatives elected by local ratepayers, and their replacement by county borough councils as the local education authorities – could be seen as moving in the Church's favour. The local education authorities were empowered to appoint education committees in rural areas, consisting of individuals with a special knowledge of the district. In practice, as the radical journal *Justice* acknowledged, this meant committees composed of 'parsons and squires' who had 'the least possible interest in the education of the children of the people, except to make them mere humble and obedient wage slaves'.

Both of these developments, rural unionization and clerical dominance of the School Managers, were to form the essential background to the strike at Burston School.

The Reverend Charles Tucker Eland was in his mid fifties when he came to Burston as Rector in 1911, shortly before the end of the Higdons' first year. He had studied at the London School of Divinity in the mid 1880s, gaining preferment relatively late and becoming Vicar of Felsted in north-west Essex, where he remained for over a decade. No portrait or photograph of him has come down to us, though he was described by one of the Burston villagers, who had reason enough to dislike him, as small and ferret-like. Eland and his wife Mary had two daughters in their late teens, Grace and Ruth, and the family inhabited the twelve-bedroomed rectory, with its 'winding paths and sheltering trees, cricket and croquet lawns, orchards and ornamental gardens'. Together with a salary of £495 a year, plus fifty-four acres of glebe land rented out to produce £86 yearly, this graceful residence was Eland's to enjoy, as one villager observed, 'because he preaches a sermon once a week to three old ladies and the sexton'.

As was customary, Eland had no sooner arrived in Burston as the new Rector than he was elected to the Board of School Managers as Chairman. By 1914 the School Management Committee was well and truly packed with the Rector's supporters. It consisted of Mrs Eland, the Reverend Charles Millard, Rector of the neighbouring parish of Shimpling, Millard's churchwarden, R. Stearne, Mr Fisher, one of Eland's tenants, and Mr Witherley, a Nonconformist who was widely held to be in Eland's pocket.

Eland's relations with the Higdons were initially polite but distant. He objected to their refusal to attend church and their preference for the Nonconformist chapel, complaining about the 'godlessness' of the village. He argued that 'The place of the school-mistress is at church and the children with her', resenting the fact that at least half the children attending Burston Council School were from Nonconformist families. Eland must also have felt threatened by the breadth of the curriculum taught by Kitty Higdon, and the school's extracurricular activities. In small ways, by teaching the girls how to use her typewriter, for instance, or through the elocution lessons she provided, Kitty was preparing her pupils for the possibility of a better life outside the village. Eland's attitude to the education of the poor remained solidly traditional. Education should reinforce their place in the social order, and not fuel their expectations beyond those commensurate with their station in life – or, as a bit of doggerel from Burston, directed at Eland, later put it, 'You teach the ground down starving man/That squire's greed is Jehovah's plan.'

The main threat to the Reverend Eland's parochial powerbase came in March 1913 with the elections to the parish council. Tom Higdon had at first resisted the temptation to become involved in local politics at Burston, wary of antagonizing farmers in the way he had at Wood Dalling. But before long he had resumed his union activities, and was unable to resist an invitation to stand as one of the farm labourers' candidates for the council. Once again Tom was involved in what he referred to as 'Parish Council Democratic Reform'. The results of the poll swept away most of the farmers' old guard, their votes failing even to get into two figures. Tom Higdon came top, with thirty-one votes, the Rector came bottom, with only nine.

From this point on, Eland pursued a vendetta against Tom Higdon, chiefly by directing an increasingly bitter campaign against Kitty Higdon's position in the school. Kitty had already been criticized by the School Managers for her extravagance in lighting a fire in the schoolroom to dry the children's clothes. She had reported that the lack of proper drainage in the playground was causing damp rot in the floorboards of the schoolroom. But she obtained permission for only limited repairs, the purchase of a wire rope for the school-bell and a larger water tank. During Eland's absence from Burston while on holiday in Switzerland with his family, there was an epidemic of whooping cough in the village. After receiving the consent of the

Vice-Chairman of the School Managers to take what action she thought necessary, Kitty closed the school for a week. On the Rector's return, Kitty was reproved at a meeting of the managers. They 'took a very serious view of her having closed the school without permission'. Matters rested until November 1913, when Eland learned that Mrs Higdon was again lighting open fires at the school without permission. On 29 November, Eland wrote to the Norfolk Education Committee that 'As Mrs Higdon seems to wish to act contrary to the Managers' wishes, and has so many complaints to make as to the present building, the Managers ask the Committee if they will kindly remove her to a sphere more genial.'

When this letter failed to persuade the Education Committee to reconsider Kitty Higdon's position at Burston, Eland produced a new, and potentially much more damaging, accusation against the headmistress: that she had thrashed two Barnardo's children when they had complained of the indecent conduct of one of the boys in the school playground. The children in question, Ethel Cummings and Gertie Stearnes, were being fostered by a Mrs Philpot, well known in the village for her temper and slovenly ways. Mrs Philpot received a weekly sum from Barnardo's for the care of the children, and this was paid to her by the Rector, as the Home's local representative.

The charges concealed a tissue of lies. The register showed that the boy who had engaged in the indecent conduct was not in school on the day the offence was supposed to have occurred. Nor had Kitty Higdon, as a professed pacifist, caned the girls and sent them home with weals on their backs, as had been alleged. Other pupils at the school knew that Kitty hadn't punished the girls. She had only admonished them for their false stories about the boy. Even the girls themselves eventually confessed that they had been put under pressure to tell these stories, and were frightened that their foster-mother would beat them if they didn't.

The Higdons wrote to Barnardo's, recommending that the children should be removed from Mrs Philpot's care, and, more questionably, stating in one letter that Ethel Cummings was a moral and mental defective and a danger to the school. Barnardo's made no attempt to investigate the situation, passing on the letter to the Rector, who made what capital he could with it. There was no basis to the charges made by the Higdons against Mrs Philpot and her foster-children, Eland told the Education Committee on 23 January 1914. 'Under all these circumstances the Managers feel at a loss what to do . . . and they consider this constant haranguing of the whole School on this unpleasant subject most tactless and detrimental to its tone and discipline. Owing to the insubordination and rudeness of the Mistress, there is no esprit de corps between her and the Managers and they find it impossible to work with her, so respectfully ask that she may be transferred.' Significantly, Eland did not attempt to press the charges of caning.

The Higdons demanded an impartial inquiry. The National Union of Teachers, with their memories of the friction at Wood Dalling still fresh, agreed only reluctantly to provide them with legal assistance. On two afternoons during the last week of February, a tribunal was chaired by three local councillors sent to Burston by the Norfolk Education Committee. At first proceedings appeared to be moving in the Higdons' favour. 'A beautiful case! A beautiful case!' exclaimed the NUT's standing counsel, confident of victory. The fire-lighting charge was dismissed on the first day before an adjournment was called. Anxious that the School Managers might not secure the verdict for Kitty Higdon's instant dismissal, Eland brought in a Norwich solicitor to act for them.

At this point the tribunal started to turn against the headmistress and her husband. A charge of discourtesy – that Kitty had failed to bow to the Rector's daughter 'as she whizzed past on a bicycle', that she had given Mrs Eland 'a cold reception' when she visited the school, and that she had ignored a greeting from the Rector himself when she passed him on the road – was upheld. The NUT counsel, according to Tom Higdon, 'gave up the fight'. He refused to call witnesses, maintaining that they were to be held in reserve for a possible slander action, and argued that the letters written by the Higdons to Barnardo's contained language that was difficult to justify.

The findings of the tribunal recommended that 'the Head Teacher should seek other employment with as little delay as possible.' The Higdons were asked to leave the council school by 31 March. Early on the morning of 1 April, the Assistant Secretary of the Education

Committee, Mr Ikins, appeared in Burston with salary cheques for the Higdons in lieu of notice and instructions that they were to vacate the schoolhouse within a fortnight. The cheques remained untouched on the schoolhouse table.

Outside, on the village green, a group of sixty-six children was lining up to form a procession. On the first clang of the school-bell, they moved off, carrying banners and wearing cards around their necks with the slogans 'WE WANT OUR TEACHERS BACK' and 'JUSTICE FOR ALL'.

The Reverend Eland, keeping well out of the way of the children's procession, but observing it from the windows of the Rectory as it passed, dismissed the strike as a nine days' wonder, or an April Fool's joke. The procession followed a prearranged route around the 'Candlestick' (an East Anglian expression for a circular walk). Violet Potter, the strikers' ringleader, played an accordion, and some of the other children had brought mouth organs, on which they accompanied the singing of the patriotic song 'Heart of Oak'. At the school-gates, they were watched by a police inspector from Diss, and received disapproving stares from two of the School Managers and the new supply teachers, who had arrived to find themselves in charge of no more than half a dozen pupils. As their tour of the village ended, the children were rewarded with glasses of lemonade, and nuts and sweets, on the small patch of green beside the Crown Inn. The procession was repeated that afternoon, and every day for the rest of the week.

The villagers' affection and unwavering support for the Higdons were in evidence on the day of their eviction from the schoolhouse, when nearly all of Burston turned out with carts and wheelbarrows to help move their belongings to the Higdons' temporary accommodation in the mill-house. In the third week of April, eighteen Burston parents appeared before Diss Magistrates for neglecting to send their children to school. A demonstration by the strikers outside the court succeeded in attracting attention from well-wishers, and enough money was collected to cover the cost of the fines.

A further set of summonses was issued by the Magistrates Court, but by now they were, in a sense, superfluous. In response to requests from parents, the Higdons, who had had no inkling that the children were going on strike, gave lessons, in the warm April weather, out on the village green. A register was kept and the teaching followed a full timetable. A disused carpenter's shop was subsequently taken over by the newly appointed School Committee. Whitewashed, and fitted out with stools and tables loaned by parents, it became the first strike school.

News of the Burston children's strike was spreading rapidly to the outside world. National papers reported that the sympathy of the villagers 'is strongly with the deposed teachers, and the opinion is freely expressed that political motives underlie the matter, Mr Higdon's views on politics being opposed to those of the Rector and the majority of the Managers'. Asked by a reporter from the *Daily Chronicle* about his membership of the Agricultural Labourers' Union, Tom replied, 'I am a Labourers' man – that's the top and the bottom of it.' The village green was the focal point for the strike and for sympathizers who travelled from miles around to express their solidarity with the villagers. Every Sunday, crowds of visitors arrived at Burston to listen to speeches on the green (or in the carpenter's shop if the weather turned showery) from members of the Norwich Branch of the Independent Labour Party. A religious service would open the proceedings, led by John Sutton, a lay preacher at Burston Chapel, and afterwards a collection would be taken in aid of the Higdons and the Parents' Defence Fund.

The Rector's church congregation had meanwhile dwindled to a handful of his personal supporters, as Methodist services, baptisms and even funerals were held on the green. If sighted by visitors attending the open-air demonstrations, Eland was likely to be chased through the village and forced to take refuge in the church. In rhymes on broadsheets, headed 'Hell for the Parson' and posted around Norwich, he was known as the 'Burston Blackbeetle':

> When the Burston Blackbeetle goes down to his doom,
>   He will ride in a fiery chariot,
> And sit in state, on a red hot plate,
>   'Twixt Satan and Judas Iscariot.

In the future, Eland would resort to ever more desperate and vindictive measures, threatening council school employees with dismissal if they did not speak out against the Higdons, and evicting glebe tenants from their property. But, undeterred, the villagers were to continue to challenge his authority by keeping their children at the strike school. The Burston Rebellion became a small beacon of hope in the struggle against social injustice and, even more importantly, a celebrated expression of the strength of grass-roots democracy.

On 15 July 1914, a large meeting was held in the village. Eighteen trade union banners were ranged around the green; a brass band came from Norwich; and a special train from London brought down hundreds of railwaymen, who had taken Burston's cause to their hearts. There were speeches, and the village children, who had started it all, sang and performed country dances.

It would be among the first of many such rallies to support the strike school in the years to come.

Not Bloody Likely

What the devil have I done with my slippers?

The soft velvet shoes, like a pair of well-aimed missiles, shot across the stage, one after the other, hitting Sir Herbert Beerbohm Tree, a foremost Knight of the theatre, bang in the face. He looked momentarily startled. Then, with dramatic effect, he stumbled slightly, located a chair behind him and collapsed into it, his eyes brimming with tears.

Tree was rehearsing the role of Henry Higgins for the first English production of George Bernard Shaw's *Pygmalion*. Rehearsals of the play, directed by its author, had started at His Majesty's Theatre in the third week of February, with Mrs Patrick Campbell taking the part of Eliza Doolittle, the flower girl who Higgins attempts to transform into a duchess by means of his science of phonetics.

It was hoped that the play would be ready for its London première in April 1914, but the signs were not encouraging, and Sir Herbert's emotional reaction to the flying slippers was only the latest in a succession of incidents which appeared to indicate that the production was in danger of disintegrating into chaos. If Tree had been in surer command of his script, he would have known that in Act IV, when Higgins returns to his Wimpole Street laboratory following Eliza's triumph at the Embassy garden party, he is assailed by a pair of slippers shied at him by Eliza, angry at the way Higgins has treated her like a mechanical doll with no respect for her feelings.

Instead, Tree was taken completely unawares by Mrs Patrick Campbell's devastating throw. He appeared to have forgotten that there was any such action in the play. 'It seemed to him,' Shaw recalled afterwards, 'that Mrs Campbell, suddenly giving way to an impulse of

His Majesty's Theatre
Herbert Tree
PYGMALION

The poster for the first English production of *Pygmalion*, April 1914, with Sir Herbert
Beerbohm Tree as Henry Higgins and Mrs Patrick Campbell (*right*) as flower girl
Eliza Doolittle

diabolical wrath and hatred, had committed an unprovoked and brutal assault on him.' While Tree nursed his bruised feelings, the entire company crowded round him, offering comfort and the evidence of the prompt book to show that the slippers were indeed part of the prescribed action. But his morale was so shattered that it was some time before he could be coaxed into returning to rehearsal.

Persistent delays to a tight schedule were among the things driving Shaw frantic. As the manager of His Majesty's, the theatre built in the French Renaissance style that he had helped to establish in 1897, Tree was just as often to be found in his office in the Dome – entertaining visitors, meeting with his business manager Henry Dana, or watching rehearsals from the dress circle with his understudy taking his place as Higgins – as he was to be seen on stage. When he did rehearse, in the improvisatory fashion that exasperated Shaw, he was frequently uncertain of his lines, or inclined to give them a touch of his own spontaneous polish. Mrs Patrick Campbell, meanwhile, was habitually unpunctual. If Tree wasn't there, she would go straight to her dressing-room, refusing to rehearse until he arrived. She had promised Shaw that she would be 'tame as a mouse and oh so obedient'. Once onstage, however, she more than lived up to her reputation as the bane of directors. She raised a host of objections: interrupting Shaw to argue with his instructions, interfering with his blocking of scenes, rearranging the furniture and protesting on the first day of rehearsals about the absence of her flower basket. She was a professional, she announced as she sailed back to her dressing-room, and wasn't prepared to rehearse without her props.

Within a week of the start of rehearsals, Shaw had stormed out of the theatre, unable to stand the temperamental behaviour of his two stars any longer. He declared loudly as he marched down the aisle that he was leaving town. In fact he only got as far as Covent Garden, and a performance of Wagner's *Meistersinger*. Tree wrote to Shaw the next day, trying to be conciliatory but nevertheless chastising him for the 'cowardly evasion' that left him 'to the tender mercies of Mrs Patrick Campbell'. He emphasized that 'of course we all have different ways of working. I find that I circle before I swoop: others appear to swoop in order to make circles afterwards.' But he appealed to Shaw to return soon. 'It is obvious that your own play needs your own spirit brooding over it.'

For each of its three principals, *Pygmalion* represented a new kind of challenge and set of departures. Tree had perhaps the most to lose. As actor-manager at His Majesty's, he was accustomed to being in control, despite his legendary vagueness about the mechanics and economics of theatre production. He had built up the theatre's name through an astute mix of repertoire: classical drama, including a dazzling succession of extravagantly mounted Shakespeare plays, and contemporary poetic drama and works by prominent British playwrights like Henry Arthur Jones, as well as a host of melodramas, farces and adaptations of nineteenth-century novels by Thackeray and Dickens.

However, in a move which signalled the general decline in dominance of the actor-manager and a new concentration on the importance of the play and its playwright, Tree had surrendered much of his power to Shaw. Understandably in these circumstances, he was unable at times to stop himself from asserting his point of view, often in opposition to Shaw's. As director, Tree had always opted for grand spectacle. His production of *The Merchant of Venice* had centred on the re-creation of a Renaissance ghetto, while his *Henry VIII* had culminated in a lavish tableau of Anne Bullen's coronation in Westminster Abbey. For *Pygmalion*, he informed Shaw that a sumptuous ball scene was needed at the end of Act III to bring home to the audience the full impact of Eliza's triumph. Shaw dismissed such suggestions as pointless attempts to gild the lily. He thought it bad enough that a taxicab drove on to the stage during the opening scene in Covent Garden. 'Really, that is the only drawback of production at His Majesty's,' Shaw told one newspaper reporter, on the trail of rumours of ructions at rehearsal. 'The scenery and adjuncts are apt to distract attention from the author's words.'

Tree was also uncomfortable in his role as Henry Higgins. He was a master of disguise, hiding behind intricate make-up and transforming his features with putty and paint for roles as diverse as Svengali, Falstaff, Micawber and Hamlet. He was able to complete this physical transformation by radically altering his carriage or stature. As

Beethoven in Louis Parker's play, this tall, lanky man had managed to suggest a short, stocky, square-set character walking in jerky strides.

The prospect of strolling on to the stage of His Majesty's in modern clothes, with the minimum of actor's tricks or histrionics, seemed, though, to defeat him. In despair Tree begged Shaw to allow the character to take snuff, adopt a limp or a Scots accent, and to vault on and off the piano from time to time. When this failed, Tree sought to make Higgins more palatable in the mould of a romantic hero. After all, hadn't Shaw subtitled *Pygmalion* 'A Romance in Five Acts'?

Tree's determination to play Higgins along romantic lines was to prove a lasting source of disagreement with Shaw. 'I say, Tree,' Shaw shouted while watching the rehearsal of the fifth act, in which Higgins asks Eliza to return to him, 'must you be so damned *Tree-acly?*' In vain, Shaw attempted to clarify the difference between Ovid's myth of Pygmalion and Galatea and his modern interpretation of it. In classical mythology, Pygmalion marries the statue which he has sculpted and brought to life. Shaw, by contrast, was adamant that Higgins and Eliza must never marry. Such an outcome, he declared, would be 'unbearable'. By the end of the play, Eliza has become an independent woman, well up to defending her independence in a battle of words with Higgins. And she has come to recognize that, unlike Pygmalion, Higgins is not a life-giver. He is mother-fixated, imprisoned by his science of phonetics, and has given Eliza a freedom greater than he himself possesses. *Pygmalion*, according to Shaw, was a romance only because 'the transfiguration it records seems exceedingly improbable.'

Like Tree, Mrs Patrick Campbell was struggling with her part. It was the first time she had appeared in a comedy. Moreover, Eliza was a far cry from the melodrama of Paula Tanqueray, Pinero's woman with a sexual past, with which she had cemented her fame. She was in her fiftieth year, already a grandmother, fighting increasing girth, and only too conscious of the fact that she was at least a quarter of a century too old for the role of an eighteen-year-old 'guttersnipe'. Shaw noticed how she insisted on having a powerful spotlight directed on her face. This was designed to disguise her age, but succeeded only in blotting out character and casting unflattering shadows. The result, he said, was that her face looked like a dinner-plate with two prunes on it. From the stalls Shaw ungallantly shouted 'Good God, you are forty years too old for Eliza; sit still and it is not so noticeable.' In his rehearsal notes, at the point where Higgins compliments Eliza as 'not bad looking', he scribbled, 'Dreadful middle aged moments'.

She was also having problems with the cockney accent in the early scenes, in spite of careful coaching from Shaw, concentrating on the 'slow – and quicker – tempo' in which she spoke her lines in her booming, sonorous voice. She had begun to suspect that Shaw had wanted her for Eliza 'for the joy' of making a fool of her. Years before, as a critic for *Saturday Review*, Shaw had praised Mrs Pat's 'instinctive' enunciation, while criticizing her affected vowels, especially the clipped English *a* through which she mimicked lady-like behaviour. In Eliza Doolittle's cockney speech cadences – into which Mrs Pat was trying to inject some rhythm 'and no comic adenoid effects' – and then Eliza's self-conscious precision when speaking as a lady, she sensed that Shaw was mocking her, perhaps even making a veiled allusion to her mother's rumoured humble profession as a circus rider.

For Shaw himself, the London production of *Pygmalion* presented an opportunity to fulfil a long-hoped-for ambition: to achieve commercial success with a new, worthwhile play in a fashionable West End theatre. After all, as he remarked, 'one has to write a box-office success now and then.' This had become all the more important to him following the heavy financial losses recently sustained by his *Androcles and the Lion*, which had opened to enthusiastic reviews in September 1913, only then to be withdrawn after barely fifty performances. Like many of his plays, *Pygmalion* had been first produced abroad. Shaw trusted that his work would be received more sympathetically in New York or Vienna than in London, where he described it as the custom of the English press, 'when a play of mine is produced, to inform the world that it is not a play – that it is dull, blasphemous, unpopular and financially unsuccessful'. *Pygmalion* had premièred successfully in Vienna in October 1913, in a German translation by Shaw's long-term collaborator Siegfried Trebitsch, with Tilla Durieux, one of the Hofburgtheater's comedy stars, as Eliza (there was some confusion in the opening scene where the backdrop depicted not St Paul's, Covent Garden, as Shaw intended, but St Paul's Cathedral). This was swiftly followed by productions in Berlin, in New York on the German-language immigrant stage, Budapest, Stockholm, Warsaw and St Petersburg.

How long, though, would it be before an English audience got to see Shaw's new play? Rumours in the press of possible delays caused by rows at rehearsals – even that Shaw and Tree had come to blows – were accompanied by mounting curiosity about the prospect of Mrs Pat playing a cockney flower girl. Intrigued, the National Cinema Company offered £100 to make a film of a day's rehearsal. Shaw turned them down flat.

But there was an unspoken, intricate subplot lurking behind all the onstage sparring between Shaw and Mrs Pat. Almost two years earlier, Shaw had declared his love for her as his 'perilously bewitching' dark-haired enchantress, and had embarked on an elaborate courtship, only to have his advances rudely rebuffed in a climactic scene at the Guilford Hotel in Sandwich, on the Kent coast, in August 1913.

An East End dona in an apron and three orange and red ostrich feathers

This was how Shaw had originally conceived the role of the 'rapscallionly flower girl' for Mrs Patrick Campbell as long ago as 1897. At that time he had hoped that the actor Johnston Forbes-Robertson – believed by many to be Mrs Pat's lover – would star opposite her as 'a west end gentleman'.

Nothing had come of this plan. But the idea for *Pygmalion* itself proved remarkably resilient. Shaw began writing the play on 7 March 1912 and completed it just over three months later. In outline *Pygmalion*'s plot owed something to an episode from Tobias Smollett's 1751 novel, *The Adventures of Peregrine Pickle*, in which Peregrine takes charge of a coarse working girl and transforms her into a fine lady. The character of Henry Higgins may have been partly inspired by the great British phonetician Henry Sweet, but he clearly owed something, too, to a dominating figure from Shaw's youth: George John Vandeleur Lee, a music teacher who had taught 'the method', and had exerted a Svengali-like influence over Shaw's mother, Bessie.

Flower girls were a familiar sight in England's big cities, in large commercial areas like Birmingham's Bull Ring, or in the principal streets of London's West End. Traditionally they alternated the selling of flowers with the sale of oranges at times of the year when the fruit was cheap. Early in 1914, attempts to move orange-sellers from outside the Drury Lane Theatre, where they had been plying their wares since the days of Nell Gwyn, had been met with angry protests, and a petition to the Home Secretary, who promised that in future they wouldn't be disturbed. It seems likely that Shaw relied on Henry Mayhew's classic portrait of mid-Victorian London street life, *London Labour and the London Poor*, for small details of the flower girl's existence. Like the better class of flower girl in Mayhew's study – specifically those who did not supplement the sale of flowers with immoral earnings – Shaw's Eliza lived in a lodging house in Lisson Grove. However, by 1914, Eliza's hat, with its three ostrich feathers, orange, sky-blue and red, was an anachronism. London flower-sellers had abandoned ostrich-plumed hats in favour of more practical ones of dark straw.

It's also not inconceivable that as he began work on *Pygmalion*, Shaw's eye may have been caught by a news item that was circulating widely in the press. This reported the story of a flower girl who was on the verge of committing suicide by jumping from Westminster Bridge when a man drove by in a pony and trap and asked her what was the matter. After some discussion she drove off with him, and in due course he set her up in business as the manager of a shop.

Little more than a week after finishing his play, Shaw read it aloud to Mrs Patrick Campbell, *Pygmalion*'s first muse, at the Westminster home of a mutual friend, Dame Edith Lyttleton. If he had been concerned that a play about 'a flower girl, using awful language . . . and having her hat put in the oven to slay the creepy-crawlies, and being taken off the stage and washed' would be beneath the dignity of his notoriously imperious star, he needn't have worried. Although she quickly began to argue with Shaw about the actor to play Higgins –

not Robert Loraine, Shaw's choice, perhaps Matheson Lang or C. Aubrey Smith (Sir George Alexander had already politely informed Shaw that he would play Higgins 'with anyone in the world but Mrs P. C.') – she thanked him for thinking she could be his 'pretty slut' and invited him to visit her at home at 33 Kensington Square. The following day, 23 June, she contrived, as she shook his hand, a brush of Shaw's fingers against her bosom, 'an infamous, abandoned trick' that sent him into seventh heaven.

He was 'violently and exquisitely in love', he told anyone who would listen. 'All yesterday,' he wrote to the actress Lillah McCarthy, 'I could think of nothing but a thousand scenes of which she was the heroine and I the hero. And I am on the verge of 56. There has never been anything so ridiculous or delightful, in the history of the world.'

To the heroine of this outrageous romance, Shaw sent a stream of effusive letters. Dropping the 'Mrs Patrick Campbell' – her stage name, derived from her marriage to Pat Campbell, killed in the South African War in 1900 – Shaw apotheosized her as 'Beatricissima' or, in a state of increasing ecstasy, as 'Stella, Stellata, Stellatissima', her second name. Mrs Pat's nickname for Shaw was 'Joey', the archetypal clown, an acknowledgement of his disarming and enraging mischievousness. Her initial response to his letters, though, dampened his ardour by telling him that she hadn't had a minute 'to answer your many funny green pages [Shaw wrote on green paper to combat his migraines]' and by signing off with her love to him – and to his wife too.

Within a month of the play reading, however, Shaw's Stella was laid up in bed, severely shaken and badly bruised after she, and her pet griffon Georgina, had been involved in a taxicab collision near the Albert Hall. Hiding two black eyes, she left London for Aix-les-Bains to recuperate. On her return she remained seriously ill and confined to bed for six months. 'My body was the nearest thing to death that life can hold,' she wrote later. 'My living mind grasped the utter futility and weariness of this business of life.'

Fortunately, Shaw was swiftly at her bedside, cajoling Mrs Pat back to life. He laughed and flirted, took photographs of her as a dark and rather heavy siren among the bedclothes, and, as she was unable to work and lived habitually beyond her means, gave her essential injections of cash. She rewarded Shaw by acknowledging her dependence, sending him 'a real love letter', while warning that she would never allow a man to kiss her unless she was certain of a wedding ring.

Playing Romeo was a delightful game. The problem for Shaw was that, in the midst of all his 'blarneying', he felt his part so deeply that he sometimes forgot he was acting. He begged Stella not to fall in love with him; but nor should she grudge him 'the joy he finds in being in love with you, and writing all sorts of wild but heartfelt exquisite lies'. Meanwhile, as he informed Lillah McCarthy, 'the deeper fidelities' remained untouched.

But did they? Charlotte, Shaw's wife of fifteen years, whom Mrs Pat unflatteringly described as generically dowdy like a suffragette, was not so sure. True, there had been a succession of Shavian romances with famous actresses, but Charlotte divined that the unresolved sexual element in her husband's relationship with Mrs Pat was of a kind that had been largely absent from his earlier dalliances.

By Christmas 1912, Mrs Pat was on the mend. She had sprung back to life, and, full of 'witcheries and devilries', was playing cat and mouse with Shaw again. Eliza Doolittle remained a vital bargaining counter between them. Shaw was convinced that *Pygmalion* needed a star actress in the role, otherwise the play would fail. Throughout the first half of 1913, the question of whether Mrs Pat would do *Pygmalion* remained undecided as she and Shaw circled one another. In the end she would commit to it, but only after appearing in *The Adored One*, a play written for her by J. M. Barrie. Shaw counselled her to take the part in Barrie's play first, as it was certain to be the more lucrative of the two, and follow it with *Pygmalion*. Under protest she took his advice. *The Adored One* opened that September and was a conspicuous flop.

'I MUSTNT be in love; but I *am*' (Shaw customarily dispensed with apostrophes, wherever possible, as superfluous, like other punctuation). In March 1913 he stole away from a meeting at Beachy Head to discuss the future of the *New Statesman* with Beatrice and Sidney Webb, and had an assignation with Mrs Pat at Brighton. Charlotte caught a whiff of this and, with 'Boundless contempt', faced Shaw with his indiscretion. 'I throw my desperate hands to heaven,' Shaw exclaimed, 'and ask why one cannot make one beloved woman happy without sacrificing another.'

However, the curtain was soon to fall on the first act of Shaw and Mrs Pat's drama. On the afternoon of 8 August, within minutes of Charlotte's departure on holiday to Marseilles, Shaw was on his way to Kent in pursuit of Stella Campbell, who had rented a cottage near Ramsgate to study Barrie's script. Arriving there that evening, after a protracted tramp across the sands, Shaw discovered that Mrs Pat had already moved to the Guilford Hotel. Here they spent two days together, Mrs Pat increasingly exasperated by Shaw's presence and unable to disguise her longing for him to go. In fact she was waiting for the appearance of her new paramour, George Cornwallis-West, Lady Randolph Churchill's youthful, estranged husband, an ex-Guards officer, and hunting, shooting and fishing fanatic. On 10 August she sent Shaw a terse note begging him to return to London – 'or . . . wherever you like but don't stay here'. At eight the next morning he knocked on her door, only to find that she had fled to St Margaret's Bay, along with her maid, chauffeur and dog.

His words, full of scorn, followed her there. She was 'a one-part actress and that one not a real part'; she was 'an owl, sickened by two days of my sunshine'. Shaw's letter ended by attacking her in terms strongly reminiscent of Henry Higgins, inveighing against Eliza Doolittle's decision to marry her young suitor Freddy Eynsford-Hill: 'Go then; the Shavian oxygen burns up your little lungs: seek some stuffiness that suits you. You will not marry George! At the last moment you will funk him . . . You have wounded my vanity: an inconceivable audacity, an unpardonable crime.'

Ah-ah-ah-ow-ow-ow-ow-oo!

'If you put a cat, a dog and a monkey into a sack together,' remarked Henry Dana, Tree's business manager, of *Pygmalion*'s rehearsals at His Majesty's, 'what can you expect but ructions?' Shaw had some photographs of himself taken which had to be destroyed because, he maintained, he looked as if he'd been in a fight. He sent one to Mrs Pat with the words 'Aren't you ashamed?', and another to Tree, inscribed 'This is your work.' He was tired of Mrs Pat's tantrums, her habit of turning her back on the other actors, or of making faces at them when anything displeased her. But her behaviour at Sandwich the previous summer also encouraged Shaw to adopt a manner of often casual, even brutal indifference towards her. 'You haven't hurt me at all,' she wrote to him in response, feigning her own brand of indifference, as opening night drew near. 'You have only bored me by your ceaseless teasing and braggarting.'

The première of *Pygmalion* was now set for Saturday, 11 April 1914, but Mrs Patrick Campbell still had one more trick up her sleeve. On Monday, 6 April, the beginning of the last week of rehearsals, she was nowhere to be seen. It swiftly transpired that she had disappeared to get married. George Cornwallis-West was a free man. Two hours after the granting of the decree absolute that had ended his marriage to Lady Randolph Churchill, he and Mrs Pat had been married in the Kensington Register Office and driven off for a three-day honeymoon at a golfing resort near Tunbridge Wells. The bride was forty-nine, the bridegroom a decade her junior.

While Tree lied brazenly to reporters in the dress-circle bar about possessing foreknowledge of his co-star's remarriage – 'naturally I was sworn to secrecy' – Shaw simply remarked that Cornwallis-West had proved a braver man than he had been. Mrs Pat arrived back just in time for the six o'clock dress rehearsal on Thursday evening. It was a dispiriting affair, attended by an invited audience that included H. G. Wells and G. K. Chesterton.

Shaw was immediately dissatisfied with the lack of rain at the beginning of Act I. Freddy was 'too dry' when he rushed in, after failing to find a cab. 'Make horrible, finer rain!' he demanded. 'Cant we get the clouds to move & the moon to come out when the rain stops?' His rehearsal notes make it clear that having to counteract any suggestion by Mrs Pat and Tree that Higgins and Eliza had a future together remained his greatest problem. Algernon Greig as Freddy was urged to make the most of his infatuation with Eliza and to 'Lean over eagerly' when he was introduced to her. When Tree as Higgins boasted about being able to pass Eliza off as a duchess in three months, Shaw exclaimed, 'Oh God, dont look at her too much . . . Higgins is interested in the challenge not the woman.' Similarly, when Higgins takes Eliza's arm as he declares her his 'consort battleship', Mrs Pat's Eliza 'must instantly throw him off with implacable pride'.

Tree had serious worries of his own. He entreated Shaw in vain to substitute 'blooming' or 'ruddy' for Eliza's 'bloody' in her sensational exit line 'Not bloody likely' – subsequently amended by Shaw to 'No bloody fear' and then restored to the original – at the end of the third act. Shaw had fallen foul of theatrical censors in the past, most notably in 1909 when *The Shewing-Up of Blanco Posnet*, his play about a horse thief set in the American West, had been banned in England on the grounds of blasphemy. But Eliza's use of 'bloody' had been passed by G. S. Street from the Lord Chamberlain's office (which was responsible for theatrical censorship) on the grounds that 'the incident is merely funny.' The word had certainly been heard on the English stage before, though it had occasionally been banned, along with the expression 'damn'. Shaw himself defended its inclusion by claiming that it was an expletive in common use 'by four-fifths of the English nation'. English dramatic censorship, however, was nothing if not inconsistent. Some weeks after *Pygmalion* opened, the censor refused to allow a licence for the performance, at London's Royal Court Theatre, of *The Supplanters* by J. B. MacCarthy, a rural postman from Ireland, because he used 'a Shavian expletive' in the expression 'Bloody brats'.

Tree remained wary of how a fashionable West End audience might react to hearing a word widely condemned as blasphemous. The foreign productions of *Pygmalion* offered no guidelines. In the Viennese production the previous year, 'Not bloody likely' had been replaced by the German word *Dreck*, meaning 'rubbish'.

Rumours that there was something scandalous about Shaw's new play, and that Mrs Pat would utter 'A Forbidden Word', had risen to a crescendo by the morning of the opening, when a *Daily Sketch* headline proclaimed that '*Pygmalion* May Cause Sensation To-Night'. The *Sketch* reporter maintained that unless the Lord Chamberlain intervened, 'a dreadful word' would 'fall with bombshell suddenness from the lips of Mrs Patrick Campbell' (the paper, intent on building suspense, was nevertheless unable to bring itself to print the dreaded word). Press interest was overwhelming, and Shaw was snapped by photographers as he made his way to the theatre after lunch.

That evening at His Majesty's, Tree approached Mrs Pat in her special dressing-room, constructed inside a tent at stage level, to beg her not to say 'bloody', or, if she must say it, to say it 'beautifully'.

The curtain was due to go up at eight. Half an hour before, the area surrounding the theatre was choked with carriages, motor-cars and taxicabs, the largest traffic jam in the West End since the coronation three years earlier. Eleven minutes late, the curtain rose on Alfred Craven's re-creation of the portico of St Paul's, Covent Garden, for what, according to the *Daily Sketch*, was expected to be 'the biggest theatrical sensation for many years'.

76 seconds

The first act, according to Shaw, went 'smoothly and well'. In the third act, Mrs Pat was superb, 'and ravished the house almost to delirium', while Tree's farcical acting 'was very funny', though the critics noticed that his dialogue, here and there, owed more to invention than to memory. As the dustman Doolittle, Eliza's father, Edmund Gurney, who had visited the House of Commons to listen to Lloyd George's speeches in order to find the right tone of contempt for the aristocracy, scored a massive hit.

There was plenty of laughter but, much to Shaw's approval, it was kept in hand and the play listened to without serious interruption. However, when Eliza's 'Not bloody likely' came, 'the performance was nearly wrecked.' The audience laughed themselves 'into such utter abandonment and disorder', Shaw told Charlotte, who had sailed to the United States three days before to avoid having to encounter Mrs Pat, that for a time it seemed doubtful that the play would be able to continue. Stanley Bell, the stage manager, timed the uproarious laughter as the audience rocked to and fro in their seats, and found that the hands of his stopwatch reached just over a minute and a quarter. It may be the longest laugh in English theatrical history.

Shaw described himself writhing in agony for the last two acts, as Tree proceeded to do the opposite of everything he had told him to do. Mrs Pat, on the other hand, was magnificent, and, to Shaw's satisfaction, when she threw the slippers at Higgins in the fourth act, she nearly knocked his head off with her second shot.

But all Shaw's careful preparations to underline the idea that Higgins and Eliza will never marry were thrown away in the play's final moments. Shaw had coached Tree in rehearsal to disregard Eliza and concentrate his attentions on his mother. Instead, the last thing Shaw saw as he exited the theatre was Higgins 'shoving his mother rudely out of the way and wooing Eliza with appeals to buy a ham for his lonely home like a bereaved Romeo'.

The furore over 'bloody' might keep audiences queuing at the box office, but it infuriated Shaw, who saw it as a distraction from the salient elements of the play, in particular his critique of the bourgeois institution of marriage. Critics – and the public – were divided over the use of the word. There had been a few boos at the end of the first night's performance. Mrs Pat said they were a protest against Tree's acting. Some suggested that they emanated from those customary theatre-wreckers, a group of suffragettes. Still others were convinced that they reflected disapproval of the 'appalling word'.

Meanwhile, newspaper columns and letters pages were filled with opinions of the word. 'Ever since Mr Shaw flung his unprintable word at the play-going public,' wrote a man to the *Sandwich Gazette*, 'my wife, who is a refined and educated woman, has regarded it as a huge joke to use the expletive on any and every occasion.' Two women, describing themselves as 'late Admirers of Sir Herbert Beerbohm Tree', protested that 'The majority of women do not wish to pay to hear these unspeakable expletives in the theatre – we hear quite enough of them at home!!' Patricia Woodcock, a twenty-year-old schoolteacher from Maidstone, wondered, in contrast, what all the fuss was about. 'I had no idea of the harmless adjective which your mealy-mouth writers found so distressing,' she told the *Daily Sketch*. 'What a stodgy provincial lot they must be. It's only in the backwoods of Manchester, Sheffield, Birmingham and Oldham that bores and stodgy puritans protest and be what they called shocked.'

The Oxford Union debated that 'This House approves the use and acceptance of a certain sanguinary expletive as a sign of a liberating influence of the English language' and voted unanimously in favour of the motion. John Corbin, an Oxford graduate, took the opportunity to show off in the *New York Times* by providing an etymology for the word. He claimed he had often used it when he was up at Balliol, where he had fallen in with a Bohemian set, as a way of shocking the stuffier dons. 'Bloody', he said, was a contraction of the Elizabethan oath 'By Our Lady', but present-day usage of the word confined it to the cockney dialect. Other correspondents fell over themselves to correct him. On the contrary, the expletive was alive and well in the extreme north of Scotland, the extreme west of Ireland and the extreme south of Cornwall.

The Secretary of the Decency League from Brighton demanded to know 'Where was the Censor . . . does he actually read the plays submitted to him?', while the Dean of Manchester described the expression as more vulgar than profane, and chastised Shaw for cheap sensationalism. From the United States, Charlotte Shaw did what she could to defend her husband's reputation. Far from being indecent, she told a reporter, he was a bashful and retiring man.

In the music halls that spring, 'What the Bernard Shaw are you doing' and 'Not *Pygmalion* Likely' became popular catchphrases. A revue at the Palace Theatre in London, *The Passing Show*, introduced a sketch, *Not Vermilion Likely*, featuring Arthur Playfair as Higgins and Nelson Keys as Eliza in a long black gown and tiara, with a bass note on the trombone taking the part of the expletive.

It was all too much for Shaw. Mrs Patrick Campbell asked him to return to *Pygmalion* on another night. 'Come soon,' she wrote, warning him about more of Tree's romantic interpolations, 'or you'll not recognize your play.' Nothing, for the time being, though, would induce Shaw to sit through another performance, or to endure more hostile criticism on account of the 'sanguinary element' in his play. Two days after opening night he had escaped all the fuss by going to Yorkshire for a week's walking and motoring holiday with a pair of his more earnest companions, Beatrice and Sidney Webb.

TWO

May to August

Honeymoon in the Sky

A high wind was blowing as he left Villacoublay, in the south-western suburbs of Paris, shortly after dawn on the morning of Saturday, 23 May, his plane spinning upwards in the air towards the northern coast of France.

Gustav Hamel had flown to the Morane-Salunier works on Thursday evening to collect his new racing monoplane. With its clipped wings, streamlined fuselage, small-capacity petrol tank, and 80 h.p. Gnome engine, the plane was capable of flying more than 100 miles per hour. Hamel could be confident that his would be the fastest machine competing in that Saturday's Aerial Derby, a circuit of 95 miles starting at Hendon, north-west of Central London. The race would be watched by thousands of spectators, including the guests of honour, the King's mother, Queen Alexandra, her sister, the Dowager Empress Marie of Russia, and the German Ambassador, Prince Lichnowsky. Hamel had been the previous year's winner of the Aerial Derby, narrowly escaping mortal danger to fly to victory. Just as he'd taken the lead, a stream of gasoline had burst over him in the cockpit, a few feet away from the exposed rotary engine. As he rapidly became drenched in fuel, Hamel had managed to put his finger over the leak, staunch the flow and keep flying. He had gone on to win the race in a record time of 1 hour, 15 minutes and 40 seconds.

In his book, *Flying: Some Practical Experiences*, co-written with the journalist and pilot C. C. Turner and published in April 1914, a month before the race, Gustav Hamel had mused upon the mystery of why a man with a perfect physique and unshakeable nerves could prove an indifferent flyer, while 'a quite insignificant-looking pupil, pale and thoughtful . . . having no inclination for violent exercise . . . would take to flying as a duck takes to water.'

Hamel certainly wasn't insignificant-looking. He was well-built, of medium height, with bright blue eyes and wavy blond hair. But he

Gustav Hamel looping the loop over Windsor Castle, 2 February 1914

did possess an undue modesty and reserve. These were all the more surprising given that, in a comparatively short time, he had become one of England's most celebrated 'heroes of the air' for the new aviation age. 'If ever there was a man born to fly, three parts a bird and the rest genius, it was Hamel,' wrote Winston Churchill, who had flown with him, and kept a framed photograph of Hamel in his office at the Admiralty. Yet, while he appeared to possess a natural aptitude for flying a wide range of machines, Hamel had a limited idea of why or how they operated. 'He used to say that he could not change a sparking plug,' wrote C. G. Grey, the most prominent of Britain's aeronautical journalists, 'but he certainly could tell where a machine felt wrong when he flew it.'

Born in 1889, Hamel was not quite twenty-five. He was the son of a German doctor, who had taken his medical degree in Switzerland before moving to London to set up a practice, and his German-speaking, Danish wife. Edward VII had been one of Dr Hamel's patients and a regular visitor to the family's Grosvenor Square home, despite the fact that Mrs Hamel had always refused to allow the King to bring his terrier Caesar upstairs into the drawing-room. Gustav had been given a traditional English public school education at Westminster School, and in 1910 the Hamel family had become naturalized British subjects. His father had hoped that his son would take up medicine, but, while travelling in France, Gustav found himself drawn to aviation after witnessing the pioneering flights of French aviators, and before long had developed into one of the Blériot School's most promising pupils.

Hamel's participation in the Hendon race in May 1914 would be watched by thousands of his adoring fans. However, as that Saturday wore on, the weather prospects for flying still didn't look promising. At Le Crotoy, on the Normandy coast, Hamel refuelled, had breakfast – it was a cardinal rule that pilots should never attempt to fly while hungry – and took off again. He then struggled for four hours in the grip of a terrible storm to reach Hardelot, south of Boulogne, only twenty-five miles away.

A westerly wind was blowing in great gusts, and Hamel faced a thick fog, of a kind which could utterly defeat the best aviator. Taking the decision to cross to Dover from Calais, instead of following his usual route from Boulogne to Folkestone, he commenced his eighteenth Channel crossing. As he did so, his plane was swallowed up by the mists hanging low over the water.

In the first seven months of 1914, aviation in England reached a new summit of popularity. The speed of progress in the development of powered flight was astonishing. It was, after all, little more than a decade since the American Wright brothers, Orville and Wilbur, had made their historic flight near Kitty Hawk, North Carolina, lasting 12 seconds and covering 120 feet. Almost three years later, in the autumn of 1906, the Brazilian Alberto Santos-Dumont, a resident of Paris, made the first flight in Europe in a strange contraption, a 'pusher' biplane with wings placed at a dihedral angle. He managed to stay in the air for a distance of 160 feet before sinking to the earth. But this was enough for the press magnate Lord Northcliffe, proprietor of the *Daily Mail*, to declare that 'England is no longer an island' and to predict that 'the aerial chariots of a foe' would descend 'on British soil if war comes'. Two years later, as French pilots flew cross-country for the first time, taking the lead in European flight, an American expatriate, 'Colonel' Samuel Franklin Cody, six foot three, with shoulder-length hair and wearing a ten-gallon Stetson, made the first mechanically powered flight on British soil, on Salisbury Plain.

The aeroplanes, designed by Cody and flown competitively by him, were too cumbersome to have much influence on mainstream design, especially in a European market increasingly dominated by the new sleeker biplane produced by the Anglo-Frenchman, Henri Farman. But Cody's successful flight did help to alleviate British fears that the Continentals had stolen a march on them. However, it was Louis Blériot's crossing of the English Channel, in July 1909, that dramatically ushered in a new period of practical aviation in England. Blériot made landfall over Dover Castle after a flight of 23½ miles in 36½ minutes. Others had made longer flights, but the significance of the crossing and the blaze of publicity surrounding it were enormous, appearing to confirm the truth of Northcliffe's remark three years earlier. More than anyone else, Blériot had convinced the British public that flying was here to stay. The Frenchman was received rapturously by crowds in Dover, and later in London, where 100,000 visitors inspected Blériot's monoplane on display at Selfridges department store.

By 1914 flying machines had improved immeasurably in reliability and performance from the fragile models made from wood and canvas in which the pioneers had made their maiden flights. In England, construction was better and materials more carefully assessed, so that there were fewer breakages in the air. Piloting skills, too, had developed to match the aeroplane's superior abilities. Aviators were growing in understanding of centres of gravity and pressure, and there was more capacity for movement in a modern aeroplane flown by a skilful pilot. The plane could be made to side-slip bodily without dropping its nose and descending in a dive. Steps were also being taken to coordinate aviators' observations of the weather with those of meteorologists, especially with regard to the analysis of the behaviour of wind currents.

Arguments still raged about the relative merits of the monoplane and the biplane – a fixed-wing aircraft with a single set of wings as against a plane with two – though the old distinction between them – that a biplane was the slower of the two crafts, but could fly for longer, whereas the monoplane could fly faster but for not so long – didn't hold with the development of more sophisticated designs.

That aircraft could now be handled with greater panache and safety was reflected in the declining statistics for air fatalities. In the British Isles in 1913, the number of recorded fatal accidents had fallen to ten, costing twelve lives. In the meantime, the length of flights had significantly increased. In 1913, according to the leading British aeronautical journal, the *Aeroplane*, a flight of 200 miles in a day by an Englishman would have been worthy of notice. In 1914 a day's flight had to be at least 500 miles to go on record. In practical flying skills, as in design, the French had taken the lead – the longest flights to date, Paris to Warsaw, for instance, had been undertaken by Frenchmen – but at London's Olympia Aero Show in March 1914, where British manufacturers like A. V. Roe and Blackburn were strongly represented, British machines were for the first time able to hold their own against foreign competitors.

The greater safety associated with flying had rapidly increased its popularity as a spectator and participant sport. At the beginning of 1914 a display at Bellevue Gardens in Manchester drew vast crowds, as B. C. Hucks, the first Englishman to 'loop the loop', ascended to 1,000 feet and made a sensational triple loop in his Avro biplane, a sight witnessed by many spectators at the Manchester City football match near by. A month later Hucks was at Hedon Racecourse, in the East Riding of Yorkshire, making six loops in a single day; and at Oxford, in March, he made a spiral descent from 300 feet, followed by a spectacular steeplechase across the city's bridges.

There was no shortage, either, of men, or women, prepared to take part in passenger flights. The Lady Mayoress of Leeds flew over the city with pilot Harold Blackburn, while Mrs Hatley Bacon of Roundhay, a suburb of Leeds, insisted that Blackburn fly over her house with her so that her children could see his plane. In February, five-year-old Billie Craig became the youngest person to date to fly in a plane, in a twenty-minute flight with B. C. Hucks around Hull.

Throughout England displays of flying proliferated. At Sheffield Aviation Week at the end of March, Harold Blackburn offered joy-rides in his two-seater monoplane, accompanied on one trip by a young woman known as 'Little Miss Independent', and, on another, by a dentist who later used a photograph of himself sitting with Blackburn on board the plane to advertise his city dental practice, and the 15s. he charged for a complete set of dentures. Later that summer Blackburn would participate in Blackpool's Pleasure Beach Flying Week, climaxing in a flight circling the Blackpool Tower. A bestselling 78-rpm record of this time, sung by Dora Whittaker, was 'Honeymoon in the Sky', and in January 1914 a newly married couple did precisely that, taking to the skies over Leeds in a monoplane.

Aerodromes, together with some seventeen flying schools, had been founded at Brooklands, Hendon, Eastbourne – which also possessed a seaplane station – Salisbury Plain, Liverpool and Windermere. Brooklands, near Weybridge in Surrey, was the oldest of these, having started in 1907. But it was Brooklands' main rival establishment at Hendon, opening early in 1911, that caught the public's imagination as the centre of British aviation and, more than anywhere else, contributed to the prevailing climate of 'air mindedness'. Hendon, also known as the London Aerodrome, was the brainchild of Claude Grahame-White, a leading impresario of early flying who, although still only in his early thirties, had managed to combine the divergent roles of showman, businessman, designer, propagandist and pioneer aviator.

A member of a wealthy Hampshire family, Grahame-White, like

other air pioneers, had been initially attracted to working in the automobile business before he was inspired by Blériot's Channel crossing to switch to aviation. At the beginning of 1910 he became the first Englishman to hold a pilot's licence, from the Aero Club de France, and that spring he raced against the French instructor Louis Paulhan for the £10,000 prize offered by the *Daily Mail* for the first London to Manchester flight.

The press coverage of the event on both sides of the Channel reached fever pitch. Although Grahame-White lost to Paulhan, his decision to fly at night – at the time an unprecedented feat – and the sporting manner in which he accepted defeat won him the adoration of the crowd. He was handsome and good-humoured, with more than a trace of the dandy about him. Subsequent prizes in air races in England, and in the United States (where, when meeting President Taft, he landed his Farman biplane on Executive Avenue in Washington, DC) cemented his reputation as the country's most famous airman. A wax figure of Grahame-White was displayed in London at Madame Tussauds, and the glamour attached to his name was further enhanced by his liaison with the American actress Pauline Chase, who was touring English theatres as J. M. Barrie's Peter Pan.

With some of the proceeds from his prize money, and a £10,000 loan, Grahame-White bought a ten-year lease on 207 acres of pasture land on Hendon Hill. Ditches were filled in and trees cut down to allow an uninterrupted view, while seventeen hangars were constructed. The Hendon site would become the best known, and most effectively organized, flying ground in the country, comprising workshops for manufacturing, flying schools and facilities for public meetings. Grandstands and pavilions were built, a clubhouse was opened, work started on a thirty-bedroom hotel, and tea-rooms and bars were provided for each of the five enclosures, where admission prices ranged from 6*d.* to 10*s.*

Under the aerodrome's general manager Richard Gates, Grahame-White's aim was to make Hendon as prominent an attraction as the London Zoo or Lord's Cricket Ground. While publicity for the opening season of international flying events in April 1912 was overshadowed by press coverage of the sinking of the *Titanic*, 'The

Hendon Habit', within easy reach of the metropolis by train, tram bus and car, quickly caught on. The most celebrated flyers, names like Hamel, Hucks, Hubert, Noel and Sopwith, were regularly to be seen taking part in stunts, aerobatics and other displays. As more special events were programmed – Ladies' Day, meetings for Boy Scouts, and shop-workers on early-closing days, and Military, Parliamentary and Theatrical Days, as well as the annual Aerial Derby – 'Enclosure Full' notices, signalling that attendance had reached saturation point, were posted more frequently. Three quarters of a million visitors went to Hendon in 1913, and it was considered 'a poor gate' at the weekend if 10,000 people weren't present. The fields near St Mary's Church at Hendon had always provided a perfect vantage point for those who wished to see the flying, but were unwilling or unable to pay. To obscure the view from the top of the hill in advance of the Easter season of 1914, screens were erected around the circumference of the aerodrome.

A journalist paying a visit to Hendon in the spring of 1914 was 'enthralled' by what he saw, reporting that 'on Thursdays, Saturdays and Sundays from 3 p.m. to dusk there is always (weather permitting) "Something doing" in the way of flying-exhibition, "Looping" and passenger flights, speed and latitude tests . . . You can have a flight as a passenger any day for a couple of guineas, and in charge of a skilled pilot it is "as safe as houses".' Another reporter praised Hendon as 'A resort of fashion – a veritable "Ascot" in London'. He was surprised at the number of cars in the enclosure, but then realized that there was no greater comfort than to 'lean back among the cushions' in a car and watch 'Hamel . . . climbing to a height of 4,000 feet, and then making twenty-two consecutive "loops" in his descent . . . Moreover an excellent tea is brought up to the car at a very moderate charge.' A writer from the *Play Pictorial* magazine seemed simply awestruck at the revolution in air travel: 'Isn't it wonderful?' he wrote. 'Fourteen years ago there was scarcely a motor on the London road, and Icarus was still considered the representative flying man.'

Accidents at Hendon were rare, though there were plenty of narrow escapes such as the occasion when Gustav Hamel nearly crashed into Colindale Avenue, the heavily pot-holed approach to the aerodrome. The first fatal accident since Hendon had opened to the public occurred in January 1914. George Lee Temple, twenty-one, the first Englishman to fly upside down, had been in bed for a fortnight suffering from flu. But he insisted on getting out his Blériot monoplane to make an exhibition flight in a strong wind. After flying around the enclosures for ten minutes at 500 feet, the plane made a sudden perpendicular plunge. As it neared the earth, a north-east wind caught the machine and, according to one eyewitness, turned it over 'just like flicking a half-penny'. The aircraft landed upside down in the centre of the aerodrome, killing the pilot instantly.

That first month of the year at Hendon also saw the setting of two records in an aerobatic display of the increasingly popular 'looping the loop'. Eleanor Trehawke Davies, a wealthy flying enthusiast, had already become the first woman to cross the English Channel when she flew as a passenger with Gustav Hamel, nearly two years earlier. On 2 January she became both the first woman and the first passenger on an English flight to loop the loop, again in a plane piloted by Hamel. Climbing to a height of 1,000 feet, Hamel executed a loop, after which he descended to about 300 feet. Ascending once more, he made a second loop, at the top of which the machine appeared to stop dead, and, after hovering for a moment or two, began to glide down on its back. A sharp nosedive returned the monoplane to its normal position. 'When you start the turn,' Hamel wrote later, 'you seem to sit still and the whole world revolves around you. The horizon disappears under your feet, and the next thing you see it coming back over your head. The whole thing is done so quickly that you don't know for the moment when you have finished. There is no unpleasant sensation except a rushing of blood to the eyes.' On reaching *terra firma* again, Miss Trehawke Davies, a semi-invalid with a heart condition, who had risen from her sickbed to take part in the flight, described flying as 'a most health-giving and nerve-steadying pursuit'.

Only ever photographed in public, coated and begoggled, with her head shrouded in a nun-like wimple, Trehawke Davies owned several aircraft, but never flew them herself. 'Flying,' argued Hamel, 'is scarcely a suitable sport for women' and 'So far no woman has become a really good pilot' – a judgement shared by Mrs Maurice Hewlett, the first Englishwoman to be granted an aviator's certificate, who doubted that women possessed the 'right kind of nerve' for flying, and compared their unsuitability as flyers with their lack of success 'at driving motor-cars'.

Women, often aristocratic ones, a testament to his family's society connections, were Hamel's most frequent passengers. Indeed, they tended to be the only ones who could afford his £250 fee for longer flights, charges which probably made him the wealthiest celebrity aviator. Lady Victoria Pery, daughter of the Earl of Limerick, claimed to be the first titled woman to fly upside down after she flew with Hamel, while the Countess of Dudley and Lady Diana Manners, as well as the actress Gladys Cooper, who was rumoured to be romantically involved with him, accompanied Hamel on more than one occasion.

A dinner in January 1914 given by Hendon aviators, under the chairmanship of Grahame-White, at the Royal Automobile Club celebrated the achievements of Hamel and B. C. Hucks as the first two Englishmen to fly upside down. The menu was served in reverse order by waiters in mechanics' overalls, with coffee first, followed by pudding, and lastly arriving at the hors d'oeuvres. Two weeks later Hamel gave a demonstration of looping the loop to George V and Queen Mary above Windsor Castle to loud cheers from assembled Eton schoolboys. The King described Hamel erroneously in his diary as 'the German aviator', but allowed the barest tremor of excitement to escape from his normally emotionless, deadpan manner when he noted that it was 'Most interesting and wonderful' to see with what ease Hamel accomplished the feat. In April the royal couple were party to another innovation for British flight when they left Dover on the royal yacht *Victoria and Albert*, on their state visit to Paris. Trailing them in his Blériot monoplane was B. C. Hucks, accompanied by a cameraman who filmed a bird's-eye view of the King and Queen's arrival in France, as the plane hovered above Calais Harbour. Hucks immediately flew the film back to England, where it was rushed off to be developed. An audience at the Coliseum in London saw the film at a matinée performance later that same afternoon.

Performance flying had added advantages in that it taught a pilot how to recover his position should a sudden gust of wind overturn his machine, and more generally helped the aviator to master his nerves in life-threatening circumstances. Some in the aeronautical industry, ignoring the fact that pioneering flight in England had always been largely financed by displays and trick-flying, regretted its lack of a more sober, scientific identity. A Theatrical Day at Hendon, in particular, was singled out for its association with 'a species of carnival' more suited to a 'third-class music-hall show'. Men 'of the class one wishes to interest in aviation', complained the *Aeroplane*, 'are not likely to bring their womenfolk to a place frequented by . . . scantily clad women of the sort commonly described as actresses'.

In the same editorial, the writer attacked the journalists and photographers who devoted space to chronicling the antics at Hendon of 'an unfortunate brat whose father happens to be Prime Minister and whose would-be ultra-smart mother insists on getting him up to look like a cross between Struwwelpeter [Heinrich Hoffmann's children's character, 'Shock-headed' Peter] and Little Lord Fauntleroy'. Eleven-year-old, curly-haired Anthony 'Puffin' Asquith, the younger child of the Prime Minister and Margot Asquith, was fascinated by flying, and had given his classmates at Summer Fields School in Oxford a lecture on aviation after being taken up by Grahame-White in his five-seater, passenger-carrying biplane, a 'Charabanc' or 'Aero-Bus'.

In spite of the *Aeroplane*'s concern, the crowds flocking to Hendon encompassed all social classes. A pit collier from Pontefract saved enough money to visit the aerodrome, only to find that the day's flying had been cancelled because of fog (Harold Blackburn promised him a free flight from his home town to Leeds to compensate him for his disappointment). John Riddey was a twenty-year-old clerk from South-East London. After finishing at Shaftesbury Grammar School, in Dorset, in July 1912, Riddey had left his Gloucestershire home in Moreton-in-Marsh, where his father was the local bank manager, to take a job at the Deptford ironworks, Frederick Braby & Co. However, living in digs in Lewisham and sharing a room with his landlady's son, Riddey found London life 'depressing', and visits to Hendon markedly lifted his spirits. On one occasion, in the early summer of 1914, he wrote home to his mother that he had been at 'some very good races'. These included seeing the French test pilot Louis Noel 'break the speed record for the aerodrome – 73.4 m.p.h., which included several corners, of course'.

Venetia Stanley was unable to resist the opportunity of flying at Hendon that summer. Asquith remained unaware of her 'exploit' until Winston Churchill let it slip one evening as they sat together on the front benches in the Commons. 'I am extremely glad that I didn't know beforehand that you were going to take yourself to wings & fly,' Asquith wrote, remonstrating with her. 'Thank God you are safely down again, and I earnestly hope you won't be in a hurry to repeat the experiment.'

One particular set-piece at Hendon, repeated regularly in the first half of 1914, was received with rapt attention by spectators, as pilots, circling at 300 feet, dropped 'bombs' made from flour-bags on to the silhouetted image of a dummy battleship, marked out in chalk on the ground below. The display was popular at night when its dazzling effect was heightened by searchlights and firework explosions.

At Brooklands, Hendon's sister aerodrome, that June, John Riddey witnessed something even more dramatic, which he described in a letter home: a mock battle during which the wounded were found 'by aeroplanes who reported their whereabouts to the Camp where they were brought in and attended to'. 'Everything was done very thoroughly in a sham way,' he told his mother, '& Queen Alexandra and Lord Roberts [the former Commander-in-Chief of the British Army] were there.'

War displays like these were designed to demonstrate to the British public that flying could be more than just exciting spectacle. At best, the government had shown little more than a half-hearted interest in the development of the military potential of aviation, something which Grahame-White had actively exposed when, in conjunction with Lord Northcliffe, he had embarked upon a 'Wake up, England' campaign as long ago as the summer of 1911. This, and a similar venture the following year, was intended to alert the country to the realities of the Aeroplane Age. With his corps of famous pilots, Grahame-White barnstormed towns and seaside resorts, spreading his gospel message: 'Aviation in England is in a state of stagnation. Our people do not realise how backward we are in comparison with other countries, and how our very existence will depend on our having a modern aerial fleet.' Of course, his motives were not merely altruistic. The continued expansion of Hendon as a manufacturing base depended upon Grahame-White's ability to attract commercial investment.

In one sense Grahame-White's campaign was preaching to the converted. Several generations had by now been raised on novels and stories containing predictions of a war in the skies. In Jules Verne's 1886 novel *The Clipper of the Clouds*, the hero Robur the Conqueror declares that the future belongs to heavier-than-air machines like *The Albatross*, a huge flying vessel, powered by electricity and lifted by horizontal propellers, employed by Robur to rout his enemies. A large amount of popular fiction in the first years of the twentieth century, especially stories for boys in weeklies and magazines, was devoted to reinforcing the idea not only that aerial warfare was inevitable, but that the British government's failure to recognize the important role to be played by the modern aeroplane in the country's future destiny would result in dire consequences. In some of these, Claude Grahame-White and Gustav Hamel appear as real-life aviation heroes, valiantly saving the day.

Undoubtedly the most influential prophet of aerial warfare was the writer H. G. Wells. With Grahame-White at the controls, Wells took his first passenger flight from Eastbourne, in 1912. Four years earlier, in his novel *The War in the Air*, he had portrayed the horrifying consequences of Germany's brutal air bombardments of the United States as heralding the collapse of civilization. Still earlier, in a fantasy story entitled 'Filmer', Wells had imagined an English inventor producing an effective flying-machine, which the War Office, failing to recognize its military potential, refused to develop. Only belatedly did Filmer win backing for his machine from the newspaper tycoon Lord Banghurst (a thinly disguised Lord Northcliffe), but in the meantime Japan had already become the world's first air power.

With the Northcliffe press behind him, Grahame-White's propaganda campaign to reverse Britain's backwardness in the air certainly hit some of its targets, forcing officials to take his views seriously, even as they distanced themselves from his more brazen exhibitionism. Both Northcliffe and Grahame-White, for example, asserted the primacy of the aeroplane over the airship, and, although scare stories about menacing German Zeppelins continued to haunt the pages of newspapers and magazines, by 1914 the British military had made a firm decision to abandon the airship as a weapon of war. Meanwhile, Italy had become the first country to make military use of the aeroplane. At war against Turkey in Libya, in the autumn of 1911, the Italians employed German-built monoplanes for reconnaissance, and towards the end of the campaign dropped four home-made bombs on the enemy.

France, Germany and Russia had announced the formation of air services for their armies in the course of 1910, making it inevitable that Britain would have to follow suit. The establishment of an Air Battalion in the spring of 1911 was followed a year later by its expansion into the Royal Flying Corps. The Royal Flying Corps comprised two flying wings, military and naval, a reserve, the Royal Aircraft factory at Farnborough and the Central Flying School at Upavon, on Salisbury Plain.

But in a variety of significant respects, the Royal Flying Corps continued to suffer from the deep-seated prejudice of senior government and army officials against military aviation, and, as a result, failed to live up to the hopes that lobbyists like Grahame-White had had for it. For a start, it came nowhere near its most obvious competitor, the French air service, in size. In a strongly worded editorial in early 1914, the *Aeroplane* felt forced to point out that the number of planes, after more than a year of the Royal Flying Corps' existence, still fell below the bare minimum, and that 'had any of our neighbours been so inconsiderate as to declare war, the resulting campaign would have been affected but little by aerial scouts on our side' (at this stage, military aviation was still conceived as primarily for reconnaissance, not offensive action).

Training, too, was deficient. In the army, flying was equated with horsemanship. The rule was simple: if you were a good rider, it was more than likely that you'd make a good flyer. Pilots were only taught to fly straight and on the level. 'Show' flying was regarded with contempt. It 'was merely selfishness and brings discredit', said Captain Frederick Sykes, commander of the military wing of the Royal Flying Corps, completely ignoring the way in which actions like looping the loop trained pilots in the mastery of their machines.

A number of fatal accidents resulted in part from this attitude. In one tragic month for the Royal Flying Corps, March 1914, no fewer than four serving officers were killed on Salisbury Plain in the space of just ten days. 'We have an absurdly small and inadequate service for our naval and military services,' said the *Daily Mail*, reacting angrily. 'Yet we have a tale of accident and death far greater in proportion than that of France and Germany.'

Some suspicion attached to the biplanes themselves that these unfortunate army airmen had been flying, especially after it was discovered that in one of them the rudder post had been weakened, leaving it half the thickness it should have been. These BE2s, as they were known, designed by the Royal Aircraft Factory, had been selected by the War Office as the standard model for the Royal Flying Corps; a slow, stable machine, incapable of going faster than 75 m.p.h., it was largely used for reconnaissance. This decision continued to attract much criticism, particularly among private manufacturers who, unlike their counterparts in France and Germany, received practically no government support, and were forced to be dependent on prize money and the proceeds from flying schools to finance the production of new models.

The government appeared reluctant to place orders with British firms. For the most part it awarded contracts to private manufacturers to produce machines of the standard model, often at a rate of only two or three at a time. Robert Blackburn of Leeds (no relation to the pilot Harold Blackburn) was a more favoured recipient of government patronage. Blackburn's Second Monoplane and his larger two-seater, known as the Mercury, had established him as one of the country's foremost aircraft designers. Originally based at a small workshop beneath a clothing factory, the Blackburn Aeroplane Company had moved in 1911 to larger premises off Balm Street,

Leeds. In June 1914, with an order to produce twelve of the Farnborough-designed BE2s, Blackburn formed a limited company, relocating to a disused roller-skating rink in the city's Roundhay Road. Here Blackburn would work on government contracts as well as on the development of machines related to his especial interest, private venture seaplanes.

The depressing fact remained, however, that the Royal Flying Corps, deprived of proper training, adequate airfields or state-of-the-art aircraft, was unfit for purpose. By the summer of 1914 the War Office had found it impossible to bring the Royal Flying Corps to its full establishment of seven squadrons, and had begun to press privately owned aircraft into action.

The contrast with the naval wing of the Royal Flying Corps could scarcely have been greater. In large measure this was due to the First Lord of the Admiralty himself, Winston Churchill. From the moment he took office at the end of 1911, Churchill had canvassed for an integral role for aeroplanes and seaplanes within the navy, for the protection of harbours and other vulnerable points, and the overall strengthening of home defence. He had recognized the necessity of building, or adapting, a ship that could act as parent for an aeroplane. Unlike the military wing of the Royal Flying Corps, with its preference for standardization, the Admiralty actively supported experimentation with a diverse range of aircraft, and listened to the opinions of the pilots who flew them. At the end of May 1914, the independence of the naval wing from its military counterpart was recognized with the splitting in two of the Royal Flying Corps, and the formation of the Royal Naval Air Service under the Admiralty's direction.

Churchill was an inveterate flyer, having made his maiden flight as a passenger in 1909. He never flew solo, or obtained his flying certificate, but with a number of different instructors he had notched up many hours of flying in nearly 140 separate flights by mid 1914. It was said that the navy hardly possessed a single plane in which Churchill hadn't flown, and for a time he was even dubbed 'the flying Cabinet Minister'.

Friends and colleagues begged him, in the words of the earnest entreaty from his cousin the Duke of Marlborough, 'to desist from a practice or pastime – whichever you call it – which is fraught with so much danger to life'. At the beginning of December 1913 Captain Gilbert Wildman-Lushington, one of Churchill's instructors, with whom he'd flown just days before, was killed as he crash-landed at Eastchurch. From that point on, the anxiety of Churchill's closest family and associates increased. 'Why do you do such a foolish thing as fly repeatedly?' the lawyer and politician F. E. Smith asked him. 'Surely it is unfair to your family, your career & your friends.'

Churchill claimed by now to know 'a good deal about this fascinating new art'. He could manage a machine 'with ease in the air, even with high winds', and, given a little more practice in landing, he believed he could fly alone 'with reasonable safety'. Aware that reported fatalities among army personnel only increased his wife Clementine's concern, Churchill tended to keep his flying secret – at least until after his latest flight had taken place. On 17 May 1914 Gustav Hamel flew Churchill from Hendon to Eastchurch, and later that same day took him flying in the area of Sheerness, in the mouth of the River Medway in north Kent. 'I spent a delightful day flying with him,' Churchill recalled years later. 'Morning, afternoon and evening we sailed about in his little Voisin monoplane.' Before Hamel set off back to London, they looped the loop six times, a story later reported in *The Times* and other newspapers. To escape the displeasure of Clementine, who was in the first months of pregnancy with their daughter Sarah, Churchill subsequently issued a printed denial that he was in Hamel's aeroplane when these manoeuvres were carried out.

Gustav Hamel had only just applied for an appointment to the reserve of the nascent Royal Naval Air Service and was soon to have given a demonstration to pilots at an air station near Portsmouth. But on Saturday, 23 May, less than a week after he'd flown Churchill to Sheerness, there was mounting concern as to Hamel's whereabouts when he failed to arrive at Hendon to take part in 1914's Aerial Derby.

Hendon was fog-bound and rainy, with visibility limited to 100 yards, and Grahame-White had no alternative but to postpone the race for a fortnight, to the disappointment of the crowds, who were slightly appeased by some displays of looping the loop in between the showers. By three that afternoon, three and a half hours after Hamel had begun his Channel crossing, there was still no news of him and the worst began to be feared. Grahame-White telephoned all the possible airfields where Hamel might have made an emergency landing, but with no success. He then alerted the Admiralty, and, under instructions from the First Lord, the cruiser *Mallard* and four destroyers put out from Dover to sweep the Channel. A flotilla of gunboats from Sheerness also joined the search, accompanied by several seaplanes. No trace of Hamel or of his aircraft was found.

Grahame-White, accompanied by Hamel's faithful mechanic Gonne, had meanwhile taken the evening boat to Boulogne, where there was still a thick haze over the Channel. At Hardelot he questioned the mechanics who had refuelled Hamel's Morane-Saulnier racer earlier that day. They assured him that the machine had been in perfect order when Hamel took off for England.

Five days later hopes of Hamel's survival were raised, only to be cruelly dashed when a report that he had been picked up by a trawler in South Shields turned out to be false. In their excitement at the news, crowds in the streets had formed around the newspaper boys in their haste to get the special editions. It was now assumed that, flying without a compass, Hamel had been carried off-course over the North Sea, where his reserves of fuel would quickly have been exhausted, causing his machine with its heavy engine to fall into the sea. The Admiralty issued a statement. Hamel 'was without question the foremost exponent in these islands of an art whose military consequence is continually increasing. His qualities of daring, skill, resource and modesty merited the respect of all those who pursue the profession of arms.' Shortly before his disappearance, Hamel had announced his next challenge: to fly the Atlantic that August.

On 29 May, a more shocking news story knocked the question of Hamel's fate from the front pages. The Scottish-built, Canadian-owned liner, the *Empress of India*, which had left Quebec bound for Liverpool, had sunk in the St Lawrence River following a collision with a Norwegian collier. The lives lost numbered 1,012, including 840 passengers, 11 more than had perished on the *Titanic* (the *Titanic*, though, had lost many more members of her crew). Among the British dead were the explorer, hunter and Conservative politician Sir Henry Seton-Karr, and the English dramatist and novelist Laurence Irving, son of the great Victorian actor-manager Sir Henry Irving, who had drowned when he jumped back into the St Lawrence in a vain attempt to save his wife.

Just over a month later, in the first week of July, a body was seen bobbing about in the sea off Boulogne. According to French reports, there could be 'no room for doubt' that it was that of Gustav Hamel.

Premonitions

In the first week of May, Sir Arthur Nicolson, Permanent Undersecretary at the Foreign Office – and as such the most senior official in that department of government – observed that he had never known such calm waters in international affairs.

This may have been due in part to the way in which the attention of each of the major powers was currently diverted by domestic issues. Britain had its unfolding Home Rule crisis. France was riveted by the prospect of the trial for murder of Henriette Caillaux, wife of the Minister of Finance, accused of shooting the editor of *Le Figaro*, one of her husband's severest critics. Russia's great cities were under threat of paralysis from major strikes, while in Germany there were mounting fears about the power of the socialists. Austria-Hungary, too, was torn by internal disputes. The Austrian Parliament had seen violent clashes between German and Czech representatives, while in Hungary there were growing tensions between the Magyars and the Romanians in Transylvania.

However, in the area of Anglo-German relations, it was also undoubtedly true that, after years of increasing antagonism at the beginning of the century, the relationship between the two countries appeared to be steadily improving. The first mark of this new spirit of cooperation had occurred in 1912 and 1913, when Britain and Germany worked well together to douse the flames of conflagration in the Balkans. The Anglo-German rapprochement continued with successful negotiations over the Portuguese colonies, and a treaty to settle the thorny question of the Berlin–Constantinople–Baghdad Railway in 1914.

Nevertheless, an underlying atmosphere of mutual mistrust and suspicion remained, never helped by the Kaiser's flamboyant and unpredictable incursions into unofficial diplomacy ('His Impulsive Majesty' was the Foreign Office's nickname for Wilhelm II). For Britain, the menace presented by Germany's growing population, her increasing military-industrial base, and her undisguised hopes of

BLESS

Bridget   Berrwolf   Bearline   Cranmer Byng
Frieder Graham   The Pope   Maria de Tomaso
Captain Kemp   Munroe   Gaby   Jenkins
R. B. Cuningham Grahame   Barker
(not his brother)   (John and Granville)
Mrs. Wil Finnimore   Madame Strindberg   Carson
Salvation Army   Lord Howard de Walden
Capt. Craig   Charlotte Corday   Cromwell
Mrs. Duval   Mary Robertson   Lillie Lenton
Frank Rutter   Castor Oil   James Joyce
Leveridge   Lydia Yavorska   Preb. Carlyle   Jenny
Mon. le compte de Gabulis   Smithers   Dick Burge
33 Church Street   Sievier   Gertie Millar
Norman Wallis   Miss Fowler   Sir Joseph Lyons
Martin Wolff   Watt   Mrs. Hepburn
Alfree   Tommy   Captain Kendell   Young Ahearn
Wilfred Walter   Kate Lechmere   Henry Newbolt
Lady Aberconway   Frank Harris   Hamel
Gilbert Canaan   Sir James Mathew Barry
Mrs. Belloc Lowdnes   W. L. George   Rayner
George Robey   George Mozart   Harry Weldon
Challapine   George Hirst   Graham White
Hucks   Salmet   Shirley Kellogg   Bandsman Rice
Petty Officer Curran   Applegarth   Konody
Colin Bell   Lewis Hind   LEFRANC
Hubert   Commercial Process Co.

A page from the first issue of *Blast*, July 1914

territorial gain and political hegemony was clear. For Germany, Britain's 1904 entente with France, and the similar alliances agreed with Japan and Russia in the first years of the century by Sir Edward Grey as Foreign Secretary, had left the country with a strong fear of encirclement, and with Austria as its only major ally.

Since 1907 Anglo-German antagonism had been rooted in an intensifying naval arms race in which Britain's new class of Dreadnought battleship had received a mighty challenge from Germany's own enormously expensive shipbuilding programme. Germany already had the greatest army in the world; this contrasted with the absence of a mass army in Britain, and with the lack of widespread support for military conscription. Now Germany constructed a fleet which threatened Britain's traditional maritime supremacy. 'The Navy,' as Sir Edward Grey had once remarked, 'is our one and only means of defence and our life depends on it and on it alone.' With an expanding German fleet at Kiel and Wilhelmshaven, just 400 miles from the British coastline, the danger seemed real enough. It forced Britain to scrap the building of smaller vessels in favour of the new type of battleship, and to organize the redeployment of its existing navy, pulling it back from duties overseas to provide the necessary home squadrons.

The Anglo-German naval race, one of the few public issues to raise intense interest at home, had convinced many that the decisive battle of the inevitable war would be fought not on land but at sea, when another Trafalgar would proclaim again that Britannia did indeed rule the waves.

Periodically Asquith's government, held to account for its rising defence budget by the large numbers of Radicals, disarmers and pacifists within the ranks of the Liberal Party, made approaches to Germany to halt the naval race. Ultimately, though, these negotiations foundered on Germany's demand, as its price for doing so, that Britain sign a neutrality pact. 'Although we cannot bind ourselves to go to war with France against Germany,' Grey wrote in 1912, summarizing the Foreign Office's response, 'we shall also certainly not bind ourselves to Germany not to assist France.'

By that time, Germany's naval challenge had slackened: it was not a race, in any event, in which it was interested in competing in the long term if it could not easily win, and the decision had been made to reallocate a portion of the country's naval expenditure to concentrate once again on the building up of the army.

In 1914 most Englishmen and women viewed Germany as their country's enemy in a future war. A meeting of the Church of England's Men's Society in the village of Downton, in Wiltshire, on the evening of 9 January 1914, serves as one illustration of this belief. The motion, proposed by the local curate, 'that war with Germany is inevitable, and that there is urgent need for immediate provision of national conscription', met with a mixed response. The vote resulted in the acceptance of the inevitability of war with Germany, but the idea of conscription was overwhelmingly rejected. In spite of the tireless tub-thumping of the National Service League, and its leader, the veteran commander-in-chief and popular war hero Lord Roberts, the British public continued to be unpersuaded about the merits of compulsory military training.

Popular conviction of the threat from Germany had been fed in the years leading up to 1914 by the unleashing of the sensational power of 'invasion scare' literature. Rolling off the presses in mass serial and book form, and filtering through from adult publications to stories for boys, these tales of the war to come were undeniable page-turners. They were full of thrills and excitement. At the same time, they were responsible for creating widespread fear about the prospect of a German invasion, while implicitly arguing the political case for more Dreadnoughts or conscription.

Erskine Childers's *The Riddle of the Sands* had established the template for the spate of scaremongering invasion literature in which Germany appeared as England's natural aggressor. Published in 1903, at a time when the German naval menace was first causing anxiety, Childers's novel was a story of enemy espionage uncovered by two English gentlemen, who witness a night-time rehearsal for the invasion of England from the German Frisian Islands, attended by the Kaiser himself. The verisimilitude of the narrative and its setting – Childers was a practised sailor around the Frisian Islands – encouraged some readers to believe that the story was true, and the book went on to sell several hundred thousand copies.

Three years later, an even more alarmist account of a German invasion of England appeared. William Le Queux's *The Invasion of 1910* was serialized in Northcliffe's *Daily Mail*, Britain's biggest-selling newspaper, with a daily circulation of almost a million copies. It was then published as a book, prefaced with an introduction by Lord Roberts. Le Queux – according to the *Morning Post*, 'an amiable and placid little man, who looked as if he caught the 9.15 from Ealing to the City every morning' – had made himself one of Britain's highest paid writers, with works of melodrama involving foreign villains and murder by outrageous methods: explosive bon-bons, a cobra in bed, tetanus in soap and rabies in ointment.

A member of the National Service League, Le Queux also wrote fiction warning of Britain's military unpreparedness for a major war. With *The Invasion of 1910* he hit the jackpot. The book simultaneously captured, and contributed to, the jittery mood of its time, appearing in twenty-seven languages and selling over a million copies. Northcliffe was canny enough to insist that, in the interests of the *Mail*'s circulation, the Germans in Le Queux's serial should pass through every sizeable town in Britain, 'not keep to remote one-eyed country villages where there was no possibility of large *Daily Mail* sales'. Another publicity gimmick was to send sandwich-men advertising the story, dressed as German soldiers, to parade through London. One eyewitness recalled the startling sight 'of a long file of veterans in spiked helmets and Prussian-blue uniforms parading moodily down Oxford Street'.

Le Queux further added to the nation's paranoia by writing lurid tales about the presence of a civilian army of German spies in England, employed as waiters, clerks, bakers, hairdressers and private servants. 'Each man,' Le Queux wrote, 'when obeying the Imperial command to join the German arms, had placed in the lapel of his coat a button of a peculiar shape . . . by which he was instantly recognized as a loyal subject of the Kaiser.'

Although this should have been dismissed for the obvious nonsense it was, many were alarmed by the spy scare, which reached its height in the years 1908 to 1910. During this period, fact and fiction often became hopelessly entangled. One Member of Parliament asked Lord Haldane, then at the War Office, for information on the

66,000 German reservists reputed to be living in the Home Counties. Another MP, acting on a 'tip-off' from Le Queux, questioned Haldane about 'the military men from a foreign nation who had been resident for the last two years . . . in the neighbourhood of Epping, and who had been sketching and photographing the whole district and communicating their information directly to their own country'. Haldane blithely responded that he thought the spies could obtain all the information they needed from Ordnance Survey maps.

Even so, the government felt forced to take seriously the potential menace from German espionage. A new Official Secrets Act was rushed through a half-empty House of Commons in the summer of 1911. A Secret Service Bureau had been set up two years earlier. A body known as MO (t), the forerunner of MI5, was charged with responsibility for domestic counter-intelligence. By July 1913 a register of aliens, from probable enemy countries, listed nearly 29,000 names.

Captain Vernon Kell ('K'), of the South Staffordshire Regiment, was the head of MO5 (g), as it was renamed in 1914. Kell was hard-working, though his department's manpower and resources were limited, and his own activities were somewhat curtailed by his chronic asthma. There was no network of German spies on the scale that Le Queux and others had so feverishly imagined. However, Kell's surveillance operation attempted to identify thousands of German reservists who were ready to sabotage railways and dockyards in the event of an invasion. From a card index of 30,000 foreigners resident in Britain, Kell's department derived a 'Special War List' of more than 200 suspects who were put under special observation. Five spies were arrested under the terms of the revised Official Secrets Act, which forbade the unauthorized disclosure of official documents. Among these was German-born Frederick Adolphus Gould, a 55-year-old cigar merchant from Wandsworth, who was taken into custody with his wife Maud in February 1914. Maud Gould had been found in possession of sensitive documents relating to the Royal Navy, which she was carrying on a train from Charing Cross to Ostend in Belgium. Three envelopes discovered under Mrs Gould's travel rug on board the train had revealed Admiralty charts of Bergen and Spithead, and drawings of engines and engine arrangements of navy battleships.

At the couple's trial at the Old Bailey at the beginning of April, Mrs Gould was acquitted after it was claimed that she'd been ignorant of the contents of the documents she was carrying. Her husband was much the bigger catch and the trail of his espionage could have come straight from the pen of Le Queux. Gould, who had spent twelve years in the German navy, had acted as a German spy for more than a decade. He had regularly corresponded with a 'Mr St.' in Potsdam – the spymaster Gustav Steinhauer – and received money in exchange for sensitive documents. Gould was found guilty and sentenced to six years' penal servitude, followed by deportation.

Reporting on the trial, several newspapers couldn't resist the temptation to raise the temperature of spy fever once more, with blatant exaggerations of the presence of German fifth columnists around England. 'Scores' of agents, according to one report, were said to 'infest' the country, 'known to one another only by numbers'. Dockyards were 'hotbeds of espionage', while women at every naval and military station 'are among the most successful spies'.

Le Queux's invasion scare story had spawned a host of imitators. P. G. Wodehouse discovered that the prospect of invasion was considered no laughing matter when his spoof *The Swoop! or, How Clarence Saved England* (1909), in which a boy scout, Clarence Chugwater, saves his country from simultaneous invasion by nine different countries, failed to find favour with the reading public. On the other hand, Saki's *When William Came*, published four years later and reprinted several times in 1914, held its humour neatly in check, though the novel's portrayal of an England actually living under Hohenzollern rule represented the ultimate nightmare vision.

The question that couldn't be easily answered, though it worried German as well as English commentators at the time, was the degree to which this rash of invasion literature contributed to a deepening of the antipathy between the two countries. In 1910 the novelist E. M. Forster had warned of the danger of the assumption that 'England and Germany are bound to fight' in his novel *Howards End*. The remark, he wrote, 'renders war a little more likely each time it is made and is therefore made all the more readily by the gutter press of either nation'.

What does emerge clearly from this strange brand of prophetic writing are the dominant ideas about what the shape of the 'next great war', as it was already called, would be. War is still cast in the heroic mould. Campaigns are conceived of as being swiftly won or lost in a single major battle, while the new weapons of destruction developed by technology are seen as possibly helping to shorten a future war, thus moderating the horror of the loss of life.

Yet all this heated excitement, together with the rough-and-ready believability of some of these tales, tended to obscure the many areas in which ties between the two countries were, by 1914, stronger than ever before. Anglo-German connections in business and trade, and in high and low culture, had been born out of admiration, a spirit of healthy competition, and occasionally harsher rivalry and consequent desire for emulation. They had been strengthened by the heavy influx of German immigrants into Victorian England. Until the last decade of the nineteenth century, and the arrival of Jews from Eastern Europe, Germans had formed the largest foreign community in Britain. In 1914 their numbers stood at approximately 57,000.

In trade, Britain was Germany's best customer, while Germany was Britain's second-best market after India. In the City of London's financial sector, the Anglo-German relationship in banking, shipping and insurance was strong and mutually interdependent. Among the governing class, several key figures were German born or educated. Lord Haldane – War Minister and Lord Chancellor in Asquith's cabinets, sent to Berlin on a special mission in 1912 that failed to achieve a compromise on naval expansion – had studied at Göttingen, which he referred to as his 'spiritual home'; Eyre Crowe, Senior Clerk at the Foreign Office, was German-born and educated, and married to one of his German cousins; Sir William Tyrrell, Sir Edward Grey's private secretary, had been educated at the University of Bonn under the auspices of his German uncle, Prince Radolin, who was German Ambassador at Paris in 1914; Prince Louis of Battenberg, a naturalized British citizen married to a granddaughter of Queen Victoria, was First Sea Lord from 1912. The dynastic relationship of the British and German royal families goes almost without saying.

Anglo-German links in the arts, sciences and the world of learning were still more impressive. 'We regard Germany as a nation leading the way in Arts and Sciences, and we have all learnt and are learning from German Scholars,' a group of British intellectuals would write in a letter to *The Times* at the beginning of August 1914. German pre-eminence in the European community of culture and learning was recognized on 3 June that year at Encaenia, the honorary degree ceremony at Oxford, England's oldest university. Germans constituted the largest body of foreign students at Oxford – thirty-four matriculated in 1913/14, compared with only four Frenchmen – and there were marked Anglophile leanings among those who subsequently returned home to form part of the Wilhelmine political and administrative establishment.

At the 1914 Encaenia, the majority of honorary doctorates were awarded to Germans or Austrians. These included the classical scholar Ludwig Mitteis, the Duke of Saxe-Coburg-Gotha, and Heinrich Lammasch, the Nobel laureate and expert on international arbitration. Richard Strauss received a doctorate in music, while Prince Karl Lichnowsky, German Ambassador to the Court of St James's, was honoured with a doctorate in civil law. Lichnowsky was enthusiastically welcomed, his popularity considered by a reporter from the *Oxford Chronicle* to be clear evidence of 'a far better feeling' between Britain and Germany 'than has prevailed for years'. The German Ambassador's presence in Oxford in 1914 seemed especially appropriate: it was exactly one hundred years since the King of Prussia's visit to the city following Napoleon's defeat and dispatch to Elba.

For their part Germans often expressed boundless admiration for English literature, particularly Shakespeare, to whom their own literary giant, Goethe, had acknowledged his indebtedness. At the level of popular pursuits, football, introduced to Germany by English settlers in the 1870s and 1880s, and horse-racing, were among England's most prized exports to Germany.

In classical music, the English bowed to the unquestioned superiority of the Germans. 'Britain is the only civilized nation without its own music (apart from ditties),' the writer Oscar Schmitz remarked in 1914 – rather unfairly, as Elgar's genius had by then long been recognized in Germany (not least because Elgar's first symphony, influenced by Brahms and Wagner, showed obvious Germanic roots). Not only were concert programmes throughout England dominated by a staple diet of works by the composers Beethoven, Weber, Mendelssohn, Brahms and Wagner, but for many years Germany had also supplied English concert halls with many of their finest conductors and soloists.

Richard Wagner was the most admired modern composer in England, and performances of his music were credited with having helped to transform the public behaviour of the English at concerts. This behaviour had sometimes been considered deplorable by German visitors, who noted that the English seemed unaccustomed to silence, and were in the habit of behaving at concert performances as if they were at a football match, eating, talking and promenading around the hall.

English audiences crowned their love of Wagner on 2 February 1914 when the first of fourteen sold-out performances of *Parsifal* took place at Covent Garden. The Bayreuth Festival's monopoly on *Parsifal* had ended as the clock struck midnight at New Year, allowing the first full-length production of the opera in England to go ahead.

E. M. Forster's *Howards End*, written and published during the years of the great naval race, makes its own nods to Wagnerian mythology and is both a plea for better understanding between the two nations, and an attempt to connect their cultures, however incompatible they might at times seem to be. Forster, who had spent some months in 1905 in north-eastern Germany as tutor to the daughters of the writer Elizabeth von Arnim, gives his two female protagonists, Margaret and Helen, the surname Schlegel. This name would have called to the minds of some of his readers the brothers Friedrich and August Wilhelm Schlegel, leaders of German Romanticism, and symbols of the more idealistic Germany that had existed before it was overtaken by Prussian militarism.

Forster saw the necessity of building a 'rainbow bridge' between the prose of England and the passion of Germany, between the more reflective and cultivated life traditionally associated with the latter, and the obsession with class, etiquette and making money pursued by the former. But in an era of Dreadnoughts and uncertain tensions on the international stage, such a bridge connecting the two nations was perhaps too much to ask for.

War with Germany may have been a spectre that continued to haunt England and the rest of Europe. But over time its power of engendering fear had steadily diminished. 'A threat that goes on for too long ceases to have the effect of a threat,' noted H. G. Wells, who had done more than anyone else to instil fears of futuristic war, and whose most recent publication, *The World Set Free*, had prophesied the advent of the atom bomb.

To some, the idea, famously advanced by the writer Norman Angell, that war itself was becoming outdated, remained influential. Angell's book *The Great Illusion*, published in 1910, had argued that even a successful war of conquest was ultimately futile, because the economic interdependence of the great industrial nations meant that war would be financially damaging to everyone involved. Angell had further stressed that the major powers were 'losing the psychological impulse to war, just as we have lost the psychological impulse to kill our neighbours, on account of religious differences'.

An 'Angellite' society was formed at Oxford University in early 1914, after a speech by Angell at the Union, at the end of the previous year, had helped to carry the motion 'That military power is economically and socially futile'. The report of Angell's visit by the undergraduate *Oxford Magazine* kept its tongue firmly in its cheek. All this talk of war between the European powers had been repeated too often to sound convincing: 'Perhaps the armies of 2913 will still be preparing for the "inevitable war".'

None the less, a spirit of belligerency stalked the land. How could it not do so, given that the rhetoric and situations of warfare were so manifest and threatening in various parts of society, aside from any predictions of a European war? By the summer of 1914 a civil war, a sex war and a class war seemed either imminent, or were already taking place. In Ireland, Unionists and Nationalists were engaged in gun-running on such a scale that they were said to outnumber British troops. The war waged by the suffragettes was accelerating its violent tactics. In industrial relations, the trade unions were promising a general strike for the autumn. As Lloyd George was to warn in July, the problems faced by the nation were 'the gravest with which any government in this country has had to deal for centuries'.

Against this background of widespread discontent, three works of art – a poem, a piece of music and a painting – seem singularly prophetic of future conflict. They are like 'preliminary skirmishes' in some as yet undefined war to come.

1. 'Channel Firing'

'All nations striving strong to make
Red war yet redder . . .'

Of the three, Thomas Hardy's 'Channel Firing' possessed the most direct relationship with current events. Written in April 1914 and published in the *Fortnightly Review* on 1 May, the poem is a parody of an apocalypse. Gunnery practice on battleships in the English Channel is so noisy that it wakes the dead in their coffins. It also sets the dogs howling, scares the church mouse and glebe cow, and makes the worms draw back into their mounds.

The dead think Judgement Day has arrived. But God reassures them that 'The world is as it used to be.' Nations, 'Mad as hatters', are still striving to make 'Red war yet redder'. So the dead lie down again, and one of them wonders out loud,

'Will the world ever saner be . . .
than when He sent us under
In our indifferent century!'

The poem's final verse emphasizes that man learns nothing from history. Hardy gives the names of three places within the sound of the booming guns. Each one represents a long-perished dynasty: Stourton Tower commemorates King Alfred's victory over the invading Danes; Camelot, King Arthur's seat, is fancifully linked to South Cadbury, where Arthur was said to have fought against the Saxon invasion; and Stonehenge, the prehistoric monument, is the symbol of an ancient British culture. All are within fifty miles of the naval base at Portland Harbour in Dorset, from where Hardy, at his home in Dorchester, could hear the Royal Navy's gunnery practice.

Hardy, who turned seventy-four in June 1914, had always been fascinated by war. As a boy, he had been moved by romantic tales of the battles of the Napoleonic Wars. As an adult during the Boer War, he admitted that 'few persons are more martial than I', and that he took 'a keen pleasure' in tactics and strategy as if they were a game of chess. But in order to do this he had to blind himself to the human side of war. For, 'directly I think of that, the romance looks some-what tawdry and worse.'

Hardy congratulated himself that the poetry he had produced during the Boer War was neither 'jingoistic' nor 'Imperial'. In his epic drama *The Dynasts* (1904–8), the first part of which imagined England's earlier invasion scare during the Napoleonic era, a hundred years before, Hardy considered the spell that overcomes people when they respond to the grotesque frenzy of war. Yet, a century from Napoleon, he was confident that 'in the fullness of time, war will come to an end.' Hardy believed that the zest for slaughter would die out, as individuals developed the power of being able to put them-selves in another's place. Furthermore, hadn't war at the beginning of the twentieth century become 'too coldly scientific' for anyone to feel like kindling a romance around it?

The rise of Anglo-German antagonism, therefore, deeply dis-turbed him. Asked in 1909 for his view of the culture of his time, Hardy had responded by laying special emphasis on 'the incubus of armaments' and on 'territorial ambitions smugly disguised as patriot-ism'. He was particularly unsettled by one example of 'invasion scare' literature, Guy du Maurier's play *An Englishman's Home*, which he had happened to see during its first West End run in 1909. Hardy thought that it was so provocative that it ought to be suppressed, since it gave Germany a reason, or an excuse, 'for directing her mind on a war with England'.

The naval arms race was the clear impetus behind 'Channel Firing'. Three months before Hardy wrote the poem, the controversy over the government's latest batch of Naval Estimates had blown up in the press. The issue of the *Illustrated London News* for 14 February 1914 con-tained a rather doleful photographic portrait of Florence, Hardy's second wife, whom he had married quietly a week before, posing with the couple's ferocious wire-haired terrier Wessex. The same publication, a few pages earlier, also included some disturbing photographs of the impact of a powerful new type of shell on the side of a ship.

'The buried people at Stinsford [the churchyard close to Hardy's house at Max Gate] hear the guns being fired at Portland,' the new Mrs Hardy wrote to a friend on 5 April, signalling perhaps the completion of the as yet unpublished poem. To Hardy the gun practice was evidence of human madness, of an urge to plunge civilization into a bloody abyss. With it came the destruction of his belief that 'common-sense had taken the place of bluster in men's minds.'

2. 'Mars, the Bringer of War'

The relentless beat of the opening bars in $\frac{5}{4}$ rhythm makes it one of the most instantly identifiable pieces in the classical music repertoire. In barely more than seven minutes, Holst's 'Mars', from his *Planets* suite, admits us to a musical world of violence and sheer terror. The hushed quiet of the start builds to a menacing crescendo, increasing our apprehension and foreboding. This gives way to fanfares from the brass and the beat of the snare drum to reinforce the metaphor of battle. At the end, a sinister fluttering of woodwind and strings is brought to a murderous finish by the brutal final cadence, which seems to reject any possibility of resolution.

In the summer of 1914, as he completed his initial sketch of 'Mars', the first in a projected suite of seven orchestral pieces, Gustav von Holst was thirty-nine (the 'von' had been added by his father, Adolph, a Cheltenham piano teacher, at the end of the nineteenth century, to make the name sound more Germanic, in line with prevailing musical fashions). Short-sighted, nervous and frail, 'looking like a learned librarian disturbed among his books', Holst combined music teaching – at James

Allen's Girls' School, St Paul's Girls' School and Morley College for Working Men and Women – with composing in his spare time.

In his thirties Holst had achieved success with his *Choral Hymns from the Rig Veda*, and his *Somerset Rhapsody*, and had received a fair amount of public exposure, though he hadn't succeeded in making a living from his compositions. However, lack of acclaim, in 1913, for his large-scale choral work *The Cloud Messenger* had seriously depressed him. He wrote that he was fed up with music, 'especially my own'. On holiday in Majorca in Spain with a party that included the writer Clifford Bax, Holst admitted to feelings of 'apparent failure'. But he also discovered that Bax shared his passion for astrology, and it was the astrological study of the planets that was already leading Holst towards the inspiration for his next major piece of music.

Holst had owned a copy of *Raphael's Mundane Astrology*, probably for several years. This guide by the astrologer Robert Cross revealed 'The Effects of the Planets and Signs, upon the Nations and Countries of the World'. What encouraged Holst to explore the subject further, however, was the work of Alan Leo, another astrologer, whose book *The Art of Synthesis* had pioneered a new approach to the subject following centuries of neglect. Leo's astrology argued against the specific prediction of events in favour of a looser approach, concentrating on character trends and the delineation of possible areas of harmony or stress.

Between six and seven hundred fortune-tellers, clairvoyants, palmists and assorted charlatans were said to be operating in London alone, but in the eyes of English law astrology was still suspect. In the spring of 1914 Alan Leo was charged under the Vagrancy Act of 1824, which forbade the activities of 'every Person pretending or professing to tell Fortunes'. In May, Leo was brought to trial at Mansion House, amid great publicity. The case was subsequently dismissed on a point of evidence.

Holst derived the characteristics of his planets from the study of Leo's work. Each one was to form a mood picture, acting as a foil to the others, 'with very little contrast in any of them', in music of a variety of idioms. His chief musical influences were Stravinsky (whose *Sacre du Printemps* had premièred in 1913) and Schoenberg's

Five Pieces for Orchestra. Significantly, Holst chose to open his suite with 'Mars, the Bringer of War'. Astrologically this was unusual, since Mercury, 'the Winged Messenger', is the first planet. But Mars, primal and aggressive, offered a dramatic and compelling start.

The altered circumstances of Holst's working life made their contribution to the creation of 'Mars'. St Paul's Girls' School's new music wing included a sound-proof room, specially constructed for Holst as Director of Music. A five-day walking tour of North Essex, in the winter of 1913, had brought Holst to the village of Thaxted, where he immediately saw the immense spire of the Church of St John the Baptist. With the church's unconventional, socialist vicar, Conrad Noel, Holst was to form a close affinity, eventually devising an annual musical festival at Thaxted every Whitsun. On a hill overlooking the village, Holst and his wife Isobel rented a 300-year-old thatched cottage, in Monk Street, as a weekend and holiday retreat. 'It stood high above the surrounding cornfields and meadows and willow trees with a view of the church spire in the distance,' Holst's daughter Imogen remembered. 'It was so quiet that we could hear the bees in the dark red clover beyond the garden hedge.'

For the Thaxted cottage, Holst purchased a second-hand piano for £12, with a light touch that suited the neuritis he suffered from in his right arm. By May 1914, the same month in which his astrological mentor Alan Leo faced trial, Holst was hard at work on 'Mars' in the tranquillity of rural Essex, or in his sound-proof room, both providing a peaceful contrast to the violence that would be found in his dramatic composition.

Did Holst set out to portray a sense of impending war in the sketch of 'Mars' that was completed by August 1914? He always claimed consciously not to have done so. But for future listeners to the work, its portrayal of the merciless horrors of mechanized warfare would be unmistakable.

3. *The Mud Bath*

If you had happened to be passing the Chenil Gallery in London's King's Road, next door to Chelsea Town Hall, in early July 1914, your eyes would have met with an arresting sight. Hanging on the outside wall of the gallery was a large canvas full of writhing, angular figures, part human and part machine, set at a sharp diagonal and presented against a bright red background.

The Mud Bath (see plate 15) was an abstract painting by David Bomberg, a 23-year-old recent graduate of the Slade School of Fine Art, and one of the most precocious and audacious of the younger generation of British artists. Bomberg was the son of a Polish-Jewish immigrant leather-worker. He had been born in Birmingham, and raised in London's Jewish community in Whitechapel. His artistic promise was recognized early. He attended evening classes given by Walter Sickert, and saw work by Cézanne for the first time at Roger Fry's epoch-making Post-Impressionists exhibition at the Grafton Galleries in 1910.

In the spring of 1914 Bomberg had exhibited in the Jewish section of the 'Twentieth Century Art' exhibition at the Whitechapel Art Gallery, alongside other Jewish artists like Mark Gertler and Isaac Rosenberg. It was a defining moment in British Modernism. Bomberg's one-man show at the Chenil Gallery in the summer of 1914 contained fifty-five drawings and paintings, charting his development from traditional draughtsmanship to the radical movement and colour of *The Mud Bath*.

The autobiographical impulse behind this painting was Bomberg's memories from his boyhood of Schevzik's Vapour Baths, opposite the synagogue in Brick Lane, close to where he'd been brought up. These 'Russian Vapour Baths', as they proudly announced themselves on a canopy projecting on to the street, were patronized by Whitechapel's Jewish residents. Whether or not there were actually facilities in the baths for a cleansing 'mud pack massage' is questionable. But the filthiness of the setting, with the accumulation of dirt under the bathers' feet as they splashed around the Baths, may have provided Bomberg with a further source of inspiration.

At a more theoretical level, too, the cleansing processes of Schevzik's Baths offered Bomberg an appropriate metaphor for what he considered to be his aims as an artist. In his foreword to the catalogue of the Chenil show, Bomberg proclaimed his intention of

1. Agnes (*above left*) and John Starchfield (*above right*) at the inquest into the death of their son Willie in January 1914, as the mystery surrounding the boy's disappearance and murder deepened.

2. Herbert Henry Asquith, Britain's Prime Minister in 1914. Asquith faced the crisis in Ireland and the outbreak of a European war with the support of Venetia Stanley, a woman young enough to be his daughter.

3. Sir Edward Carson – champion of Ulster Unionism at the height of its resistance to Home Rule for Ireland – inspects a band of armed Ulster Volunteers in the spring of 1914.

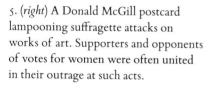

"NOW AINT THAT A SHAME, I BET IT'S THEM SUFFRAGETTES DONE IT !!"

4. (*above*) The suffragette Mary Richardson and the axe with which she slashed Velázquez's *Rokeby Venus* at the National Gallery in March 1914.

5. (*right*) A Donald McGill postcard lampooning suffragette attacks on works of art. Supporters and opponents of votes for women were often united in their outrage at such acts.

6. (*above left*) Kitty and Tom Higdon, the teachers at the centre of the Burston School Strike. Five years older than her husband, Kitty was a pacifist with an unbending sense of her own rectitude, while Tom was something of a firebrand.

7. (*above right*) Violet Potter, the plucky and determined fourteen-year-old who led her classmates in a strike against the sacking of their teachers.

8. Mrs Patrick Campbell as Eliza Doolittle, the common flower girl whom Professor Henry Higgins passes off as a duchess in Shaw's *Pygmalion*. The English production of the play opened in 1914, beset by disagreements between its stars and the playwright–director, and by the controversy caused by Mrs Pat's use of a shocking expletive on stage.

9. A theatrical cartoon advertising *Pygmalion* at His Majesty's, Herbert Beerbohm Tree's theatre. The play ran up to the end of July in 118 sold-out performances, and could easily have continued for much longer.

10. (*above left*) A typical scene at Grahame-White's Hendon Aerodrome in the first half of 1914. Spectators watch as a Breguet biplane crosses the line at the start of a race.

11. (*left*) One of the heroes of the new aviation age, Gustav Hamel, described by Winston Churchill as three parts bird, the rest genius.

12. (*far left*) The First Lord of the Admiralty, Winston Churchill, photographed after flying over the fleet. Nicknamed 'The Flying Cabinet Minister', Churchill was instrumental in securing the formation, in 1914, of a Royal Naval Air Service, independent of its military counterpart.

13. Isobel Holst, the composer's wife, in the sitting-room of the Thaxted cottage that she and Holst rented as a weekend and holiday retreat. The second-hand piano purchased by Holst for £12, on which he composed parts of 'Mars, the Bringer of War', can be seen to the left.

14. Gustav von Holst – as he was known until 1918, when he dropped the 'von' by deed poll – looking like a bespectacled librarian.

15. David Bomberg's *The Mud Bath*, first exhibited in London in the summer of 1914.

16. A pair of clerks remove their jackets as they walk in Hyde Park during a hot spell in June 1914. The English weather that summer was by no means as remarkable as myth would have us believe, and parts of the country saw plenty of rain and below-average temperatures.

17. Ladies at the Henley Regatta in July 1914, showing off the latest fashions.

To BUCKINGHAM PALACE!

To DEMAND VOTES FOR WOMEN

To PROTEST AGAINST TORTURE

To CLAIM EQUAL TREATMENT
FOR MILITANT ULSTER MEN AND
: MILITANT SUFFRAGISTS :

DEPUTATION TO THE KING
Led by MRS. PANKHURST

Thursday Afternoon, May 21st, at 4 p.m.

An Irish deputation which demanded citizen rights was received by King
George III. in person in 1793. Why should not the Women's Deputation be
received in 1914 by King George V?

David Allen & Sons, Ltd., London, Harrow, Etc.   [P.T.O.

18. A poster advertising the suffragettes' deputation to the King at Buckingham Palace on 21
May, the militants' final planned demonstration before the outbreak of war. The occasion was
marked by brutal attacks on the women, and multiple arrests.

stripping art of all 'irrelevant matter'. He was interested in decoration only if it occurred accidentally. 'My object is the *construction of Pure Form,*' he wrote emphatically. 'I hate the colours of the East, the Modern Medievalist, and the Fat Man of the Renaissance.'

Displayed on the wall of the Chenil Gallery, garlanded with Union Jacks (matching the painting's colour scheme), and alternately rained upon and baked by the sun, *The Mud Bath* attracted a range of responses. Horses drawing the 29 bus used to shy at it as they came round the corner of the King's Road; there were traffic jams outside the gallery; while some passers-by were said to ignore the painting because they didn't recognize it as a picture.

Bomberg's *Mud Bath* stood out as a campaign banner for English avant-garde art. In 1914 the London art scene was in a state of ferment. The pictures on display at that summer's Royal Academy exhibition – including works by Orpen, Munnings, Laura Knight and John Singer Sargent (the portrait of Henry James slashed by the suffragette Mary Ward) – were criticized for being staid and conservative, and unresponsive to developments in contemporary art. Even the bad paintings were dismissed for being 'not quite spirited enough'. The artist C. R. W. Nevinson summed up the malaise in the establishment art world by saying that the annual summer exhibition at Burlington House had been much the same for the past fifty years.

By contrast, 1914 was also a year when new ideas and displays, experimental and dynamic, were exploding on to the radical art scene, and exciting heated comment among critics and commentators. Clive Bell's polemical *Art*, published in January, propounded his influential theory of 'significant form', namely that lines and colours combined in a particular way stir our aesthetic emotions. That same month, the philosopher T. E. Hulme announced the end of naturalistic art and the rebirth of older geometrical forms comprising stiff, angular lines. Exhibitions meanwhile seemed to provide the capital with a never-ending succession of ground-breaking shows: the London Group at the Goupil Gallery; 'Twentieth Century Art' at Whitechapel and Bomberg at the Chenil; Gaudier-Brzeska at the Grafton; the Italian Futurists at the Doré; and that spring's well-attended, much praised display of 'Modern German Art' at the Twenty-One Gallery.

The founder of Futurism, Filippo Marinetti – whose manifesto had declared a desire 'to glorify War', along with 'militarism, patriotism, the destructive arm of the Anarchist, the beautiful Ideas that kill, the contempt for women' – was in London publicizing his movement. Between the autumn of the previous year and the summer of 1914, he delivered more than ten lectures in the capital. At the Coliseum in June, Luigi Russolo, the Futurist composer and noise artist, assembled twenty-three of his *Intonarumori*, or noise organs, on stage to perform a 'Grand Futurist Concert of Noises'. The poet Ezra Pound described it as 'a mimetic representation of dead cats in a fog-horn'.

Pound had given the name to an English art movement that owed much of its spirit of violence, theatricality and angry, condemnatory propaganda to the example of Marinetti and the Futurists. 'Vorticism', suggesting a spinning flow of perpetual motion, was really a misnomer for the rigid, angular style taken up by the painter Wyndham Lewis and his small band of adherents. Coldness and hardness, 'reflections of steel and stone in the spirit of the artist', were to be the guiding aims of the Vorticists, in opposition to the Futurists' emphasis on blurred motion, intended to mirror the chaotic speed and energy of modern life.

But what mattered most about Vorticism was not so much its principles and philosophy, which remained airy-fairy and ill-defined, but its artistic call to arms. Vorticists have been aptly called the shock-troops of British Modernism; or, to put it another way: in common with later generations of angry young men – and women – they were sticking two fingers up at the establishment, subverting it and calling on supporters to turn their backs on tradition, in particular Victorian tradition, to create something dynamic, forceful and new.

Undoubtedly, the Vorticists' most important, and energetic, act of belligerency was the publication, at the beginning of July 1914, of the first issue of *Blast*. Sandwiched between bright puce covers – or 'steam-calliope pink', as Pound described the colour – with huge black sans serif typography, Lewis's declaration of war blasted England first, 'from politeness', for being the 'dismal symbol, set round our bodies, of effeminate lout within'. Its climate was cursed 'for its sins and infections'. As 'Primitive Mercenaries in the Modern World', Vorticists swore to purge the nation of 'its luxury, sport, the famous English "Humour", the thrilling ascendancy and idée fixe of Class', responsible for 'producing the most intense snobbery in the World'.

Individuals and Institutions were lined up on opposing sides to be contrastingly blasted and blessed. Elgar, Beecham '(Pills, Opera, Thomas)', the Bishop of London 'and all his posterity', Galsworthy, Captain Cook and 'Clan Strachey' were among the blasted; Charlotte Corday, Cromwell, a suffragette (Lillie Lenton), a trade unionist, an Ulster rebel (Sir Edward Carson), the champions of the air (Hamel, Grahame-White and B. C. Hucks) and, naturally, England's 'maritime prowess' were singled out for unbridled praise.

David Bomberg refused to add his signature to those of the eleven artists, nine men and two women, subscribing to the manifesto presented by *Blast*. Indeed he went so far as to threaten Wyndham Lewis with legal action if he reproduced any of his work. Bomberg wished to maintain his freedom from partisan movements, and his one-man show at the Chenil was a demonstration of this. However, his art, near-abstract, geometrical and mechanistic, clearly had so much in common with the professed beliefs of Vorticism as to be almost indivisible from them.

Wyndham Lewis was obsessed with war, later admitting, as he looked back over his life, that 'With me, war and art have been mixed up from the start.' In the early months of 1914, Lewis had been working on a large-scale canvas, now lost, entitled *Plan of War*. The painting's strict emphasis on geometrical form made it appear suggestive of the lines of battle drawn up on a battlefield.

In a related way, though for the time being less apparently, Bomberg's *Mud Bath* seemed to offer an uncomfortable premonition of a future type of combat that was already being talked about, though it remained scarcely envisaged: trench warfare.

Adlestrop

1. From a Railway Carriage

Early on the morning of 24 June – Midsummer's Day – the writer Edward Thomas, and Helen, his wife of fifteen years, were making hurried preparations to catch a train. They were on their way to visit the American poet Robert Frost at Leddington, near Ledbury, on the Gloucestershire–Herefordshire border. Leaving Thomas's parents' house, a handsome Victorian villa at 13 (later 12) Rusham Road, Balham, where they had been staying, the couple made their way up Nightingale Lane to take the underground, or maybe the 36 bus, to Paddington Station.

Thomas was thirty-six years old, tall and spare, with sun-bleached hair and a haunted look of melancholy that flickered periodically across his pale blue eyes. We can imagine him wearing a jacket of homespun tweed, with a rucksack slung across his shoulder, and carrying a sturdy walking stick in his strong, craftsman's hands. There was perhaps a trace of elation in his step. He had been in London for only a few days, and had, after all, been 'born and bred a Clapham Junction man', but he could not get out of London fast enough, relishing the thought of escaping the city to journey westwards into the countryside of Gloucestershire and Herefordshire. 'Let us get out of these indoor narrow modern days . . . into the sunlight and the pure wind,' his literary hero Richard Jeffries had written, in words that Thomas had long regarded as 'a gospel' or 'an incantation'.

Before leaving the house in Rusham Road, Thomas had written a brief note to his friend, the writer Eleanor Farjeon, explaining that 'We are just starting for Ledbury and are in a real hurry', and mentioning that on the previous evening he and Helen had been to the ballet at Drury Lane. That summer's season of German and Russian opera and ballet at the Theatre Royal, under the direction of Sergei

136 LONDON, OXFORD & MALVERN

For Local Tables see pages	Down Trains.		a.m.	a.m.	a.m.	p.m.	p.m.	p.m.	p.m.
26 to 35	LONDON (Paddington) ...	dep.	10 20	11 5	1120	12 30	...	1 0	1 40
	Ealing (Broadway) . .	,,			10 53	12 41		.	
82, 83	Bournemouth (Central)	dep.	...	..	...	10 2..	...	...	
	Portsmouth Town ,,		...	..	...	9 35	..	...	
	Southampton Town(for b'ks) ,,		9N8	..	...	11a10	..	...	
26 to 35	Reading . . .	dep.	11 11	..	12 8	1 30	..	.	
	Didcot . . . . . ,,		...	..	12M 6	1 10	..	.	
	Oxford	arr.	11 44	.	12 43	2 5	..	.	
. .	OXFORD ...	dep.	11 52		1247	2 18	2 25	.	
. .	Wolvercot Platform . . . ,,				12 53		2 31		
...	Yarnton . . . . . . ,,		W		12 57		2 36		
.	Handborough (for Bleuheim) . ,,		12 7			2 30			
...	Charlbury . . . . . ,,		12 19			2 41	STOP		
.	Ascott-under-Wychwood . . ,,		12 26			2 48	.		
.	Shipton (for Burford) .... ,,		12 31			2 53	.		
.	Kingham . . . . ,,		12 40			2 58			3*14
159	Chipping Norton . . . . { arr.		1 33			3 36	...		3*36
	{ dep.		11M52			.			
159	Bourton-on-the-Water . . arr.		1 26			3 36			3*30
	Cheltenham (St. James') ,,		2 7			4 18			4*18
...	Adlestrop . . . . dep.		12 48	...		STOP			...
...	Moreton-in-Marsh . . . ,,		12 59	.		.			..
141	Shipston-on-Stour . . . . { arr.		1 52	...		.			
	{ dep.		11 55			.			
...	Blockley . . . . dep.		1 6	...		M			
..	Campden . . . . ,,		1 13	...		p.m.	M		
...	Honeybourne . . . . ,,		1 24	1 51		3 42	3 49		
159	Broadway (M) . . . { arr.		2 16	2 16	.	3 26	3 26		
	{ dep.		...	1 22	...	.			
158	Stratford-on-Avon . . . . . { arr.		1 57			.	3 25		
	{ dep.			1 30	...	.			
.	Littleton and Badsey . . dep.		1 30	1 57	.	3 49	3 56	.	
...	Evesham .... ,,		1 38	2 2		2 4	3 55	4 2	
.	Fladbury . . . . . ,,		1 44			2 11			
.	Pershore . . . . . . ,,		1 54			2 18			
.	Stoulton . . . . ,,		2 0						
...	Norton Junction . . . . . . ,,		2 6						
.	WORCESTER (Shrub Hill) arr.		2 12						3 55

Right-side notes running vertically: "Via Stratford-on-Avon", "THURSDAYS AND SATURDAYS ONLY.", "Via Stratford-on-Avon", "Luncheon and Tea Car Train.", "Will not run on Bank Holidays."

The railway timetable for the Great Western stopping service to Worcester and Malvern, showing the 10.20 a.m. train taken by Edward Thomas on 24 June 1914

Diaghilev of the Ballets Russes, and the sponsorship of the patent-medicine manufacturer Sir Joseph Beecham, was currently mesmerizing London.

Fashionable and political society was flocking to Drury Lane. Members of the aristocracy and native and foreign royalty were there, as well as the Asquiths, but so, too, was a more ordinary class of capital-dweller whose taste in opera and ballet was being considerably broadened by the programme of performances. Edward Thomas had already seen Mozart's *Magic Flute*, still virtually unknown in

London (and described by one contemporary critic as 'a striking example of great gifts misdirected'), which had opened the season. On 23 June he was part of the audience for an evening of music by Richard Strauss, including the English première of Strauss's one-act ballet *The Legend of Joseph*, conducted by the composer himself, with colourful and flamboyant costumes designed by Léon Bakst and choreography by Michel Fokine. However, this transposition of the biblical story of Joseph to 'a fanciful setting' in Renaissance Venice, with troupes of oriental slave-dancers, boxers and wrestlers, did not find favour with Thomas. He disliked the music and thought the ballet itself was a failure, but was returning none the less to Drury Lane the following week for *The Spectre of the Rose*, renowned for its star performer Vaslav Nijinsky and his ethereal leap across the stage.

At Paddington, Thomas and his wife boarded the 10.20 a.m. Great Western stopping service to Worcester and Malvern. It was probably a train with four carriages, a third-class at each end with two composite middle carriages, consisting of one first and one third-class compartment in each. The Thomases travelled third class. Some of Edward Thomas's paternal relations had been employed at the Great Western Railway works at Swindon, including his uncle Harry, who was a fitter there in the 1880s, while his father, Philip Henry Thomas, had entered the civil service as a staff clerk for light railways and tramways at the Board of Trade.

If railways could in some sense be said to be in his blood, they had also formed the subject matter for two of Edward Thomas's short prose sketches, and a chapter in his book *The South Country*, about his wanderings in southern England. In one of the stories, 'A Third-Class Carriage', the only thing said to commend a small English town or village is its railway works. In 'Death by Misadventure', written a few years earlier, all the men in the carriage drop their newspapers to their knees, without any appearance of emotion – 'in short with a railway carriage expression' – to scan the name of the station. A man has fallen underneath the engine. 'Some of us were dimly pleased to have had an experience which not everyone has every day.' The body is extracted and placed on a stretcher. 'The scent of death had not taken a minute to reach those women whose sons and husbands and fathers and lovers include some . . . who are destined to die bloodily and unexpectedly.' The 'guilty train' begins to shunt forward again. 'There was not a sound except the hissing of the steam.'

Passing through Battersea Park, Thomas jotted down a description, in one of the field notebooks that always accompanied him, of 'the sea of slate and dull brick'. At 11.44 the train reached Oxford, where Thomas had been an undergraduate at the turn of the century. Here he observed the 'tiers of pure white' in the sky 'with loose longer masses above and gaps of dark blue above haymaking and elms'.

'Then we stopped at Adlestrop,' Thomas's notebook continues. It was 12.48 p.m. Through the willows he heard 'a chain of blackbirds' songs . . . & one thrush & no man seen, only a hiss of engine letting off steam'.

Adlestrop was – and is – a small rural parish, of about 150 inhabitants, approximately three miles east of Stow-on-the-Wold, bounded on its north-east side by the River Evenlode, which, in 1914, ran behind the Down platform at the station. Had Edward Thomas stepped off the train, he would no doubt have been delighted to discover, as a keen and inveterate walker, that the road crossing the village was a route of considerable antiquity, part of the old Cotswold Ridgeway, which dated back to Anglo-Saxon times. He might also have made his way up to the church, and to the rectory where Jane Austen had stayed on several occasions with her relatives, the Leighs, and which may have inspired her portrait of Edmund Bertram's Thornton Lacey Parsonage, and its surroundings, in *Mansfield Park*, published exactly a hundred years earlier.

But instead, all Thomas may have noticed from the window of his railway carriage were the 'country noises brushing the surface of a deeper silence', the growing heat of the sun in the middle of the day – and the name of the station. Several stops on and the train came to a halt outside Campden

by banks of long grass willow herb & meadowsweet, extraordinary silence between the two periods of travel – looking out on grey dry stones between metals & the shiny metals & over it all the elms willows & long grass – one man clears his throat – a greater than rustic silence.

These were 'brief unrestrained impressions of things lately seen', which, as Thomas had recently told Robert Frost, he was writing every day, perhaps as a bridge to the poetry he wanted to write, but which somehow still eluded him.

The impressions of 24 June recorded by him in his notebook were also an illustration of what his friend Jesse Berridge once described as Thomas's 'extraordinary talent for giving an intense significance to a single, almost momentary, experience', making it instantly unforgettable. Six months after his railway journey through the Gloucestershire countryside, Edward Thomas would conflate the sights and sounds of that Midsummer's Day to write one of his earliest poems, composed in the remarkable outpouring of creative energy with which he ended the year and began 1915. In so doing, the sixteen lines of 'Adlestrop' would become a fragile remembrance of English countryside and English character in the summer of 1914, an unobtrusive record of what appears to be a set of random impressions and sensations; or, what Thomas himself had once described as 'an enduring echo of we know not what in the past'.

2. Weather Obsessed

Few writers have evoked the changing patterns of the weather as powerfully, or as intensely, as Edward Thomas. Whether it was 'the north wind' making 'an invasion with horizontal arrows of pricking hail'; the hot sky on a summer's day, 'blue without pity and changing to a yellow mist near the horizon'; or 'the heavy and lasting rain', the 'early momentous thunderdrops, the perpendicular cataract shining . . . at night the little showers' – Thomas's descriptions of weather brim over with acute observation and pointed metaphor. In his latest prose work, *In Pursuit of Spring*, published in April 1914, Thomas had depicted himself on a walking and cycling pilgrimage from London to the Quantock Hills, in which he described the climatic cycle of one season passing into another, searching for 'Winter's grave' and awaiting the regenerative force of spring's return.

Thomas's descriptions of English weather were honed and refined on long walking expeditions. E. M. Forster may have had Edward

Thomas in mind, several years earlier, when he portrayed Leonard Bast, 'such a muddle of a man, and yet so worth pulling through', in *Howards End*. Like Thomas in an earlier work, *The Heart of England*, Bast escapes the city to walk out into the countryside on its western fringes, sometimes at dead of night. Rainy conditions rather than sunshine were best for walking, Thomas used to claim, as they forced the walker to gaze downwards in the direction of his feet, noticing animal life in the hedgerows and in no man's land, the colloquial term for the green strip running along country roads. Strenuous walks across country often helped to abate Thomas's feelings of depression. The rhythmical movement of his feet over 'rough, tussocky' terrain was both a stimulant to thinking and an influence on the development of Thomas's poetic style, in prose and, eventually, in poetry.

The summer of 1914 had, according to Thomas, begun 'dirtily enough'. Although temperatures in parts of England at the beginning of the last week in May had reached eighty-two degrees Fahrenheit in the shade, these had been succeeded by a wintry start to June, breaking records for the month and making it the chilliest for thirty years. A savage frost in Warwickshire had been followed by hail, heavy rain, flash floods and increasingly violent thunderous conditions throughout southern England.

On the evening of Sunday, 14 June, John Riddey, the clerk from the Deptford ironworks, last glimpsed enjoying himself at the Hendon air races, witnessed 'one of the biggest thunderstorms I have ever seen'. At his lodgings in Tressillian Road, Lewisham, in South-East London, he found 'all the male folk paddling about downstairs with no shoes & socks on, bailing the water out of the basement. I picked up some hail stones as large as my thumb nail.' That day, seven people – four of them children – were struck by lightning and killed on Wandsworth Common, while several others were struck and injured. A married couple, sheltering under a tree, were among those killed. Their baby, lying in a perambulator, remained untouched by lightning (apparently because of the rubber tyres of the pram). Storms in the south of prolonged intensity raged on and off all day, setting electric bells ringing and causing enormous disruption to telephone and telegraph lines.

Within a few days, temperatures in many parts of the country had risen to above normal for the time of year. From Silverdale, the village that stands on Morecambe Bay, close to the Cumbrian border in Lancashire, where he was staying with the poet Gordon Bottomley, prior to his visit to London, Edward Thomas wrote to his wife that he had 'contrived to get more pleasure than almost ever before out of the weather'. He had taken a morning bathe in Haweswater, and watched as the misty heat enveloped the hills and the sea.

'This has been a year of years for weather,' Thomas continued, more than a little prematurely, but he must have had hopes that a run of bad summers was coming to an end. The previous two had been disappointing: 1912, with one of the coolest Augusts on record, had effectively been a year without a summer; and 1913's summer months had also tended to be cool. Furthermore, it had rained on 15 July, St Swithin's Day, fostering fears, in line with proverbial lore, that a further forty days of rain would follow – though in fact 1913's rainfall had stalled at average levels for the time of year. The so-called 'Halcyon Summer' had been that of 1911, when temperatures had soared to a record peak of one hundred degrees, and when the unrelenting heat was widely believed to have exacerbated the outbreaks of violence during the prolonged period of industrial unrest.

Would the summer of 1914 match, or even exceed, the record set by 1911's? Parts of the Northern Line on the London Underground were in the process of introducing new ventilation systems just in case it did. Electric fans were in increasingly common use in many public places. Meanwhile, as Edward Thomas passed through Adlestrop on 24 June, on his way to stay with Robert Frost, the temperature in the shade of the stationmaster's house reached exactly eighty degrees.

3. Elected Friends

Robert and Elinor Frost, and their four children, were renting a cottage at Leddington in north-east Gloucestershire, so near to the Herefordshire border that Edward Thomas sometimes referred to Leddington as being in the adjacent county. Frost had sailed to

England in 1912, after selling his New Hampshire farm and giving up a job as a teacher of psychology. This was Frost's last-ditch attempt at making his name as a poet by achieving recognition in England, following almost two decades of critical neglect in the United States. He planned to live a simple life in the English countryside, and claimed to have always wanted 'to live under thatch', though the first house inhabited by Frost and his family was a bungalow in Beaconsfield. Frost's friends, the poets Lascelles Abercrombie and Wilfrid Gibson, persuaded him to move closer to them in a remote area of rural Gloucestershire, to experience the real English countryside, rather than a suburban version of it. The Frosts' new home, Little Iddens, wasn't thatched either. It was also small, consisting of five rooms and only basic amenities. However, it possessed a picturesque charm, with its black-and-white timber frame, brick floor and open beams, and an old iron pump for water. Frost settled here into a colony or tiny nest of poets, at three corners of a triangle with the village of Dymock at its centre. Abercrombie, its first resident, rented The Gallows, a pair of cottages at Ryton, to the south-east of the village. Gibson lived at The Old Nail Shop, a thatched cottage at Greenway Cross, to its west. In 1914 the Leadon Valley, in which Dymock lies, was lush and fertile, full of orchards of apples, pears and plums, and fields of soft fruit stretching across a vast expanse of land.

Edward Thomas had initially visited the Frosts at Little Iddens for a week in April 1914, soon after the Frosts' move there, when Dymock's famous crop of daffodils was turning the meadows yellow. 'Edward Thomas, who is a very well known critic and prose writer has been here,' Elinor Frost wrote to her sister. 'Rob and I think everything of him. He is quite the most admirable and lovable man we have ever known.' Thomas was returning now with Helen, partly in order to arrange lodgings for a longer visit that August with his wife, and children: Merfyn, fourteen, Bronwen, eleven, and Myfanwy, nearly four years old.

The friendship between Thomas and Frost had developed rapidly after their first introduction, at the beginning of October 1913, at St George's vegetarian restaurant in St Martin's Lane in London, a popular meeting place for poets and writers. But it was more than simply a love of literature that cemented their relationship. It was as if each saw himself mirrored in the other. Frost at thirty-nine was the older by four years, but both were tall and fair-haired – though Frost's hair colour was closer now to grey – with pale blue eyes. Both had endured disappointment as professional writers: Frost from a lack of recognition, Thomas from the 'hack work' taken on to support his family, which hampered his search for a literary form that suited him, and made him fear that he would never produce writing worthy of his talent. Both men, too, were encouraged by the devotion of their loving wives, while suffering on occasion from levels of despair that made them at worst suicidal. Frost on one occasion had flourished a revolver in his wife's presence, threatening to kill himself, or her. In Thomas's case, he had considered taking his own life in 1908, striding out of his Hampshire home one day with a revolver in his pocket. Five years later, in October 1913, the month he met Frost, Thomas had been talked out of a suicidal 'design' by the writer Walter de la Mare. 'I think I have now changed my mind,' Thomas told de la Mare afterwards, 'though I have the Saviour in my pocket.'

Thomas's 'accursed tempers and moodiness' were at times frightening in their ferocity, and utterly bewildering to his wife, Helen. A crisis point had been reached in the autumn of 1911. Physical weakness accompanied Thomas's violent mood swings, making him more miserable and dejected than ever, and alarming Helen to the extent that she feared at times for her husband's sanity. A course of treatment under Helton Godwin Baynes, a pioneer of psychoanalysis, who later studied under Jung and worked as his assistant, achieved some limited success the following year. Baynes encouraged Thomas in a process of self-interrogation, providing a spur for his experiments in autobiography, memories of his childhood in fictional and memoir form, which he was beginning to work on.

However, he was unable to overcome the worry and depression brought on by financial hardship and constant overwork. Between 1910 and 1912 alone, Thomas produced twelve books. In *The Happy-Go-Lucky Morgans*, a fictional portrait of his childhood and teenage years in London, Wiltshire and Wales, published in 1913, he offers a reflection of himself in the character of Mr Torrance, described as 'a doomed hack' who is forced to survive by writing 'hasty compilations, ill-arranged, inaccurate, and incomplete, and swollen to a ridiculous size for the sake of gain'. One such piece of grinding toil, written in tandem with his autobiographies, was *A Literary Pilgrim in England*, a book he grew swiftly to detest. No sooner had this been dispatched than he was at work on another despised anthology, *The Flowers I Love*.

Reviewing continued to make an essential contribution to Thomas's income. In the decade and a half since coming down from Oxford, he had written roughly 1,500 signed book reviews and seventy articles, and had won a reputation as an influential and discerning critic (Walter de la Mare said that he must have been a critic of rhymes in his nursery). Harold Monro had been anxious to include him in the launch of the Poetry Bookshop in January 1913, though Thomas's subsequent review of the bookshop's initial enterprise, *Georgian Poetry 1911–1912*, had fallen short of the enthusiastic reception Monro must have hoped for. Soon afterwards, Thomas had also been one of a panel of judges chosen to select the best poem published in Monro's *Poetry Review*. Thomas had opted for a poem by Wilfrid Gibson, but the majority decision of the judges was to award the £30 prize to Rupert Brooke for his 'Old Vicarage, Grantchester'.

Criticism, though, brought Thomas little money or satisfaction, and, increasingly, was produced at a massive cost to his well-being and self-respect. 'Journalism is as tedious and meaningless as a clerk's work,' Thomas had once written, a point of view he confirmed in the spring of 1914, after losing his regular reviewing berth on the *Daily Chronicle*, when he contributed an article entitled 'Reviewing: An Unskilled Labour' to the journal *Poetry and Drama*. In the past he had sometimes imagined another world in which he would pursue a kind of writing that was, as he put it, 'more like me'. The last chapter of *The Happy-Go-Lucky Morgans*, written in 1913, in which the narrator recalls the magical power of the incantation of a poem by Shelley, almost seems to presage Edward Thomas's belief in a new kind of literary future for himself.

The award to Thomas of a grant of £100 from the Royal Literary Fund in February 1914, in response to an application in which he had described his rapid fall in earnings and the sharp decline in his health, allowed him some temporary respite from money worries. After months of a peripatetic lifestyle, his decision to make Yew Tree Cottage, in the village of Steep in Hampshire, the house to which the Thomas family had moved the previous summer, his permanent base could be construed as evidence of a greater stability of mind. His relationship with Robert Frost was encouraging him to think of other kinds of practical and artistic solutions to his existence as a writer. Thomas was wavering over the possibility of uprooting his family for a life in America, accompanying the homesick Frosts back to New Hampshire when their time in England came to an end. Most of all, Frost was helping Thomas to see himself in a vital new guise: as a poet.

In May 1914, a month before his arrival in Leddington on his latest visit to the Frosts, Thomas had written to Robert Frost, wondering 'whether you can imagine me taking to verse. If you can I might get over the feeling that it is impossible – which at once obliges your good nature to say "I can".' Reading Thomas's latest book, *In Pursuit of Spring*, left Frost in no doubt that there was a poet lingering, concealed in the shadow of the prose writer, and when they were together, Frost would read aloud passages from the book – in his 'vurry Amur'kn' deep and pleasant voice' – as if they were poetry, to encourage Thomas to write 'in verse form in the same cadence'.

Other friends and acquaintances had already admired the poet in Edward Thomas before he wrote a line of poetry, and in that sense Frost's advice amounted to no more than what people had been telling Thomas for years. W. H. Davies, the Welsh poet and autobiographer, had recognized that Thomas was 'essentially a poet' from reading *The Happy-Go-Lucky Morgans*. 'You noticed probably in reading the book that every person described in it . . . are one and all just Edward Thomas,' Davies wrote to Richard Garnett. 'A poet trying to write prose fiction often does this.' Eleanor Farjeon, who had become a close, and uncomfortably infatuated, friend of Thomas in 1912, remembered asking him whether he'd ever written poetry, only to receive the answer, 'with a short self-scornful laugh', that he couldn't write poetry to save his life.

In fact Thomas may have been formally attempting to write poetry for some months now, perhaps as far back as the autumn of 1913. Although Thomas would later generously tell Frost that he was the 'only begetter' of his poetry, the evidence suggests that he was well along the road to fulfilment as a poet before he met him. And while in subsequent years Frost would occasionally contribute to the mythology surrounding their friendship – which was sometimes compared to great literary relationships and collaborations from the past, like that of Wordsworth and Coleridge, or Verlaine and Rimbaud – he also acknowledged that Thomas's evolution as a poet had been largely independent of him, and that 'Anything we may be thought to have in common we had before we met.'

They did share a common conviction that poetic language should abandon literary ornamentation – 'to wring all the necks of my rhetoric – the geese', as Thomas put it – and move closer to colloquial speech. In his review, later that summer, of Frost's second collection, *North of Boston*, the book that finally catapulted Frost to international fame, Thomas wrote that 'These poems are revolutionary because they lack the exaggeration of rhetoric . . . The metre avoids not only the old-fashioned pomp and sweetness, but the later fashion also of discord and fuss. In fact, the medium is common speech and common decasyllables.'

Throughout the three days of the Thomases' June visit to the Frosts at Leddington, it was 'always hot weather', as Thomas recorded in his notebook. The two men sat talking in the garden under a tree, and continued their conversation on long walks across country. '1914 was ours,' Frost was to recall. 'I never had, I never shall have another such year of friendship.'

On the Thomases' first evening with them, 24 June, the Frosts took their guests to call on Wilfrid Gibson and his wife Geraldine, who were enjoying an idyllic existence, 'a Heaven of delight', at The Old Nailshop, a part-thatched red-brick and timber-built house at the junction of the Dymock–Tewkesbury road, by the side of the lane to Leddington. Also present were their neighbours Lascelles and Catherine Abercrombie from down the road at Ryton, and Rupert Brooke, recently returned from a year's travel in Canada, the United

States and the South Seas. Brooke, according to Edward Thomas, was 'browner & older and better looking after his tour'.

Thomas and Brooke were old friends. Although separated in age by almost a decade – Brooke was still only in his mid twenties – Thomas had taken a keen interest in the younger man's work. They had stayed with each other at Grantchester, Brooke's Cambridgeshire haunt, where visitors were encouraged to go barefoot and swim naked in Byron's Pool, and at one of the Thomases' earlier homes in Hampshire, which had proved conveniently close for Brooke's assignation with Noel Olivier, a shy, entrancing Bedales schoolgirl with whom he was tormentedly obsessed.

Like everyone who came into Brooke's orbit, Thomas was conscious of the younger man's beauty. 'He stretched himself out, drew his fingers through his waved, fair hair, laughed, talked indolently, and admired as much as he was admired . . . He was tall, broad and easy in his movements. Either he stooped, or thrust his head forward unusually much to look at you with his steady, blue eyes. His clear, rosy skin helped to give him the look of a big girl.'

Astutely, Thomas understood that Brooke's appearance and personality were inextricably linked, 'and helped one another'. He had reviewed Brooke's only collection of poetry to date, published at the end of 1911, suggesting that copies 'should be bought by everyone over forty who has never been under forty', and foreseeing promise in Brooke's future as a poet.

While in the South Seas, Brooke had written a number of new poems, among them 'Heaven', his satire on religious belief, and sent them back to his adoring patron, Eddie Marsh, in England. The best of these had appeared in *New Numbers*, a series of anthologies of verse by Abercrombie, Gibson, Brooke and John Drinkwater. The first two issues, bound in grey paper with a cover price of 2*s*.6*d*., were guaranteed against loss by Marsh, and had sold about 700 or 800 copies each, easily covering costs as well as attracting favourable reviews. Brooke's work predominated in the third number, containing five of his most recent poems, including 'Tiare Tahiti' and 'The Great Lover', with its jarring opening phrase 'I have been so great a lover'. The third volume was still in production on the June evening of Brooke and Thomas's visit. One can imagine Thomas looking on perhaps slightly enviously as he was shown the finished copies from the latest issue in the poets' joint enterprise. Lascelles Abercrombie packed the magazine into parcels; his wife Catherine addressed the envelopes to subscribers; and Wilfrid Gibson licked the stamps, giving himself a mild attack of glue poisoning in the process.

The merriment that evening was undoubtedly fed by the drinking of copious quantities of the local cider and perry, made from cider apples and perry pears. Even Robert Frost, who had arrived from New Hampshire a teetotaller, had succumbed to its inviting flavour. Long afterwards, Wilfrid Gibson captured the conversation and laughter of the occasion – though he erroneously dated it to a July evening, 'On nineteen fourteen' – in his poem 'The Golden Room':

> . . . In the lamplight
> We talked and laughed; but for the most part listened
> While Robert Frost kept on and on and on
> In his slow New England fashion, for our delight,
> Holding us with shrewd turns and racy quips,
> And the rare twinkle of his grave blue eyes?
> [. . .]
> Now, a quick flash from Abercrombie; now,
> A murmured dry half-heard aside from Thomas;
> Now, a clear laughing word from Brooke; and then
> Again Frost's rich and ripe philosophy,
> That had the body and tang of good draught cider
> And poured as clear as a stream . . .

4. God! I will pack, and take a train, And get me to England once again!

A little more than three weeks earlier, Rupert Brooke had been on a train heading from Plymouth into London's Euston, having returned to England after an absence of a year. The train steamed into the station several hours late, but a faithful reception committee, of Eddie Marsh, the actress Cathleen Nesbitt, who, nominally at any rate, was

Brooke's current love interest, and the musician Denis Browne, was there to meet him as he stepped on to the platform.

As the *Philadelphia*, his ship from New York, entered Plymouth Harbour on 5 June, Brooke had caught his first whiff of England from the strong smell of newly mown Devon hay wafting across the water, which he sniffed 'ecstatically' while leaning over the taffrail. It would take time for him to acclimatize to English – and especially London – life again after the simplicity of his existence in the 'paradise' of the South Sea Islands, inhabited by 'dear good people, with their laughter and friendliness and crowns of flowers'. The weather initially came as a bit of a shock. 'What a *cold* summer we've been having,' he wrote from Rugby, while making a dutiful visit to his mother. Before long, though, he was experiencing 'glorious' days, when 'the air is so heavy . . . with the scent of hay and mown grass and roses and dews and a thousand wild flowers, that I'm beginning to think of my South Sea wind [as] pale and scentless by comparison!'

Launching himself back into metropolitan society, Brooke attended a party at Marsh's flat for his homecoming, where the guests included Harley Granville-Barker, Lillah McCarthy, Duncan Grant, Hugh Walpole, Duff Cooper, as well as his *New Numbers* collaborators, Gibson, Abercrombie and Drinkwater. At dawn the guests gathered in Gray's Inn Fields to watch Brooke perform a Hawaiian siva-siva dance. A week later, on 18 June, Brooke was present at Drury Lane for the British première of Stravinsky's *Le Rossignol*. He was hoping to get tickets for Shaw's *Pygmalion*, now in its third month at His Majesty's, though he admitted that he didn't have 'any very great hopes' for the play.

Brooke's time out of England had been extremely productive. He had written his finest poems to date, as well as some of his freshest and most original journalism. Moreover, in Tahiti, on the final leg of his travels, he had found some personal happiness – and sexual fulfilment – with a native girl of Mataia, called Taatamata, who became his mistress.

All this had formed a marked contrast to the atmosphere of poisonous recrimination and twisted bitterness in which Brooke had departed in May 1913. For more than a year prior to his departure, Brooke had been in a state of complete mental breakdown. He had been paranoid and delusional, alternately unhealthily needy and cruelly mistrusting of his closest friends, full of self-loathing, and talking openly of suicide.

The immediate cause of Brooke's mental collapse was the insane jealousy and sense of humiliation he had felt when the woman to whom he'd loosely attached himself declared her love for someone else. Warm, plain, dependable Ka Cox, with her wide, swaying hips – who no doubt answered Brooke's desire for what he once described as 'sleepy mother-comfort' – revealed her infatuation with the artist Henry Lamb in December 1911, provoking an emotional maelstrom. Brooke persuaded Ka to be his lover, before throwing her over, full of contempt and passionate resentment at what he saw as her betrayal of him. Brooke's confusion was only exacerbated by simultaneous entanglements, most of them chaste, with a number of women: Noel Olivier, Elisabeth van Rysselberghe, Phyllis Gardner and Cathleen Nesbitt, to whom Brooke was first attracted towards the end of 1912.

But this crisis also offered evidence of darker, murkier strands in Brooke's personality that had deeper roots further back to his childhood and undergraduate days. His unremitting hatred for Lytton Strachey – who, Brooke believed (unjustifiably, as it turned out), had stirred up the attraction between Ka Cox and Henry Lamb – opened up a well of poison directed against Strachey, his brother James (one of Brooke's intimates since their schooldays) and other members of the Bloomsbury set. In the most acute phases of his breakdown, Brooke vented his spleen against Jews, women and homosexuals. He seemed desperate to draw a veil over his own experience of homosexuality, and was obsessed by the idea of 'cleanliness', his own as well as that of others, a puritanical trait inherited from his bossy, controlling, much-feared mother, habitually referred to by Brooke as 'the Ranee'. 'God damn you,' he had exploded at James Strachey. 'God bum roast castrate bugger and tear the bowels out of everyone . . .' The poet famous for celebrating a pastoral idyll of Englishness turned his back on the country that had witnessed his disintegration with a nasty flourish. 'I shall, with great pleasure, give orders that England is to be wiped out, *sunk*, and *deleted*,' he wrote jubilantly as he embarked on his tour.

On his return to England in June 1914, Brooke appeared – to use his own word – 'rejuvenated'. There were disturbing signs, however, that not all his personal difficulties had been put to rest. Even before boarding ship for England, he was once again relieving himself of an animus against the country of his birth, and London especially, where the pavements were 'greasy' and 'the ways are full of lean & vicious people, dirty, hermaphrodites and eunuchs, Stracheys, moral vagabonds, pitiable scum'. Back in London, he began to be awkwardly possessive of Cathleen Nesbitt, resenting the independence of her acting career. A chance meeting with Lytton Strachey, at the performance of *Le Rossignol*, at which Brooke turned on his heel and marched away as Strachey approached him, showed that there was no realistic hope of reconciliation there.

The Cambridge idol, with his artfully disarranged hair and boyish stunts that had turned distinguished men like Henry James to mush, had revealed his feet of clay. As Brooke rushed about the country that summer, seeing old friends and making new ones, he seemed reluctant to take stock. Fundamentally he believed his life to have been a failure and, in the absence of marriage or children, he gave no indication of knowing in which direction to strike out next. Brooke's destiny in the summer of 1914 – like that of Edward Thomas – appeared to hang in the balance.

Summer Mayhem

George Pike, thirty years old and a motor-fitter's mate at Tilling's bus yard in Peckham, had been drinking all afternoon. His wife had left him six months earlier for a new life in California, and he was still struggling to cope with the situation. After the pubs had closed, in the early hours of 7 June, he was wandering back home to Pimlico when he reached the bottom of Constitution Hill and decided to scale the ten-foot wall of Buckingham Palace.

Climbing over the spiked railings, he jumped on to a small lawn and hid for a while in the shrubbery, before scaling a further wall and entering the Palace through an opening in the basement. He then went up to the sleeping quarters of the royal servants on the sixth floor, taking a circuitous route, that brought him close to Queen Mary's rooms. Pike removed his clothes and dressed in a morning coat, waistcoat and shirt, also appropriating a walking stick, cigarette case and clock. Entering another room, he was challenged by the Queen's page Mr Copple, who happened to be awake and gave chase. Arrested by his pyjama-clad adversary, Pike was taken away by the police.

After George V interceded on his behalf and requested that Pike should not be punished severely, the Palace intruder was released from Bow Street police court with a lenient sentence: he had to pay a surety of £20 to keep the peace for six months. The incident, Pike admitted, was 'a foolish freak, the result of domestic trouble', and fuelled by alcohol. What had encouraged him to enter the Palace were the newspaper reports, two weeks earlier, of the suffragette rally at Buckingham Palace, when Emmeline Pankhurst and a deputation of militants had rushed the Palace in an attempt to present a petition to the King. 'I had heard that the suffragettes had wanted to get into Buckingham Palace,' Pike explained, 'and wondered if it was possible.'

Emmeline Pankhurst being seized by Chief Inspector Rolfe outside Buckingham Palace, 21 May 1914

The militants' planned demonstration at Buckingham Palace had been advertised since January with appeals to women all over the country to join it, and an invitation to the general public to come and see that the brutal attacks on suffragettes by the police on Black Friday, four years earlier, were not repeated. Unsurprisingly, Reginald McKenna, the Home Secretary, had advised George V against receiving the deputation. However, Mrs Pankhurst, claiming that women had a greater right to have an audience with the King than men, as they had no part in parliamentary government, was undeterred. McKenna's advice, she informed the King, was 'unconstitutional and disloyal', and, in spite of the refusal, declared that the deputation would wait upon him at Buckingham Palace on 21 May. Three major aims were stated in the publicity for the event: to demand the parliamentary franchise for women, to protest against forcible feeding, and to claim equal treatment for militant suffragettes and militant Ulster men, who continued to go unprosecuted despite their taunt of open rebellion in the face of government.

On the afternoon of 21 May as many as 2,000 police, mounted and on foot, had been posted in the neighbourhood of the Palace: at the top of Constitution Hill, along the Mall and opposite Wellington Barracks, with a force also patrolling the grounds and courtyard of the Palace. By 3 p.m. enormous crowds had gathered to watch as the ranks of one hundred suffragettes marched from Grosvenor Square to Wellington Arch, at the south end of Hyde Park. The order had been given to drive them away, with as few arrests as possible. Some of the women, veterans of the violent battles of the past, carried clubs and horsewhips, and threw eggshells full of red, yellow and green paint. 'The police got hold of them in dozens,' reported one bystander, 'and threw them back amongst the crowd. On the women came again, and each time they came back the police took greater liberties with them – twisting their arms, punching them and tearing their hair.'

Those women who entered the Mall by Admiralty Arch found themselves in a crowd of straw-hatted middle-class youths holding up walking sticks to which they had tied comic effigies of suffragettes. The Palace windows were crowded with people watching the scene, and there were detectives on the roof. Every now and then a woman would rush out from the throng of spectators into the cordoned area in front of the Palace, only to be caught by the police and flung back into the crowd. Then the straw-hatted youths would turn on her, pulling at her hair and shouting 'You ought to be burnt!' before being dispersed by mounted police arriving at a gallop, and driving the crowd away. One woman penetrated the cordon, only to slip and fall and be arrested by police.

At 4 o'clock, a shout went up and Mrs Pankhurst, who had slipped through almost unrecognized to the gates of Buckingham Palace, was pushed by her supporters into the arms of the police. She looked weak and exhausted, but was immediately seized by the bear-like Chief Inspector Rolfe, who lifted her in his arms and carried her within the cordon guarding the open space in front of the Palace. Here she was placed in a taxi and driven away to Holloway to complete the sentence she had started in March before being discharged, suffering from heart pains. The photographs of Rolfe lifting the tiny figure of Mrs Pankhurst, white feathers billowing from her dark toque, from the ground, with a man in a boater at their side, apparently supporting him or remonstrating with her, became one of the most iconic images of the suffragette movement (Rolfe died of a heart attack a fortnight later).

In Holloway, Mrs Pankhurst immediately began her eighth hunger and thirst strike, and was released on 27 May after five days. She was taken to 34 Grosvenor Place, a house from which, the press noted ominously, 'she can overlook the grounds of Buckingham Palace', and was due to return to Holloway in a week's time, though once again she eluded rearrest. 'On Sunday it was reported that I was dead,' she wrote to Ethel Smyth from Grosvenor Place, 'and I don't think McKenna would have been sorry if that had been the result of the horrible bear's hug that huge policeman gave me when he seized me. Fortunately for me I have "young bones" or my ribs would have been fractured . . . Lying here my heart swells at the thought of our women. I shall never forget how, when we saw the Wellington Gates closing on us as we marched towards the park, they dashed forward, flinging themselves against them to prevent their being shut, returning again and again to the charge, their tender bodies bruised and bleeding.'

Sixty-six women and two men appeared at Bow Street on 22 May to answer charges connected with the Buckingham Palace demonstration. Pandemonium overtook the proceedings. Shouts drowned the voices of officials, a man on a cornet started to play the 'Marseillaise', and eggs and flour were thrown around the court. A woman defendant flung a boot at the magistrate, who deftly caught it and handed it to an assistant.

Following the crushing of their demonstration at Buckingham Palace, the suffragettes unleashed a summer of mayhem in the capital and other parts of England, slashing paintings, planting bombs and burning churches. The day after suffragettes attempted to petition the King, a charity performance at His Majesty's Theatre of Henry

Arthur Jones's melodrama *The Silver King*, in the presence of King George and Queen Mary, was repeatedly interrupted by militant outbursts. A petition was thrown at the royal couple when they arrived at the theatre, and as the curtain rose on Herbert Beerbohm Tree, taking a busman's holiday from *Pygmalion* in the role of an ancient rustic, a woman mounted her seat in the stalls and shouted to the royal box, 'Your Majesty, why do you permit –', before being bundled out. Five women in other parts of the theatre had to be ejected. Several were chained to their seats, and before one particularly violent woman could be removed, the arm of her seat had to be broken.

Three days later, at the Epsom Derby, there were widely expressed fears that the race might again be disrupted by suffragette protest and that someone might attempt to imitate Emily Davison's fatal action of a year earlier, when she had thrown herself in front of the King's horse. Rows of wooden rails with iron bars every three inches had been constructed at the point at Tattenham Corner where Davison had made her dash, and 3,000 police were drafted in for the occasion. In the event, the only dramatic occurrence was a woman's arrest for firing a toy pistol and scorching a policeman's leg. She wasn't a suffragette, though. 'It was purely high spirits,' reported the *Daily Mail*, 'and not to advance the cause of women.' The race itself was considered one of the least exciting of recent years. The King's horse Brakespear finished sixth, while, in a comparative novelty, the race was won by a French-bred and trained colt, Durbar II, a result which stunned the crowd into silence.

The London Season had begun, marked by a series of court balls and levées at Buckingham Palace. The first of these, on 4 June, saw one of the two formal presentations of the year's debutantes. That evening, hundreds of young women, dressed in their finery of white and cream-beaded court-dresses, with their hair up, plumed with ostrich feathers, waited with their mothers, and their fathers and brothers – uniformed, or in black velvet jackets and knee-breeches – to take part in this ceremony, which set the seal on their coming-out. Among them were Elizabeth Asquith, the Prime Minister's younger daughter, and Elsie, the second child of the writer Rudyard Kipling, 'white from top to toe, and her bouquet likewise'.

A roll of drums announced the start of what the United States Ambassador Walter Hines Page had called 'the best-managed, best-mannered show in the world'. George V and Queen Mary sat in the Throne Room, a circle of duchesses to one side of them, and a canopy from the Indian Durbar over their heads. For two hours, to the accompaniment of soft music, the file of debutantes and older women passed in front of the dais, to curtsey and receive in acknowledgement a brisk regal nod.

At 10.45 the smooth-running of this scene was thrown briefly, and almost imperceptibly, off course. Only those closest to the throne knew what had happened. Most people thought that a debutante had fainted. Lady Blomfield, widow of the Gothic revivalist architect Sir Arthur Blomfield, had just curtsied to the King and was making her bow to the Queen, when her daughter Mary suddenly went down on one knee, stretched out her hands towards the King and addressed him with the words, 'Your Majesty, for God's sake do not use force –' Immediately, at a signal from the conductor, the orchestra in the gallery began to play louder, and, with a minimum of fuss, two gentlemen-in-arms removed the young woman before she could finish her sentence. The queue of debutantes filed on as if nothing had happened.

'You see that a Miss Bloomfield [*sic*] last night knelt instead of curtseying & implored the King to stop torturing women,' the Earl of Selborne, who had displayed some sympathy with the constitutional suffrage movement in the past, though not with its militant counterpart, wrote to his wife. 'A rare plucky girl I call that – she had a perfect right to be there & she made no silly scene when they quietly led her off.' Margot Asquith agreed about Mary Blomfield's quiet scene-stealing. As Asquith told Venetia Stanley, Margot and their daughter Elizabeth had been 'close at hand during the suffragette scene at the Court, and say that the young woman did her part very well'. By contrast, Carrie Kipling, Rudyard's wife and Elsie's mother, came away from the occasion disgusted at Mary Blomfield's behaviour, claiming that an important rite of passage had been ruined for her daughter. George V, always a stickler for close observance of the rules of etiquette, metaphorically threw up his hands, commenting in his diary, 'I don't know what we are coming to.'

That sense of revulsion was shared by members of the Blomfield family, who issued a statement saying that they were 'sick and disgusted to a degree'. Lady Blomfield, a convert, like her daughter Mary, to the Baha'i faith, the monotheistic religion founded in nineteenth-century Persia, swiftly disassociated herself from her daughter's act ('Lady Blomfield had been enthusiastic for militancy of the most extreme kind, so long as it was committed by other people's daughters,' Sylvia Pankhurst later noted caustically). Parts of the foreign press, meanwhile, were even more outraged by this 'invasion' of the court than British newspapers, and took advantage of the incident to run extensive commentaries on the inability of the Asquith government to suppress militant extremism. The *New York Times* went so far as to suggest that the prison authorities should get rid of the 'odious expedient' of forcible feeding and allow the militants to starve themselves to death. Reporting on this, the London *Times* warned 'that if we are unable to cope with this outbreak of domestic violence and unreason, our reputation will be lowered in the eyes of the world'.

And there seemed no end in sight to suffragette defiance. At the International Horse Show at Olympia, four days after Mary Blomfield's protest, a suffragette made a further demonstration in front of the King and Queen. It was perhaps unrealistic to hope that a Peace Ball at the Albert Hall, on 10 June, to celebrate the centenary of the signing of the Treaty of Ghent in 1814, and one hundred years of Anglo-American peace, would pass unnoticed, and, sure enough, a suffragette rushed up to the royal box at the climactic moment to make the obligatory plea: 'How can you talk of Peace, when women are being tortured in prison for their cause?'

The Peace Ball was described as 'a multi-coloured phantasmagoria'. Its camp splendour included a tableau of Columbus on the poop of the *Santa Maria*, and one of Sir Walter Ralegh and the Virginian Settlers; processions headed by Lady Maud Warrender as Britannia, leading fifty of the tallest women in England in gold helmets and breastplates; and Mrs John Astor as the Statue of Liberty, with a trail of women, followed by their blue trains powdered with silver stars, as the forty-eight states of America. Among them,

Mrs Lewis ('Loulou') Harcourt – the New York-born wife of the Colonial Secretary, a particular *bête noire* of the militants because of his outspoken opposition to women's suffrage – represented one of the states. As the suffragette was led away, there was the surreal spectacle of ladies in fancy dress striking at her with their programmes and fans.

In the face of continual harassment from the militants, the monarchical nerve was beginning to tremble just a little. In the Waterloo Chamber at Windsor Castle on 14 June, George V summoned Lord Selborne to see him, and revealed that he had received threats from suffragettes against his life. 'He told me that he & the Queen felt very much the way they were being treated . . . He told me that he was now receiving threatening letters every day and that very morning he had had one to say that the next thing they would have to shoot him and would.'

But the tide of public feeling had gradually turned as the exploits of 'the wild women' had moved from relatively harmless acts to more dangerous incidents threatening life and property. The *Daily Mail* reported that its offices were being inundated by letters from indignant readers asking why it should be the duty of the police to protect the detested 'suffs' from the fury of the public (an ironic response, given the police's manifest brutality towards militants at many public meetings). In the Commons, Opposition backbencher Lord Robert Cecil warned that 'the irritation of the public . . . is growing every day. There are very distinct symptoms that members of the public will take the law into their own hands. That means what is called "lynch law".'

Violence against the suffragettes and their supporters was indeed much in evidence that June. At the milder end of the spectrum there was the small but angry crowd that greeted the Bishop of London, Winnington-Ingram, after he gave permission for a memorial service to Emily Davison at St George's, Bloomsbury ('She died for women', the service sheet announced, proclaiming Davison's martyrdom).

More disturbing were the sporadic attacks on militants and their property. At Hastings, on the South Coast, a van carrying suffragette banners, posters and other literature, in their distinctive green, white and purple colours, was smashed to pieces. A speech by a suffragette in Birmingham had to be abandoned after her dress was set on fire amidst cries of 'We'll teach them to insult the King!' Later in the month, Lloyd George was addressing a garden party in Denmark Hill, South London, when a suffragette heckled him. She was set upon by some of the partygoers, and her clothes torn in a struggle. When a clergyman, the Reverend C. A. Wills, of the church of St John the Evangelist in Angell Town, Brixton, voiced his support for her by shouting 'Give enfranchisement to women', he found himself silenced with a handkerchief placed over his mouth, and being unceremoniously thrown into a nearby lake. Another man standing on the bank then jumped into the water and repeatedly tried to duck him, cheered on by amused bystanders.

In the House of Commons, on 11 June, the Home Secretary, acknowledging 'the recent gross rudenesses which have been committed against the King', sought to answer his critics, who argued that the government's policy against the suffragettes had completely failed. He examined in turn the various solutions to the problem of the militants currently being pressed on him by members of the public, refusing, however, to discuss the option of giving them the vote.

The most popular of these, he admitted, was that forcible feeding should cease and that the suffragettes should be allowed to die in prison. But, McKenna countered, to let them die would be 'the greatest incentive to militancy which could ever happen', earning these women, who combined 'hysterical fanaticism' with undeniable courage, 'the crown of martyrdom'.

Deporting suffragettes – to St Kilda, the remotest part of the British Isles, was one suggestion – rather than imprisoning them, would not resolve the difficulty either, but merely place it at a distance. As for certifying suffragettes as lunatics, McKenna declared that he had never come across any doctor who would be prepared to take such a step.

In the debate that followed, the different treatment meted out by the government to the Ulster militants, who, like the suffragettes, preached open rebellion, but who had not faced prosecution, was once again rehearsed. It was left to Josiah Wedgwood, the Liberal member for Newcastle-under-Lyme, speaking out against his party, as so often during his parliamentary career, to draw attention to the practice of forcible feeding as 'an abomination', and one that history might well come to regard as a crime.

The temper of the parliamentary debates on the question of women's suffrage at this time left no one in any serious doubt that, whatever the past trickery involved in denying both suffragists and suffragettes a fair decision on their case, there was no chance, in the summer of 1914, that political discussion of the question of women's enfranchisement would proceed while the violence of the militants persisted. Responding to suffragette heckling at a Birmingham meeting on 13 June, the Labour MP for Blackburn, Philip Snowden, a noted supporter of women's suffrage, told his audience that 'the women's actions during the past year had so set the clock back that the suffrage question was temporarily as dead as Queen Anne.'

———

Following the Curragh débâcle, which demonstrated to the government that Ulster's resistance to Home Rule would not be overcome by force, Asquith had quickly bounced back personally and, to some extent, politically. The Prime Minister enjoyed his new responsibilities at the War Office, where he had taken over the job of Secretary for War after Colonel Seely's departure, and was elated by his enthusiastic reception in Scotland when he went up to Fife to seek re-election as MP for East Fife (until 1918, a Member of Parliament had automatically to stand again for his seat when accepting any cabinet office).

Aside from Home Rule for Ireland, the Asquith government was struggling to get another leftover from Gladstonian days on to the statute book. The Welsh Church Bill was a complicated piece of legislation to disestablish the Welsh Church. A new budget, introduced in May, also presented problems. It had to correct the £5 million deficit from the increase in naval expenditure agreed by Lloyd George and Churchill back in January, while attempting to introduce increases to income tax and death duties in order to fund a programme of grants to local authorities for education, expanded aid to children, and road and sanitation improvements. This was essentially a follow-up to the 'people's budget' of 1909, as well as a preliminary bid to win the General Election of 1915. The war against poverty and illness was 'as real a war as ever carried on against a foreign foe', Edwin Montagu, Chief Secretary to the Treasury, reminded members as he rounded up the budget debates.

In spite of opposition to the budget from wealthier Liberal Members, and worries on the horizon about the question of further concessions to Ulster, Asquith's relaxed, devil-may-care temperament appeared to have been restored. He played a lot of golf, one way, as the German Ambassador, Prince Lichnowsky, observed, in which he steeled his nerves. Lichnowsky, who had arrived at the Court of St James's in late 1912 with a determination to foster good Anglo-German relations, stayed that June at the Asquiths' country home at Sutton Courtenay. Unfortunately Asquith found both the Ambassador and his wife Marie to be rather trying guests. 'He is loquacious and inquisitive about trifles,' Asquith told Venetia Stanley, while the Princess – whose combination of black socks and white boots, along with her 'crazy' tiaras, offended Margot Asquith's fashion sense – 'took possession of the piano-stool, and strummed & drummed infernal patches of tuneless music for the rest of the evening'.

Asquith's need for Venetia Stanley remained essential to his well-being, and he continued to pour out letters to her, full of personal and political confidences. 'Short as it was – far too short – I thought we had a delicious time,' he wrote to her on 11 May after one of their assignations, 'and the drive back to-day was a thing to remember.' Writing a month later, he told her, 'You know how I love sharing things with you'; and, in a further letter, 'Talking with no one else does me so much good.' On the whole, Asquith was untroubled by the risk of his relationship with Venetia being publicly exposed, though he admitted that he hated 'even the possibility of gossip about us'. That possibility seemed fairly slight. Newspapers showed little interest in the subject of the Prime Minister's female companions. Asquith was, in any case, as Lichnowsky subsequently noted, well known to be 'fond of the ladies, especially the young and pretty ones', and Venetia Stanley was unlikely to be singled out. When Asquith travelled to Penrhos, Venetia's parents' home, at

Whitsun 1914, with his daughter Violet and Venetia as his companions, the local paper, the *Holyhead Chronicle*, didn't trouble to mention the third member of the party. However, in the course of the holiday, Asquith, with Venetia and one of her pet penguins, was snapped by an enterprising *Daily Mail* photographer, standing outside Lord Sheffield's home. 'The Premier and the Penguin' was the heading of the published photograph, with 'the Hon. Miss Venetia Stanley' only captioned in the small print underneath (see p. 25).

This Whitsun holiday had marked a difficult patch in Asquith's relationship with Venetia. If you read between the lines of the letters he sent her immediately afterwards, it's clear that she had tried to check the power of his obsession, somewhat alarmed by the strength of his dependence on her, and bowing to pressure from her mother, Lady Sheffield, who was unhappy about the Prime Minister's interest in her daughter. Mindful that Edwin Montagu was as determined as ever in his romantic pursuit of her, Venetia appears to have warned Asquith that he would not always be the only man in her life. The result was that Asquith left Penrhos 'with some bright memories and a *sad* heart'. In the mournful little note he wrote to Venetia before his departure, he quoted Beaumont and Fletcher's words from *The Maid's Tragedy*: 'They have most power to harm us whom we love.'

The salient aspects of their relationship, though, for the time being stayed the same. Not even the hint of a reproach from her could dampen his ardour. 'My darling the thought of you is a joy & inspiration to me,' he told her the next day, enclosing for her interest a letter from Lloyd George for 'your possession in some safe & secret receptacle'. Despite the rebuff, Asquith depended on Venetia as much as ever. For, at Penrhos, she had saved him from what he later described as 'something very like despair' over the continuing crisis of Irish Home Rule, and the question of the settlement of the Ulster problem by some acceptable form of compromise.

By Whitsun 1914, the Home Rule Bill had passed the Commons for the third time, amid scenes of uproar, immune from amendment or rejection by the Lords. Rather than including changes at a committee stage of the main bill, Asquith had decided on a separate Amending Bill, to incorporate whatever exclusion proposals for

Ulster had been agreed between the government, the Unionists and the Irish Nationalists, led by Redmond and John Dillon. As the Ulster Volunteers and their Nationalist counterparts, the National Volunteers, which by now outnumbered Carson's force and were proving difficult for Redmond to control, continued to drill and import arms, the dire predictions of civil war in Ireland were every day becoming more of a reality. Time for reaching an accommodation on settlement terms for Ulster was running out. This was recognized only too well by the King, who, in April, had sent 'a rather hysterical letter', as Asquith described it to Venetia, to his Prime Minister, emphasizing 'the terrible position in which I shall be placed if that solution is not found'.

To satisfy the King, and to take advantage of the conciliatory hints dropped in the Commons by Edward Carson, Asquith had once again resorted to secret negotiations with Carson and Bonar Law, the Conservative leader, in the 'silken tents' of Edwin Montagu's house at Queen Anne's Gate. There were rumours among his own supporters that Carson's thoughts of matrimony – he would marry his second wife, Ruby Frewen, that autumn – were diverting him from major political issues and softening his attitude.

Nothing could have been further from the truth. For, while Carson and Bonar Law agreed to the procedural issue of an Amending Bill, there would be no movement on the deadlock created by Carson's insistence on the exclusion, with no time limit, of the bloc of six Ulster counties – four largely Protestant, and two, Fermanagh and Tyrone, not quite evenly balanced, with Catholics just in the majority – from the operation of the Home Rule Bill. The Curragh, and the gun-running exploits in April at Larne, had decisively strengthened the Ulster Unionists' hand. That the Unionists' own resistance was now well organized, and that Asquith was only too aware that he could not order the army to fire on Ulstermen, placed Carson and Bonar Law in a powerful bargaining position, increasing their confidence of securing the exclusion of Ulster on their own best terms.

Given this state of affairs, Asquith's decision to use the Amending Bill merely to repeat his offer of March – that each Ulster county could opt out for a period of six years – seemed utterly futile. The

King protested the uselessness of the offer since the proposal had already been rejected by Ulster. A small cabal in cabinet, led by Lloyd George and Sir Edward Grey, tried to persuade Asquith that the battle over the question of a time limit was lost, and to accept that 'all the fight will be over area.'

Perhaps Asquith hoped that, as the pressure intensified, all parties – the Opposition, Irish Nationalists and Ulstermen – would recognize the urgent necessity of breaking the deadlock by coming willingly to the negotiating table, with the intention of brokering a compromise.

If this was so, he was to be sadly disappointed. On 23 June, the Amending Bill was introduced in the House of Lords. A week later, the Lords, with its Unionist majority, transformed the bill to fit the most extreme of Unionist demands: all nine counties of Ulster were to be excluded, without plebiscites, and without a time limit.

The granting of Home Rule to Ireland had reached yet another impasse.

Meanwhile, a spark blew across the highly inflammable tinderbox of European nationalism in the Balkans. On Sunday, 28 June, Archduke Franz Ferdinand, heir to the Habsburg throne, and his wife, Sophie, were assassinated by a Bosnian Serb student, Gavrilo Princip, while visiting Sarajevo, the capital of the Austro-Hungarian province of Bosnia-Herzegovina.

In England, the weekend of 27–8 June had been a scorching one. Most of the governing and political elite were out of London, enjoying the good weather in the countryside. The news of the assassination on Sunday night led to the hurried recall of newspaper editors and leader writers. Henry Wickham Steed, foreign editor of *The Times*, returned to his office at 7 o'clock to find the place in turmoil. Beyond an obituary of the Archduke, there was scant material about the crime and still no clue as to its meaning.

The Archduke had gone to Sarajevo to take part in the annual army manoeuvres. He had chosen a bad day for his visit: 28 June was a date loaded with symbolism, as the anniversary of the humiliating defeat of the Serbs by the Turks at the Battle of Kosovo in 1389. It was also Serbia's national day, and a focus for Bosnian Serbs' hatred of their Habsburg overlord. As the imperial party drove through the city, six young conspirators were dreaming of the moment when Bosnian Serbs – totalling 42.5 per cent of Bosnia's population – would be freed from Austrian oppression and become an integral part of Serbia, the only independent hope for Slavs living under foreign rule in the Balkans.

The timing of Franz Ferdinand's arrival in Sarajevo may have been tactless, but he was delighted to have the rare opportunity of appearing in public with his beloved wife Sophie Chotek. She was the mother of his three children, and his 'entire happiness'. Yet, as a mere countess, Sophie had been considered too lowly for an imperial Habsburg marriage. In order to marry her, Franz Ferdinand had been forced to sign away the rights to the Habsburg succession of any children of the marriage.

Security for the visit was extraordinarily lax. One of Princip's group threw a bomb at the archducal car. It bounced off before exploding and injuring two officers on the Archduke's staff. After Franz Ferdinand's official welcome at the Town Hall, he asked to be driven to the hospital to visit the injured members of his party. On the way there the chauffeur took a wrong turning and drove straight into the path of Princip himself. Princip had never been considered by his instructors to be much of a shot, but he took decisive advantage of this sudden opportunity, firing two bullets at the passengers seated in the back of the car. Sophie died almost immediately. The Archduke bled to death on the drive to the hospital.

The trail of the conspiracy led incontrovertibly back to Serbia. While Princip and the other 'Young Bosnia' conspirators were a home-grown terrorist movement, Serbian officials, as Austria immediately suspected, had tolerated and even assisted in the assassination. Princip, and two other associates, had been trained in Serbia by the Black Hand, a secret organization committed to unifying all Serbs by violent action. They had been given their weapons in Belgrade, and smuggled them across the Austrian border back into Bosnia in May. The head of Black Hand, Colonel Dragutin Dimitrijević, known as 'Apis', was the head of Serbian military intelligence. Serbia's cabinet and Prime Minister, Nikola Pašić, may not have been involved in the plot to kill Franz Ferdinand. But Pašić had been undoubtedly aware that armed men had crossed the border, and his only response had been to send Austria an ambiguous warning.

From Belgrade, in the days following the assassination, Pašić made conciliatory overtures towards Austrian leaders in Vienna. At the same time, he tried to evade anything that might implicate him, or his government, in the crime. The 84-year-old Emperor Franz Joseph, for whom the death of his heir presumptive was the latest in a string of tragedies following on the suicide of his son Crown Prince Rudolf and the murder by an anarchist of his wife, the Empress Elisabeth, returned to Vienna, where anti-Serb riots were taking place, to discuss Austria-Hungary's next step.

In 1912 and 1913 Austria-Hungary had three times almost gone to war to reduce the power of Serbia. But on each occasion militant diplomacy had saved the day. Would this again be the case? Or would the views of the Austrian Chief of Staff, General Franz Conrad von Hötzendorf, who had called for war against Serbia more than fifty times, be allowed to prevail? And, if it was to be war, how would it be possible to contain the action and prevent other powers, in particular Russia, leader of the pan-Slavic movement, from rushing to Serbia's defence?

In London, two days after the assassination, Sir Arthur Nicolson, the British Permanent Undersecretary at the Foreign Office, once more asserted his view of the relative calm in international waters, writing to the British Ambassador in St Petersburg that 'The tragedy which has just taken place in Sarajevo will not, I trust, lead to further complications.'

On the same day, Asquith gave his '"obituary" on the Austrian royalties' in the Commons, expressing the 'indignation and deep concern' of the House at the murders, which he described as 'one of those inscrutable crimes which almost make us despair of the progress of mankind'. The Archduke and his wife had visited England as recently as the previous November, when they had stayed as guests of King George and Queen Mary at Windsor Castle. Surprisingly, given Franz Ferdinand's reputation – in the words of A. C. Benson –

as 'a curious, dumb, reserved, uncomfortable sort of man', the couple had won the hearts of the British people. 'Never have such exalted guests [received] a more cordial welcome from the great British public,' the *Daily Chronicle* had remarked at the time. This affection was borne out by the reaction to the assassination of George Cecil, the eighteen-year-old grandson of the Conservative Prime Minister Lord Salisbury. George, a prize cadet at Sandhurst, who had joined the 2nd Grenadier Guards early in 1914, was training at Purfleet Camp in Essex. On hearing the news of the shooting he immediately asked his mother Violet to buy a memorial engraving of the Archduke for him from a local print shop.

Unlike Gavrilo Princip and the other Bosnian plotters, who had failed, fatally, to recognize that the Archduke was a more far-sighted advocate of reform than other Habsburgs, and not without sympathy for Slav national aspirations, many British commentators gave Franz Ferdinand credit as a man 'of great ability'. The journalist Edith Sellers wrote a glowing commemorative article about 'The Murdered Archduke' and observed that 'Had he lived . . . he would have held together the diverse races over whom he would have ruled, and would have kept rival States at bay.'

'Everyone horrified and throwing up their hands,' the writer Edmund Gosse confided to his diary on 29 June, from the House of Lords, where he was librarian. In the ten days that followed, the rumours of planned Austrian action against Serbia that were flooding out of Vienna created a certain uneasiness in the British press, with the *Morning Post* on 6 July going so far as to predict that the Austrian response might lead to a 'European war'.

After that, though, things settled down considerably. Foreign Office reports contained no more significant comments about the assassination, and on 6 July Sir Arthur Nicolson wrote that he didn't expect anything to come of the affair. Drawing a line under it all, the *Daily Mail* noted with supreme confidence that Emperor Franz Joseph 'may be trusted to handle the situation wisely, to resist the extremists, and to realise that a policy of reconciliation will be the noblest monument to the sacrifice of the dead'.

For most British people, possible repercussions from the murder of an Austrian Archduke and his wife caused no perceptible alarm. Bloody outrages in the Balkans were common enough occurrences, and usually soon subsided. They seemed in any case irrelevant to the larger issue of European peace.

Instead, thoughts of war focused closer to home. The assassination hadn't succeeded in driving news of impending civil conflict in Ireland from the headlines. Newspapers across the country were providing almost daily reports and pictures of both Irish Nationalist and Ulster forces mustering volunteers and transporting arms.

At Kiel Yachting Week, in northern Germany, at the end of June, the biggest sailing event in the world, a squadron of the British Fleet, consisting of four battleships and three cruisers, had anchored alongside the German Imperial High Seas Fleet. The Kaiser had donned the uniform of a British Admiral of the Fleet and boarded the battleship *King George V*, where German officers received a cordial welcome from their British counterparts.

Lady Maud Warrender, who had starred as Britannia earlier in the month at the Albert Hall Peace Ball, was among the guests also on board ship. At dinner she was seated next to Admiral Tirpitz, Secretary of State of the German Imperial Navy Office, and together they discussed the events in Ireland. Tirpitz expressed his doubts that there would be any trouble, as 'you English people are too sensible.' Maud Warrender shook her head violently in disagreement, and bet the Admiral a sovereign 'that there will be Civil War in Ireland a month from now'.

On 11 July, the Earl of Crawford, a Unionist peer, wrote to Lady Wantage, reporting on Lord Northcliffe's recent 'grand tour of inspection' of Ulster:

> Northcliffe says that the number of rifles is large, the amount of ammunition enormous. Stores of food are accumulated at all strategic points. Practically every motor in eastern Ulster is at the disposal of Carson. Meanwhile Capt. Craig [Unionist MP for the Ulster seat of East Down] . . . has effected a capture of all the petrol in Ulster. There is a strong desire to precipitate matters, not to await further

shilly-shally on the part of the government. I am anxious that the Ulstermen shall be kept closely in hand but every day that passes exacerbates them more.

. . . Here is an episode of last week . . . The Nationalists heard that arms were stored in a farmhouse two or three miles from London-derry. They called out a battalion of Volunteers to raid the place and late at night they started on their expedition. Capt. White heard of it, rushed off in his motor to intercept them, and only managed to do so with difficulty, and about a quarter of a mile from the farm. He headed the men off with his motor and drove them back into Derry.

He did not know, neither did the Nationalist Volunteers (all armed with Revolvers), that at that very moment there were lying entrenched all round the farmhouse 800 Ulster Volunteers armed with rifles, and with fifty rounds of ammunition apiece. Fancy if the Nationalists had reached their objective – if Capt. White had had a puncture in his tyre. There were about ten minutes between this forced retreat and a pitched battle.

Just over a fortnight later, the Irish National Volunteers would organize their own gun-running expedition at Howth, near Dublin, from Erskine Childers's yacht *Asgard*. This was a brilliant bit of show-manship that matched the daring, if not the scale, of the UVF's operation at Larne the previous spring. Unlike Ulster's gun-running exercise, however, this one ended in bloodshed. The intervention of the police and the army caused violent scuffles with a Dublin crowd, and the regular troops opened fire, killing three Nationalists and injuring thirty-eight others.

With the Irish situation deteriorating so rapidly – and with the pressing urgency for the Amending Bill to receive the Royal Assent at the same time as the Home Rule legislation – Asquith had finally given in to the repeated request that the King had been making for some weeks now. This was that Asquith and Bonar Law, Redmond and Carson, each with a single supporter, should attend a round-table conference at Buckingham Palace, referred to by George V, with disarming modesty, as 'my house'. The King's response to Asquith's letter, accepting this course of action, was described by Margot

Asquith as possessing 'bad grammar but quite intelligent and keen. H[enry] says he [George V] is *exhausted*, & for the first time in his life feels himself a *real* monarch.'

More informal negotiations with nominated representatives of every party had taken place throughout the first half of July. Asquith's main object in these was to try to narrow down the differences, as Lloyd George and Grey had suggested, to a question of geography. The stumbling block appeared to be acceptable partitions of the counties of Tyrone and Fermanagh, where the presence of large Catholic populations made a solution even more difficult than in the four northern counties. The conference, as Asquith informed the King, might be unable to attain a definite settlement, 'but it will certainly postpone, and may avert dangerous and possibly irreparable action'. In the circumstances, delay was the best he could hope for.

'It was a great satisfaction to me that you were so clear that this is the right course, my darling counsellor,' Asquith wrote to Venetia on 17 July, after they had discussed the prospects for the Buckingham Palace conference. The next day Asquith wrote again from the Royal Yacht *Victoria and Albert*, moored in Portsmouth Harbour and awaiting the King's review of the fleet at Spithead. As a mark of economy, a test mobilization of the navy had been substituted for the normal navy manoeuvres.

Apart from the King and the Prince of Wales, the only other dignitary staying on board was Prince Albert, the King's second son and a midshipman in the home fleet, and 'a bit better than his brother'. 'I have felt ever so much happier & more hopeful since our talk,' Asquith admitted to Venetia. The only thing to sour his contentment the next day was the publication 'in the two Northcliffe organs', *The Times* and the *Daily Mail*, of the details about the conference.

The final composition of the group of politicians facing each other around a table in the 1844 Room of the Palace (named after the year in which Tsar Nicholas I had stayed there) was Asquith, Lloyd George, Redmond and Dillon, and Bonar Law, Lord Lansdowne, Carson and Captain Craig, representing the two Irish and two British parties. Beforehand Bonar Law had informed the King's private secretary Lord Stamfordham that there was so little prospect of agreement that he wouldn't have been prepared to enter into a conference, 'except in deference to the wishes of His Majesty'. The first meeting was held on 21 July, the final one three days later. Margot drove Asquith to Buckingham Palace on the first day and sat in her car, parked on the Palace forecourt, longing to listen to the exchanges for herself inside the conference room. While she was sitting there, a suffragette attempted to deliver a petition to the Palace.

'I am afraid I was rather a "grumpy" companion yesterday,' Asquith wrote to Venetia following the initial meeting, 'but as always happens your comradeship & counsel and understanding were worth more than a King's ransom.' The subjects singled out for discussion had been the questions of area and time limit. Area was discussed first – and, as a result, the debate over time limit was never reached, as Asquith's letter to Venetia proceeded to explain:

> We sat this morning for an hour & a half, discussing maps & figures, and always getting back to that most damnable creation of the perverted ingenuity of man – the County of Tyrone. The extra-ordinary feature of the discussion was the complete agreement (in principle) of Redmond & Carson. Each said 'I must have the whole of Tyrone, or die; but I quite understand why you say the same'. The Speaker who incarnates bluff unimaginative English sense, of course cut in: 'When each of two people say they must have the whole, why not cut it in half?' They wd. neither of them look at such a suggestion . . . Nothing could have been more amicable in tone, or desperately fruitless in result . . . I have rarely felt more hopeless in any practical affair: an impasse with unspeakable consequences . . . Isn't it a real tragedy?

Still, Asquith maintained his composure. Lunching with the Prime Minister, Count Harry Kessler, dandified patron of the European arts and librettist for Strauss's *The Legend of Joseph* (which Asquith had disliked as much as Edward Thomas), recorded that 'he seemed cheerful, as if he hadn't a care in the world.' On 23 July, the penultimate day of the conference, Asquith was unable at the last minute to attend a lunch party given by Kessler at the Savoy because he had to see the King to keep him abreast of developments. 'The situation in Ulster seems very serious,' Kessler wrote. 'England stands before a civil war.

Yesterday the Irish Guard before the Palace gave the Irish nationalist leaders an ovation.'

At a garden party, given that afternoon by Margot Asquith for 1,600 guests – from which Asquith hoped to slip away to be with Venetia – Kessler talked with Winston Churchill, his mother, Lady Randolph Churchill, and Prince Lichnowsky, the German Ambassador. Lady Randolph 'said that the Ulster Conference had as good as failed. Lichnowsky asked how it would end. "Blood, blood," said Churchill.'

On 24 July, Asquith announced to Venetia 'a black letter day in my Calendar'. The conference had indeed failed, amid tears from some of its participants. 'At the end the King came in, rather *émotionné*, & said in two sentences . . . farewell, I am sorry, and I thank you.' Asquith intended to proceed with the original Amending Bill for exclusion by county option, with a fresh clause about the 'power of option' at the end of the initial time limit. But it was no more than a prolongation of a parliamentary farce, which wouldn't settle anything.

However, the miracle of the unexpected in politics suddenly intervened, and transformed everything. On the afternoon of Friday, 24 July, after Asquith had reported to a meeting of the cabinet on the winding-up of the conference, 'the quiet grave tones', as Winston Churchill recalled them, of Sir Edward Grey's voice were heard, reading from a document that had just been brought to him from the Foreign Office. It was Austria's ultimatum to Serbia, demanding a series of damaging and humiliating concessions from the Serbian government, and a commission to investigate the assassination of Archduke Franz Ferdinand. An answer was required within forty-eight hours. In the opinion of Sir Edward Grey, this was 'the most formidable document ever addressed by one State to another that was independent'.

In Churchill's later memorable words, 'The parishes of Fermanagh and Tyrone faded back into the mists and squalls of Ireland, and a strange light began immediately but by perceptible gradations to fall and grow upon the map of Europe.'

Asquith recognized immediately that this was the most dangerous situation in Europe for forty years. 'We are within measurable, or imaginable, distance of a real Armageddon,' he wrote to Venetia, 'which would dwarf the Ulster and Nationalist Volunteers to their true proportion.' It meant 'almost inevitably' that Russia would come to the defence of Serbia, in defiance of Austria; and that, should this be the case, it would be difficult 'both for Germany & France to refrain from lending a hand to one side or the other'.

It was, he admitted, a 'blood-curdling prospect'; but he went on to add, 'Happily, there seems to be no reason why we should be anything more than spectators.'

Recoiling from the Abyss

On the afternoon of Saturday, 25 July, the day following his announcement to the cabinet of the terms of Austria's ultimatum to Serbia, Sir Edward Grey left London to resume his normal weekend routine. The Foreign Secretary found the city oppressive at the best of times, and never more so than in summer. 'There is the aggressive stiffness of the buildings,' he once wrote, 'the light all day striking upon hard substances, and the stuffiness of the heat from which there is no relief at night.'

Grey's refuge was a small cottage, in reality little more than a wooden shack, at Itchen Abbas in Hampshire. It was a single-storey building built on brick foundations, with a brick chimney and a corrugated-iron roof painted red. Its walls were covered in a mass of creepers, honeysuckle, roses and clematis. There were no gravel walks, the writer W. H. Hudson, a close friend of Grey, noted, 'nor other gardener's abominations . . . and no dog, nor cat, nor chick, nor child – only the wild birds to keep one company'. The cottage was hidden from the road, at the end of an old avenue of lime trees, on a slope within fifty yards of the River Itchen. On the other side was a small chalk quarry, a favourite nesting place for many different species of bird, including a pair of kingfishers, which Grey had fenced off as a miniature sanctuary.

It was on a stretch of the River Itchen that Grey had developed his passion for dry-fly fishing as a schoolboy at Winchester College. In the 1880s, as the young MP for Berwick-upon-Tweed, near his family estate at Fallodon, Grey had started to spend weekends on this part of the river, staying at an inn in Itchen Abbas, and subsequently borrowing a fishing lodge from his cousin Lord Northbrook. Then, in 1890, Grey and his wife Dorothy had the cottage constructed. But their real life continued to be lived outdoors. The opportunities for trout fishing on that part of the river were excellent. Walking or

Sir Edward Grey's cottage at Itchen Abbas, Hampshire

cycling in the surrounding countryside, equipped with his field-glasses, Grey could also draw on his exceptional knowledge of birdlife, an expertise that would lead in time to Grey becoming a prominent figure in campaigns for the protection of wild birds and the creation of bird sanctuaries.

'It was something special and sacred, outside the ordinary stream of life,' Grey wrote of their rural idyll at Itchen Abbas, after Dorothy's early death in 1906, in a riding accident. They were a childless couple. Dorothy had made clear her strong aversion to the physical side of marriage from the outset, and they had lived together as brother and sister, in the spirit of Dorothy and William Wordsworth, their favourite poet and the 'high priest' of their study of nature. Dorothy Grey's dislike of the city was even more pronounced than her husband's. In their early years together, she had constantly fulminated against the wickedness of London life, 'with its unworthy aims, mistakes, and general devilishness', giving Grey cause while she was alive to doubt his long-term prospects as a politician at Westminster.

By the summer of 1914, however, Grey, at fifty-two, had been a widower for eight years, and was approaching his ninth anniversary as Foreign Secretary. He was widely respected for his dignity and for the authority he brought to his office, though criticized by some of his colleagues for his insularity and detachment. Politics, as Beatrice Webb noticed disapprovingly, was only an episode in Grey's life. He certainly would much rather have caught a three-pound trout on the dry-fly than have made a successful speech in the House of Commons. At Itchen Abbas he maintained the simple way of country life that he and Dorothy had started, 'subconsciously' regretting the advances of 'the Victorian Industrial Age' – 'as if anything could be good that led to telephones, and cinematographs and large cities and the *Daily Mail*'.

Grey had been suffering from heavy personal as well as professional strains in the course of 1914. At the beginning of the year he had given up smoking on his oculist's advice, owing to increasing anxiety about his sight. He found that he could no longer see the ball accurately when playing squash, nor was he able to pick out his favourite star in its constellation. His abstention from smoking, however, hadn't improved the situation, and at the end of May a specialist examination confirmed that Grey had a serious infection in both eyes. In time it was predicted that he would probably lose the ability to read while still being able to distinguish light from darkness. Grey's consultants advised him that, at some point in the future, he should take time off work and go away for six months. He had already planned to attend the clinic of a specialist in Germany that summer at the end of the parliamentary session. That was before the pace of European events forced him to postpone his visit.

The Foreign Office in Whitehall, in its palatial Gilbert Scott building from the 1860s, was experiencing a period of internecine struggle and tension. Grey's relationship with Sir Arthur Nicolson, his Permanent Undersecretary, was severely strained. Nicolson's zeal for closer alliances with France and Russia (where he had been Ambassador at St Petersburg) in order to check German aggression, combined with Lady Nicolson's outspoken support for Ulster, did not endear him to Grey. Nor were Nicolson's rivalry with Grey's private secretary, Sir William Tyrrell, and his long-running feud with the Assistant Undersecretary, Sir Eyre Crowe, exactly conducive to the smooth running of the department. Nicolson longed to move to Paris as ambassador, and Grey could not wait to be rid of him. Moreover, the serious rise in the volume of paperwork produced by the Foreign Office, coupled with the failure to employ more staff to deal with it, threatened system overload. All in all, the Foreign Office was not in the best shape to face a major crisis.

While the rest of the cabinet continued to be heavily preoccupied with the turmoil surrounding Irish Home Rule, Grey had spent the first weeks of July anxiously seeking information about Austria's likely reaction to the assassination at Sarajevo. An interview with the German Ambassador, Prince Lichnowsky, on 6 July, had resulted in serious concern about the measures 'of a rather strong character' which Vienna intended to inflict on Serbia. But Grey's anxiety had been allayed somewhat by Lichnowsky's assurances at this and subsequent meetings that Berlin was intent on restraining her Austrian ally. The Austrian ultimatum, with its 48-hour deadline, delivered to Serbia on the evening of 23 July, came therefore as something of a shock, though Crowe had been attempting to warn Grey for days that German actions in Vienna suggested something very far from conciliatory. The chances of localizing the conflict and of persuading France to hold back Russia from taking any action in the interests of her Serbian ally had now all but disappeared.

But Grey continued to place trust in the idea Britain might be able to act in the role of mediator, as it had during the Balkan Wars in 1912. Even Austria's rejection of Serbia's response, late in the day on Saturday, 25 July, did not reduce his efforts for peace. From Itchen Abbas, early on the Sunday afternoon, he sent two telegrams to Nicolson in Whitehall, authorizing the proposal for a four-power conference to resolve the mounting crisis. Germany refused point-blank to take part on the grounds that it would amount to a court of arbitration. This was a serious blow to Grey's hopes, and on his return to London he reported the collapse of the plan to the cabinet. 'There's some *devilry* going on in Berlin,' Grey was heard to exclaim with unaccustomed passion in his voice as he waited to enter the cabinet room.

Germany's negative response to Grey's request for cooperation led him to move closer to Nicolson and Crowe's interpretation of events. 'Our interests,' Crowe had argued in a Foreign Office minute, 'are tied up with those of France and Russia in this struggle, which is not for the possession of Serbia, but one between Germany aiming at political dictatorship in Europe and the Powers who desire to retain individual freedom.'

The question that remained uppermost over the course of the next week, as an inexorable sequence of events pushed Austria, Germany, France and Russia into mobilizing for war, was whether Britain would, in Crowe's words, 'idly stand aside, or take sides'. Would a decision by Grey to align the country with its entente partners, France and Russia, act as sufficient deterrent to Austria and Germany and prevent their being drawn into a major war? Or was it more feasible, and more logical, given Grey's consistent refusal to turn alliances into formal obligations, for Britain to continue to play a detached role until such time as cabinet and public opinion gave positive signals in favour of intervention?

Of course, Grey was correct in his assumption. There was 'devilry' in Berlin, though it would remain impossible until long afterwards to obtain an accurate reading of all the signs. Ambassador Lichnowsky was little more than a dupe, 'left in complete ignorance' by his German masters, as he later admitted, 'of most important matters', while relaying ambiguous messages back to Berlin about the likelihood of Britain's neutrality if it came to war.

What Grey couldn't have known was that the 'war party' in Germany – the military hawks, a group that included the Reich Chancellor Bethmann Hollweg, Foreign Minister Gottlieb von Jagow and Admiral von Tirpitz – had triumphed. They had seized upon the antagonism between Austria and Serbia to provoke a Continental war, making it appear to the outside world that it was Austria, not its German ally, that was working towards a European conflagration. Disturbed for some time by the rapid growth of Russian military power, Germany had calculated that if war between the two countries came in two years' time, it would do so under much less advantageous conditions for Germany than those that existed in 1914.

The German General Staff were confident that a war against France would be over in forty days, especially if Britain could be persuaded to stay out of the war, at least in its early stages, giving Germany just enough time to defeat France by means of a lightning strike through Belgium.

As Austria declared war on Serbia on 28 July and began preparations for the bombardment of Belgrade, and Germany, Russia and France moved closer to ordering general mobilization, Sir Edward Grey embarked on some last-minute tightrope diplomacy, still hoping to preserve peace and keep Britain's options open. In the days ahead, Grey would tell the German and French ambassadors exactly the opposite of what they hoped to hear: hinting to Lichnowsky that Britain might be drawn into the conflict on France's side, while at the same time denying to the French Ambassador, Paul Cambon, that Britain had any binding obligation to assist his country.

'Our action is held in suspense,' Herbert Samuel, President of the Local Government Board, wrote to his wife in the final days of July, 'for if both sides do not know what we shall do, both will be the less willing to run risks.' But Samuel knew that the time for a final decision was running out, and that 'We nineteen men around the table at Downing St[ree]t may soon have to face the most momentous problem which men can face.'

Nothing but a miracle could now avert a war, Asquith informed Venetia Stanley on Wednesday, 29 July. With a majority of the cabinet supporting neutrality, that still did not necessarily mean a British war. However, the first precautionary steps for 'a possible outbreak of hostilities' had been taken. The fleet had been prevented from dispersing after the test mobilization earlier in the month, and on 28 July, Winston Churchill, as First Lord of the Admiralty, had ordered the Royal Navy to Scapa Flow. From his yacht on Start Point, the most exposed peninsula on the Devonshire coast, the writer Hilaire Belloc watched 'a procession of great forms, all in line, hastening eastwards'.

The decision had also been made to send warning telegrams to all the military, naval and colonial stations, ordering them to be in a state of readiness. 'We must not be caught napping,' Asquith explained to his wife. Margot was amazed at the speed at which the provisions of the 'War Book', carefully prepared instructions for this precautionary period, were put into action. 'All these wires were sent between 2 & 3.30, marvellously quick,' she wrote in her diary, adding that she had never seen Asquith 'so keen outwardly'.

Venetia, well out of the mainstream, staying with her parents at Penrhos, had wondered whether lack of time and the pressure of the crisis might lead the Prime Minister to cease writing regularly to her. Asquith hastened to reassure Venetia that his need to share everything with her was greater than ever. He longed to join her '& the dogs & the penguin on the rocks', but, as that proved impossible, the next best thing was to receive her daily letters and keep her in touch with the 'ever shifting currents' of events. She sent him a piece of white heather for luck, and he yet again admitted that he would have been lost without her love and understanding. However, as so often in a crisis, Asquith stayed calm and unruffled.

And the white heather appeared to have brought him good fortune. The only blessing to emerge so far from the gloomy European scenario was that 'the whole Irish business' had been 'put into the shade by the coming war'. The suddenness of developments had surprised everyone. On 30 July, Asquith was sitting in the Cabinet Room surrounded by a map of Ulster, and files of population and religion statistics, preparing for the second reading of the Amendment Bill, when he was called to an unexpected meeting at the Conservative leader Bonar Law's 'rather suburban looking' villa in Kensington.

Here Asquith found Bonar Law himself along with Sir Edward Carson. They placed before him a significant proposal. Given the deteriorating international situation, both men were anxious to postpone the legislation dealing with Ulster's exclusion from Home Rule. For Britain to advertise her domestic problems at such a time might, they said, act as an impediment to the search for peace. Carson had come to see it as his patriotic duty to place the country's interests before those of his Ulstermen.

Asquith accepted the offer after consulting Grey and Lloyd George, as well as Redmond, who was equally prepared to make concessions at a time of international tension, and anxious not to be outdone by the patriotism of the Ulsterians. The Home Rule Bill became law but its operation was suspended until the Amending Bill could be passed.

This chapter appeared closed for the present, and with it passed the threat of civil war in Ireland for the foreseeable future. But war in Ireland had been replaced by something altogether deadlier. Venetia Stanley joked that it was like cutting off one's head to get rid of a headache. As news of the postponement of the Amending Bill spread around the Speaker's Gallery in the Commons, Margot Asquith was confronted by a group of ladies, including the Unionist 'diehards' who had shown such insolence to her face throughout the entire session, pressing for more information.

'Good Heavens, Margot, what does this mean?' one of them asked. 'How frightfully dangerous! Why the Irish will be fighting tonight – what does it all mean???'

'It means your civil war is *postponed*,' Margot replied, 'and you will never get it . . . if you read the papers you'll find that we are on the verge of a European War.'

Asquith's assessment on 30 July was that the European situation had deteriorated to 'at least one degree worse than it was yesterday'. Alarmed by Lichnowsky's reports that Britain might not after all stay out of a war, Germany had made a clumsy bid to secure British neutrality by promising that if Germany defeated France, French territorial integrity would be maintained. This pledge, however, did not extend to France's colonies, nor was there any guarantee that Belgian neutrality would be respected. Grey, in 'a white heat of passion' that no one who knew him had witnessed before, replied forcefully that the British government would neither desert France nor bargain away Belgium's neutrality.

In the series of cabinet meetings taking place over the next few days, the overall response was much less transparent. It was becoming clear that Asquith was going to have to find a compromise to hold his government and the Liberal Party together. A split in the cabinet at this stage seemed inevitable, with a majority of ten ministers – Morley, Beauchamp, Simon, Harcourt, Samuel, Pease, McKinnon Wood,

Runciman, Burns and Lloyd George – supporting various shades of neutrality and non-intervention, in opposition to the Prime Minister and the Foreign Secretary. Churchill was the most bellicose member of the pro-war group, automatically downcast the moment that prospects for peace brightened, and keen for any enterprise that would give him the opportunity to show off the navy. John Burns, President of the Board of Trade, leaning over the cabinet table and shaking his clenched fists, was the most resolute opponent of war.

The ultimate intentions of Lloyd George, the Chancellor, were difficult to gauge. He seemed jittery and undecided, and talked at one point of retiring to his native Wales. As the major champion of economy and reductions in naval and military expenditure, he was the natural leader of any anti-war party. He was also receiving warnings from C. P. Scott, editor of the *Manchester Guardian* and self-appointed head of the Liberal press's campaign against intervention, that any man pressing the government into embarking on a war would never lead the country as Prime Minister. Yet not so long ago, at the time of the Agadir dispute in 1911, Lloyd George had appeared to threaten Germany with military or naval retaliation in defence of French interests, after the German gunboat *Panther* had sailed into the Moroccan Atlantic harbour. Which way would he side now?

As much as three quarters of the Liberal Party in the Commons, Asquith estimated, was against war. The view of most Liberal members was that Britain should make an immediate declaration that in no circumstances would it play any part. The Conservatives were broadly pro-interventionist, though their leader, Bonar Law, told Grey that he doubted that his party would be overwhelmingly in favour of war unless Belgium was invaded.

The press were divided in opinion and effectively cancelled each other out. The Northcliffe press, together with other Conservative papers, had advocated intervention, and the need for Britain to align with France, from an early stage. On 29 July the *Pall Mall Gazette* put the case succinctly: 'We pray that this dread issue may be averted. But, if it be raised, our duty is clear. We must stand by our friends with the most prompt resolution, and with the whole of our might.' At the other end of the spectrum, a paper such as the *Daily Chronicle* emphasized that 'This is after all a Continental war, and Britons may again thank God for their insular position.'

Most of the provincial press advocated neutrality at this point. The *Yorkshire Evening News* claimed that it was 'certainly to Great Britain's interest that she should keep out of the quarrel' owing to the fact that there were 'plenty of domestic matters to occupy her for the present'. The *Huddersfield Daily Examiner* went further. It was the 'nation's fixed resolve' not to be involved in any European conflict in any circumstances, 'short of direct attack'.

The City had also been urging the government 'to keep out at all costs' as the international crisis spread to the foreign exchange markets. The vast and complex structure of credit around the world appeared to be on the verge of collapse. On the morning of 31 July, in the words of the *Economist*, came 'the final thunderclap'. The London Stock Exchange was closed, and the Bank rate was raised from 4 to 8 per cent in an attempt to halt cash withdrawals (the next day it was raised to 10 per cent, and not reduced again until 6 August, when it went back down to 6 per cent). A huge crowd, drawing gold, formed outside the Bank of England. A single peal of Lloyd's Lutine Bell was heard ringing out, traditionally a herald of bad news. General mobilization had been proclaimed in Russia. The following day, 1 August, Germany declared war on Russia and started to mobilize. France's mobilization in recognition of its alliance with Russia appeared inevitable.

The issue of Britain's response in the event of Germany's violation of Belgium's neutrality had been brought to the cabinet's attention on 29 July, but no firm stance had been taken. The Prime Minister, summarizing that day's discussion for the benefit of the King, acknowledged that if such an eventuality were to arise, the matter would be one of policy rather than obligation. The 1839 Treaty of London, which had recognized the independence of the kingdom of Belgium, had given each of its signatories – Britain, Austria, Prussia, France, Russia and the Netherlands – the right, but not the duty, to intervene if Belgium were invaded. This right applied in law, whether or not Belgium resisted attack or called for assistance from the appropriate signatory powers.

However, it was impossible to know in advance how the Belgians would react in the event of an attack. They might offer no resistance to German invasion and make no call on Britain for help. They might covertly have decided to be pro-German. While it was widely accepted that Germany would have to send its armies through Belgium, in order to make an effective attack on France, it was by no means clear what route they would take. This had significant ramifications for the destruction of Belgian independence. If German forces confined themselves to the smaller, southern tip of the country, to the south of the River Meuse, such a route might not be regarded by the Belgian government as constituting a substantial enough violation of their borders to warrant an outside appeal. And even if such circumstances did provoke a request for assistance, the British government might consider itself bound neither by moral obligations nor by strategic considerations to act.

Late in the afternoon of 31 July, Grey asked the French and German governments whether they would respect the neutrality of Belgium, provided that all other powers did the same. France replied in the affirmative. Germany's response was tantamount to a refusal.

To some waverers in the cabinet, resistant to going to war in order to preserve the balance of power in Europe against the threat of German hegemony, the option of rushing to the defence of Belgian neutrality was beginning to appear more attractive. One of them, Herbert Samuel, put the case that they were 'not entitled to carry England into the war for the sake of our goodwill for France, or for the sake of maintaining the strength of France and Russia against that of Germany and Austria'. But intervention, he thought, might be conceivable to protect the independence of Belgium, 'which we were bound by treaty to protect'.

The cabinet as a whole seemed intent on continuing its brinkmanship, still refusing to authorize an official statement about British intentions should war come. Cambon, the French Ambassador, was summoned again to the Foreign Office, only to be told in a 'rather painful' interview that the cabinet's position remained unchanged, and that Britain was under no obligation to help France.

Sir Eyre Crowe, the Assistant Undersecretary, unwilling to recognize the pressure Grey was under in trying to avoid an irrevocable split in the government, sent him a strongly worded minute. There might be no formal alliance between the two countries, but Britain nevertheless had an obligation to France through the 'moral bond' of the entente, which 'can have no meaning if it does not signify that in a just quarrel England would stand by her friends'.

Crowe, and his superior, Sir Arthur Nicolson, viewed Grey's failure to take a firm position on entering the war with a mixture of despair and alarm. Seeing Grey pacing his room and biting at his lower lip, Nicolson asked him whether it was true that he refused to support France at the moment of its greatest danger. 'You will render us,' Nicolson continued angrily, 'a by-word among nations.' Crowe, white and drawn, repeating the words 'the poor French', with tears streaming down his face, claimed that Grey wasn't equipped by upbringing or study to understand the sinister depths of the German mind.

On the evening of 31 July, Edmund Gosse dined with his friend Lord Haldane, the Lord Chancellor, at Haldane's house in Queen Anne's Gate. Grey, who was staying with Haldane, was in the drawing-room when Gosse arrived, and put a good face on the crisis, telling him that he had 'not lost all hopes of a settlement'. Later, though, when they were alone in the study, Haldane admitted to Gosse that 'a European War was now inevitable', and that 'he was persuaded that we should hardly keep out of it.' Haldane found the attitude of the waverers among his cabinet colleagues incredible. For him, the terms of Britain's friendship with France made all notion of neutrality impossible. 'The German fleet,' he predicted to Gosse, 'will sail down the Channel bombarding [Le] Havre and Cherbourg, and smashing the northern coast of France. But people like Harcourt [the Colonial Secretary, among the ten cabinet members arguing for non-intervention] say, "What business is it of ours? Let us be benevolently neutral!" '

On 1 August, Grey dined at Brooks's with his parliamentary private secretary, Arthur Murray, and played a game of billiards. Keeping his resignation letter in reserve, Grey told Murray that he intended to have his 'tussle' with the cabinet on the following day.

In the country at large, the developing crisis possessed something of the impact of a dormant volcano that had unexpectedly erupted. It was only in the last week of July that most families in England began to have an inkling of the danger posed to them. Suddenly they opened their newspapers to be confronted with the astonishing news of a threat of war, not from Ireland, but from the continent of Europe. Two *Times* editorials, on 30 and 31 July, headed 'Lowering Clouds' and 'Waning Hopes', commented on the emerging sense of gravity and national emergency. Reading these, Kathleen Isherwood thought it 'so extraordinary that in a few hours Home Rule and Ireland have sunk into insignificance'. From Teignmouth, in Devon, Dorothy Holman expressed her similar astonishment: 'the papers are nothing but war, war. Ulster has gone into oblivion so have all other subjects. It is so sudden. I never heard the vaguest suggestion of it till Sunday [26 July].'

The closure of the London Stock Exchange on Friday, 31 July, and the resulting wave of financial panic, awakened many people to the seriousness of the situation. To some it seemed that the dire predictions of Norman Angell in *The Great Illusion*, about the unprofitable nature of modern war, were coming true. Kate, Lady Courtney of Penwith, the Quaker and peace activist, noted in her diary that the 'severe crisis in the City seems to have sobered people, and let loose the tongues of those who object to our being drawn in [to the war], but hesitate to speak out. It looks as if the Liberal rank and file will at last mobilise and put pressure on the government.'

The headlines, though, were growing more ominous. 'Europe Drifting to Disaster' was emblazoned across a late edition of the *Daily Mail* on the morning of the Stock Exchange closure. 'The situation abroad is looking very serious now, isn't it?' the young Deptford clerk, John Riddey, wrote home to his mother that day. 'I hope I shan't have to go & fight.' At Victoria Station on that same Friday, Mary Coules, who was leaving for a family holiday in Worthing, noticed the 'hundreds of coastguardsmen – Naval reserve, I suppose – all with kit bags and straw hats . . . This was the first inclination we had of any likelihood of war. One of the men called out as we passed him "We're here for the Germans."'

For anyone connected to an army or naval reservist, or living near an army or naval base, the prospect of war was becoming impossible to ignore. At midnight on the 30th, the first military personnel on leave in England began to be recalled to their units. A cricket match the following day at Lord's broke up when reservists were abruptly ordered to leave. By Sunday, 2 August, the order had gone out for naval mobilization. In Hull and Grimsby, and in the East Anglian fishing ports, large numbers of reservists received their official telegrams, while in the fishing communities of the West Country, thousands of reservists were called up by telegraph boys and policemen knocking on their doors.

At Brixham, in Devon, nearly every family was affected by mobilization, and the annual regatta had to be abandoned. In Cornwall, at Looe, large numbers of men mustered by the quay and were marched off to the station, headed by the town band. Thirty miles away at Falmouth, naval mobilization was proclaimed by the town crier, and some 200 reservists were quickly rounded up by police and volunteers. At Barrow-in-Furness, in Cumbria, officials from the Vickers Shipyard, designers and builders of warships as well as aircraft, announced that the annual week's holiday, due to begin on 5 August, was cancelled. At the same time, foreign crews were being hurriedly recalled home. One hundred and fifty Austrians set sail from Grimsby for Hamburg, and on 2 August French reservists returned from London stations.

From Westcliff-on-Sea, a seaside resort near Southend in Essex, Hallie Eustace Miles recorded on 1 August that 'the air is full of whispers of coming trouble: and the rumours of war are becoming more and more alarming and more and more persistent; it is even said that War has already been declared.' Bessie Rayne, a suffragette living in a London suburb, reported, also on the 1st, that there was 'All sorts of conflicting news but war seems certain.' Trying to forget the 'rumours of war', she immersed herself in preparations for that weekend's tennis tournament. For Clement Webb, a theologian at Oxford University, the last days of July and the first ones of August, 'under the shadow of the European Crisis', were more difficult to get through. On Saturday, the 1st, Webb wrote that 'One lives under a cloud and can think of little else . . . Things could scarcely look blacker.'

Georgina Lee, a middle-class London woman, whose husband was legal secretary to the Archbishop of Canterbury, felt that the sense of 'impending calamity hanging over everyone' broke down the 'ordinary reserves of English people'. At lunchtime on Friday, 31 July, she was stranded at Paddington Station on her way to the village of Cossington in Somerset for the Bank Holiday weekend. The shunters working on the Great Western Railway had gone on strike a few hours earlier, and she and other delayed travellers sat in the waiting-room, discussing the recent tumultuous events, while their children played with their spades and pails on the dusty floor. An elderly man told her, 'in listless tones', that he had worked for the Stock Exchange for the past forty years, 'and had never known it close in a crisis, nor seen so many failures in a few hours'. When she reached Cossington, Lee and her husband spent a day walking around the 'picturesque' neighbourhood, barely noticing the scenery, 'so busy were we, discussing the chances of war in all its aspects'.

But the British people should continue to hope for peace, the *Daily Mail* counselled on 1 August, 'if only because no irrevocable step has yet been taken'. *The Times* agreed that there was still a chance of averting 'this supreme catastrophe'. Much of the population now realized the imminence of war, but people's reactions continued to be in a state of flux. Many were undecided, and for some it seemed beyond belief. The writer Wilfrid Scawen Blunt was convinced as late as 2 August that Asquith's government was on the verge of announcing Britain's neutrality. On 1 August, the Archbishop of Canterbury, Randall Davidson, replied cautiously to an invitation from Dr Ernst Drylander, the eminent German Lutheran and Chief Court Chaplain to the Kaiser, asking whether the Anglican Church would take part in a celebration of the 400th anniversary of the Reformation in Germany in 1917. While anxious about international developments, the Archbishop took the opportunity to say that 'war between two great Christian nations of kindred race and sympathies is, or ought to be, unthinkable in the twentieth century of the Gospel of the Prince of Peace.'

Special prayers for peace were offered in Anglican churches all over the country on Sunday, the 2nd, by order of the Archbishop. Similar instructions were given to their clergy by the Roman Catholic bishops. Most Church of England clergy prayed for peace and for divine guidance for the government, while commenting on the gravity of the situation. 'A week ago,' observed the vicar of St Matthew's, Torquay, 'little did we imagine the calamities which were to come so suddenly upon the Continent of Europe.' A vicar in the parish of Wallington in Surrey presented a more doom-laden scenario to his congregation, declaring that 'we were in the face of the most terrible catastrophe in the memory of living man.' The Dean of Manchester Cathedral went further, sermonizing on 'the duty of every Englishman' to continue to pray for peace so long as peace was possible, and to support the government loyally if war broke out.

Some individual Anglican clergy did use their sermons on that Sunday to oppose war. The Bishop of Lincoln asked parishioners in Cleethorpes 'to pray to God to keep our people from war', and told them that 'a continental war could be nothing short of disastrous when one thought of the militarism of Europe, of the hell of battlefields, of the miseries of wounded, of ruined peasants.' He declared that England had no quarrel with Germany and that 'to go to war without reason was tempting providence. Moreover it would inflict upon our industrial community one of the most terrible curses possible to inflict.' In Newmarket, the Rector of St Mary's must have struck terror into the minds of his listeners. He warned them that 'no town in England was now safe. At night it might be turned into a smouldering ruin and its inhabitants into blackened corpses.'

Nonconformist chapels, upholding venerable peace-loving traditions, were generally more condemnatory in their opposition to war, especially in the Midlands and the industrial North, the heartland of neutralist sentiment. It was in places like Huddersfield, in West Yorkshire, dependent on the wool trade, that the strongest fears of the economic dislocation likely to result from war were to be found. These were also the areas from which the socialist and trade union opposition to the war drew their greatest strength. In Huddersfield the two combined when meetings in St George's Square on 2 August, called by the Independent Labour Party and the Trades Council, in support of striking engineers, turned into anti-war rallies.

More than 100,000 people took part in anti-war demonstrations around the country on Sunday, 2 August. Some were organized by socialist and Labour protestors, calling for a workers' strike against the war. Others united a wide cross-section of people from different backgrounds in opposition to the war – but then, as one Labour MP noted, 'terrible danger made strange bedfellows.' Still others were of a religious inspiration.

At the Birmingham Bull Ring, George Cook told the assembled crowd of around 2,500 that 'the workers already had on hand an industrial battle for better economic conditions which was far more important than entering into a war with their brothers on the continent.' At the Market Cross in Carlisle, in Cumbria, a large crowd massed 'for the purpose of passing a resolution in favour of the neutrality of this country in the complications that have arisen in Europe'. A similar resolution was passed at Scarborough and sent to Sir Edward Grey. S. C. Joad attended two meetings in the Midlands on Sunday evening. 'At one its original religious theme was adhered to, but the other became a pacifist meeting . . . at which it was urged that even at this last hour, efforts to avert war should not cease to be made.'

The largest of the socialist demonstrations was held in Trafalgar Square, during a heavy downpour of rain, on the afternoon of 2 August. As many as 15,000 people were present. Described in one Labour newspaper as far bigger 'than the most important suffrage rallies', it passed a resolution in favour of international peace and solidarity. It also deplored 'the impotency to which the democracy of Germany had been reduced' and called on the British government 'in the first place to prevent the spread of war and in the second . . . to see that the country is not dragged into the conflict.'

Edmund Gosse, on his way to see Lord Haldane again at Queen Anne's Gate, travelled on the tube that afternoon and noted that 'although the train was rather full, no one seemed conscious of anything unusual; people were chatting calmly of their own affairs.' At Trafalgar Square he stepped outside the tube station and immediately found himself 'confronted by a dense crowd'.

A procession with tawdry banners of magenta and emerald-green, with a plentiful flutter of tinsel, and accompanied by a blaring band, passing westwards down the Strand. The main inscription called upon England to 'Stand Clear!' and there were banners with 'Think what War will cost!' and 'What business is it of yours?' The trampling of feet was almost drowned by the vulgar music, and I found it impossible to cross the Square at first. I noted the absolute silence of the crowds looking on; there was no applause and there was no hissing; all one can say was that London . . . took no more notice of the procession than of the Salvation Army . . .

Gosse's account of the Trafalgar Square rally is slightly at odds with other reports of the demonstration. These described heckling from middle-class youths who 'shouted patriotic songs until a heavy shower of rain dampened their enthusiasm and the mounted and foot police who had arrived to avert trouble found themselves with nothing to do'. Perhaps Gosse had arrived too early or too late to observe them. Some of these 'rowdy clerks' may have been the same youths in straw-boaters who had participated in the attacks on suffragettes at Buckingham Palace two months earlier. That evening these youths joined the crowds moving down the Mall and gathering outside the Palace, the beginning of a nightly vigil that would continue every evening for the next week.

It was unprecedented for the cabinet to meet on a Sunday. On 2 August it did so twice. Shortly before the morning session, news of the German invasion of Luxembourg reached London. A violation of Belgian neutrality now seemed a bygone conclusion. It would be impossible for German troops to get out of Luxembourg without crossing Belgian territory, except by way of a very narrow bottleneck through France.

The morning cabinet was a long and difficult meeting, lasting for almost three hours, from eleven to nearly two o'clock. Grey outlined Britain's obligation to assist France and proposed forbidding the German Fleet's use of the English Channel as a base for hostile operations against the French. McKenna, the Home Secretary, responded that the Channel should be neutralized to both France and Germany. But half-measures were pointless, Grey replied. 'If the Channel is closed against Germany *it is* in favour of France . . . either we must declare ourselves neutral, or in it.' And if the majority voted in favour of neutrality, he would resign.

A letter from Bonar Law, read out by Asquith, in which he and Lord Lansdowne pledged the support of the Conservative Party in favour of intervention, must have strengthened the resolve of the pro-war party in the government. If there did turn out to be a split in the cabinet, those favouring intervention, who included the Prime Minister, Grey and Churchill, might be in a position to form a war coalition with the Unionist opposition.

At last a decision was reached. Germany was to be informed that any naval action in the Channel by its fleet would not be tolerated. John Burns promptly resigned, insisting that this amounted to a declaration of war against Germany. He was persuaded to postpone his resignation until that evening's cabinet. Shortly afterwards, the cabinet broke for lunch.

Edmund Gosse had reached Haldane's house after his walk across Trafalgar Square during the anti-war demonstration. He immediately came upon Sir Edward Grey conducting the French Ambassador, Paul Cambon, whom Grey had just informed of the cabinet's decision, to his waiting carriage. Cambon looked 'pinched and bent; I noticed a bright spot of colour on his cheek-bones, his white hair and beard seemed whiter than ever'. Grey greeted Gosse with the words, 'What do you think I am going to do? I have a clear hour and I am going up to the Zoo, to spend it there among the birds.' His attitude struck Gosse 'as very curious, and rather inscrutable. All his features were sharpened; he looked tired, but his strong eyes were bright and calm.'

Inside the house, Haldane, who had hardly slept for forty-eight hours, told Gosse, in the deepest confidence, that 'war is now certain' and that 'We cannot keep out of it', though the government had done its 'very best'. Asquith, he said, 'had been wonderful . . . in grasp of the moving situation . . . It is all like a huge cinematograph show, seen through a mist.'

Referring to the split in the cabinet, Haldane said that there were four members who were resolute about the impossibility of Britain's leaving France 'in the lurch'. Haldane knew already that the deciding factor in persuading other ministers to stay would be Lloyd George. He was the 'invaluable mentor' who was still 'wavering'. If he decided to move in favour of intervention, others might follow.

German invasion of Belgium was the decisive issue that might allow Lloyd George and the other waverers to reconsider their positions. At the second cabinet meeting, on Sunday evening, Grey made a strong case that substantial violation of Belgian territory would compel Britain to take action. By the end of the cabinet, at around 8 o'clock, John Burns had reiterated his intention to resign. The intentions of the others remained undeclared.

Late that night at Downing Street, with the future of his government still in the balance, Asquith composed a letter to the French Ambassador, pledging for the first time Britain's support for France if it were attacked by Germany. After sending it by messenger to the French Embassy, the Prime Minister suddenly became convinced that, in the dim light of his sitting-room, he'd misaddressed the letter to the German Embassy instead. Fortunately, the note of 'enthusiastic gratitude' that arrived from the French confirmed that Asquith had been mistaken.

Outside, the distant roar of the crowds 'perambulating the streets and cheering the King at Buckingham Palace' could be heard into the early hours. Quoting the words of his predecessor Sir Robert Walpole, in a letter the next day to Venetia Stanley – 'Now they are ringing their bells; in a few weeks they'll be wringing their hands' – Asquith observed that 'War or anything that seems likely to lead to war is always popular with the London mob', adding with disgust, 'How one loathes such levity.'

Bank Holiday

War clouds were not the only thing that was dampening the prospects for August Bank Holiday Monday, 3 August. Despite the fact that temperatures in some parts of the country during the first week of July had soared as high as ninety degrees, much of the rest of the month had been cooler – in some places, ten degrees below normal temperatures for the time of year – as well as cloudier and changeable, with thunderstorms in central England causing considerable havoc.

For the Bank Holiday weekend, there was a mixture of heavy rain and sunshine. In the West Country, and some areas of the North-East, for example, rain was unrelenting across the three days. But the southern and south-eastern coasts, favourite destinations for holiday crowds, enjoyed brilliant sunshine, fresh breezes and billowing clouds. That weekend, a newspaper at Dover, in Kent, announced, perhaps a little over-optimistically, the sale of 'a wonderful new toilet discovery': 'Creme de Luxe', which guaranteed protection for the skin 'from the heat and glare of the sun'.

England's summer Bank Holiday on the first Monday in August had been introduced in 1871 by the Liberal MP Sir John Lubbock, primarily to provide holiday relief for bank employees and other white-collar workers (exactly a hundred years later, it was officially moved to the last Monday of the month following a five-year trial period). Although initially unpopular with manual workers, who weren't entitled to wages for enforced breaks, St Lubbock's Day, as the holiday continued to be widely known in 1914, had quickly become a staple fixture in the calendar. Throughout the country, hundreds of thousands of working men and women enjoyed themselves in carnivals and entertainments at home, or embarked on day trips to the countryside and seaside.

'Virtue must lie somewhere, I suppose, in Bank Holiday excursions,'

Children on a South Coast beach, August 1914

wrote Mabel Rudkin, a resident of Dover, in Kent, of August 1914's holiday. 'Otherwise, ordinarily sensible men and women would not cram themselves and their families into suffocating trains, trams and buses; risk crashes in cars racing four abreast; scramble for hastily cooked poached eggs and lukewarm coffee, in airless tea-rooms; and queue up patiently for almost any seats at any entertainment.'

Families, who had taken advantage of tickets at unprecedentedly low prices for railway excursions to a variety of seaside resorts, faced disappointment. Two companies, the North-Eastern Railway, extending through Yorkshire, County Durham and Northumberland, and the South-Western line from Waterloo, through Surrey, Berkshire and Hampshire, had felt 'compelled to cancel all excursions' owing to the European crisis. Those who had planned holidays to Continental destinations were similarly disappointed, while some more cautious holiday-makers opted for a last-minute cancellation of their plans in view of the economic dislocation that was widely feared, and, in some places, already evident. Agnes Smithson, about to go on her annual holiday to Tenby, in Wales, with her parents and brother, was dismayed when her father suddenly announced the cancellation of their trip. She later remembered that 'A moratorium [had been] declared on all payments and banks were closed, and he was afraid of the result for the family textile business,' Joseph Smithson's of Halifax, in Yorkshire.

Nevertheless, many destinations reported record attendances. At Worthing, in East Sussex, the abandonment of excursions on two railway systems attracted even larger crowds than usual to the town. Just along the coast, Brighton was 'as crowded as ever', despite 'the thunderings of war', with rowing and sailing boats, pleasure steamers and motor coaches packed to overflowing. Whitby, the North Yorkshire seaside town, saw a large influx of visitors, while the seafront at the north-eastern resort of Roker in Sunderland was inundated 'by huge numbers'. The focus for Sunderland's celebration of the Bank Holiday spirit was its East End Carnival, where there were contests in a range of age categories for the best children's hair and teeth, a fancy dress competition, and prizes for illuminated houses and 'comic decorated houses'.

In some parts of the country, though, there was a noticeable absence of what one Sussex newspaper termed 'the usual holiday enthusiasm'. At Worthing, for instance, it was noted that 'the war scare seemed to have a subduing effect on amusements and relaxations.' In Cornwall, where horse shows, wrestling matches and other Bank Holiday attractions had seen a low attendance, it was claimed that 'people did not feel like amusement', while the disappointing turnout at the county's Newquay Carnival was accounted for by people's concern about the unfolding crisis.

The one absorbing topic of conversation on the seafronts, beaches, and in restaurants, cafés and other public places, seemed to be the possibility of war. 'Will England be brought in?' was the question on many people's lips. In Roker, 'wherever a crowd collected the news was discussed with much earnestness. At night the streets presented an animated appearance until a very late hour. Groups of people gathered at street corners arguing about the rights and wrongs of the war. For the most part they were quiet and orderly.' There was a heavy demand for the special war editions of newspapers, an outward sign of the dread and foreboding which lay at the back of so many people's minds. The newsboys had been swift to take advantage of this, charging more for special editions, and forcing editors to intervene and print front-page warnings to their readers that prices remained as normal.

The atmosphere in the capital on the 3rd also appears to have been muted. 'To see the crowds wandering round London you would not think anything was happening,' Ethel, wife of Rear-Admiral Beatty, wrote to her husband. The London correspondent of the *Manchester Guardian* reported 'that no one seemed to want war. There were no war songs or war talk except by way of a joke or forecast.' Many Londoners were spending the Bank Holiday in their customary way. There were large numbers in the parks, in the Zoological Gardens, at Earls Court and White City. Madame Tussauds had rapidly put together a new exhibit, 'The Crisis of Europe' – with wax models of King George, the Emperor of Austria, King Peter of Serbia, 'and Other Reigning Sovereigns' – and did brisk business. Grahame-White's Hendon Aerodrome, on the other hand, recorded one of its sparsest crowds on record, and there were smaller race attendances at Sandown.

A favourite spot for Londoners on an August Bank Holiday was Hampstead Heath, where the annual Cockney Carnival took place. From the Vale of Health up the hill to The Old Bull and Bush, Jack Straw's Castle and the Spaniards Road, pubs were open all day long, there was a fair, and market stalls, tea gardens, and the spectacle of costers in their gala finery dancing to the music of the piano-organ and melodeon.

But even here the mood was different from usual. A local paper reported that the 1914 carnival had been 'a dismal affair . . . Many attempts were made to infuse gaiety into the proceedings, but even when these attempts were partially successful, incongruity was afforded by the harsh and discordant voices of news vendors shouting out the latest war news . . . Nowhere was there the slightest sign of "Mafficking" and it was obvious to the observer that the idea of war was distasteful to all.' 'Mafficking' was a reference to the boisterous celebrations that had accompanied the news in London of the relief of Mafeking, the British garrison town in South Africa, in 1900 during the Boer War. Memories of the spectre of 1900, and its brand of discreditable jingoism, which had appeared at times dangerously out of control, was to be a constant point of reference in descriptions of the English crowds of August 1914.

In the evening, holiday crowds flocked to the picture palaces and music halls. Nationwide there had been a trend in the previous two years towards considerable investment in cinemas. A sizeable town might now have as many as ten or fifteen cinemas – compared with only two or three music halls, or theatres – the larger ones containing 1,000 seats, with prices at threepence, sixpence and a shilling, and a change of programme of up to three times a week (London had almost 400 film venues by 1914).

Considerable concern had recently been expressed about the potential provided by the cover of darkness in cinemas for acts of indecency, consensual or otherwise. 'The cinema cad' was an increasing problem, and plans were under serious consideration for 'women only' sections of film halls. As the controversy, earlier in the year, surrounding the murder of Willie Starchfield had shown, there were also fears that films depicting violence and other types of crime were acting as encouragement to would-be criminals. On the night of 3 August, Sunderland's Wheat Sheaf Picture Hall was showing the feature-length *Monsieur Lecoq*. Lecoq was based on Émile Gaboriau's character, a scientifically inclined detective employed by the French Sûreté, and a major influence on the creation of Conan Doyle's Sherlock Holmes. The film was advertised as 'full of sensational incidents', though the management were anxious to assure patrons that there was no risk of implanting dangerous ideas in the minds of audiences, particularly those of younger patrons. Presentations at the cinema for the immediate future included a number of Keystone Comedies, part of 1914's 'Chaplin boom', starring Mack Sennett's new find Charlie Chaplin, in his popular persona as 'The Tramp'.

Across town, at the Empire Theatre, the *Sunderland Daily Echo* noted how 'the war spirit is now invading our music halls.' The 'Marseillaise' and 'God Save the King' were played by the orchestra before each performance, with the audience standing during the national anthem, 'and cheering heartily at the conclusion'. The Schichtl Brothers, a variety act, were on the bill, but their appearance had to be cancelled when one of them was summoned back to Germany to join the army. During the second house, the German Consul visited the theatre and informed a member of the Vega Trio that he must report to the Consul's Office first thing the following morning, and that he, too, would soon be returning to Germany for enlistment in an army unit.

The weather had been fine that afternoon for the Bank Holiday cricket match at Kennington Oval, where 17,000 spectators watched Surrey play Nottinghamshire. Surrey won the toss and scored 472 for five wickets, a performance largely due to Jack Hobbs's record innings of 226 runs.

Some of those present felt that even at the Oval there was an atmosphere of foreboding, which suggested that many in the holiday crowd had their minds on graver matters than cricket. From where they sat on the balcony of the pavilion, members of the Surrey

County Cricket Club could see the flag fluttering over the Houses of Parliament, where, just after three o'clock, the Foreign Secretary, Sir Edward Grey, rose from the front bench to make the most momentous speech of his parliamentary career.

At the meeting of the cabinet on the morning of 3 August, the imminent German invasion of Belgium, coupled with the appeal to George V by King Albert of the Belgians for diplomatic action to protect his country's neutrality, had decisively swung Lloyd George's attitude in favour of intervention. 'I stay. It's Belgium,' he whispered in the ear of another waverer, Lord Morley, as they filed into the Cabinet Room, to which Morley replied that 'German bullying of Belgium does not alter my aversion to the French entente policy.' Lloyd George made an impassioned plea to the other non-interventionists not to go, and, in the event, of the ten original waverers, only two – Burns and Morley – resigned. At the last moment, there was a 'slump in resignations', as Sir John Simon and Lord Beauchamp elected to stay, their decision at least in part a result of having listened to Grey's remarkable speech. Asquith's government was secure for the foreseeable future.

The Commons chamber had not been as packed for almost twenty years – not since Gladstone's introduction of his second Home Rule Bill in 1893 – and additional seating had to be provided, with chairs placed across the gangway. In the Press Gallery sat the Lord Chief Justice and the Archbishop of Canterbury, while Count Benckendorff, the Russian Ambassador, was present in the Diplomatic Gallery. As Grey rose to take his place at the dispatch box, there was a prolonged cheer from both sides of the house, and then the buzzing of voices ceased and there was a dead silence. 'His face was passionless and sharply cut like a bird's,' reported one witness of Grey's performance, which lasted for about an hour; 'his voice was clear, with no warm tones in it, his language was wholly unadorned, precise, simple, accurate, austerely dignified.'

'He had his papers in his hands,' wrote Edmund Gosse, another spectator who was scrutinizing Grey closely, 'but I could not tell how much he read and how much he spoke.' In fact, as Grey's parliamentary private secretary later testified, the speech had hardly been prepared at all. Asquith described it afterwards to Venetia Stanley as conversational in tone, '& with some of his usual ragged ends', but 'extraordinarily well reasoned & tactful & really *cogent*'. Gosse agreed that the speech was 'without clap-trap of any kind, and even without passion or emphasis'. At the start Grey seemed to be tentatively feeling his way. He outlined the historical background to the ties of friendship with France, dating from the military conversations that had taken place between the British and French general staffs since 1906, but stopped short of arguing that this entailed an obligation to act. Instead, Grey appealed to the individual conscience by urging that every man 'look into his heart, and his own feelings, and construe the extent of the obligation for himself'.

In a similar fashion, Grey dealt with the past assurances given to the French government that Britain would not stand aside if the Germans entered the English Channel and launched an attack against the undefended coasts of France. 'We could not stand aside,' he told the House, 'and see this going on practically within sight of our eyes, with our arms folded, looking on dispassionately, doing nothing. I believe that would be the feeling of this country.'

Turning to Belgium in the second half of the speech, Grey quoted Gladstone's words from 1870, saying that Britain had a right, rather than an obligation, under the terms of any treaty to defend that country's neutrality. He asked whether it was possible that 'this country . . . would quietly stand by and witness the perpetration of the direst crime that ever stained the pages of history, and thus become participators in the sin'.

'Our extreme peacemakers were for the moment reduced to silence,' Asquith wrote later. Indeed, many of the Liberals sitting behind the Foreign Secretary appeared to be in a state of sombre acquiescence, while such applause as Grey received came from the Conservative benches rather than from his own party. Bonar Law immediately rose to reiterate the Opposition's support. On behalf of the Irish Nationalists John Redmond – in Gosse's words, 'a born orator, with a voice of honey' – said that the government might withdraw its troops from Ireland with immediate effect, leaving the defence of Ireland from foreign invasion to the bands of Volunteers, Nationalist

Catholics and Protestant Ulstermen fighting side by side. Only Ramsay MacDonald, leader of the Labour Party, spoke on behalf of the not inconsiderable minority who still resisted war. He remained unconvinced either that the country was in danger, or that its honour was involved.

The Foreign Secretary's statement, concluded Christopher Addison, a Liberal MP and staunch critic of Grey's policy, had 'crushed out all hope of peace and of our being able to keep clear'. From the chamber, another Liberal, the Quaker Arnold Rowntree, scribbled a note to his wife that 'the country will be at war in, I fear, very few hours. Grey's speech has of course made a great effect but it really is a damning indictment of the Balance of Power – Grey's pet policy.'

To Beatrice Webb, expressing the more general estimate of Grey's essential trustworthiness, 'the public mind' had been 'cleared and solidified' by the speech. Kate, Lady Courtney of Penwith, Webb's elder sister and a prominent internationalist, correctly saw Grey's declaration about German violation of Belgian neutrality as 'the rock on which all the anti-war feeling [was] shipwrecked.' The issue of an unprovoked attack on defenceless Belgium by barbarous Germany had injected a new sense of moral purpose into Britain's involvement in the oncoming war, a development recognized by George V when he wrote in his diary on the evening of the 3rd that public opinion 'had been entirely changed' by Grey's speech, and that 'everyone is [now] for war and for helping our friends.' But it was their Belgian friends that most British people saw as needing their urgent assistance. At Salisbury Railway Station, for instance, at lunchtime the next day, there was 'much talk' among waiting travellers of Belgium, 'none of the needs of, nor of our obligation to, France'.

'Hands off Belgium – Violated Treaties' ran the headline in the *Daily Telegraph*. 'A straight lead at last', declared the *Morning Post* with undisguised relief, before observing that 'Substantially, England is now a united nation.' 'We are bound,' said the *Daily Mail* resolutely, 'as Sir Edward Grey stated, by pledges in the case of Belgium. We are going to stand by those pledges . . . Orders have been given to back Sir Edward Grey's words with deeds. The Navy is mobilized; the British Army is mobilizing.' The *Manchester Guardian* maintained its opposition to the war, referring to Grey's 'strange blunder'; but other papers that had hitherto opposed intervention underwent a sudden process of conversion, the *Birmingham Gazette*, one of the most significant of provincial papers, going so far as to praise Grey's 'frank and honest recital'.

Grey had returned from the Commons to the Foreign Office to help draft an ultimatum to Berlin, to expire at midnight (Central European Time; 11 p.m. Greenwich Mean Time) the next day, seeking an assurance that Belgian neutrality would be respected. Outside Parliament the arrival and departure of ministers was being greeted by what Asquith described as 'cheering crowds of loafers & holiday makers', while small boys ran around the precincts of Westminster waving flags. None the less, the Conservative evening paper the *Globe* emphasized the 'Quiet and orderly' nature of the crowd. 'Downing Street itself was kept clear by police – a duty easily managed by a handful of men, so correct was the behaviour of the crowd.' News of Germany's declaration of war against France had reached London that afternoon. The German invasion of Belgium would begin the next morning.

It was getting on for dusk, and Grey was visited by an unidentified friend, perhaps the journalist J. A. Spender. As the two men stood by the window of Grey's room, overlooking St James's Park, the lamplighter was turning up the gas lamps in the courtyard below. It was the occasion for Grey's only memorable and much-quoted remark, 'The lamps are going out all over Europe; we shall not see them lit again in our life-time.' There is the slight incongruity of Grey being prompted to produce a metaphor about lamps being extinguished by the sight of lamps being lit, as has sometimes been pointed out. But, just as poignantly, the image of lamps going out may also have been a conscious, or unconscious, reflection on Grey's part of his declining powers of sight. He was fast approaching his own personal descent into semi-darkness.

The Bank Holiday was extended, during Commons' business on the 3rd, for another three days, to Thursday, 6 August, in order to prevent a run on the banks. When the banks opened their doors again at the end of the week, the public would discover that, rather than receiving their money in gold, they were to be paid in the new legal tender of Treasury notes: £1 notes in black, and ten-shilling notes in red. 'The notes are small and very plain & clear [and] are printed on stamp paper with the watermark GR frequently repeated,' noted Ada Reece from West London, wife of a medical officer at the Local Government Board. This would be the first time that the state had issued paper money since the end of the seventeenth century.

Ada Reece was trying to cope with her mother-in-law's panic and distress about the banking crisis. 'The poor old Mater had been crying all night,' she wrote in her diary on 3 August, 'afraid she would lose her money.' Mrs Reece herself was facing a bit of financial embarrassment at home. With the banks closed until Friday, she was unable to cash her weekly housekeeping cheque, and was forced to borrow money from her cook.

Food prices had been on a steep rise since the weekend, and, following Grey's announcement, they rose more sharply still. 'Stocks are exhausted and [the] prices of the remainder are going up hourly,' Ada Reece recorded after an unsatisfactory morning's shopping on 4 August. She considered that 'a moderate buying was prudent, but one hears of such immoderate orders. And those of us who are calmer are forced to buy now before the greedy seize all.' The amount of business, in the opinion of one London shopkeeper, was 'unprecedented'.

On the afternoon of Tuesday, 4 August, Asquith, accompanied by his wife and daughter Elizabeth, drove to Parliament to make a statement to the Commons. The Prime Minister informed MPs that the German government had stated, through Prince Lichnowsky, their ambassador in London, that their reason for disregarding Belgian neutrality was to forestall a French attack across Belgium. 'We cannot regard this as in any sense a satisfactory communication,' Asquith commented, 'with dignity and composure', according to the Conservative *Daily Graphic*. He announced therefore that an ultimatum had been sent to Germany, due to expire at midnight.

'Those words,' Margot Asquith wrote in her diary, 'called forth a roll of cheers from every part of the House.' Afterwards she saw her husband briefly in his room. 'So it is all up?' she asked him. 'Yes, it is all up,' he replied. He had tears in his eyes. Later Asquith wrote to Venetia Stanley, still at her parents' home at Penrhos, telling her about the day's events, and that the House of Commons had taken the news 'very calmly'. Winston Churchill, 'who has got on all his war-paint, is longing for a sea-fight in the early hours of to-morrow morning . . . The whole thing fills me with sadness.'

As they had for days now, holiday crowds drifted around White-hall and Palace Yard, cheering the appearance of ministers, and making a spontaneous move towards Buckingham Palace as evening came. From the Commons on Monday the 3rd, the MP Arthur Ponsonby had made an initial reference to 'bands of half drunken youths waving flags', which he saw as signalling the beginning of 'war fever'. Beatrice Webb was struck by the mixture of elements in the crowds, 'hooligan warmongers and merely curious holiday-makers', though she also noted that there was 'no enthusiasm about the war', and that it was 'on the part of England, a passionless war'.

Other commentators emphasized an overall absence of fevered excitement among the London crowds, or suggested, like Webb, that for some of them the developments surrounding the war were simply another form of Bank Holiday diversion. There were large numbers of people on the capital's streets on 4 August, reported the *Cambridge Daily News*. However, they 'were not excited or demonstrative, but they were intensely interested'. The writer Irene Cooper Willis remembered no 'jubilation' outside the House of Commons or in front of Buckingham Palace. Instead she felt that 'there was more tension than excitement during the last two days of peace in London.' For her part, Ada Reece thought that West End visitors 'seemed unusually quiet', while the Earl of Crawford observed that 'London on the whole behaves well.' Kate Courtney heard people passing her house singing patriotic songs, but admitted that the crowds were 'not mafficking badly' and were 'on the whole serious'.

This state of affairs was mirrored in other parts of England on 4 August. In Newcastle-upon-Tyne, Reverend Mackay wrote that 'there were no great demonstrations of excitement. The people took things very calmly.' At Worthing, Mary Coules described the atmosphere as 'a queer, subdued flutter of excitement' rather than anything more overtly enthusiastic. At Oxford, where students' *viva voce* exams were interrupted by men removing furniture to allow the Examination Schools to be converted into a military hospital, the singing of 'Rule Britannia' could be heard as a distant refrain throughout the evening.

The mathematician R. W. M. Gibbs was standing on the pier at Bournemouth as the countdown to war expired. 'The band . . . played patriotic and martial airs. There was some cheering towards the end, but not nearly so much as one would have expected as the pier was packed with a Bank Holiday crowd. A gentleman who was with me and had recently returned from Colorado expressed surprise. He said "An American crowd would have gone crazy."'

At New Mill, a small village near Holmfirth, six miles outside Huddersfield, a solemn bell on the evening of the 4th summoned almost the entire adult population, 500 people, to bear witness to their convictions in support of peace. Although war now seemed inevitable, the villagers passed a resolution in favour of Britain's neutrality 'in the present crisis'. As the *Huddersfield Examiner* reported the next day, the villagers of Holmfirth had the satisfaction of knowing that, whatever the outcome, they had made their stand for peace.

In the streets surrounding Trafalgar Square and Westminster, as the decisive eleventh hour approached, men carrying placards with the words 'Why War?' were allowed to proceed without fear of being stopped. A taxi-driver who shouted 'Down with Germany' received no response, as the crowd was reportedly 'in no humour for demonstrations of this kind'. As the evening wore on, larger crowds assembled in front of the gates of Buckingham Palace. The Earl of Crawford stood there for an hour, between ten and eleven, and wrote of 'Twenty thousand people, calm, respectable, anxious: all there to see the King, and very hearty in the welcome they offered when he appeared (for the third time that night) at his windows.' Other sources offer widely varying, much lower estimates for the Buckingham Palace crowds, anywhere between 1,000 and 10,000, with the suggestion that they were heavily populated by young, middle-class men.

At the eleventh stroke of Big Ben, a swarm of people congregated around Downing Street and Parliament Square, spontaneously breaking into 'God Save the King'. They then rapidly dispersed in all directions, the more excited among them running along the streets shouting 'War! War! War!' For many ordinary people, the past few days had encompassed an extraordinary range of different emotions: depression, anxiety, fear, excitement, curiosity being chief among them. Now, like a cork bursting from a bottle, the tension was released after a week of uncertainty. Later that evening the Earl of Crawford watched 'the vulgar and ostentatious patriotism of a crowd which surged round Piccadilly Circus – waving flags – men sitting on the top of taxis, women too, all so excited as to be quite ridiculous'.

In the Cabinet Room at 10 Downing Street, Asquith and Grey had been among those waiting for the expiry of Britain's ultimatum to Germany. The most optimistic of Grey's words in his speech of the previous day had been largely overlooked by journalists. In them Grey had told the country that 'if we engaged in war, we shall suffer but little more than we shall suffer if we stand aside.' Asquith's private presentiments were both more prescient and full of foreboding when he told Venetia Stanley that 'We are on the eve of horrible things.'

The timing of the first Glastonbury Festival of 'Music, Dance and Mystic Drama', as it advertised itself, could hardly have been more unfortunate. The festival was the brainchild of the composer Rutland Boughton, and the intention had been to build a temple theatre for this annual event, including seating for 1,200, and to employ the Beecham Symphony Orchestra, on loan from its founder Sir Thomas Beecham.

Instead, the new Glastonbury Festival, in Somerset, opened on Wednesday, 5 August, the first day of Britain's war with Germany, to a heavy downpour of rain and diminished ambitions. Without a new theatre or large orchestra, Boughton had been forced to settle for the Glastonbury Assembly Rooms and a grand piano.

A last-minute change in the programme, however, seemed wholly appropriate. Rather than the promised scene from Wagner's *Parsifal*, a short choral work by the British composer Sir Charles Stanford, *The Last Post*, was substituted in acknowledgement of the overwhelming cataclysm of world events.

As the mournful trumpet echoed around the Assembly Rooms, set against the dramatic background of the Abbey ruins, where King Arthur is reputedly buried, it must have seemed like a melancholy valediction to the hope and optimism of a passing era, and recognition of England's emergence into a different world.

THREE

August to December

A Different World

The shock of the news of war reverberated around the country. '*We are in*,' the novelist John Galsworthy wrote in his diary, as he struggled with the nightmare of this 'appalling fact'. 'The horror of the thing keeps coming over one in waves; and all happiness has gone out of life.'

For some people, the rush of events was almost too great to take in. 'It is simply crushing, the suddenness & awfulness of it all,' commented David Robson from Malvern in Worcestershire; while to Elsie Stephens in Penryn, Cornwall, it seemed that 'Everything has come on us like a sudden thunderstorm.' An Essex resident, Mrs A. Purbrook of Hornchurch, summed up the widespread feeling of disbelief when she wrote that 'just a week ago I don't think that, in spite of the newspaper scares, any one of us, the uninitiated public, thought there would be war – and certainly they never really imagined that England would be in it. The final development has been most rapid.'

So rapid, in fact, that the declaration of war was responsible for a number of premature births. Dorothy Holman, who was considering offering her services as a nurse, visited her local hospital in Exeter on 5 August, the day after war was declared, only to be turned away because 'they were frightfully busy with the premature babies caused by the shock of war.' Several suicides of London financiers, already under pressure from the panic in the foreign markets and the closure of the Stock Exchange, were reported in the press during the first weeks of August. One of them, Victor Leveson, a forty-year-old stockbroker, was described as having been depressed by 'the terrible state of things'. He had drowned himself in his bath.

Because Britain's ultimatum to Germany had expired in the final hours of 4 August, most people only discovered that the country was at war on the 5th. On that morning, in Wellington, Somerset, the cook in Mary Lees's household rushed without knocking into the

Digging trenches at Folkestone, Kent, September 1914

dining-room, where her mistress was writing letters, and blurted out, 'Oh Ma'am, Oh Ma'am, War! War! War!' Beatrice McCann's postman bicycled uphill from Hungerford, eight miles from her village, to get the news to her. Mill-workers at Worsall, North Yorkshire, had their morning break extended so that they could read about Britain's war with Germany on the church notice board in the village. Much of the population heard the news from paperboys, who were rushing about in the early hours of 5 August, shouting 'War!' Irene Rankin, attending extension lectures at Cambridge University, recalled being unable to sleep that night because motor-bikes kept starting up outside her lodgings 'making a terrific noise'. The next morning she discovered that men from Pembroke College had gone to London by motorcycle in the hope of getting into the army as dispatch riders.

For many holidaymakers, the news brought an abrupt change to their plans. Lucian Hunt and her three brothers were in Broadstairs with their mother when war was declared. Their father immediately sent a telegram 'telling us to come home by the next train as all the trains to the coast would be requisitioned for troop transport, and we might not be able to get home for some time'. A. D. Gardner, a medical student cruising the Norfolk Broads with friends in a small cabined sailing boat, remembered being both 'excited and upset by the news, because although it had been a possibility for some time, we had been glad to believe it wouldn't really happen'. He cut short his holiday immediately, unlike William Johnson, who returned to London on 8 August, after a short time away at Saltfleetby, near Grimsby, completely ignorant of recent developments in world events.

'We are living in a different world!' the Surrey businessman F. A. Robinson exclaimed in the opening entry of his diary, started specifically for the purpose of recording the war. The most immediate manifestations of this new order of things were the emergency powers assumed by the state. Already, in the first days of August, a series of royal proclamations had anticipated the declaration of war by banning the use of wireless telegraphy by merchant ships in Britain's territorial waters; prohibiting the flying of aircraft over the British Isles and the export of specified warlike materials; and authorizing the control of the railways by the government. On 8 August the Defence of the Realm Act became law. At not much longer than a paragraph, the new Act attempted to prevent the passing of information to the enemy, while ensuring the security of the country's transportation system. The acronym DORA summoned up a mental picture of a crabby and pinched maiden aunt, malicious and interfering, and it didn't take long for the legislation to be caricatured and lampooned as such. At the end of November, the Act was expanded to outline a wider range of possible wartime offences, further extending the power of the state over the lives of ordinary Englishmen. In time, DORA would assume control in matters as diverse as a citizen's right to fell a tree, keep homing pigeons, buy a drink for a friend, whistle for a cab or consort with a prostitute.

'Every train that steams out of London, every cart in the street, is assumed to be commandeered by the government for the purposes of war,' Beatrice Webb observed on 5 August. Ada Reece, the London housewife – whose doctor husband was about to receive his call-up papers, ordering him to Territorial camp on Hounslow Heath – had recorded 'the glorious news' of war in her diary, qualifying her enthusiasm with the admission that 'we undertake hostilities very gravely and reluctantly.' On 6 August she went for a walk in gusty rain from Queen's Road to Marble Arch, delighting in the novelty of seeing 'many Khaki uniforms about', but also bemoaning the shortage of buses: 'they say 400 chassis have been requisitioned by the government.'

It was announced that the railway passenger system had returned to normal within four days of the outbreak of war, though inevitably the ongoing mobilization of Regulars and Territorials that month caused disruption to services, especially to the south of London. During the first twenty-four hours of embarkation, trains were arriving at Southampton Dock every ten minutes. In spite of this, the needs of August holidaymakers weren't overlooked. On 22 August, on the day when the British Expeditionary Force was facing its first major action – followed by its 'great retreat' to the River Marne – an additional excursion train, the 8.15 a.m. from Victoria to Brighton, none the less managed to be scheduled.

Railway stations provided the most visible, and often poignant, manifestations of the war in its early days. 'There is no cheering, no great ovations, no wild enthusiasm,' the Reverend James Mackay wrote of the departure of soldiers leaving immediately for France from Newcastle-upon-Tyne Station on 6 August, 'just a great stricken mass of humanity, broken hearted as a mother who has lost her only child.' The same day, a reporter from the *Eastern Daily News* watched a group of Territorials leaving Norwich with a spring in their step. The men 'sang their favourite melodies with vigour and shook hands cordially with friends who came to have a last word with them . . . Girls rushed forward with merry laughter just to tap their military friends on the back and receive a warm glance of recognition as a reward.' Troops setting off from Bury were given a farewell from a concertina band, playing 'Scotch Airs' and 'Tipperary'. Only as the train pulled out of the station did the mood of the music turn sombre. The band struck up 'Auld Lang Syne' and continued playing until the last carriage disappeared around the bend towards Manchester.

D. H. Lawrence's impressions of departing Reservists, which appeared in the *Manchester Guardian* on 18 August, were less roseate:

They were young men, some of them drunk. There was one bawling and brawling before the ticket window; there were two swaying on the steps of the subway shouting, and ending, 'Let's go an' have another afore we go.' There were a few women seeing off their sweethearts and brothers, but, on the whole, the reservist had been a lodger in the town and had only his own pals. One woman stood before the carriage window. She and her sweetheart were being very matter-of-fact, cheerful and bumptious over the parting.

'Well, so long!' she cried as the train began to move. 'When you see 'em let 'em have it.'

'Ay, no fear,' shouted the man, and the train was gone, the man grinning.

On mobilization, the British Army possessed just eighty motor vehicles and 25,000 horses. A magistrate sat early on the first day of the war, hurriedly signing warrants to authorize the seizure of vans, cars and horses. Broad Walk in Kensington Gardens was lined with cars waiting for government inspection. To Beatrice Trefusis on 5 August, 'The first visible sign of anything unusual' was 'the appearance of a few yeomanry men who have come here & are buying all the available horses in the neighbourhood . . . & rushing off with them'. Horses were essential for transportation, reconnaissance and raiding parties, and within twelve days the army had successfully impressed 165,000 of them. The great haulage companies, larger department stores and municipalities were among the major suppliers of horses, but the railway companies secured exemption of their animals from compulsory purchase on the grounds that they would be of greater assistance to the war effort in conveying soldiers and their equipment to railway stations. Farmers, forced to do without their finest animals, relied on breeding mares for work in the fields – thereby reducing the numbers and quality of the next generation of animals – and experimented increasingly with the use of motor-tractors.

The War Office's price guidelines for the purchase of horses indicated that £70 was an appropriate price for an officer's charger, but in a number of cases of an 'extravagant nature' more than double that sum was paid. An average working-horse could go for as little as £35, which is what William Pead of Lichfield received for each of his brewery horses, requisitioned by the West Yorkshire Regiment. 'Poor brutes, their lives will probably be short,' he commented after watching them being led away, a sentiment echoed by Hallie Eustace Miles, who witnessed 'a sad procession' of horses being marched through the streets of Looe in Cornwall, and thought to herself that 'even they have to take their share!'

In the village of Manaton, on Dartmoor, John Galsworthy came close to losing his favourite horse, Peggy, only to retain her when the army declared the horse unfit to serve. A Wigan schoolgirl, Freda Hewlett, was so distraught that her pony Betty might be seized, after losing two other beloved horses to the army, that she wrote directly to Lord Kitchener, newly appointed at the War Office, begging him to spare Betty. 'It would break our hearts to let her go,' she wrote on 11 August. 'We have given 2 others & 3 of our own family are now fighting for you in the Navy.' She signed herself on behalf of her family, 'your troubled little Britishers'. Happily, the War Office bureaucrats were touched by the letter, and Betty won her exemption.

Defences being urgently erected around the country against possible invasion were also bringing home to people the reality of the new situation. On 8 August, Will Eaves, from Plymouth in Devon, was astonished to find that 'trenches are being dug all along the coastlines ... and this evening I was confronted by a barbed wire entanglement and a redoubt of sandbags.' Gladys Cruickshank saw trenches being dug in the dunes at Newhaven and thought that 'They looked so curious in the bare and smooth downs.'

The lights of London were lowered for the first time five weeks into the war, on 11 September, and subsequently in other big cities, as protection against the risk of enemy air attacks. The peals of Big Ben were silenced the following month. John Burns, the outgoing Local Government minister, who had resigned from the cabinet after it became clear that Britain was going to support France, saw the 'shrinking gloom' as indicating 'for the first time in a darksome way that Britain is at war'. In a letter from London to his brother stationed with the East Lancashire Regiment, W. W. Collins wrote that 'no high electric standards are lit & very few lamps; every light is obscured as far as possible.' *The Times* journalist Michael MacDonagh found it impossible to read a newspaper as he travelled home on the Clapham tram from Westminster. The light was dim and 'The car was specially fitted with blinds, and before we crossed Westminster Bridge these were drawn by the conductor for the purpose . . . of disguising the course of the river from hostile airmen, should they attempt a raid on London.' Hallie Eustace Miles and her husband started refusing all evening engagements, as 'it is ever so weird at night, and so danger-ous too'. By contrast, Ada Reece found the experience of a hair-raising drive along darkened streets 'quite exciting' (at the end of the year, all London vehicles were obliged to carry a rear red light to prevent accidents).

H. G. Wells poured scorn on the new lighting regulations. 'I admit the risk of a few aeroplane bombs in London,' he wrote to *The Times* in October, 'but I do not see why people should be subjected to dan-ger, darkness, and inconvenience on account of that one-in-a-million risk' (later in the war, a cartoon in the London journal *The Passing Show* poked fun at the enforced darkness by depicting a soldier with multiple wounds, 'injured not on the Somme, or in the Salonika but in the Strand').

London at night may have been shrouded in darkness, but in the daytime, in common with other parts of England, it was basking in warmer temperatures following the week of heavy rain and claps of thunder that had heralded the coming of war. An Indian Summer was in prospect, as dry, sunny days lingered on into the autumn months. John Galsworthy eulogized this late summer's 'singular beauty': 'The perfect weather, the glowing countryside . . . the quiet nights trembling with moonlight and shadow and, in it all, this great horror launched and growing'.

Robert Bridges, the poet laureate, observed similarly, on 27 August, that 'I have never in my life known so beautiful an autumn, nor so prolific a general harvest.' He found it 'strange' that the remarkable weather should coincide with the solar eclipse that had occurred sev-eral days earlier, and came close to suggesting that there was some mysterious portent in the coincidence of the eclipse and the death of Pope Pius X on 20 August.

The writer Katherine Mansfield sent a friend, back in her native New Zealand, a snapshot of London in the first weeks 'of this frightful war':

> There are camps of soldiers in the parks and squares, in the streets there is always the sound and sight of soldiers marching by. The big white trains painted with the red cross, swing into the railway stations carrying their sad burdens and often at the same time other trains leave with boys in khaki, cheering and singing on their way to the front. At night London . . . is darkened, and huge searchlights sweep the sky and the hundreds of . . . newspaper boys run up and down the streets like little black crows . . .

The raising of a volunteer army – voluntary because of deeply ingrained British hostility to the idea of conscription – provoked massive change and upheaval in the lives of thousands of English families in the war's early months. In August 1914 Britain did not possess an army capable of fighting a major Continental war. Indeed, given that the larger proportion of defence spending had been concentrated on the navy, many people at the outset confidently awaited news of a decisive British naval victory.

In reality, five divisions of the small professional army, the British Expeditionary Force, were dispatched to France and concentrated near Maubeuge, to help stem the German attack, while Lord Kitchener, the hero of Omdurman, who was appointed Secretary of State for War on 5 August, set about organizing the recruitment and training of a mass citizen army.

Asquith had immediately taken the decision to give up the War Office, a position he'd held in conjunction with the premiership since the Curragh crisis, and, as he informed Venetia Stanley, 'install Kitchener there as an emergency man, until the War comes to an end'. This was generally a popular decision, especially in the press and with the public, though placing a somewhat dictatorial Field Marshal in the cabinet was a bit like allowing a bull into a china shop. For his part Kitchener asked God to preserve him from politicians.

'There is no doubt that Lord K. has already found his place as national mascot,' Edmund Gosse wrote within weeks of Kitchener's appointment. On 6 August, Parliament authorized an increase in the army of half a million men. The next day, the first recruiting appeal appeared – 'YOUR KING AND COUNTRY NEED YOU' – printed in the national colours, red, white and blue, and calling for an addition of 100,000 men, aged between nineteen and thirty. A call for a further 100,000 was made three weeks later, when the age limit was raised to thirty-five and a special appeal was addressed to married men. On 5 September, the famous image of Kitchener with level-eyed frown and pointing finger, by Alfred Leete, a graphic artist and prolific designer of posters for, among others, Rowntree's, Guinness and Bovril, made its first appearance on the cover of the weekly *London Opinion*, and was displayed on hoardings throughout that autumn. To Margot Asquith, the Secretary for War made 'a great poster'. However, Leete's design was not initially part of the official campaign, unlike posters issued by the Parliamentary Recruiting Committee, and its immediate effect may consequently have been limited.

There was a rush to the colours in these first few weeks, as was only to be expected. Between 4 and 8 August, 8,193 men enlisted. Passing the recruiting headquarters in Great Scotland Yard, off Whitehall, Michael MacDonagh observed 'a big throng of young men still in straw hats, waiting their turn to get in and . . . "take the King's shilling"'. On 7 August, the crowd of applicants was so large that mounted police had to restrain them, and the gates were opened to admit only six at a time. 'There was no cheering and little excitement,' *The Times* noted, 'but there was an undercurrent of enthusiasm, and the disappointment of those who failed to pass one or other of the tests was obvious.'

However, the response to Kitchener's appeal from London far outweighed that of the provinces: for example, the 1,100 recruits enlisted in London on 9 August represented roughly 40 per cent of the national total for the day. Furthermore, the system of army bureaucracy was failing to keep pace with the needs of the campaign, with an inadequate number of recruiting stations simply unable to cope with the flow of volunteers. On 24 August, enlistment fell dramatically. It would pick up again before the end of the month, but the true surge of patriotic enthusiasm would have to wait until the first ten days of September.

'England is already a different place than it has been for years past,' Frederick Oliver, managing director of the firm of Debenham & Freebody, wrote to his brother in Canada when the war was barely a month old. 'I had not conceived it possible that a nation could be born again so quickly. This war even now has undone the evils of a generation.'

The suffragettes, for so long a thorn in the side of the Asquith government, and increasingly a danger to themselves and the general public, laid down their hatchets, home-made bombs and other weapons, and declared a truce in their campaign for the vote. From the headquarters of the Women's Social and Political Union, a message was sent out to its membership, instructing them to bring a halt to all militant activities until the crisis was over. The National Union of Women's Suffrage Societies, representing the constitutionalists, travelled along a more difficult path to patriotism. As hopes of peace faded on 4 August, 2,000 of its members had taken part in a protest against war at the Kingsway Hall in London. They would soon be immersed in an internal debate about the extent to which they should support the war effort.

For Emmeline and Christabel Pankhurst, the transition was much smoother. On 10 August, Home Secretary McKenna responded to the announcement of their truce by agreeing to an amnesty: all suffragette prisoners were to be released unconditionally. 'With that patriotism which has nerved women to endure endless torture in prison cells, we ardently desire that our country shall be victorious,' Mrs Pankhurst told readers of the WSPU newspaper, *Votes for Women*. On her first reappearance on a public platform, at the London Opera House on 8 September, she neglected to mention the subject of votes for women, choosing instead to focus with admirable foresight on a new cause, the idea of food rationing for wartime Britain.

To Mrs Pankhurst's more fanatical shock troops, like Mary Richardson, slasher of the *Rokeby Venus*, this came as a serious disappointment. Richardson could hardly believe that the campaign had been abruptly terminated without the securing of the vote, though, true to form, she would later place herself right at the centre of its final phase. In her autobiography, Richardson portrayed herself as the last suffragette to be released from Holloway. In fact, when war broke out, Mary Richardson was already far from prison, recovering from acute appendicitis and about to be sent on a prolonged convalescence to Madeira. The doctor treating Richardson recorded one of the signs of the suffering she had endured in her struggle to win the vote: the deep and painful scars inside her mouth, inflicted by the fingernails of prison officials in the process of forcing food down her throat.

Another aspect of the country's internal dissension instantly became less threatening. As soon as war was declared, trade union leaders called 'an industrial truce'. Strike action was immediately reduced. Less than 6 per cent of the 451,000 strikers in Britain for the year were involved in action between August and December 1914; and from the autumn to the end of the year, only 161,437 working days were lost to strikes, 1.6 per cent of the 1914 total. Opposition to the war itself all but evaporated, as the socialist and Labour leaderships reversed their pre-war positions and promised support. Speakers for 'Stop the War' campaigns found themselves shouted down and facing violent obstruction from hostile audiences.

A new source of unrest, however, had quickly raised its head. The panic-buying and hoarding of food, which had commenced in late July, continued unabated into mid August with renewed intensity. In communities across England, mass buying, together with the constant variation in prices – the price of flour and butter in some areas changed as much as three times a day – provoked tension and ill-feeling. On 5 August a Kensington woman recorded in her diary that 'The well-to-do-people in London have, in quantities, lost their heads. They are buying enormous stores of food, as if for siege provisions . . . Among the very poor there is indignation at rich people laying in . . . stores, and they say burglars, and people who may starve later, are marking the houses where it is done, in order to raid them later on.'

A day earlier, Miss G. West, from Selsey in Gloucestershire, had reprimanded her neighbours, who had already lectured her on the evils of hoarding, for their hypocrisy, when she found them stocking up on vast quantities of meat and margarine. With the cost of a four-pound loaf soaring from 5½*d.* to 8*d.*, a scale of maximum retail prices was drawn up, but never properly put into effect. In these circumstances, the food reformer Eustace Miles (husband of the diarist Hallie Miles) patronized the poor by lecturing them on the need to masticate their food more thoroughly, lessening the bulk required, and on the practice of 'gentle but deep and full breathing'.

The anxiety caused by hoarding led to eruptions of violence. There was a food riot in Bermondsey in East London on 7 August, with the arrest of twenty women; another one the following day at Hitchin, in Hertfordshire, when police used batons to disperse the crowd. At Long Sutton, in Lincolnshire, customers threatened to raid local bakers for raising the price of loaves to 7*d.* Their threats succeeded in forcing the price back down to 5*d.* In Cambridge, panic about hoarding led to a rush, not only on food but also on revolvers and other weapons. There were fears that these might be used to fire on starving crowds intent on seizing provisions.

Happily, as the food panic subsided in the second half of August, so too did the risk from these more extreme scenarios. 'Business as Usual' was the face which Britain was presenting to the outside world. This slogan was introduced by big shopkeepers like Harrods of Knightsbridge, anxious about the likelihood of economic turmoil in the first days of war. It was quickly adopted by other traders and advertisers, and popularized in turn by pronouncements from members of the government such as Winston Churchill. The self-confidence of the phrase, though, disguised a mixed bag of fortunes. Trade and employment would suffer heavily for much of the rest of 1914 (the slump in employment, of course, boosting recruitment to Kitchener's Army). The East Coast fishing industry, Yorkshire's woollen industry, Lancashire's cotton trade, and Cornwall's china clay, tin mining and fishing industries were among the hardest hit. But, as the war progressed, some trades found themselves able to adapt to the new conditions, especially when, like the woollen industry, their goods were in enormous demand from the army. In Huddersfield, for example, factory workers were called in from late September to work overtime, even on Sundays, to produce the khaki cloth urgently required for the new recruits. By November, they would be turning out 250 miles of khaki cloth every week.

The demand for war news, hardly surprisingly, was insatiable. But as William Pead observed from Lichfield in early August, 'Everyone is eager to buy papers in which we find little war news and what there is is mostly unreliable.' Four days into the war, Pead noted that the 'usual foolish rumours were rife' of 'great Naval victories and a German invasion of Scotland'.

The press naturally played a vital role in publishing such unsubstantiated rumours, but hearsay spread by word of mouth, and embellished with each subsequent retelling, had a habit of sending them soaring into realms of fantasy. The appetite for news of German spies and espionage was an obvious illustration of this, fed by the pre-war spy fever stirred up by the stories of the writer William Le Queux. A suspicious accent, strange appearance or unusual set of actions could immediately implicate anyone unfamiliar to the community. On 4 August it was reported that a German spy, Herbert Jan Krewitz, had been captured at the Humber estuary seaport of Grimsby. The arrest of Krewitz, who was caught reading a German book while resting on a country walk, caused enormous excitement, though he was quickly identified as a Russian and set free. In Alresford, Essex, two women followed someone they believed to be a stranger and slashed the tyres of his bicycle. This alleged 'spy' was later revealed to be the local coastguard. Such incidents had their comical element, but there were occasions when spy-catching had a tragic outcome. At the army town of Aldershot in Hampshire, in late August, J. E. Carroll, a deaf and near-sighted man, was shot and killed by sentries – presumably because he failed to respond to their call of 'halt' – as he took a well-known local walk close to a railway line.

The most famous rumour of these early months of war – perhaps, from the British point of view, of the entire conflict – was that thousands of Russian soldiers had passed through Britain on their way to the Western Front. 'Everybody had a friend whose aunt's butler had seen them,' wrote Winifred Towers, to whom the thought of the Russians did much to cheer the wartime gloom. 'They were reported from every part of the country; many of the stories were vague & far fetched & some were very amusing, as the one of the old lady who was sure that Russians had gone through Willesden because she had heard them stamping the snow off their boots on the platform, but many were really authenticated & first hand, some even semi-official.' A 'very decided' denial of the story was issued by the Press Bureau, but this did nothing to break the hold of this most popular of wartime rumours over vast swathes of the population.

The lack of firm news created a sense of foreboding in ordinary citizens like William Pead, the Lichfield brewer. As the first wave of panic and emergency began to subside in this state of 'phoney war', Pead noted in his diary that 'There is a general feeling of the need to brace oneself to meet danger.'

In the first minutes of 5 August, not long after the expiry of Britain's ultimatum to Germany, Rebecca West gave birth to a son, Anthony, at 'a raw-boned house' perched on a cliff facing the Wash. As West's child hadn't been due until September, one might almost believe that Anthony's premature birth was a result of the shock surrounding the declaration of war. When the mists of chloroform cleared, West looked at her squealing son, 'not with the passive contentment of the mother in peace-time, but with the active and passionate intention: "I must keep this thing safe."'

At twenty-one, Rebecca West already possessed a budding reputation as a promising writer and fearless controversialist. She had made a name for herself partly through her outspoken attacks on convention. Unfortunately, the throwing over of convention in her own life had led to six months' isolation in furnished lodgings in a Norfolk seaside town, posing as 'Mrs West' while she waited for her illegitimate baby to be born. Anthony's father, H. G. Wells, was a hundred miles away at the time of his son's delivery, at his family home at Easton Glebe in the Essex countryside, where he lived with his wife

Amy Catherine, or Jane, as he called her, and their two sons. Wells had met Rebecca in 1912, after she had attacked his notion of the emancipated woman in a sarcastic review of his novel *Marriage*. He at once fell in love with her wit, intelligence and liquid brown eyes, she with his exuberance, energy, avuncular protectiveness – and fame. In time-honoured fashion, Wells was a middle-aged man conquering his fear of ageing through an affair with a much younger woman. Rebecca was exciting, 'a physical necessity', even. The trouble was that he still needed Jane to provide the balance of his existence. 'He hadn't thought the affair out,' Wells acknowledged in the thinly dis-guised autobiography of *Mr Britling Sees It Through*, his bestselling novel of the war years. 'And it kept on developing in just the ways that he would rather that it didn't.'

Wells pronounced himself 'radiant' at the news of his son's arrival. 'I keep on thinking of your dear dear, dear grave sweet belovèd face on your pillow and you and it,' he wrote to Rebecca. He visited them every few days on complicated cross-country rail journeys, and wrote regular letters. But his mind found a welcome relief from these pri-vate tensions in the enormity of the national catastrophe. 'Nothing to say very much but war, war, war,' he wrote hurriedly to Rebecca a few days after the birth.

To Wells the outbreak of the conflict was 'like the shock of an unsuspected big gun fired suddenly within a hundred yards'. He had often played with the idea of war in his imagination, and it had formed the basis of many of his books. Yet at heart he had never believed that a great European war would really happen. His feelings of nervous apprehension had been evident at a holiday fête and flower show, at Easton, on the afternoon of 4 August, when he got into a heated discussion with George Bernard Shaw. Shaw 'said that it served us right. We could have seen it coming if we hadn't been blackmailed by Edward Carson over Ulster.' 'Never mind about that now,' Wells riposted, in the high-pitched voice that he was unable to control whenever he was excited.

At home that evening, Wells started work on an article that would crystallize his ideas about the purpose of the conflict and what he hoped its outcome would be. As he worked into the night – sparing a thought perhaps for Rebecca and her as yet unborn child – he began to see the coming of war as opening the way 'to disarmament and peace throughout the earth'. The forces controlling Germany – Prussian militarism as sharply distinguished from the German people – had to be crushed. But this would only be the prelude to a new world order, which would abolish the nation state and introduce a peace settlement guaranteed by all the world powers: the first step towards the World Republic that Wells had originally espoused in his novel *The World Set Free*, published earlier in the year.

'Never has any state in the world so clamoured for punishment,' Wells raged in a spate of belligerent rhetoric. 'Every sword that is drawn against Germany now is a sword drawn for peace . . . By means of a propaganda of books, newspaper articles, leaflets . . . we have to spread this idea, and *impose upon this war* the idea that this war must end war.'

The article appeared in the *Daily News* on 14 August, and became the first piece in Wells's collection published a month later under the title *The War That Will End War*. Like his *alter ego* Mr Britling, Wells 'could no more help having ideas about everything than a dog can resist smelling at your heels'. More than anything, he worried about being irrelevant to current events, in the role of spectator rather than participant. It was in order to combat this fear that he threw himself into producing as many 'shrill jets of journalism' as his considerable energy could manage. This initial collection of wartime writings attacked food hoarding, a practice he attributed to 'the vehement selfishness of vulgar-minded prosperous people and to the base cunning of quite exceptional merchants'; called for the involvement of the United States in the war; and for an end to 'Kruppism', the private manufacture of arms. It also envisioned an eventual peace conference to provide a new map of Europe.

The phrase 'The War That Will End War' was eagerly embraced by people searching for an idealistic explanation for the conflict and passed rapidly into circulation. Wells may have been its author, but the gist of the slogan had been encapsulated in the poem 'Casus Belli' by Harold Begbie, published in the *Daily Chronicle* a week before Wells's original article appeared. 'War, for the end of War' was the first line of Begbie's quatrain. 'Why do our cannon roar?' it goes on to ask. 'For a thousand years of Peace', comes the answer. By October, Wells's phrase was well known enough to be mocked, as well as scorned, by the socialist and pacifist journalist T. W. Mercer, in his poem 'The Climax'.

> But, lo! a wonder passing all, –
> Wells preaches War for peace!

The world of entertainment was doing its bit for the war effort. At theatres and music halls, programmes began with the National Anthem, though spontaneous bursts of 'Rule Britannia' from the audience tended to distract and disconcert the actors and variety artistes, catching them unawares. The singing of the 'Marseillaise' usually brought the entire auditorium to its feet, while the Russian National Anthem was generally less warmly received because of ambivalence towards the oppressive Tsarist regime. In September, the War Office wrote to the managers of the major variety theatres, asking them to add songs like 'Fall In!' to their repertoire, 'with a view to encourage enlistment'. 'Recruiting plays' like *England Expects* (London Opera House) – with Phyllis Dare singing 'We don't want to lose you but think you ought to go' – *John Shannon Reservist* (Empire Theatre, Shoreditch), *Your Country Needs You* (Tivoli Theatre, Manchester) and *The Hem of the Flag* (Hippodrome Theatre, Woolwich) were soon an established part of the bill.

At cinemas, the pictures thrown up on the screen of Lord Kitchener and Sir John French, commander of the British Expeditionary Force, were 'so loyal, and thrilling and realistic', wrote Hallie Eustace Miles, that the audience 'nearly burst with enthusiasm and excitement'. In one startling innovation at Southampton, Messrs Bacon and Hood, proprietors of the Palladium, a Stockport cinema, rented premises in the high street and set up a 'cinema rifle range'. Images of German soldiers were projected on to a reversible screen and the public were 'invited to get their own in' against the enemy.

The final performance at His Majesty's Theatre of Shaw's *Pygmalion* had taken place in the last week of July, after a run of 118 performances.

It could easily have gone on for longer, but Beerbohm Tree, who had never felt comfortable in the role of Higgins, was bored and wanted to go on holiday. This left Mrs Patrick Campbell, who was taking the production to New York, to remonstrate in vain that 'It is quite absurd that the notice [of closure] should go up at the end of a £2,000 week!' Tree returned to his theatre in August with 'a play of moving spectacle and stirring patriotism', a revival of Louis N. Parker's *Drake*. The topical relevance of 'The Father of the Fleet', as the play referred to Drake, singeing the King of Spain's beard and defeating the Armada after a nonchalant game of bowls, would not be lost on contemporaries. For once, Tree decided not to take a leading part. Instead he observed the workings of the special effects, including a stately Spanish galleon at full sail, from the front stalls. At the end of 1914, His Majesty's would mount a large-scale adaptation of *David Copperfield*, with a nostalgic ideal of England represented by a huge painted backdrop of Canterbury Cathedral, and Tree in the kind of scene-stealing dual role he relished, doubling as Dan'l Peggotty and Micawber.

The response to the war in London's major concert halls was much less clear-cut. For example, the Queen's Hall Promenade concerts, conducted by Sir Henry Wood, planned to open their 1914 season on 15 August, with a programme that included Richard Strauss's *Don Juan*. On the day, however, Tchaikovsky's orchestral fantasy *Capriccio Italien* was substituted instead. The following week, the traditional evening of Wagner was replaced by Franco-Russian music.

Modernist music like Strauss's wasn't to everyone's taste and – so the argument ran – his exclusion could be dismissed as a special case. But would more traditional Germanic repertoire like Bach, Beethoven and Brahms face a similar ban? And was it possible, in this climate of opinion, for Handel and Mozart still to be represented at the Proms? Proms officials toyed with the idea of limiting the ban to all German music written since Germany's unification in 1870. Then, just before the end of August, a note was inserted into the concert programme 'emphatically contradicting statements that German music will be boycotted during the present season' and asserting that 'The greatest examples of Music and Art are world possessions and unassailable even by the prejudices and passions of the hour.' Strauss was reinstated; and, in the weeks that followed, the Queen's Hall echoed with the music of Bach, Mozart, Beethoven, Mendelssohn and Liszt.

Shaw, in high glee at this defeat for cultural chauvinism, recounted the episode for the benefit of his German translator:

> In London . . . the usual series of nightly cheap orchestral concerts called Promenade Concerts announced patriotically that no German music would be performed. Everyone applauded the announcement. But nobody went to the concerts. Within a week a programme full of Beethoven, Wagner and Strauss was announced. Everybody was shocked; and everybody went to the concert. It was a complete and decisive German victory, with nobody killed.

At Wellington House in London, on a warm, early September afternoon, a group of eminent writers sat round a table covered in a blue cloth and lit by bright yellow sunshine. They were there at the invitation of C. F. G. Masterman, Chancellor of the Duchy of Lancaster and head of a new propaganda department, to discuss the drafting of a manifesto in support of British involvement in the war.

Not one of the twenty-five writers present was a woman (an invitation might conceivably have been extended to that formidable lobbyist and opponent of women's suffrage, Mrs Humphry Ward, but her signature, with those of three other women, found its way on to the 'Authors Declaration' in support of the Allies, published in *The Times* on 18 September). All were over forty years old, many of them by at least two or three decades. Nevertheless, their enlistment was testimony to a belief in the primacy of the written word in the task of counteracting the effects of German propaganda, and of convincing neutral countries, in particular the United States, of the righteousness of Britain's cause.

The Wellington House roll-call includes forgotten, as well as some unjustly neglected writers, in addition to many whose names still mean something to us today. Wells and Hardy were there, and so, too, were Galsworthy, Conan Doyle, Barrie, Masefield and Chesterton.

Notable absentees were Rudyard Kipling and Shaw. Kipling was initially excluded, at Sir Edward Grey's insistence, because of his high Tory politics and connections with American Republicans. There was no place at the table either for Shaw. He had made clear from the outset his conviction that 'we are sacrificing ourselves to an insane cause.' Three months into the war, he advised English and German soldiers to shoot their officers and go home. His pamphlet *Common Sense about the War* – 'the more thoroughly we realize that war is war, and death death, the sooner we shall get rid of it' – appeared in November and sold more than 75,000 copies before the end of the year. But it made Shaw an international pariah.

Surveying his fellow writers at Wellington House that September afternoon, the novelist Arnold Bennett noted afterwards that 'The sense was talked by Wells and Chesterton' and, rather more noncommittally, that Thomas Hardy 'was all right'. Later in the year, Chesterton would publish *The Barbarism of Berlin*, arguing that England was fighting for 'the long arm of honour'. Hardy, full of sorrowful misgivings about the war, went home from the meeting and composed his 'Song of Soldiers' ('Men Who March Away'), displaying public confidence that 'Victory crowns the just.' As for the intensely pro-French and pro-Belgian Bennett, he soon proved to be Masterman's most prolific propagandist, speedily producing *Liberty: A Statement of the British Case*, and rivalling Wells with countless newspaper articles on the subject of the war. A photograph of Bennett's face, with its dyspeptic expression, on the side of London buses, advertising his latest article or column, became a familiar sight.

The published manifesto, signed by fifty-two writers, declared it to be Britain's 'destiny and duty . . . to uphold the rule of common justice between civilized peoples, to defend the rights of small nations, and to maintain the free and law-abiding ideals of Western Europe against the rule of "Blood and Iron" and the domination of the whole Continent by a military caste'.

The defence of the rights of small nations, specifically Belgium, struck the strongest chord around the country. Germany's invasion of Belgium had given Britain's entry into the war an overriding sense of moral purpose. '[W]e had to stand by Belgium,' Beatrice Webb conceded privately, concluding that 'If this little race had not been attacked', the war would not only have been 'positively unpopular', it 'could hardly have taken place'.

Individual attitudes continued to evolve. In many people's eyes the war was now nothing less than a battle to crush German barbarism and for the defence of civilization itself. The war that would end war was also seen in some quarters as an opportunity for the country's moral and spiritual regeneration. On 5 August, Beatrice Trefusis had only been able to think of the war's 'horribleness and ghastliness', commenting on 'How barbarous the world still is! & . . . How little removed from the primitive, even in this 20th century.' Five weeks later, she recorded in her diary that 'my feelings have changed . . . The horrors & suffering, thoughts of which obsessed me so much at first, seem now small in comparison with the tremendous power for good to the whole Empire. It is a fine thought – this whole Empire rising as one man to fight, not so much for material things, but for honour & spiritual progress – against a doctrine of militarism & military force.'

'Honour' had become England's watchword for 1914. It would be enshrined by Rupert Brooke, after he'd witnessed the fall of Antwerp and the city's surrender to the Germans in early October, on service as an officer in the Royal Naval Division. The third of Brooke's *1914* sonnets would express his belief that 'Honour has come back, as a king, to earth.' The word seemed to pepper both private and public pronouncements. 'I'm glad England has gone into the war,' Lionel Gibbs wrote to the Reverend George Bell, his old Oxford tutor, in mid August. 'She could not have kept out of it and kept her honour.' At a service of intercession at Canterbury Cathedral on 21 August, the Archbishop of Canterbury, Randall Davidson, told the congregation that 'Our conscience as a Nation State and people is, as regards the war, wholly clear. We might, I suppose, *for a time*, have stayed out of it. But it would have been at the loss of England's honour, England's chivalry to weaker people's plighted word.' Until the Allied armies had 'utterly crushed the Germans', the wife of Major D. G. Johnson told her husband in a letter in September, 'there can be no Peace with Honour.'

'Gallant' or 'Plucky Little' Belgium came further to the fore in the last week of August, as reports began to reach England of atrocities committed against Belgian civilians by the German Army, which was by now occupying nine tenths of the country. Additionally, on 29 August, shocking photographs of the fourteenth-century Belgian city of Louvain after its sacking by the Germans appeared in the British press: the smouldering, devastated wreck of historic buildings, together with the destruction of the University Library, a wanton case of cultural vandalism, with the loss of 250,000 books, 800 incunabula and 950 manuscripts.

Inevitably some of the more lurid reports of German atrocities were either wholly manufactured or grossly exaggerated; but still more had their veracity tested in the course of the war and were confirmed to be completely authentic. The difficulty was to distinguish between the two different kinds of report. In the first six weeks of war, there were undoubtedly thousands of horrifying instances of rape, cold-blooded murder and spontaneous massacre, committed by marauding German troops against Belgian civilians, including women and children, and members of the clergy. But blatantly unfounded reports were also given an enthusiastic hearing: of children with their hands and feet sliced off, of slaughtered babies stuck on bayonets and roasted over the fire, or of soldiers lying injured on the battlefield, all with their noses cut off. For the more credulous, such stories proved irresistible. Ada McGuire, a schoolteacher from Wallasey, Cheshire, related a bizarre couple of tales in a letter to her married sister Eva, who was living in the United States:

> [T]here is a soldier now lying in our Fazakerley military hospital who has had legs, arms, ears, and nose cut off and his eyes are out. His father called to see him. They begged him not to see him, but he would and the shock has turned his brain. I do not vouch for this, but have heard it from two different sources. A gentleman in a train was talking to a friend of his. A. T. was in the same carriage. He said a couple he knows well wished to take a Belgian child as they had no children. To their horror the child sent to them had no hands. They had been cut off!

After hearing a similar tale, of a surgeon's hands being cut off by Germans on the rampage in a Belgian town so that he'd never be able to practise again – which he seems to have accepted without question – Rudyard Kipling reported to his American publisher that 'Germany is running this war . . . without the faintest regard for any law human or divine.' Carefully sifting reports of atrocities against the Belgian population, and seeking corroborative evidence for them, the mathematician R. W. M. Gibbs concluded that they proved that Britain's entry into the war had been right, and that 'not one man out of a hundred has any doubts but that our action was justified.'

'Murder, lust and pillage', to use the words of the Bryce Committee, appointed by the government at the end of 1914 to investigate alleged German outrages in Belgium, contributed to a defining image of the enemy as the 'Hun'. Atrocity stories assisted recruitment by reinforcing the idea of the war as a moral crusade. They also raised dark fears that England might face a similar fate should it be overrun by German invaders. 'If they do come here,' exclaimed Ada McGuire, 'they will have no mercy on us, and oh! their cruelty is appalling.' Carrie Kipling informed her mother that 'It's our turn next unless we can keep them out.'

These fears intensified with the arrival in England, in late August, of the first Belgian refugees, fleeing the invading German forces and bringing with them more horrifying tales of Germanic bloodlust. This was the greatest flood of immigration to the country since the arrival of the Huguenots following the Revocation of the Edict of Nantes at the end of the seventeenth century. In the course of the next two months, 200,000 men, women and children arrived, 11,000 disembarking in one day from Folkestone following the Fall of Antwerp in early October. The well-to-do came first. At Oxford University, C. C. J. Webb offered assistance to one professor from Louvain at the beginning of September, 'who has reached Folkestone with his wife & two children, but has nothing else left in the world'.

Next came the forcibly dispossessed. In London two large depots for refugees were organized under the supervision of the Metropolitan Asylums Board. One was at Alexandra Palace, the other at the Earls Court Exhibition Centre, a compound of thirty-five acres, where the exhibition 'Sunny Spain' was hurriedly closed to provide shelter in the vast Empress Hall. 'On Sunday night over 1,700 slept there,' ran the report of an eyewitness in the depot's first week, 'and on Monday evening 500 more were expected. Imagine receiving, registering, classifying, and making arrangements for bathing, feeding, and sleeping this huge family, in an empty building. The bathing is done at public baths nearby, and the able-bodied feed in a huge dining-room with rows upon rows of tables.'

Michael MacDonagh described the 'most pitiable state' of the Belgian refugees arriving at Victoria Station. 'I should say all classes of society were represented in those parties which I saw, but the main bulk of them obviously were peasants – dark-complexioned and undersized, most of them.' The dispersal of refugees around the country was coordinated by the War Refugees' Committee, while some 2,500 local relief charities and reception committees were set up. There were concentrations of Belgians in London and the seaside resorts, which had plenty of out-of-season accommodation to spare. Great care was taken to ascertain the social class of the refugees so that they could be placed with British people of equal standing. Measures were also put in place to ensure that Walloons and Flemings, Belgium's two distinct cultural and linguistic groups, with a history of mutual hatred and distrust, were kept apart.

According to one newspaper in Keighley, West Yorkshire, 'The appearance of these unfortunate fugitives in our midst has brought home to our people the horrors and miseries of war in a way that hardly anything else could have done.' There was an initial outpouring of sympathy and generosity towards the Belgians from all sections of society. After several weeks, Keighley reported that nearly £400 had been raised to provide for the town's fifty-one refugees. But the refugees could also be objects of an unhealthy curiosity. Mill-workers at the Yorkshire town of Bingley in early November were so excited about receiving their 'share' of refugees that false rumours of their arrival left the crowds turning at the station to meet them bitterly disappointed. At Nantwich, in Cheshire, there was a sense of anti-climax when their party of Belgians turned out to be dressed not in rags and tatters as expected, but in smart clothes.

For some, the experience of accommodating refugees left their altruism wearing a bit thin. Miss G. West and her family in Gloucestershire, who had offered to take in two refugees, were sent six members of the Leughels family at the end of September. On 20 November she reported that 'Belgians getting on pretty well though they are a bit exacting about their food and garments. Mrs refused a charming little red coat because "red does not suit fair babies".' She went on:

> Other people's Belgians are not so amiable. Those in Woodchester do their own catering and run up huge bills, buying only the best joints and quantities of butter and eggs. The lady who looks after them says that the only thing that brings a passing smile to their faces is roast pork so although it is awfully dear she can't refuse it to them. Most people agree that they are fat, lazy, greedy . . . and inclined to take all the benefits heaped on them as a matter of course.

By the end of the month, the Leughels had left the West household, to be reallocated elsewhere, after an incident when M. Leughel came home at one in the morning 'drunk as a cork'.

The more empathetic could see that difficult behaviour in the cases of some of their Belgian guests arose as a result of the horrifying experiences to which they'd been subjected. However, as far as Mary Coules was concerned, 'Belgianitis' had 'quite abated' by the end of 1914. 'The Belgians are not grateful,' she confided to her diary. 'They won't do a stroke of work, and grumble at everything, and their morals . . . ! It may be true enough that Belgium saved Europe, but . . . save us from the Belgians!'

How long would this war, already being labelled 'Great', last? Estimates in these early months differed enormously (the easy slogan, 'over by Christmas', said to have been on the lips of much of the population in 1914, appears to be a fabrication of post-war myth). 'From three weeks to three years have been suggested as the probable duration of the contest, with every variety of intermediate estimate,' *The Times*'s military correspondent reported on 8 August, arguing that a 'short, sharp war' was 'probable' because it was essential for Germany to deliver a swift, devastating blow against France. The Archbishop of York, Cosmo Gordon Lang, writing two days earlier, disagreed with forecasts of a short war. It was 'the first time there has been a struggle of this magnitude since our country became democratic', he told Lord Robert Cecil, 'and it is very difficult to know how the mass of people will stand the strain. At present I do not think they realise how long and exacting it will be.'

Vera Brittain, writing at the beginning of September to her future fiancé Roland Leighton, admitted that she was 'quite without an opinion' of her own. Reports she had read of an imminent battle were large and decisive enough to suggest that the war might be over in a month, while 'others speak of it being a slow business likely to last three years.' Opinion divided families. In the second week of October, Beatrice Trefusis quoted Kitchener's conjecture in the House of Lords of a three-year war, against her brother's assurance that the end was a 'matter of [a] few months' away. Irma McLeod of Horsham, in West Sussex, meanwhile, expressed alarm in mid October, when her husband wrote suggesting that the war might still be going at Christmas.

In fact, the German advance on Paris had been decisively halted by retreating Anglo-French forces at the Battle of the Marne, in the first week of September, destroying German hopes of a rapid victory in the West. The battle on the Western Front was about to descend into a bloody period of deadlock and attrition. On 16 September, Sir John French issued the British Expeditionary Force with its first instructions for trench warfare. By November, with the opposing armies embedded in trenches running from the Alps to the English Channel, there could be no expectation any longer of a short war.

Understanding this, Walter Hines Page, the American Ambassador in London, wrote of the necessity for his adoptive country to accustom itself to a different kind of life: 'to a routine of double work and to an oppression of double gloom. Dead men . . . maimed men, the dull grey dread of what may happen next, the impossibility of changing the subject, the monotony . . . the consequent dimness of ideals, the overworking of the emotions, and the heavy bondage of thought.' It was a stark vision of a future that most English men and women in the autumn of 1914 had scarcely begun to recognize for themselves.

All the King's Men

On Sunday, 30 August 1914, a group of thirty women were out in the streets of Folkestone in Kent, taking part in a strange new recruitment ritual. Catching sight of any man of military age not in uniform, the women immediately stepped forward to hand him a white feather, or pin one to his lapel.

The aim of this deliberate act of public humiliation was to shame 'idlers and loafers' into enlisting. A white feather was commonly recognized as a mark of cowardice and inferior breeding. In the sport of cock fighting, some game birds had white feathers in their tails, and so, in common parlance, to show the white feather was to turn tail.

The term had taken on a renewed symbolism in 1902 with the publication of A. E. W. Mason's popular adventure novel *The Four Feathers*. Mason's leading character, Harry Feversham, quits his regiment as it is about to leave for the Sudan. He receives four white feathers as a result: three from fellow officers, and one – a white ostrich feather plucked from her fan – from his fiancée Ethne. In order to redeem himself, Harry dons Arab disguise, leaves for the Sudan, and comes to the aid of the officers who dishonoured him when they are attacked by Dervishes, saving their lives and proving his bravery. Harry Feversham's story had had particular resonance in the period just following the Boer War, a time when fears were being voiced about the condition of British manhood, arising from the poor quality of army recruits.

Admiral Charles Penrose Fitzgerald was the man responsible for orchestrating the Folkestone rally in August 1914. In his early seventies, and a resident of the seaside town, Fitzgerald had a long and distinguished naval career behind him, during which he had commanded several frontline warships. In retirement, he had issued stark warnings about the danger to Britain presented by the expansion of Germany's navy. As a long-term member of the National Service

A cartoonist's view of Kitchener's call to arms, 1914

League, Fitzgerald had been a peacetime campaigner for the implementation of mandatory military service in Britain. In the absence of conscription at the start of the war, he remained committed to his view that 'in a free, self-governing country, every sound man of military age ought to be, not only willing, but *ready*, to fight for his country.'

The towns of the English Channel ports, with their centuries-long history of impressment, may have offered a favourable environment for the introduction of a 'White Feather Brigade', as this novel method of enlistment for Lord Kitchener's Army soon became known. A notice in the 'Personal Column' of *The Times*, headed 'ENGLAND'S DISGRACE', the day before Fitzgerald sent his band of women out on to the streets of Folkestone, had advertised as 'WANTED, a PRESS GANG in FOLKESTONE' for the 'Capture of 1,000 able-bodied "knuts" [a "knut" was a term for a fashionable, showy young man], idlers, and lady-killers'. It's impossible that anything like a tally of 1,000 men was achieved by the Folkestone brigade. But, whatever the direct inspiration for Fitzgerald's scheme, there can be no doubt that the idea quickly caught hold of the public imagination. In neighbouring Deal, two days later, the experiment was repeated. The Town Cryer paraded the streets crying, 'Oyez! Oyez!! Oyez!!! The White Feather Brigade! Ladies wanted to present the young men of Deal and Walmer who have no one dependent on them the Order of the White Feather for shirking their duty in not coming forward to uphold the Union Jack of Old England. God save the King!'

The response from the women of the town was immediate and overwhelming. White feathers were eagerly distributed to any man who appeared to fit the description of 'selfish shirker'. The practice spread rapidly around the country. The precise extent of the White Feather campaigns, which continued even after a system of military compulsion was introduced in 1916, has always been difficult to estimate. In later years, many women who had been active participants were understandably reluctant to come forward and admit that they had played a part. Nevertheless, from their persistent appearance in letters and diaries of the time, and from the way in which they quickly became part of popular and press culture – especially the culture of the Northcliffe press – from the early months of the war, it's clear that the distribution of white feathers was widespread.

This threat of public humiliation was evidently something to be feared. 'The bellicosity of these females,' as Michael MacDonagh observed, 'is almost as terrible to the young man who has no stomach for fighting as an enemy with banners and guns.'

The handing out of white feathers by groups of roaming females was certainly cruel and sometimes misdirected. Stories abound of the indiscriminate presentation of this 'emblem of cowardice', like that related by Macleod Yearsley, a London doctor, who recalled a young man home on leave, dressed in mufti, being given one, in spite of the fact that he had just been awarded the V. C.

Yet a voluntary system, charged with enlisting hundreds of thousands of civilian men for Kitchener's new armies, partly depended on this mobilization of women in the cause of recruitment. Asquith's government was adamant that it would not introduce conscription, and consequently a spirit of unofficial compulsion prevailed. Before long it was difficult to move around the streets of London, and other major cities, without encountering the display of some image demanding the enlistment of more recruits, whether it was the taxi-cabs, omnibuses, and illuminated tramcars bearing placards and notices of Kitchener's call to arms, or the thousands of posters spinning off the presses from the Parliamentary Recruiting Committee. Women, as wives, mothers, daughters, friends, were integral to this branch of the government's propaganda campaign. Passively, they stood for everything conjured up in the notion of 'home' that the British Army was said to be defending. Actively – and more invidiously – they were called upon to send their menfolk to war by shaming them into volunteering, if necessary through refusing to be seen out with them unless they were in uniform, or by casting aspersions on their masculinity. As one early recruiting leaflet, addressed to 'MOTHERS' and 'SWEETHEARTS', put it: 'If you cannot persuade him to answer his Country's Call and protect you now *Discharge him* as unfit!'

The playwright Henry Arthur Jones, soon to be embroiled in

unpleasant disputes with Shaw and Wells over his allegations that the writings of both men were traitorously pro-German, emphasized the new role that a nation at war expected its women to undertake. From the Reform Club on 29 August, he wrote that 'The English girl who will not know the man – lover, brother, or friend – that cannot show an overwhelming reason for not taking up arms – that girl will do her duty and will give good help to her country.'

Jones's view had been echoed in a letter to *The Times* the day before. Miss A. M. Woodward, a woman from London, argued that women had 'a wider duty' than the knitting and sewing of garments for the troops:

> Young men ... must be persuaded to think what this war really means and what the terrible consequences may be if we fail to appreciate its magnitude and its meaning. So I am commencing a little missionary work. To-morrow I mean to give a leaflet to every man who is a possible recruit. I shall watch for them on the tram, in the street, at cricket and tennis grounds, at the theatre, at the restaurant, and I hope that the single appeal 'from the women of England' will at least rouse their thought and possibly help them to act.

From this it seems more than likely that Miss Woodward was herself an early recruit to a 'White Feather Brigade'.

England may have expected every woman to remind a man of his duty, but the motivation behind the presentation of white feathers varied widely. For those women whose menfolk were in training or already at the Front, the sight of an apparently unenlisted man could represent a serious affront to decency. Other women were keen to participate in the fighting vicariously by personally ordering out recruits. Among female patriots of this class, it was almost a badge of dishonour not to have made all possible efforts to persuade male friends 'to take the King's shilling'. This was an attitude exemplified by Iris Holt, in Lewes, Sussex, who wrote proudly in September 1914 that she did not have 'a single friend or relation eligible to serve who is not doing so'. Conversely, Irma McLeod, from Horsham, could only express her sadness at what she saw as the 'absolutely hopeless outlook' for her friend Evie when Evie's fiancé was rejected by the army. 'I wish I could do something for her,' she sympathized. Some women used the sanction provided by the campaigns as a useful cover for a flirtatious encounter. Later the writer Compton Mackenzie would offer another explanation for the provocative gesture: he was sure that 'idiotic young women' handed out white feathers to boyfriends of whom they'd grown tired.

For the self-consciously modern woman, the emergent young 'flapper', prizing her independence, white feather giving possessed a thrill of transgression – all the more so since it seemed to flout conventional rules of behaviour between the sexes. Suffragettes, currently being urged by Mrs Pankhurst to suspend militancy and do all they could for the war effort, may have discovered something of the risk-taking appeal of their former peacetime activities in handing out feathers. It was also an opportunity to take a form of subtle revenge on some of their former male assailants, a chance to wield a new kind of sexual power in public, while reminding men that their rights of full citizenship made it incumbent on them to fight.

While Mrs Pankhurst appeared at recruitment rallies advocating conscription and compulsory war work for women, the degree to which her supporters were involved in the rampant white feather campaign sometimes ascribed to them is open to question. Travelling on a bus, on his way to a dinner party, Macleod Yearsley remembered coming across 'an aggressive looking lady of uncertain age, evidently a suffragette, as she carried a copy of *Votes for Women*'. Also on the bus were three young men in khaki. 'Suddenly she addressed me in a loud voice. "Are you not ashamed of yourself, standing there in evening dress? . . . Why aren't you *doing* something for your country, a fine young man like you? Look at these splendid fellows in khaki . . . doing their duty while you play the coward."'

Yearsley's response was swift and damning. He was a hospital surgeon, he told her, and responsible for a number of the wounded. He was also drilling recruits two days a week. In addition, he was well over military age. After the woman, with a certain bad grace, made an apology, Yearsley pointed to the issue of *Votes for Women* she was holding and 'gave her the knock-out blow': 'Before you obtain *that*, madam, you have much to learn, including how to restrain yourself

19. An anti-war demonstration in Trafalgar Square on the afternoon of 2 August, during the final days of peace. In England, the first week of war was marked by heavy downfalls of rain.

20. The crowd in front of Buckingham Palace at midnight on 4 August 1914, awaiting the expiry of Britain's ultimatum to Germany. Onlookers described them as respectful, generally calm, but also anxious.

21. (*left*) The Lord Chancellor, Lord Haldane, soon to be the object of widespread attacks because of his German connections, with the Foreign Secretary, Sir Edward Grey, photographed coming from the cabinet meeting on 28 July, the day Austria declared war on Serbia.

22. (*above*) The forlorn figure of the German Ambassador, Prince Lichnowsky, walking across Horse Guards Parade, his hopes for peace between Britain and Germany defeated.

23. Removing the Imperial insignia from the door of London's German Embassy in the first days of the war.

24. (*above*) Young men waiting to enlist at the Central London Recruiting Depot, Great Scotland Yard, in early August. The crowd was so large, with only six men admitted at a time, that mounted police had to restrain volunteers. A fortnight later, however, enlistment fell dramatically.

25. (*left*) Albert Knowles (*centre*) being sworn in on enlisting with the 'Leeds Pals', later the 15th Battalion, The Prince of Wales's Own (West Yorkshire Regiment), at Leeds Town Hall, in August 1914. The commanding officer, Colonel Walter Stead, stands to the left. Knowles fought in the Battle of the Somme in 1916. Badly gassed, he was invalided out of the army, but his health never recovered and he died shortly after the end of the war.

26. Horses commandeered by the army in Hampshire.

27. George Cecil's battalion, the 2nd Grenadier Guards, receive acknowledgement from the King as they pass Buckingham Palace on their way to Victoria Station en route to France, 12 August 1914.

28. (*top*) Belgian refugees arriving in London in 1914, regarded with curiosity by onlookers.

29. (*above*) The Rectory of Great Leighs in Essex, where Andrew Clark wrote his diary and compiled his record of the war's influence on the English language.

30. (*right*) A notice posted at Clark's church of St Mary the Virgin to inform parishioners of the progress of the war, and later pasted into his diary.

The second week's official Bulletin.

Summary of Saturday's Official War New
[Posted: in Great Leighs, Sunday 23 August 1914]
Belgian retirement on Antwerp and German entry into Brussels confirmed
Artillery attack on Namur in progress.
So far most engagements reported during war have been relatively unimportant
Eastern campaign has hardly begun.
In West, German failure during three weeks to deliver big attack that earlier might have seriously embarrassed operations of French Armies constitutes a noteworthy advantage.
General military position satisfactory.
Rumours of casualties among British troops again officially denied.

31. A scene from the hit play *The Man Who Stayed at Home*, which opened in the West End in December 1914. Daphne presents the hero, Christopher Brent, with a white feather for cowardice, which he proceeds to use as a pipe cleaner.

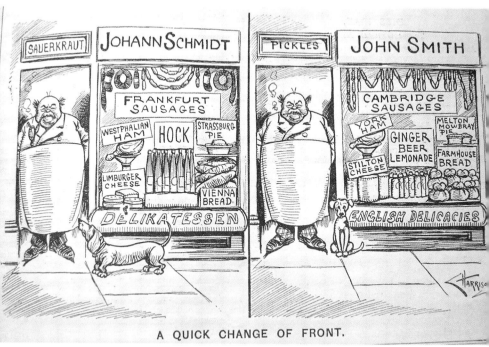

A QUICK CHANGE OF FRONT.

32. A *Punch* cartoon poking fun at the sudden necessity, on the outbreak of war, for German shopkeepers in Britain to anglicize their names.

33. The German spy Carl Hans Lody, closely guarded during his trial, in October–November 1914, in the Middlesex Guildhall at Westminster. Lody's dignified bearing and mild-mannered behaviour did not square with the public's image of sinister German espionage agents.

34. The telegram notification of Lody's execution by firing squad within the precincts of the Tower of London.

35. 'Remember Scarborough!', a poster from the painting by Edith Kemp-Welch, issued in the wake of the German naval bombardment of the East Coast towns in December 1914. Unfortunately, expectations that the German attacks would have a beneficial effect on enlistment soon proved unfounded.

and the folly of judging by appearances.' Completely vanquished, the suffragette sloped off the bus at the next stop. Yearsley sank back into his seat, 'with a sigh of contentment'.

The folly of judging by appearances was demonstrated repeatedly: soldiers on leave, dressed in civvies, suddenly finding themselves the recipients of white feathers; men who had done their best to enlist, only to be rejected by the military authorities as not up to standard, subjected to public taunts; most shocking and reprehensible of all, the instances of wounded men being presented with feathers while they were at home awaiting treatment. One man, preparing to be admitted to Roehampton Hospital to have an artificial leg fitted, was given a feather. He stood up as best he could on his healthy leg and waved the stump of the other one in the perpetrator's face.

An unnamed correspondent in *The Times* in September complained about the way in which his failure to be accepted by the army had left him open to being treated like a shirker. 'I have volunteered but they would not look at me,' he wrote. 'There must be a large government badge for the disqualified. Until we receive this . . . the only badge we have [is] the WHITE FEATHER.' In the autumn of 1914, the entertainer Frank Pettingell – presumably one of the disqualified – wrote and performed a musical monologue for the 'Men Who Are Left Behind', entitled *We Cannot All Be Soldiers*, expressing the pain of rejection as well as the subsequent humiliation:

> There is many a single young fellow who is snubbed by stronger folks
> Who give him the white feather and play other well-meant jokes;
> And the girls all turn their noses up and eye him with contempt,
> For they don't Know that Nature has made that man exempt.
> And he'll grit his teeth and suffer, and he'll feel a beastly pain
> When he sees the Khaki uniform and hears the bugle's strain.

The white feather may have been the prerogative of the female patriot, but there is evidence to suggest that some men were far from averse to handing them out. In Devon, Maurice C. Bolt received a card in the post with a feather sewn on the back from 'A Retired Man, White Feather Brigade'. The accompanying note accused him of 'unmanly and cowardly behaviour', and asked why he allowed others to risk their lives while he stayed at home. The sender, being above the age of military service, was conveniently free to pressure eligible, younger men to take part in the war. Similarly, a disabled man, also from Devon, describing himself as a member of a White Feather Brigade, claimed to have been sending out feathers since the beginning of the war. Across the county, there were more than a dozen men, almost all above military age, later reported as having taken part in a white feather postcard campaign.

The success rate of White Feather Brigades in persuading men to enlist has, of course, gone unrecorded. It's possible that many more men joined up out of fear of receiving a feather, and of being branded a coward, than did those who actually received one. In time, public revulsion against the distribution of white feathers would reduce their effectiveness as a recruiting tool. Helen Hamilton's poem 'The Jingo-Woman' later expressed, with real ferocity, a woman's scorn for the other members of her sex who took part in this ugly manifestation of female patriotism ('I'd like to wring your neck,/ I really would!/You make all women seem such duffers'). Asquith's government, too, did its best in the end to distance itself from the practice. The implication behind the White Feather Brigades – that the Liberal government was emasculated and that, rather than leading the country in a time of national emergency by forcing men to fight, it was dependent on the fairer sex to 'beg' recruits for its war effort – hardly served as effective propaganda, at home or abroad.

However, even among the vast majority of women who played no active part in white feather campaigns, there remained a widespread hostility to men seen as 'shirking their duty', together with the underlying assumption that if a man refused to fight, he was less of a man and unfit to be not only a citizen, but also a husband or father. This kind of impugning of masculinity was apparent in such publicity stunts as the one depicted in a photograph in the *Daily Chronicle*'s weekly *War Budget*. This shows a petticoat hanging from an upstairs window. Beside it a working-class woman holds out a placard inscribed with the words 'SERVE YOUR COUNTRY OR WEAR THIS'. It was present, too, in the popular recruiting song

'I'll Make a Man of You', sung originally by Clara Beck in *The Passing Show* in the final months of 1914.

By the close of 1914, the white feather was sufficiently a part of the cultural landscape to be caricatured in Lechmere Worrall and J. E. Harold Terry's hit play *The Man Who Stayed at Home*, in a scene in which the hero accepts a feather from Daphne, a 'gushing' young woman, and then proceeds to use it as a pipe cleaner. 'More than half the girls in the Tennis Club have decided to do the same thing,' Daphne offers by way of explanation for her behaviour, though she admits that others say she'd be better employed in 'knitting comforters' for the troops.

But in November the public was reminded of the potential for tragedy threatened by the white feather campaigns, when the case of Robert Graves of Harrogate reached the coroner's court. A white feather had been pushed through the letter-box of his lodgings. According to his landlady, Graves, who had been declared unfit for army service, 'had taken this action very much to heart'. He was unable to talk of anything but the war, and could neither eat nor sleep. Finally he committed suicide. 'The white feather action was a cruel, wicked thing to do,' the coroner declared in recording his verdict, 'and should cause lifelong regret to the person responsible.'

Ironically, at the end of August, just as the white feather campaigns were getting under way, there was an astonishing upsurge in recruitment, for the first time in weeks.

Enlistment at the start of the war, as has already been noted, had initially been strong in London. However, the provinces had been much slower to respond. Overall there was disappointment that the call to arms had not been received with more enthusiasm. Nationally, poor returns were attributed to congestion at recruiting offices, and to widespread misunderstanding that the appeal for 100,000 recruits – which Kitchener announced in the House of Lords on 25 August as 'practically secured' – might not represent the limit of the government's requirements. In the meantime, the organization of public recruiting meetings was stepped up, and efforts were made to improve the machinery of recruitment. More doctors were engaged for the medical inspections, and there was a sharp increase in the number of recruiting stations. In Central London, a marquee was erected on Horse Guards Parade to accommodate the overflow of volunteers waiting at Great Scotland Yard.

The sudden upturn in recruitment numbers occurred almost overnight. The change was followed by the Lichfield brewer, William Pead, in his diary. On 25 August he had written critically of 'four sturdy young men in the prime of early manhood', with whom he had struck up a conversation while travelling in a charabanc on holiday. 'They did not appear to think that the call to arms appealed to them in any way,' Pead noted, 'nor did they seem to be the least interested in the war news. They spent the ride singing comic songs and in chaffing passers-by. And they are typical of many others at present.'

Just over a week later, on 4 September, Pead noticed that a remarkable change was taking place at the local barracks, a few miles from his home. 'Crowds of young men are enlisting,' he wrote. 'A continuous stream of them are passing up to Whittington Barracks.' He described them as 'slightly organized', as they were drafted off at about 1,000 men a time to various depots, and reported that 'They have neither arms nor uniforms and present a sorry spectacle.'

This rush to enlist was being repeated throughout the country. On 25 August, a report in *The Times* had given the British public its first news of the Battle of Mons. An editorial noted ominously that 'The battle is joined and has so far gone ill for the Allies.' A leader on the same day stated that 'Yesterday was a day of bad news' and warned that 'more must follow'.

The so-called 'Amiens dispatch', published in the paper on 30 August, duly delivered these further bad tidings. A graphic eyewitness account by the correspondent Arthur Moore, who had lately joined the retreating British 4th Division, described, in somewhat alarmist terms, the fate of what he called a 'broken army'. Moore told *Times* readers that losses were very great, and that he had seen 'the broken bits of many regiments': 'We have to face the fact that the British Expeditionary Force, which bore the great weight of the blow, has suffered terrible losses and requires immediate and immense reinforcement. The British Expeditionary Force has won indeed imperishable glory, but it needs men, men, and yet more men.'

The impact of this news had a striking and immediate effect, as recruiting fever gripped the country. On 25 August, just over 10,000 men volunteered, the first time a five-figure total had been achieved in a single day. In the final week of August, and the first fortnight in September, a true burst of patriotic enthusiasm seized the nation. In the week between 30 August and 5 September, 174,901 men joined the army, including 33,204 new recruits on 3 September, a figure that would prove to be the highest enlistment total for any day of the entire war. The enthusiastic response in London was reflected in other major cities, as Moore's stirring article was syndicated to local newspapers. In particular, Birmingham, Manchester and Newcastle all delivered strong returns.

The second week of September saw a continuation of this surge across Britain, as 136,160 men signed up. In the midst of this, on 10 September, Parliament was asked to sanction Kitchener's appeal for a further 500,000 men (a second 100,000 had been approved on 28 August). Reporting to Venetia Stanley on the 'tremendous pace' in recruiting, Asquith admitted that before long it would become impossible to meet the demands of the new army for uniforms and arms (soon afterwards the Prime Minister drove past some members of Kitchener's new army, the majority of them not yet in khaki, but wearing 'East end costumes', and had to admit that 'such a rabble' had rarely been seen). All the same he didn't think it desirable to dampen down the current wave of enthusiasm.

Nevertheless, with limited accommodation for the new soldiers while they were in training, and anticipated shortages in uniforms and weapons, something had to be done to stem the rush. Furthermore, recruiting stations were once again suffering from serious congestion. At many London recruiting offices, according to one report, men were queuing for up to eight hours to enlist. Consequently, on 11 September, the War Office announced that the minimum height requirement for recruits bound for the infantry (apart from ex-Regulars) would be raised to five feet six inches (the minimum chest measurement was also increased).

James Brady, from Rochdale in Lancashire, later recalled that the news of the retreat from Mons 'spread like wildfire casting gloom' around the town. The message around the country, however, was clear: volunteers were urgently required to take the place of dead men in the British Army's depleted ranks. On 28 August, Alexander Thompson, a solicitor's clerk from Newcastle, informed his mother that 'unless the Allied forces' prospects are better on Monday than they are at present . . . I will join Kitchener's Army.' A few days later he enlisted with the 9th Battalion Northumberland Fusiliers. The shock reverberating from the news of Mons also strongly influenced Andrew Buxton, a member of a Quaker family, who worked in a senior position at the Westminster branch of Barclays Bank. 'I know you don't want me to enlist,' he wrote to his sister on 31 August, 'but I cannot help thinking it my duty from every point of view . . . to do so soon – say next week or the week following.' He, too, volunteered not long afterwards.

Jimmy Carpenter, twenty-five, from Walthamstow, a clerk at a firm of provision merchants at London Bridge, also made up his mind to enlist that week. With his cousin Albert Dixon, he made his way to the recruiting office near St Paul's on 7 September. After two hours' waiting, they were admitted for their medicals, which both of them passed, and then, along with eight others, they raised their hands to swear an oath to serve King and Country for the duration of the war. To their disappointment, Jimmy and Albert were enlisted in the Royal Sussex Regiment; they'd hoped for the Cornwalls or the Royal East Kent Regiment (the Buffs), but felt a sense of pride, as they received their first day's pay of 1s.6d. before leaving the recruiting station.

Having enjoyed an evening at a Music Hall, the cousins spent the next day making preparations for their departure. At Whitehall the following morning, as 'all kinds and classes of men' formed up, Jimmy and Albert received money for rations before being marched off to Victoria. Reaching Chichester Barracks, the two men managed to transfer to the Buffs and were sent immediately to begin training in camp at Purfleet. Here, with some soldiers in their battalion wearing increasingly soiled civilian clothes, and others sporting a mixture of bowler hats, khaki tunics and ordinary trousers, they spent the mornings drilling and marching, while attending lectures in the afternoons. They were moved to another camp in Shoreham, and then to billets in Worthing, receiving their inoculations for foreign service in November. It would be another nine months before Jimmy Carpenter and Albert Dixon left Folkestone for France, as part of 'a fit and fully trained battalion', all of them, as Jimmy later proudly recalled, volunteers.

The recruiting boom came to an abrupt end on 12 September. The following week, the daily average fell to 6,382 from a five-figure total almost double that. It had been a brief, but extraordinary run of success for the new mass army. Between 4 August and 12 September, nearly half a million men had enlisted, more than 300,000 of those in the fortnight after 30 August. By the end of November, a fortnight after Asquith sought Parliament's approval for a further million volunteers, enlistment had reached just over one million.

The downward trend in recruitment figures, however, continued, much to the government's alarm. The returns for October showed a huge drop, down by as much as two thirds from September. As a result, the minimum height standard was reduced, and the age limit extended to thirty-eight (the dental regulation, which required each new recruit to have four opposing molars in good condition, was also relaxed). One new initiative was the creation of 'Bantam' battalions for men of between five feet and five feet three inches in height. This idea arose after a Durham miner walked from Durham to Birkenhead, and was rejected as too short at every recruiting office he visited. In all, twenty-four Bantam units would eventually be raised.

In November, recruitment improved slightly during the period of the First Battle of Ypres, when the tide of fortune appeared once again to be turning against the British Expeditionary Force. But never again would recruitment approach the peaks of those September days.

What were the factors forcing or encouraging men to 'volunteer'? And what stood in the way of men enlisting?

Broadly speaking, the response across England from urban

communities was much more robust than that of agricultural ones. Autumn 1914's harvest was an especially rich and plentiful one, and undoubtedly played a considerable part in slowing down rural recruiting. Additionally, farmers were sometimes accused of attempting to keep labourers on their farms by offering them an increase in wages, convincing them that working on the land was a patriotic act in itself and as vital to the country's interests in wartime as going off to fight.

In country areas, particularly in the more outlying districts, recruiting agents often experienced difficulty in conveying the gravity of the situation to ordinary people, let alone in making them understand basic factual information about the war. 'No one living in the busy rush of towns can have any conception of the ignorance, and therefore incredible indifference, of our countryfolk,' a 'villager' wrote to *The Times* at the end of August. 'There is a determined minimizing of any suggestion of danger and a blind belief that . . . there is no need to lift a finger, since there are plenty doing all that may be necessary elsewhere.' The Reverend Llas, from Haywards Heath, suggested that lantern-slide lectures about the war should be provided to combat 'congenital slowness of apprehension'. Some form of public information service might well have been usefully deployed in the farther flung parts of Cornwall, where, according to one local, ignorance about the war was 'appalling', and where, in one remote village, a postman was once asked to resolve an argument between a husband and wife over whether Lord Kitchener was British or German.

In Cornwall, one of the remotest and poorest parts of England, national news was often difficult to come by, and current events seemed in any case to be scarcely a priority for much of the population. However, even during the last days of August and the beginning of September, when volunteers throughout the country were flocking to recruiting offices after the news from Mons, the county's recruitment figures for that week recorded the enlistment of only seventy men. The reason for this, and the poor attendance at recruiting meetings, was revealed in the local press. Many Cornishmen were still smarting from the brutal methods used by the authorities to smash the clay miners' strike the previous year. 'We don't forget' was the shout at one meeting, while a clay miner told a reporter, 'Let the gentry go and fight, what is it to do with us?'

In neighbouring Devon, known before long as 'unpatriotic Devon', where enlistment figures remained well below the national average for the rest of 1914, the general attitude to the war appeared to be one of almost studied indifference. Admittedly, this state of affairs was not helped by the snail's pace at which the recruiting machinery for the county operated at the outset. Seven weeks passed after the declaration of war before the Devon branch of the Parliamentary Recruiting Committee established itself. In the southern and eastern parts of the county, in particular, there was still the problem of men having to walk long distances in order to find a recruiting station where they could enlist. In short, there was a palpable lack of emergency about Devon's reception of the war. The local press failed to print recruiting advertisements, and there was little news of the war in the papers. Posters put up in post offices, town halls, restaurants and pubs were torn down, and recruiting depots and buildings vandalized. Recruiting agents, dispatched by the National Service League, became a familiar sight, much resented around the county as they made door-to-door calls, harassing and goading men of military age into volunteering. In some desperation at the lack of response to their calls for volunteers to do their patriotic duty, the Parliamentary Recruiting Committee issued a seven-page pamphlet addressed to 'Men of Devon', reminding them that 'Never in all the mighty story of the English people has the Motherland been faced by a more tremendous task or threatened with dangers so terrible.'

In urban communities, economic necessity was the significant factor in forcing men to enlist in the first months of war, when many industries were hard hit by the curtailment of production. Unemployment, which had stood at 2.8 per cent in July, topped 7 per cent in August, subsiding slightly to 5.9 per cent in September, before falling with each successive month. The recruiting boom in late August and early September therefore coincided with a widespread recession, and many men must have joined up because they simply could not afford to do otherwise.

Unemployment figures may do much to explain the initial rush to the colours, but what remains more mysterious is the question of what subsequently persuaded working-class men from comparatively well-paid jobs to leave and join the army. In 1914 the army paid privates 8s.9d. a week (about the same rate of pay as an agricultural labourer), which, with food and clothing allowances, amounted to 13s.9d. This none the less remained a modest figure in comparison with the average weekly wage packets for police constables (72s.), coal miners (33s.) or builders (29s.).

But then, across all social classes, a variety of pressures was being brought to bear to encourage men to enlist. For the privately educated middle and upper classes, there was the peer pressure of the old school tie. One alumnus of Uppingham, in Rutland, a school with a strongly militaristic ethos, wrote to another former pupil, J. E. B. Gray, at the end of August, to tell him how 'ashamed' he was that he'd so far failed to enlist:

> To think that a great strong chap like you are, should, as yet, have done *nothing* for this country is really a shame. That is not only my opinion but that of all the O. U.s [Old Uppinghamians] . . . who *are doing something*. It may interest you to know that there are now 26,000 names of possible officers on the War Office list. At present we 'hopefuls' are drilling hard every day with the 'Inns of Court' O. T.C. [Officers Training Corps], and have mostly had our names down *since the day War was declared*. I really *do* think you are a slacker! What you had better do is to ENLIST AT ONCE. Soldiering is pleasant work, take it from me. Now hurry up and get a job for your country *needs* you. *Don't wait* for others to give you a lead!

A sense of community affiliation and loyalty, and of common interests, was at its strongest in the recruiting drive known as the 'Pals' Battalions, in which men volunteered with other members of their families, with friends, and alongside colleagues from work. The idea that men might be more willing to serve if they could do so with people they already knew originated at the War Office, with the Director-General of Recruiting, Major-General Henry Rawlinson.

Rawlinson organized the raising of a battalion composed of men who worked in the City, which, by 27 August, was already 1,600 strong. However, it was Lord Derby in Liverpool who set the example of locally raised battalions that was adopted countrywide. At a recruiting meeting in the city on 28 August, Derby announced that he intended to try to raise a battalion consisting solely of local men. Within days, sufficient numbers had enlisted to fill four battalions.

Birmingham and Leeds were among the other major cities immediately raising their own battalions as public expressions of civic pride (after mid September, the War Office banned further locally raised units unless they were authorized according to the government's own preferred timetable). Although some battalions were made up of working-class recruits, a major strength of the scheme as a whole was that it made middle-class recruitment socially acceptable. There was a definite degree of class consciousness in the desire of large numbers of young men from similar backgrounds, and possessing comparable non-manual skills, to volunteer together as one unit. In Leeds, the battalion of 1,000 men raised for the city included solicitors, schoolmasters, shop assistants, tax collectors and articled clerks. An excited crowd of 20,000 waved the pals off from the new railway station, a marked contrast to the restrained departure of ordinary recruits, who, it was reported by one Leeds newspaper in October, received a glance of curiosity, but nothing more.

In the world of sport, so many rugby players volunteered in pals' groups that the season had to be abandoned soon after the start of the war. Football, on the other hand, attracted increasing public criticism throughout the autumn of 1914, with the Football Association facing demands that the game should be voluntarily abandoned for the duration of the war. The *Daily Chronicle* observed that 'About two thousand men, all of fighting age and in the peak of physical condition, are employed week by week in playing matches which attract hundreds of thousands of other men whose place is also in the colours.' Recruiting speeches from army sergeants at half-time were now a common feature at Saturday matches, though they achieved little conspicuous success. Michael MacDonagh noticed that the sandwich boards being carried around the grounds no longer showed evangelical messages concerned with eternal salvation: they had been replaced by posters which interrogated the crowd with questions like 'Are You forgetting there is a war on?' In December a public meeting took place at Fulham Town Hall to launch the Footballers' Battalion. Its chairman, the MP William Joynson-Hicks, urged footballers to volunteer to protect their wives and daughters from the threat of German atrocities. Professional football lasted barely one wartime season, and was suspended the following spring.

Employers were in a special position to pressure men into enlisting. Some great landowners, like Lord Wemyss in Gloucestershire and the Earl of Lonsdale in Cumberland (the latter issued a recruiting poster, printed in his racing colours, with the words 'Are You a Man or Are You a Mouse?'), threatened servants on their estates with dismissal if they failed to enlist, and even provided transport to take them to the recruiting office. Lord Burnham at Beaconsfield, in Buckinghamshire, made the offer of £10 to every worker on his estate who was prepared to join up. In November, Buckingham Palace let it be known that the monarch's state coach would not be in use at the state opening of Parliament because no fewer than eighty-nine royal servants were at the Front.

Aquascutum, the luxury outfitters in London's West End, took out an advertisement in the *Tatler* stating that 'we think it absolutely necessary for every single man between nineteen and thirty to answer his country's call.' The store offered to pay 'half his present salary to any of our present employees while serving', promised to keep a position open to await the volunteer's return, and furthermore gave the assurance that, in the event of a parent, or parents, being dependent on the volunteer, 'full salary will be paid to him during his service.'

Other, less exalted, firms were by no means as generous in the offers they made to their employees. Edward Thomas, on a journalistic assignment across England, 'listening to people, in railway carriages, trams, taverns . . . talking about the war', was told wherever he went that employers were dismissing younger men to drive them to enlist. ' "Not exactly to drive them," said one, "but to encourage." ... They suggested the "Government" had put the employers up to it, or that "It don't seem hardly fair" or "It comes near conscription, and only those that don't care will give up good wages and leave their wives to charity." '

John Riddey, the young Deptford clerk, was anxious to volunteer at the beginning of September, despite his mother's advice that he 'wait a bit'. The iron manufacturers where he worked had only enough materials for another two months, and there were fears that the firm might soon be forced to close down. A notice from head office informed employees that those who enlisted would have jobs found for them after their discharge, 'as far as possible'. 'Not very generous of them, I think,' Riddey observed to his mother. Several days later, he was able to report better news. His manager had told him that if he volunteered, 'they would pay half salary until further notice.' In the meantime, Riddey asked his mother to reconsider her objections to his enlisting. 'I'm getting quite ashamed to be seen in the street; in fact I hear that in some districts girls are handing white feathers to all young fellows seen about not in uniform.'

'The White Feather: A Sketch of English Recruiting' by Arnold Bennett, written for the American market and published in *Collier's Weekly* in October 1914, captured the predicament of a man, with wife and children, who finds he cannot afford to enlist. In this topical story, Cedric Rollinson learns that the manufacturing company for which he works as a manager will keep the place open of any employee who joins the colours, and will pay his family the difference between his soldier's pay and his company salary.

Rollinson tells his wife that he intends to seek a commission as an officer. 'His wife startled him by answering seriously: "I've been wondering about it too, dearest." In a moment they both knew that the matter was decided. He must go . . . His wife cried and started to prepare things for him.'

However, Hawker Maffick, the cunningly named director of the firm – who amuses himself by placing messages to 'shirkers' in *The Times* and *Morning Post*, along the lines of 'Cotton wool and glass case will be provided free of charge to any young man who does not feel equal to joining the army' – tells Rollinson that the company is only willing to make up the pay of manual workers, not of managers, whose salaries cost considerably more.

Rollinson realizes that if he enlists, his family will face hardship. 'He had to choose between his country and his wife and family, and he chose.' He tells Hawker Maffick, 'Very well, sir ... I must stay here.'

On the way home that evening, Rollinson encounters three smartly dressed girls. One of them stuffs a white feather into his waistcoat, with the words 'That's all you're short of, you coward. Why don't you enlist?'

There was really no monotony of type among these recruits, though the great majority wore dark clothes and caps, had pale faces tending to leanness, and stood somewhere about five foot seven ... Clean and dirty – some of them, that is straight from the factory – of all ages and features, they were pouring in. Some might be loafers, far more workers. I heard that of one batch of two hundred and fifty at Newcastle, not one was leaving less than two pounds a week. Here and there a tanned farm labourer with lighter-coloured, often brownish, clothes, chequered the pale-faced dark company. The streets never lacked a body of them or a tail disappearing.

Edward Thomas's description of a line of prospective recruits, during the recruitment boom in September, emphasizes the absence of uniformity in their appearance. The same might also have been said about the personal motives that were driving the volunteers of 1914 to join up. For the factors encouraging men to enlist were as complex and diverse as human nature itself.

Undoubtedly, for some men, like Captain Bruce Baily, who wrote at the end of August that 'nothing would please me better than to die fighting for my country', a sense of patriotic duty was paramount. Others welcomed the chance to exchange a monotonous existence for a more adventurous life. Edward Robinson of Yarnley, near Leeds, admitted that his patriotism wasn't very deep, and that Belgian atrocities 'didn't cut much ice', but that he was 'fearfully sick of a humdrum life that led nowhere and promised nothing'.

Many enjoyed the chance to be with friends, to earn a secure, shilling-a-day income for the first time, or to evade the responsibilities of wives and children. Some recruits had a more sinister motive: the desire to escape a criminal past by reinventing themselves and assuming a new identity in the army. Nor did most men volunteer in a great wave of patriotic enthusiasm. A large proportion bided their time before enlisting, making a pragmatic assessment of when the country had the greatest need of their services, or holding back until they could be sure that their families would be adequately compensated for their absence by the state payment of separation allowances ('excessive drinking' among women, which led to a new government order at the beginning of November, preventing women from drinking in public before 11.30 in the morning, was partly attributed to the anxiety caused by delays in the payment of these allowances).

The reaction of parents or wives to a man's decision to enlist could also vary widely. For every mother who attempted to dissuade her son from enlisting – like Mrs Tully of Peckham, in South-East London, who wrote 'My heart is broken' at the top of a letter in which her son informed her that he had volunteered without her permission – there were others who actively sought their sons' departure on wartime service, or who showed a marked ambivalence about whether they should stay or go. Ada Reece's son Harold was up at Cambridge, studying medicine, when the war began. He had hoped to apply for a commission through the University's Officers Training Corps, but was forbidden by his father on the grounds that it would be too expensive. Harold's subsequent 'want of enthusiasm' for enlisting made his mother 'ache with shame', and she suffered inner rage at the thought that 'he should be the only boy I know who is allowed to do nothing', and dreaded 'the moral effect of him being left out of this great enthusiastic movement'.

What is beyond dispute is that the pressure to enlist, whether exerted by family, friends or complete strangers, was often overwhelming and difficult to resist in these early months of war, as a letter in the autumn of 1914, from William Orchard to his father, giving his reasons for volunteering, shows:

We are in the thick of it, large employers are sacking their young employees in order that they should be compelled to do their duty and enlist, and those who don't enlist for whatever reason are looked upon as funks and shirkers so you can imagine my feelings, as I can't bear to be thought a funk . . . I told Phil [his girlfriend] . . . that I shouldn't join unless forced to but I simply *must*.

Was this an expression of England's finest volunteer spirit, or conscription by the back door? An article in *Bystander*, in December, was in no doubt about the distinction:

Men who put on uniform as a result of exhortation by squires, parsons, retired officers, employers, schoolmasters, leader-writers, politicians, cartoonists, poets, music-hall singers and old women of both sexes are not volunteers; they are conscripts, but conscripted by the wrong people in the wrong way.

Dim Fading Hope

To be senselessly tossed and retossed in stale mutilation
From crater to crater. For this we shall take expiation.

But who shall return us our children?

In peacetime, this forest of beech trees set in hilly countryside, with its glimpse of distant greenery through the dense woodland, had a reputation as a place of natural beauty. But in November 1914, after several months of war, it had taken on a more macabre aspect.

A small party, including English officials and an Anglican clergyman, had been driven in a Red Cross car, some fifty miles north-east of Paris, to the town of Villers-Cotterêts. From here they had travelled a short distance further along the road to Vivières, stopping at the edge of the forest to begin the examination of a mass grave which had been discovered there.

The grave was marked by a plain wooden cross with some evergreen wreaths lying on top of it. A number of khaki caps had been found close by, suggesting that English soldiers were buried in the forest. This was confirmed by an inscription to this effect in French, written on the cross, which in turn had been taken from some writing in German scribbled in purple pencil on one of the neighbouring trees. But the inscription was almost illegible, and it was difficult to see whether the figure for the number buried there was twenty or two hundred.

The marshy top soil soon gave way to a dry, powdery mud with a faint smell of putrescence. In the murky November light, six labourers dug away at the ground, forgoing rest periods to complete the job as quickly as possible. The burial pit turned out to be about twenty-five feet long and twelve feet wide. Before dusk on the first day at least twenty corpses had been disinterred. Many more were evident in successive layers underneath, the bodies lying huddled and

The grave at Villers-Cotterêts, northern France, November 1914

entangled just as they had fallen after being thrown hurriedly into the pit.

The next day a further sixty corpses were disinterred and examined. Identity discs were removed from some of the soldiers' bodies. In no case was it possible to identify a body by its features. For, having been smashed and thickly coated with clay and blood, the faces were often unrecognizable.

On the morning of the third day, when nearly eighty bodies had been exhumed, the remains of the first officer to be discovered, immediately identifiable through the clothing, were lifted from the pit and placed on the ground. A second corpse was found, its disc intact, then a third. This last lacked a disc and its long riding boots had gone, but it was clear from the buttons and uniform that this was the body of an Irish Guards officer. One of the party present muffled his face with a handkerchief and fought hard to control his emotions. From the general shape of this officer's figure, he could see that the remains must be those of his brother. Any uncertainty was removed when a small gold watch bearing the officer's name was suddenly revealed as the sleeve of the uniform was lifted. This body was also placed on the ground beside the others, and then, almost immediately, with barely a pause for breath, the grisly process resumed.

———

Back at the very beginning of August, as the British cabinet remained split on the vexed issue of whether or not to come to the aid of France, eighteen-year-old George Cecil announced his intention of resigning his commission in the Grenadier Guards and entering the French Foreign Legion should Asquith's government fail in its obligation to its ally.

With the declaration of war, it rapidly became clear that George Cecil's time in England would be short. On 11 August, the day before he was due to be sent to the Front with the first troops of the British Expeditionary Force, to join the 4th Guards Brigade, George dined with his mother, Violet Cecil. They met at the Cecil family's London home, 20 Arlington Street, just behind the Ritz Hotel in Piccadilly, and Violet noted how jittery George seemed. 'The long strain of excitement, uncertainty and fatigue was telling on him,' she recalled later, and he could hardly eat anything. After dinner, George took a cab to the Garrick Club, where, in the early hours of the next morning, he wrote his Will and enclosed it in a letter to his mother. 'Cox [his bankers] will send you this *only* if the worst has come to the worst,' George told her. He wanted his younger sister Helen to have his shares and any cash remaining in his bank account. His father, Lord Edward Cecil, currently out in Egypt as financial adviser to the Egyptian government, was to be given his watch. 'I want you to keep my sword,' he continued to Violet, 'as after all it is an emblem of sorts . . . Otherwise distribute my few goods as you think fit. God bless you.'

The 12th of August was a 'grilling hot day'. At Chelsea Barracks, George's battalion of the 2nd Grenadier Guards was the last to set off for Victoria Station. 'I saw Mummy cry for the first time in my memory after George had gone out of Barrack square,' Helen Cecil wrote in her diary. They said their final farewells at Nine Elms Station, near Vauxhall, as the soldiers departed for Southampton to cross the Channel to Le Havre on the *Cawdor Castle*. Running along the platform as the band struck up 'God Save the King', Violet and Helen were just in time to thrust baskets of plums and pears through the window to George as the train left the station. The noise was 'tremendous' with the soldiers' cheering. 'Every window had 3 or 4 hands thrown out.' Violet's last sight of her son was of 'his flushed excited face' behind his friend John Manners. She waved until the train passed out of sight. 'The thing I could hardly bear was a mother who burst into tears when the train went.'

In one of his first letters home, George informed his mother and sister that the weather was boiling, that he had been inoculated for enteric (typhoid) fever, and that things were 'comparatively peaceful'. Initially Violet had been more afraid for her son's health 'than I am of the bullets'. She wrote that 'at 18 to undergo such a strain as *this* campaign seems to me excessive.' On 27 August, George sent a more ominous report from the position the 2nd Grenadiers had established in an area of Picardy in northern France, following their retreat from Mons. 'We had a most strenuous time,' he wrote in an uncharacteristically illegible hand, struggling to form the letters with a pencil by the light of a flickering candle. 'We marched right forward by stages up to the front. Then this evening, just as we were sitting down to dinner, the alarm was given that hostile cavalry had been seen quite close to the town. Soon sounds of very heavy firing were heard.'

At Great Wigsell, her home on the Kent–Sussex border, which she had rescued from dereliction and lovingly restored to something of its original style as a Jacobean manor house, Violet waited anxiously for further news. She reported what little she learned of George's movements to his father, Lord Edward Cecil, thousands of miles away in Cairo. The suspense aggravated Violet's health. She had difficulty sleeping, and on 23 August, the day of the Battle of Mons, had woken at 6.30 a.m. believing that she heard rifle fire. On 4 and 5 September she recorded in her 'War Diary 1914' that she was experiencing bad fainting fits which left her unable to stand, adding that 'these are the days that frighten me.'

At forty-two, Violet Cecil – 'Lady Ned', or Lady Edward Herbert Gascoyne-Cecil, as she was more properly known – was one of the most remarkable women of her generation. She came from a distinguished family. Her father, Admiral Frederick Maxse, had been a Crimean War hero. Her elder brother, Ivor Maxse, was the Brigadier-General commanding the 1st Guards Brigade out in France (Violet's other brother, Leo, was the owner-editor of the right-wing *National Review*). All the Maxse children were fierce imperialists and ardent Francophiles. For her part, Violet had acquired her love of France as a young woman studying drawing near the Boulevard Saint-Germain on the Left Bank. She was passionately attached to art and literature. She had met Degas in Paris, been admired by Burne-Jones, and became acquainted with George Meredith and Oscar Wilde through her parents' circle of friends. While in Paris, she had also begun a life-long friendship with Georges Clemenceau, the future Prime Minister of France.

Violet was tough, domineering and combative ('You should . . . never argue with the Maxse family about the French Revolution or anything else. It is a pure waste of breath' were Lord Edward's words of caution to his children). These traits, combined with her radical thinking and committed atheism, did not endear her to her husband's family, the Cecils of Hatfield House. Lord Edward Cecil, fourth son of Robert, Marquess of Salisbury, three times Conservative Prime Minister, had married Miss Maxse in a whirlwind romance in 1894. The wedding register, containing the signatures of Salisbury, Balfour, Asquith and Joseph Chamberlain, attested to the bridegroom's political heritage; while the bride's artistic bent was represented by the presence at the ceremony of six poets: Alfred Austin, George Meredith, Alfred Lyall, Edward Arnold, Oscar Wilde and Wilfrid Scawen Blunt.

Georgina Salisbury had confidently predicted that Hatfield would 'overpower' her new daughter-in-law. But neither the house nor the family succeeded in taming Violet. The Cecils disapproved of 'the competitive air' of her conversation in society, her extravagance, her love of haute couture and her predilection, while staying at Hatfield, which had only two bathrooms, for constant hot baths. Most of all, they deplored Violet's 'heathenry'. The Cecils were pious Anglicans, and religion was an integral part of the family's life. 'They were certain that they had the key to all essentials and that this lay in the

Anglican Church,' Violet once wrote. During the early years of her
marriage, various family members attempted in vain to bring this
heathen closer to God. At one time Violet was sent for instruction to
Arthur Winnington-Ingram, later the Bishop of London. 'I spent
some hours with him,' Violet remembered, 'and I was not asked to
go again.'

The Cecils' hopes that a clever wife for 'Nigs', as the family called
Lord Edward, would have a beneficial effect on this late developer
were also to be largely disappointed. Lord Edward possessed a vola-
tile and, at times, melancholy temperament, complicated by a concern
for his own spiritual well-being, but lightened by his peculiar brand
of facetious humour. As a young man he had failed to pass the exami-
nations for admission to the Royal Military College at Sandhurst.
Instead he obtained a commission in the militia, the local volunteer
force, and from there had made a smooth transition to the Grenadier
Guards after his father, the Prime Minister, had interceded on his
behalf with the Duke of Cambridge, the army's Commander-in-Chief.

From then on, Lord Edward's career path showed promise. He was
aide-de-camp to Lord Wolseley, the general commanding British
troops in Ireland, and, soon after his marriage, was appointed to serve
in the same capacity to the sirdar (commander-in-chief) of the Egyptian Army, Sir Herbert Kitchener, on the eve of his conquest of the
Sudan. Lord Edward saw his first action in the field at Omdurman, in
September 1898, fighting against the Dervishes. 'It was very exciting
and not a bit brutalizing,' he told his older brother Lord Robert, 'as
one does not at all realize that the enemy are men.' The following
summer, Lord Edward received orders to sail for South Africa. With
the outbreak of war, he suffered the ordeal of the entire 217 days of
the siege of Mafeking. Afterwards, he could never bear to speak of his
experiences there, but his stocking of the town's supplies with four
times the amount of stores considered necessary by the British government had undoubtedly proved decisive in Mafeking's survival.

The Relief of Mafeking, in May 1900, ended a period of protracted separation for Violet and Edward. However, it also marked
the beginning of their prolonged estrangement and the effective
breakdown of their marriage. Violet had travelled with her husband

to South Africa, staying in Cape Town with Cecil Rhodes at his estate, Groote Schuur, and with the British High Commissioner, Sir Alfred Milner, at Government House, while she campaigned to improve the state of the military hospitals. But when Lord Edward sailed to Egypt in the spring of 1901, following his secondment to the Egyptian Army, Violet did not accompany him. Even after he established himself in Cairo as an undersecretary, she refused to make her home there. Violet was in love with Alfred Milner, who was raised to the peerage and accorded a hero's welcome on his visit to London at the conclusion of the South African War. Already discreetly Milner's mistress, she became his constant companion after 1907 when he returned permanently to England, to a farm at Sturry Court, near Canterbury. Violet's meetings with Lord Edward were by then limited to the month or two of home leave that he took each year, in the spring or summer.

This was naturally very hard on the two children of the marriage, George, born in 1895, and Helen, six years later. However, despite missing their father, they thrived at their new home at Great Wigsell, the house of pale golden stone, set in the richly wooded landscape of the Sussex Weald, with farm buildings and twenty-five acres, which Violet and Edward scraped together the money to buy in 1906. Eight miles away, in the Burwash Valley, at the Jacobean manor of Bateman's, the twin of Great Wigsell, lived Violet's close friends, Rudyard Kipling, his American wife, Carrie, and their two children, John and Elsie. Violet was a fervent admirer of Kipling's writing, and shared his vision of spreading the values of Western civilization throughout the British Empire. She was also one of Carrie Kipling's few intimates. Sharp-tongued, a hypochondriac and ever watchful of her husband's movements, Carrie Kipling was widely disliked, but the two women formed a friendship of mutual trust and confidence. In the children's stories contained in *Rewards and Fairies*, published in 1910, Kipling immortalized the countryside where he had chosen to put down roots. In the poem 'If', prefaced to one of the book's historical fantasies, he evoked the virtues of stoicism in the face of adversity, and the determination not to be deterred from one's task, for the benefit of his son, John (from whom the character of 'Dan' in

Rewards and Fairies was drawn), and his generation of young men, who would shortly come of age.

George Cecil, two years older than John Kipling, was sent to Winchester College. Mother and son were extraordinarily close. Violet wrote to him every day and allowed him to accompany her on her annual trip to Paris, where on one occasion he dined with Clemenceau, soon to be the outgoing Prime Minister of France. George, she noted with pride, was 'not a bit forward and yet quite taking his share'. Like Violet, he possessed a distaste for all things metaphysical and had inherited her strength of personality, 'I insist' being one of his characteristic phrases.

As a child he had been drawn to the military almost as soon as he could walk and talk. When his father was under siege at Mafeking, George was given a toy cannon which fired peas at toy Boers on the nursery floor, and with news of Mafeking's relief, and of Lord Edward's release from captivity, four-year-old George had taken a leading role in the celebrations in Hatfield Park, lighting an enormous victory bonfire with a red, white and blue taper.

At Winchester, where it was more or less compulsory to join the Officer Training Corps, George took part in the parades and mock battles with enthusiasm. In 1912 he won a prize cadetship to Sandhurst. 'He has come on splendidly – sage, as ever and altogether delightful in his account of the new life, and keen as mustard,' Rudyard Kipling reported to Violet, after meeting George in London for dinner at Brown's Hotel. In January 1914 George passed out of Sandhurst and joined his father's old battalion, the 2nd Grenadier Guards, at Chelsea Barracks. Tall and strong, with wavy blond hair, George met the minimum height restrictions of the Grenadiers, whose size as well as their discipline had given them a reputation as formidable opponents.

Kipling later recalled George, while still a cadet at Sandhurst, forecasting the disposition of British troops in a war with Germany. 'We shall be sent to prolong the French left – *here!*' he said, pointing at his atlas. 'We shall not have enough men to do it and we shall be cut up. But with any luck I ought to be in it.'

At Great Wigsell, on 8 September, Violet had just finished dressing when her normal routine was punctured by the arrival of a letter from one of George's fellow officers. It informed her that George had been wounded and was presumed missing, following his part in an action fought near the town of Villers-Cotterêts by the rearguard of the fourth brigade, a week earlier on 1 September. Ten days of marching and fighting by the 2nd Grenadier Guards following the British defeat at Mons had managed to frustrate the Germans' outflanking movement. In a circular clearing in a forest called Rond de la Reine, two miles north of Villers-Cotterêts, George's company had taken up its position on the morning of the 1st. However, they had failed to see their enemies, Brandenburgers from the 35th Regiment, coming at them from the east because of the thickness of the foliage of the trees. In the small enclosed space of the forest, George's platoon had fought desperately for their lives while attempting a counterattack, a bayonet charge against the Germans to cover the retreat of companies of Coldstream and Irish Guards. 'The enemy ran in upon them from all sides,' Kipling wrote later in his history of the Irish Guards, 'and the action resolved itself into blind fighting in the gloom of the woods, with occasional glimpses of men crossing the rides, or firing from behind tree-boles.'

Those Grenadiers missing after the battle included 160 'other ranks' and three officers, among them George and his friend Second Lieutenant John Manners. As she tried to keep a tight hold over her emotions, Violet telegraphed Lord Edward with the devastating news concerning his son. Only to him could she admit subsequently that her dreams were filled with images of 'My darling, darling boy', often 'with some terrible injury in his beautiful face – and suffering – suffering'.

To the flood of letters from well-wishers in the next few weeks, she sent out a carefully worded reply. She thanked them for writing about George, observed with pride that he had withstood 'ten days' marching and fighting very well, but until I can hear something I am most terribly anxious. "Missing" with a barbarous enemy may mean so much.'

Was it possible that George could have survived such an onslaught of bullets, fired at point-blank range? Violet clung to various possible scenarios: that he was lying unidentified in some French hospital; that he might have been taken as a prisoner of war; or, the most terrifying possibility, that a wounded George might have crawled to take shelter in a French house, where he remained, too hurt to move. 'I have every reliance on George's resourcefulness and brain,' she wrote. 'But he may be too ill to think.'

One thing was certain. Violet was not going to stay passively at home, while she waited for further news. 'My boy is everything in the world to me,' she told Philip Ashworth, another Grenadier, 'and I want to leave no stone unturned.' She mobilized all the connections she could in an attempt to uncover more information about George's fate. Her cousin Ernest Maxse, working at the British Consulate General in Rotterdam, was asked to make inquiries to discover if the Germans were holding George prisoner. Violet travelled to London, 'terribly distressed and looking very ill', to make similar requests of the War Office, and of Walter Hines Page, the American Ambassador in London. But they all drew a blank. 'So far,' Violet explained to Lord Edward, 'the Germans have refused to open a war Bureau to give names and conditions of the wounded.' She appealed to Georges Clemenceau, who reported, after making inquiries, that he had been unable to trace George in any village, hospital or household. Privately he believed that Violet's son had been captured by the Germans.

Through her brother-in-law Lord Robert Cecil, Violet was able to seek assistance from the Wounded and Missing Enquiry Bureau, which was in the process of being set up by a small group of British Red Cross Society volunteers in Paris. Robert Cecil was a backbench Conservative MP, out of step with his party on a number of key issues, including tariff reform, the power of the House of Lords and the case for women's suffrage, which he supported. Cecil's work for the Red Cross in France was eventually to convince him that war prevention was the only worthwhile political objective.

In these early months of war, news about the work of the Bureau spread by word of mouth, and in the press. What began as a trickle of inquiries about the fate of missing officers soon became a flood of requests for information about other ranks, especially the ordinary soldier. The War Office sent only the briefest messages to relatives declaring simply that their man at the Front had been declared 'Missing in Action' on a given date. Free of charge, the Wounded and Missing Enquiry Bureau offered support – and hope – for those with nowhere else to turn. The Bureau's team of voluntary searchers sent out inquiries to hospitals, combed hospital wards and convalescent homes, and interviewed regimental comrades of the missing, often embarking on the time-consuming task of sifting conflicting evidence about an individual's survival. Sometimes, a missing soldier would turn out to be alive, in a hospital bed or interned in a prison camp. More often than not, the work of the Bureau would provide relief to the family in the form of confirmation that their husband, son or brother was indeed dead, killed in circumstances that the Bureau was able to describe and buried in a certain spot. The worst outcome was where there was an absence of definite news and no alleviation, therefore, of the suffering of the family in question.

Violet was offered a seat in the Red Cross motor-ambulance in which Lord Robert and other Bureau volunteers were travelling to the battlefield near Villers-Cotterêts to investigate the disappearance of hundreds of 'missing' soldiers on behalf of their distraught relatives. She seized upon this opportunity, despite Alfred Milner's efforts to dissuade her on the grounds that the trip was too dangerous. 'The difficulty was that the Battle of the Aisne, which has now been raging for 3 weeks, is very near that part of the world,' she wrote to Lord Edward following her return at the end of September. 'Villers-Cotterêts was last week, I daresay it is still – the headquarters of the French army.' As it turned out, Violet felt obliged to give up her place in the ambulance to a nurse, but with the help of Clemenceau, who obtained a pass for her to visit prohibited areas, and the loan of a car from Myron Herrick, the American Ambassador in Paris, she reached the battlefield and its surrounding areas on 26 September to search for traces of her son.

She found some poignant relics there, including men's pocket books, 'signed by my boy'. With the assistance of the French doctor who had remained at Villers-Cotterêts throughout the German occupation, she checked the hospital register of all the patients, but could find no sign 'of any of our 3' officers. Dishearteningly, the village schoolmistress – who had already been interviewed by Lord Robert Cecil, informing him that among the prisoners marched away by the Germans was 'a very young, very big and fair officer speaking excellent French [George had passed the exam for a French Interpretership in June 1914]' – was unavailable for questioning. Everything 'was despairingly vague'. All Violet could ascertain from local people was that a number of unwounded prisoners had been rounded up in the church, while the English wounded had been sent to two hospitals.

At every turn, the results of inquiries about George, which appeared initially to promise so much, latterly proved to be a cruel illusion. The 'fitful hope and racking uncertainty', Alfred Milner wrote, observing Violet's distress, continued after she returned to Great Wigsell. Awaiting her was a telegram reporting that the United States Consul-General in Berlin had maintained 'verbally' that George's name was on the list of wounded officers taken as prisoners of war to Aix-la-Chapelle. But no sooner had her hopes been raised than they were dashed again when two conflicting reports of George's death emerged, one from a drummer boy who said he'd buried George and John Manners, the other from a returned prisoner who claimed to have seen George killed by a shell.

'I don't feel as if George could be dead,' Violet wrote to Lord Edward, 'but that is simply because I saw him last so well and full of life. My instincts tell me he is alive – my reason that he is dead.'

Britain's aristocracy was taking the lead, in the autumn of 1914, in the rush to the colours. After decades of being widely attacked as redundant and parasitic, the upper classes were keen to prove themselves, and saw the war as their supreme opportunity to do so. Some members of patrician houses, like George Cecil, were already in the Regular Army when the war started, but others in the Territorial Force made a vital contribution to the fighting in the months before Kitchener's New Army was trained and equipped. Still more young aristocrats were quick to volunteer, worried that the war would be over before they had the chance to get to the Front. Older grandees played a part by encouraging recruitment in their localities. 'If I had twenty sons,' Lord Derby told the West Lancashire Territorial Association, 'I should be ashamed if every one of them did not go to the front when his time came.' Titled ladies, meanwhile, like the Duchess of Westminster, or the Dowager Duchess of Sutherland, threw themselves into nursing work, organizing hospitals in northern France or setting up ambulance units in Belgium.

Fergus Forbes, son of the Irish Earl of Granard, was the first peer, or son of a peer, to be killed, at the Battle of Mons, on 23 August. The sons of Baron Willingdon and of the Earl of Aylesford; the younger brothers of the Duke of Devonshire and the Earl of Durham – all were among those killed in the course of the next two months. By the close of 1914, the death toll amounted to six peers, sixteen baronets, ninety-five sons of peers and eighty-two sons of baronets.

There was concern early on that the monarchy, by failing to send its men to war, might not be seen to be doing enough. The twenty-year-old Prince of Wales, who had been commissioned in the Grenadier Guards, had expressed a 'very vehement' desire to be sent to the Front, but Kitchener was 'equally determined that . . . it would be in every sense wrong to let the Prince go'. Lord Hugh Cecil, another of George Cecil's uncles, raised the matter with the Archbishop of Canterbury, Randall Davidson, on 19 September. Lord Hugh believed that it would be 'a great political disaster' if the Prince of Wales were killed, but that his death would possess the considerable advantage of covering 'the monarchy in glory'.

There has been so much sacrifice splendidly borne in this war that people won't like the King not risking anything. How many only sons have already fallen! – & the King has five . . . The patriotic zeal of the classes nearest the throne is wonderful. I left Lady Airlie, whose husband was killed in S.[outh] Africa, scheming to get all her three sons out to the front before the war is over. I have myself nine nephews of fighting age – all of them are in one or other military forces – all are volunteering for active service – except the two who have already gone, one of whom is back here wounded, the other is missing & either a prisoner or too probably killed – I don't pretend to be patriotic myself & shall be heartily glad if some of the nine fail to pass the doctor – but I note the patriotism of others. Believe me the King's five sons will be stones around his neck unless the Prince of Wales goes.

The publication, on 3 September, of the long-awaited first casualty lists for the British Expeditionary Force – 'The Toll of War', as it was headlined in the press – followed by further returns on 5, 7 and 10 September, brought home the extent of the aristocracy's sacrifice. 'But oh that new list!' exclaimed Mary Drew, Gladstone's daughter, of the 'Roll of Honour' released from General Headquarters on the 9th, which contained George Cecil's name among the missing, along with other members of aristocratic families. 'Aubrey Herbert [second son of the Earl of Carnarvon] wounded and missing – Ld. Edward Cecil's only son; Ld. Maurice Fitzgerald, the fine young boy Ld. and Ly. Manners' son, and lots more dead and wounded . . . It is most unspeakable the horror of it all.'

Writing to Venetia Stanley on 9 September, Asquith commented on the identical casualty list, shortly before its publication, and noted the appearance of George Cecil's and John Manners's names. He feared that they might have been 'too impetuous' and taken as prisoners. 'On the other hand they may be able to straggle back, as so many of the "missing" have done & are doing.' Asquith was not alone in being struck by the extraordinarily high proportion of missing contained in the casualty statistics. In the returns for 3 September, the total 'missing' came to over 4,000, 95 officers and 4,183 other ranks. A substantial number of these, unaccounted for in the confusion of the aftermath of battle, did indeed manage 'to straggle back'. Just occasionally, the press would print a notice like the one carried by *The Times* later in September, which reported that Canon Lister of Newcastle had heard through the Red Cross that his son Captain G. D. Lister, previously included among the missing, had passed through Brussels as a prisoner in the course of the previous week. But for the families of the remainder, as the Reverend Denys Yonge, Vicar of Boreham in Essex, noted in his diary, 'the list of missing = frightful anxiety', an anxiety relieved only by confirmation of the loved one's death.

If the editor of the *Daily Express*, R. D. Blumenfeld, is to be believed, the horrifying novelty of the casualty lists soon wore off. 'The first eight or ten casualties had as much publicity as all the rest put together,' Blumenfeld wrote in his diary as early as 24 October. 'People discussed the deaths of young second lieutenants with bated breath. Gradually the familiarity of the thing became apparent. You receive the news of the death of your friends as a matter of fact.'

The first lists, however, may well have been a spur to the writing of Laurence Binyon's famous commemorative poem 'For the Fallen', which was published in *The Times* on 21 September. The poem was composed in the wake of news of the losses at Mons, as Binyon sat on a Cornish cliff, gazing out at the ocean at Polzeath. Its central stanza, echoing the language of Shakespeare and of the King James Bible, was an unforgettable expression of the wartime nation in mourning:

> They shall grow not old, as we that are left grow old:
> Age shall not weary them, nor the years condemn.
> At the going down of the sun and in the morning
> We will remember them.

'And so the horrible see-saw goes on.' These were Rudyard Kipling's words to a friend in early October, describing Violet Cecil's distressing predicament: not knowing for certain whether her son was dead or alive, 'and letters of condolence *and* congratulation crossing each other and harrowing her soul. Meanwhile the boy's father thousands of miles away and cut off from all save letters and wires.'

The Kiplings were doing all they could to support Violet. Rudyard Kipling gave practical help by making inquiries of his own through official channels about George's fate, hoping to break down the 'German wall of official silence' about the English prisoners they were holding. 'I can't tell you to still hope as we do,' Carrie Kipling wrote to Violet after this proved unsuccessful; 'only nothing *has* been proved has it? And we have *not* seen the list of prisoners. That George does not write is nothing; he is not allowed to.' Always present in their minds, as they concerned themselves with the question of George Cecil's survival, must have been fears for their own boy John.

On his seventeenth birthday in August, John had visited recruiting stations in Hastings and Maidstone, but had been declared unfit for military service by both of them owing to his extremely poor eyesight (his 6/36 vision meant that he had difficulty deciphering the second line of a standard eye chart). His father then turned to his old friend Lord Roberts to help obtain a commission in the Irish Guards for John. In mid September, John reported for duty as a second lieutenant at Warley Barracks in Essex, the headquarters of his regiment's reserve. It was no coincidence that, soon afterwards, Kipling's health began to be affected by the tensions of the war, and he would sometimes wake in the night suffering from sharp, neuralgic pains on one side of his face. Carrie Kipling faced up to the reality of their situation, writing in October that 'There is no chance that John will survive unless he is so maimed from a wound as to be unfit to fight. We know it and he does . . . but we must give and do what we can and live on the shadow of a hope that our boy will be the one to escape.'

The 'dim fading hope' of finding George Cecil alive was finally snuffed out on 19 November, when the digging party, working at a shallow grave near Villers-Cotterêts, uncovered the body of a fourth officer. The buttons on the uniform showed that the man had been a Grenadier, but no disc could be found. However, from the description of George Cecil's figure supplied to the party – and especially from the size of his boots – there was no doubt that these were his remains. The identification was confirmed when the initials 'G. E. C.' were revealed on the front of his vest.

A telegram informed Violet of the terrible news. She in turn sent one to George's father in Egypt: 'grave opened George believed identified broken hearted Violet Cecil'.

Violet was overcome by the 'crushing' thought of 'all the years of our lives' that 'must be lived without him' and mourned '*the fearful waste* of his promising life'. She tortured herself, imagining George's last minutes. How long had he been in agony before he died and was 'thrown like carrion into a pit'? 'When I think of the inhuman waste of a beautiful life I can hardly endure myself to be part of a world where such things were possible.' Three buttons cut from George's uniform, together with a piece of the vest he was wearing when he was killed, were returned to Violet. She wore a fragment of the vest in a locket around her neck for the rest of her life. For a relic of his only son, Lord Edward chose the crucifix given to George at his baptism by his godfather and uncle, Hugh Cecil. He had it engraved with the epitaph 'Died for his country September 1st 1914 near Villers-Cotterêts in France having continued Christ's faithful soldier and servant until his life's end'. There could be no meeting of minds between husband and wife on the subject of George's 'future life'. To Violet, death was 'the Great Dissolver'. 'Your beliefs are incredible to me,' she wrote to Edward in one painful exchange, 'and my consolation different to yours.'

With Rudyard Kipling's assistance, Violet was able to piece together the story of George's final hours. In early December he reported to her on the enormous efforts he had made, having interviewed three of George's men who were convalescing at Gatcombe House, on the Isle of Wight. With the aid of a map showing the Grenadiers' positions on 1 September, Kipling was able to question the men and sift the reliability of their evidence. One of them, Private Titcombe, he described as 'slow, unlovely, thick skinned and phlegmatic', and consequently not at all the type, he thought, who would embroider or vary his statements. The most valuable witness, though, was Private Snowdon, another soldier from one of the platoons of George's company, who had been discovered recovering from his wounds in a London hospital. According to Snowdon's account, George had come upon the German attack in a sunken lane and shouted to his men to 'Charge lads, and we'll do 'em in yet.' George was first hit in the hand, and then shot through the head. 'Snowdon says the fire was then coming from all quarters,' Kipling told Violet. 'He thinks George was the last officer on his feet.'

Violet was now the closest she would ever come to an account of her son's dying minutes. But where would she find any sense of the consolation she'd referred to in her letter to Lord Edward? The answer came from a perhaps surprising source.

The bodies of the ninety-four men exhumed near Villers-Cotterêts were carefully laid out in an enlarged grave. An Anglican clergyman and a Catholic priest said prayers for the dead at graveside before the bodies were covered with earth, and a temporary wooden cross erected over them. The burial of the four officers, by contrast, was a more ceremonial affair, consistent with their status. They were interred in pine coffins in the local cemetery, their funeral attended by the mayor and members of the French military, and marked by the firing of a cannon salute. In death as in life, officers were given preferential treatment. In late 1914 there was as yet no suggestion that there should be uniformity of burial across all ranks.

The families of the private soldiers were also denied something that Lady Violet Cecil had obtained by virtue of her class, status and influence: information concerning the fate of their missing loved ones. Coming to terms with George's death, Violet later offered consolation to the grieving working-class families whose menfolk had served under him. Many had received only the barest notification from the War Office that their son, brother or husband was 'missing'. Violet took it upon herself to inform them, where she was able, that the bodies of their missing relatives had been located and given a respectful burial.

The many dozens of letters from grateful relatives, testifying to this extraordinary act of compassion on Violet Cecil's part, are extremely moving. Charlotte Jamieson admitted that her family had wondered how her brother had died, and would certainly never have found out the truth had it not been for Lady Violet. Violet Oldershaw thanked her for the details she'd provided 'from the bottom of my heart'. Eveline Meadows expressed her relief: 'I could not get to know whether my husband died from disease or wounds, I have sent to the [War] Office twice.' John Meagher wrote to Violet that it was 'always a matter of deep anxiety to me and his mother to know how he died because the only previous accounts all differed and seemed unreliable'. Some of Violet's correspondents gave insights into the experience of hardship, and told in passing of how the deaths of loved ones had impacted on their own lives. Catherine Laffey was a 'heart-broken mother' who had already lost two sons in the war and considered suicide: 'I got out of drowning as I am getting afraid I drew more trouble on myself.' From Liverpool's Royal Infirmary,

Elizabeth Wallace wrote that 'My trouble was twofold as I lost my eldest girl & the Father inside ten months and my baby was only nine months the day He [her husband] was killed so it quite broke my health up.'

'It is a consolation to have a grave to cry and pray over and to know he was buried with his comrades.' Apart from the reference to praying, these were sentiments with which, as a grieving mother, Violet Cecil could wholeheartedly concur.

A Country Parish in Wartime

Is it conceivable that ordinary men and women could have been oblivious to the war in its early stages? The recollections of Olive May Taylor certainly suggest that ignorance of the war's existence was at least possible. In 1914 Taylor was sixteen years old and working as a domestic servant on a small farm in a remote area of Humberside. She later claimed that 'England had been at war three months before I knew', and that when a farm boy had told her about the war, one day in November 1914, she had refused to believe him. 'How could this be?' she asked herself years later. 'Why had I not known that England had declared war on August the fourth that year?'

Miss Taylor's complete lack of awareness of the war – if accurately remembered – obviously represented an extreme case. But the evidence of other personal records suggests that an attitude of indifference to the war in its first months was not unheard of. The diary of the suffragette Bessie Rayne for August and September alludes to the war briefly in passing, but is much more taken up with descriptions of shopping expeditions and plans for family birthday parties. Similarly, the diary account for August of Miss E. Barkworth, from Devon, demonstrates a marked lack of interest in the war. Miss Barkworth spent the month going to the beach and reading Dickens.

In marked contrast to these manifestations of 'war indifference', however, were the many daily or weekly journals initiated by men and women with the specific purpose of recording their observations of the rapidly changing sequence of world events, and the impact they were having on their own lives. Frederick Robinson, for example, a businessman from Cobham, in Surrey, began his daily record on 22 July 1914, just as the international situation was beginning to darken, and continued it, more or less unbroken, for the next four years.

The Reverend Andrew Clark, Rector of Great Leighs, Essex

What would in time prove the most ambitious and remarkable English diary of the war years was the product of a Scottish-born clergyman, the Reverend Andrew Clark, the Rector of a small country parish in the village of Great Leighs, in Essex. It was born partly out of Clark's deep regret that he had failed to keep a diary during the

South African War, when he first came to recognize the interest and historical value of the letters sent home by men from Great Leighs on active service, and the peculiarity of rumours about the war which passed around the village. By the end of 1914 Clark had already completed the first eight volumes of a diary that would eventually stretch to ninety-two notebooks comprising a total of over three million words. Each of the notebooks, tied shut with red ribbon, measures eight by six and a half inches, and every entry is signed and dated by its author, as if to set the seal on its authenticity for posterity. Clark depended on shorthand to make quick notes of conversations he'd had or of information handed on to him, transcribing these into the full record once he was back in his study at the rectory.

As a diarist, Andrew Clark eschews personal detail. In the course of the war, he suffered the death of his wife, though he makes no reference to this bereavement in his record, merely observing a few days afterwards that mourning was difficult to obtain because of the enormous number of casualties on the Western Front. 'The War Diary', Clark noted, 'is – above all things – a village diary.' It is in essence a diary of small things, an account of the echoes of the war as they resound in an English rural parish, and their effect on the everyday lives of ordinary people. Clark's overriding concern at all times was to set down what he observed about the effects of the war on his parish, or what he learned from others. He was well placed to interpret noises from the outside world, given his connections in Oxford, his friends and contacts in neighbouring Essex towns, and his relatives in Scotland.

Great Leighs was – and, to some extent, still is – 'a wide and thinly peopled parish'. In 1914 its population consisted of 614 people, and the village, nestling between Chelmsford to the south and Braintree to the north, was described as 'singularly isolated', despite being within forty miles of London. The Great Road, where most villagers lived, had long since 'ceased to throb with through traffic', while the building of the railway in the 1840s had completely bypassed Great Leighs. In order for Clark to reach Oxford, where he was regularly employed as an examiner by the University, he had to be driven the six miles to Chelmsford in a pony cart to catch the up-train to Liverpool Street, then make his way across the city to Paddington and out into the countryside once more.

The life of Great Leighs was, to use Clark's own description, 'self-centred'. It revolved around the work of its farms, its smithy, its wheelwrights and its carpenters. Conscious of the fact that the villagers didn't have access to newspapers, and that they rarely visited neighbouring towns, let alone large metropolitan centres like London, Clark acted as a purveyor of information concerning the war. During the South African War, he had posted makeshift bulletins of war news on a brick pillar on a wall opposite the blacksmith's shop. From August 1914, official bulletins, introduced as part of a new government policy, were displayed at country post offices every Saturday, containing the latest, though 'as a rule . . . extremely meagre', war news. Clark pinned up a copy each weekend in the church porch, in time for the Sunday services, afterwards pasting several of the notices in the pages of the diary.

Andrew Clark was the lynchpin of his small, scattered community. His portly, ungainly figure was a common sight, shuffling along the narrow lanes of the village. Clothed in his black clerical garb, and wearing the 'wide-awake' hat that indicated his Anglo-Catholic sympathies, Clark was like a taller, Anglican version of Chesterton's Roman Catholic priest Father Brown (who also happens to hail from Essex). Encountering villagers on the way, he treated them with sympathy while listening intently to whatever they might have to tell him. It was no accident that, in his other role as scholar and antiquarian, Andrew Clark was the editor of the seventeenth-century writers Anthony Wood and John Aubrey. He shares with them an extraordinary aptitude for the collecting and recording of information, and an insatiable appetite for the quirks and idiosyncrasies of human behaviour. One can almost feel Clark's delight registering on the diary page as he relates the story of the confusion of an aged maidservant at Painfield Hall, in nearby Braintree, who is imprisoned in a time warp from sixty years earlier, in the era of the Crimean War: '[She] cannot be put right as to the enemy we are at war with now, but imagines it as in Crimean days. She heartily wishes them [*sic*] Russians were shot; they are cruel; and to think of the way they are killing our men.'

Clark was in his late fifties at the outbreak of war, having been born in 1856 at Dollar, Clackmannanshire, in Scotland, the son of Robert Clark, a farm worker, and his wife Eliza. Clark's academic gifts were recognized from an early age, and he benefited from the wide curriculum and excellent teaching of the local school. In 1871, at fifteen, he attended St Andrew's University. Four years later he went up to Balliol College, Oxford, and the following year he won a scholarship to Lincoln College.

Clark took a double first in Greats in 1879, and returned briefly to St Andrew's before being elected to a fellowship at Lincoln, where he was a college tutor and a lecturer in logic. He was ordained in 1884 and became the chaplain of Lincoln as well as the incumbent of two Oxford churches, All Saints and St Michael's, Northgate. He also took a wife at this time, Mary Walker Paterson, five years his senior and a daughter of the Provost of St Andrew's. They settled in North Oxford, and their first child, Mary, was born in 1887. She was followed, almost a decade later, by another daughter, Mildred.

Meanwhile, Clark's scholarly interests centred on the rich collections preserved in Oxford's college archives and in the Bodleian Library. Among other works, he compiled and edited Anthony Wood's *Antiquities of the City of Oxford*, wrote Wood's *Life and Times*, and produced an edition of John Aubrey's *Brief Lives*, based on the original manuscripts.

It may have been Mary Clark's aversion to the university's social life that led her husband to apply, in 1894, for the living of Great Leighs, which was in the gift of Lincoln College. He took his first service as Rector there on Palm Sunday of that year, and so engrossed did he become by 'the duties of this most scattered parish' that he doubted at first whether he would ever find the time to continue with his writing and editorial work. However, Clark was indefatigable and had soon immersed himself in local history, contributing to the *Essex Review* and attempting a systematic record of his new parish from the reign of Elizabeth I onwards.

Clark's church of St Mary the Virgin has a long and complex history. Its circular west tower (of which there are a number of other examples in the county) was constructed of flint, Roman tiles and puddingstone, and built on Saxon foundations. St Mary's possesses a twelfth-century nave and a fourteenth-century chancel, together with a distinctive Norman archway, as well as various nineteenth-century additions. Close to the church, off the Boreham Road, stood the Rectory and Lyons Hall, a fine old house that had been in the Tritton family for more than a century. In 1914 Lyons Hall was home to the current Squire and Lord of the Manor, Joseph Herbert Tritton, a director of Barclays Bank, which had been formed in the final years of the nineteenth century from the family banking firm of Barclay, Bevan, Tritton & Co.

Tritton and his wife Lucy come across in Clark's diary as a kindly, but somewhat stiff and slightly forbidding couple. (A hint of Tritton's character is to be found in his comments to the Institute of Bankers on the three cardinal virtues for a banker: 'Incredulity, Affability and the Power to say No'.) The Trittons took their squirearchical duties seriously. They were generous in their provision of local philanthropy, ferrying the sick to the hospital in one of their cars, and paying for a new village pump and church clock, while their four daughters – there were also five sons – were active in good works. The relationship between Squire and Rector was mutually respectful, and had grown in time to be a productive working partnership. But some uneasiness between them had long been evident as a result of their differing attitudes to religion. The Squire's Quaker-based Evangelical fervour found little to commend in Clark's Anglo-Catholicism. To offset the effects of Clark's High Church services, Tritton erected a corrugated-iron shed on his property, known locally as the 'Tin Tabernacle', which was intended to offer a sanctuary to the village's Nonconformists.

The Reverend Clark had often thought of devoting some of his spare time to writing a history of Oxford during the English Civil War. In August 1914 he suddenly turned from projects like this, lending a voice to the past, and began work on recording the life of his parish in the present, for the benefit of the historians of the future. He started writing his diary on 19 August, making irregular entries as he attempted to reconstruct a record of the days he'd missed from earlier in the month. By 24 August he was maintaining it regularly, 'day by day', and had given the first volume a preliminary title: 'Echoes of the 1914 War'.

Daily life that first autumn of the war started early for the Rectory household. Its occupants tended to be woken at 'earliest dawn' by the noise of the steam scarifiers working at neighbouring farms. Following the army's requisition of farm horses, these scarifiers had taken the place of horse-drawn ploughs, breaking up the soil for seedbed preparation and the planting of essential foodstuffs. If the sound of farm machinery failed to rouse them, then the 5 a.m. reveille played by a bugler at a nearby cricket ground, where hundreds of Territorials were bivouacked, would certainly have succeeded. Another loud echo of the war descended on the Rectory soon after breakfast every morning: the discharge of heavy firing from gunnery practice, not far away on the coast at Shoeburyness, which caused all the windows in the Rectory to rattle violently.

The Trittons took the lead in implementing emergency preparations for the parish. Fears of food scarcity, after reports of rising prices and riots in Essex town stores, encouraged members of the family to issue instructions to villagers about the necessity of sowing vegetable seeds, especially for onions and carrots, in every garden, large or small. Directions from Lyons Hall, however well intentioned, were not always welcomed. In October, advice from Lucy Tritton and her daughters to the Great Leighs cottagers about the need to practise domestic economy by cooking inexpensive but wholesome meals, such as macaroni cheese, were dismissed by some as 'patronizing', and the recipes as 'more costly than ordinary'. Women in the village were also quickly enlisted in knitting and sewing for the troops. Mrs Tritton sent out directives for knitting socks: 'Needles – no. 15. Wool – either 4 ounces best Scotch fingering or 5 ounces second quality.' In time, they would graduate to producing sand bags for the front line.

Great excitement surrounded the arrival of troops in Great Leighs. A brigade of 6,000 Territorials marched through the village in mid

August. 'There's never been a sight like that in Great Leighs,' exclaimed Old Collins, a former under-gamekeeper, respected as the village patriarch. Andrew Clark immediately closed the Church School so that the children could see the 'troops in movement'. Two of the regiments on this occasion were 'hopelessly' footsore, and two trainloads of them had to go on to Braintree by rail from Sudbury. 'The first marches ought to have been short and slow,' Clark commented in his diary. 'It is said they were *19* miles a day, on bad roads, in blazing hot weather, with heavy kit!!!' Tired and dirty, these soldiers bought ginger beer and lemonade from the village shop and St Anne's Castle, reputedly the oldest licensed premises in England, and lay on the grass, chatting and bantering with the villagers, who brought them apples and plums. 'One of the men had a woman's head tattooed on his arm; and was told that he was taking his girl's photograph with him to the war. Another man told the folk about him that he was going to bring back half the Kaiser's moustache.'

To the children, any soldiers were 'a beautiful sight', and inspired imitation. At Little Waltham, the adjacent village to Great Leighs, a small boy was seen 'marching a run of boys of his own size, along the road, preceded by a boy (doing duty as "the band"), whistling "It's a long way to Tipperary", the marching-tune of the regiments this year.' In Braintree High Street, a row of little children were observed with their noses flattened against the window of the local bookshop, watching 'a partly moving apparatus showing a fort, a railway, sentries, cavalry, infantry, Territorials in uniform, kilted Highlanders . . . They had been there . . . for hours.'

Great Leighs itself did not directly experience the billeting of soldiers at a time when troops were being assembled for France and camps were still under preparation. The appearance therefore of any man in army uniform continued to be something of a novelty. But Clark's diary gathered reports of the impact of billeting on other areas. For instance, he learned that the billeting of Scottish troops, many of whom were from fishing communities, on poor cottagers in Bedford had not been successful, as they 'smelt as if they never washed'. Closer to home, in Chelmsford, a Territorial division of the

Warwickshires disgraced themselves, when men and officers were seen drunk in the streets, night after night. As a result, the Warwickshires were moved into camp at Colchester, and the Berkshires replaced them in the billets they'd vacated, though Clark suggested that at least some of the fault lay with the citizens of Chelmsford. They were 'possessed with the idea that all men who enlist are the waifs and strays who enlisted in the old evil days of the army. They have not yet awoken to the fact that the men of the new army are gentlemanly fellows, and expect gentlemanly treatment.'

The local recruitment meeting, soon to become a regular feature of Great Leighs life, and a focal point for discussion of the war, congregated for the first time in the barn at Lyons Hall, on Sunday, 6 September, a day of fierce heat. 'As is usual in an Essex village', the women entered the barn first, the men waiting outside until all the women had gone in. Clark was among those seated on the platform, along with Tritton, the chairman, and assorted local dignitaries, including a representative of the Territorials, a veteran of the Boer War and speakers from both major political parties.

Tritton, whose eldest son, Alan, was at the Front serving as a captain in the Coldstream Guards, emphasized that

> One cause stands out before all others, and can be expressed in four words: Germany meant to fight. We were bound to our neighbours, the little Kingdom of Belgium . . . [and] the great French republic . . . I do want to say to the fathers and mothers of these two parishes [Little Leighs was also represented] – do not stand in the way of your son's going to fight for the country. This I can say as one who has given a beloved son to do the same.

Major Taylor, from the Territorials spoke next:

> Lord Kitchener appeals to every man of nineteen to thirty-five to enlist . . . but not on the usual conditions. Ordinarily a man enlisted for twelve years; now he enlists only for the period of this war . . . To every working man who may think of serving his country at this crisis I would say – don't worry about your family in your absence: they will be well looked after . . .

Five days later, at another meeting, the process of actual recruitment began. The response was disappointing. The presiding Colonel
attributed the reluctance of young men to come forward to shyness
in the presence of the 'ladies' in the audience. He predicted that for
every man who came forward at the meeting, 'four or five offered
themselves next day'. Some men, it was true, were reported by Andrew
Clark as preparing to do so. Albert Wright, 'one of the strongest
young farm-hands', had announced his intention of volunteering, as
had Jimmy Lewin, 'the "boy" who drives Mann's [the baker's] cart',
though 'as this rests on his own statement this is not believed'.
Another man, Edward Baker, was eager to enlist, but Clark thought
it would be surprising if he was accepted: 'He is narrow-chested;
stammers; and has a big operations scar.' The son of the head-gardener
at Lyons Hall also wanted to volunteer, but his chest measured only
33½ inches, half an inch short of the required minimum. He had
therefore invested in a pair of dumb-bells to build himself up, and
would apply again in a fortnight's time.

According to Clark, however, there was already ill-feeling in the
village 'against lads who are of age and physique to enlist and who
have not done so' – and he set down in his diary the names of three
who had failed to come forward. Equally, though, there was resentment against any pressure being brought to bear to force men at Great
Leighs to join up. When a footman at Lyons Hall volunteered, there
were rumours in the village that he had not done so entirely of his
own volition, and that the Squire may have played a part in exerting
influence on him. A group of 'farm-lads' who were admonished
about enlisting retorted that 'they were waiting for the farmers' sons
of the district to show them the example.'

'The country lads say,' Clark noted, 'and to my mind justly, "If so
many men are needed by the country, let the country say all *must*
go."' But as yet there was still no widespread political support for the
introduction of conscription. As for Andrew Clark himself, he was
far too old to fight, so in what wartime capacity might he serve his
country? His younger daughter Mildred, who was going to study
medicine at her father's old university, St Andrews, had enrolled as a
Voluntary Aid Detachment nurse at Braintree Hospital (the VAD

scheme had been introduced in 1909, under the auspices of the British Red Cross and the St John Ambulance Association, to assist the professional military nursing service in the event of a national emergency). Clark chose to join the local branch of the Special Constabulary. Nationally this was a body of private citizens of above military age, called upon for at most a couple of nights a week, for several hours at a stretch, to stand guard over reservoirs or electrical works, patrol the streets and enforce the new lighting restrictions (among the more illustrious special constables in the autumn of 1914 was the composer Sir Edward Elgar, pounding pavements in the Hampstead district of North London).

At the end of August, Clark described the details of his new appointment. 'Every Special Constable will have his warrant card, with his name, empowering him to act, and his baton. At present there are in Essex only 975 batons and 1,682 Special Constables already enrolled.' The baton was not to be carried in a provocative manner, but kept inside a pocket in the right trouser leg. An armlet badge and a whistle also went with the job. Clark took part in the drill organized in a village field, and caused 'Prodigal amusement' among the other participants as he was pulled and shoved, and 'hustled into unexpected positions'.

Yet, as time went on, he felt increasingly the futility of his duties as a special constable. He was not alone in this respect in Great Leighs, where numbers for recruits of the new constables had quickly fallen from forty to twenty-five by the time of the swearing-in ceremony in early September. The patrolling of the roads in his parish appeared utterly pointless, for there was nothing in the village that the enemy would wish to destroy: no reservoir, no railway station, no wireless station, no barracks. Moreover, villagers living in fear of German invasion were often alarmed by the sound of footsteps outside their homes late at night or in the early hours of the morning.

Clark's disillusion was compounded by the man selected to lead the local branch of the constabulary. Sir Richard Pennefather, an ex-officer of the Metropolitan Police, was benign but fussy, and 'very full of terrors', like so many other people, of the threat from German spies 'prowling about to blow up bridges and cut down telegraph poles'. Pennefather elicited near-hilarity among his constables when he related an experience from one of his recent spy hunts. Suspicious of a man discovered sheltering beside a haystack on a wet evening, Pennefather and his patrol immediately seized him, but had to let him go after finding no bomb or other incendiary device about his person. 'It was irresistibly comic,' Clark observed wryly, 'that a man in authority should be ignorant of the common tramp and his habit on wet nights, of sleeping rough.'

Rumours – of spies, sabotage by enemy agents, or the ubiquitous Russian soldiers, with bushy black beards, passing through England – were reported by Clark in the pages of his diary, mostly without any accompanying assessment of whether they were true or not. A spy dressed as a nun was said to have been arrested at Felsted; a chemist in Braintree, who was asked for 'a quantity of poison' by someone with a foreign accent, reportedly managed to send a message to the police, who arrived just in time to arrest 'the alien subject'; Clark learned of a Belgian girl, recovering in the Convent at Bocking, whose hands had been 'hacked off' by German soldiers; and two of the Territorials who'd marched through the village in August were rumoured to have died the next day, one from pneumonia, the other from blood poisoning (both these were later confirmed to be fictitious). It was characteristic of the village mind, Clark believed, 'that it is too feeble to accept simple fact, it has to add legendary details'.

The impressions that reached Clark in Great Leighs of actual fighting at the Front were necessarily more limited. In October, he reproduced one eyewitness account he'd received of an ambulance train that had stopped at Derby Station:

> The wounded seemed to be in berths in tiers at each side. There were some pitiable cases. One man had lost both legs. One man tried to wave his hand, but was too feeble except just to raise it. There were several from the battlefield, their boots still in a horrid state with Belgian mud.

More chilling was Clark's report of an encounter he'd had that autumn with a sergeant of the South Staffordshires, on the return train journey from one of his visits to Oxford. The sergeant, who had served in the British Army as a Regular for almost two decades, told Clark that the Boer War had been 'a picnic' in comparison with the present conflict: 'In several of the actions he had seen more shells discharged in twenty minutes than he had seen in the whole course of the South-African War. He said that this war "is not fighting, but murder".'

————

Among the mass of books, letters and other documents in the rectory study were a pot of glue, a pair of scissors and editions of five news-papers, delivered each day: the *Scotsman*, the *Star*, the *Daily Express*, the *Daily Telegraph* and the *Evening News*. These papers were the materials that Clark drew on for the other regular project which he began in the early days of the war, his 'English Words in War-Time'.

Andrew Clark was fascinated by language and its uses. He some-times jotted down the unusual forms of speech that he heard among the villagers. A thunderstorm in Great Leighs was a 'tempest'; frogs were 'little Jacobs'; mud was 'slud'; and a woodpecker was a 'waffle'. He had also long been an enthusiastic reader of the new *Oxford English Dictionary*. The OED, under the editorship of James Murray, another Scotsman, was still ongoing, thirty years after its first fascicle, cover-ing the words in the range 'A to Ant', had been published by Oxford University Press. By 1914 the dictionary had reached the letter *S*. That October saw the appearance of its latest instalment, for the words 'Speech to Spring', though the departure on active service of many men from the Press meant that production of the OED had inevitably slowed.

'Each section of the Dictionary as it comes out I get & peruse with rapt attention,' Clark had told Murray in 1900. Clark was counted as 'a friend' of the dictionary, one of the experts called upon to provide assistance in the definition and usage of 'historical, legal, philosoph-ical, scientific, and technical words'.

Clark recognized the outbreak of war as presenting him with a rare opportunity. Here was the chance to document developments in the English language at a significant point in history, as they were occurring. Like the diary, Clark's study of language in wartime focuses on the everyday, the ordinary and the ephemeral. In his notebooks, Clark provided the words or expressions thrown up by the war with a tentative definition, while offering examples of their current usage from 'slips', clippings from newspapers that were pasted alongside each entry. He collated every word against the evidence of the published *OED*, noting whether it was 'adequately represented', 'not directly found' or 'apparently absent'. In time Clark hoped that his work would go some way towards filling linguistic gaps for lexicographers compiling the dictionary in the future. By the end of October 1914, he had completed four notebooks containing roughly 4,000 entries. Eventually, sixty-five volumes would be placed in the Bodleian Library's archive in Oxford.

The first months of the war supplied Clark with a rich crop of new words and phrases. In the wake of the German destruction of Louvain, at the end of August, Clark noted the appearance in the press of the expression 'Hun-like methods', and located the first use of the word 'Hun' as a noun ten days later. The term 'Shirker' was in use by 29 August, and its related noun, 'Slacker', noted not long afterwards. The growing practice by women of handing out white feathers to able-bodied men who had failed to volunteer was quickly included as one of the entries in Clark's notebook for September, though his definition strayed across the line of strict lexicographical impartiality: 'To show "*the white feather*" is the long-standing proverbial expression to be deficient in courage. At the beginning of the war hysterical feminists made themselves objectionable by sending "white feathers" to young men who had not enlisted.'

The less contentious of these novel usages included to 'shatter the nerves', described as 'an expression in constant use'; 'the fog of war', defined as the 'withholding of information as to events in the theatre of war', another phrase reportedly 'much in use Aug–Oct 1914'; and 'battalions of chums', an early variant of the more common expression, 'pals battalions'. 'Siege-war' was, according to Clark, 'a compound noun much in favour Sept–Nov 1914', an attempt to convey through language a new type of conflict, very different from the traditional war of movement. Not all of Clark's words necessarily had a wartime background. 'Non-starter' was recorded as an interesting new term, though it was documented with a quotation from an unnamed source as 'A non-starter – The Kaiser, who was nominated only two months ago as the next recipient of the Nobel peace prize'.

Many of Clark's entries for the first letter of the alphabet related to the new terror from the skies, the aeroplane and the threat of aerial bombardment. In 1912, the year in which Britain, lagging behind its foreign competitors, had established its Royal Flying Corps, James Murray had lamented the absence from the dictionary of the 'terminology of aeroplanes and aeronautics'. Clark more than compensated for this. 'Airmanship', 'Aviator', 'Aerial raider', 'Aerial scouting', 'Air offensive' and, more ominously, for the letter 'B', 'Bomb-dropper' were all carefully glossed by him.

Reference to a current fear sweeping England was contained among Clark's entries for the letter *Z*: *Zeppelinphobia*. Great Leighs itself displayed symptoms of this new phobia, and there was much talk in the village that autumn about how long it might be before England faced invasion by German airships. Even the sighting of an aeroplane over the rectory grounds was sufficient to produce a combination of alarm and awe from the Rector and his household, causing them to rush out of the house and observe its movements closely.

At noon each day, by order of the Squire, the church bell of Great Leighs was rung so that those hearing it might pause and offer a prayer 'for all who have joined the Colours'. A list posted inside St Mary's recorded the names of villagers serving in the armed forces. At the beginning of the war the number stood at thirteen. In spite of the initial reluctance of some to come forward, this figure would soon double and eventually rise by fivefold, reflecting approximately one in ten of Great Leighs' total population.

The sacrifice of young men that the war called for, which Andrew Clark had alluded to in passing in a sermon in early August, made its mark on the village for the first time in mid October. Dick Fitch, aged nineteen, was one of twelve children of a farm labourer and had joined the 2nd Regiment as a Regular some fifteen months earlier. Dick's mother, Sophia – who was to suffer the loss of three more of her sons in the war – called on the Reverend Clark to have the application signed for the return of her son's effects.

At the summit of Great Leighs' social hierarchy, one of J. H. Tritton's sons, Alan, had been with the Coldstream Guards in France since the beginning of the war. Details of Captain Tritton's experiences on the Western Front, relayed to Andrew Clark by his mother, Lucy, found a place in the diary. 'We had a letter from Alan this morning,' Mrs Tritton wrote to Clark in a letter that was pasted beside the diary entry for 30 October. 'He has been in for a good deal of fighting and again three of his brother officers have been wounded and three killed, yet he is preserved.' In the third week of November, Alan Tritton came home for a week's leave, and was reported as being 'very well and in excellent spirits'.

On 29 December, Clark received a letter from Tritton. 'The blow has fallen.' Alan Tritton had been killed in France three days earlier. Later details emerged of the circumstances of his death. A tall man, he had been passing along a trench when he was shot through the head by an enemy sniper.

Andrew Clark organized a joint memorial service, at Tritton's request, for Alan and for Dick Fitch (and for Dick's brother Arthur killed weeks afterwards). Publicly remembering someone from the bottom of the social scale at the same time as someone from the top seemed to Clark to express a sense of community, which, in a different way, his diary of echoes from the war also seeks to affirm.

A Spy in Every Stranger

The Tower of London, one of the capital's most historic landmarks, was a scene of some commotion early on a bleak, foggy morning at the beginning of November. For the first time in over 160 years the Tower was to witness the execution of a prisoner of state. Not since the beheading of the Jacobite Lord Lovat, on Tower Hill, in 1747, had anyone been executed in the Tower's precincts; and it was more than 300 years since a prisoner – Elizabeth I's favourite, the Earl of Essex – had been executed within the fortress's walls. A long wooden shed, situated between the inner and western outer walls, near the Martin and Constable Towers, was set to be the place of execution. It had been built before the war for the Tower's garrison to use as an indoor rifle range.

At 7 o'clock the prisoner, Carl Hans Lody, found guilty just three days earlier of being a German spy, was led from his cell at 29 The Casemates, the Victorian apartments at the rear of the curtain wall. The firing party, eight guardsmen from the 3rd Battalion Grenadier Guards, were lined up on the veranda of the Tower Main Guard. A procession, headed by the Chaplain, solemnly reading the Burial Service, was followed by the prisoner, with an armed escort marching on either side of him, and the eight guardsmen bringing up the rear.

For the Chaplain, it was an unnerving experience. His voice trembled as he intoned the words of the service, and his hands, carrying the prayer book, shook visibly. The escort and the firing party, too, were far from comfortable. The slow march was taking its toll on their nerves, and they gave the impression of wanting to get their task over with as quickly as possible. None had shot a man in cold blood before.

Only the condemned man appeared calm. At thirty-seven years old, Carl Lody, dressed simply in shirt and trousers, was of medium height, with dark hair parted in the middle and searching blue eyes.

Teutonic Barber. "SHAFE, SIR?"
Customer. "YE-ES—— THAT IS, NO!——I THINK I'LL TRY A HAIR-CUT."

A *Punch* cartoon from September 1914, illustrating the widespread suspicion that German spies were masquerading as barbers

He walked steadily, his face upturned to the sky. At the end of the veranda, the Chaplain started to take the wrong turning. Lody quickly stepped forward and, with a polite smile, took the Chaplain's arm and gently guided him in the right direction towards the doorway of the rifle range.

Inside, Lody was seated and his limbs bound to the chair. The offer of a bandage for his eyes was refused. 'Are you all ready, Sergeant-Major?' asked the officer in charge. 'All ready, sir,' came the reply. The officer raised his stick and brought it down swiftly. The sound of a single volley echoed out. The figure in the chair gave one convulsive shudder and fell forward, limp and bloody.

––––

'Fear of espionage is very great and one smells a spy in every stranger.' These words, describing wartime Britain's spy fever, had formed part of Carl Hans Lody's final report to his paymasters in Berlin, dispatched via an intermediary in Stockholm, but intercepted before it could reach them by the British postal censor. August 1914 saw a limited number of arrests in Britain of Germans on suspicion of espionage. Far greater, though, was the sharp rise in imaginary espionage on the outbreak of war. Indeed, at times this spy mania verged on a state of mass hysteria.

'There is a genuine spy peril, and a stupid spy scare,' declared the Conservative MP and keen spy catcher, William Joynson-Hicks, speaking in a Commons debate in the autumn of 1914, 'and it is very necessary to distinguish between the two.' Unfortunately the task of making that distinction was by no means as clear-cut as was sometimes maintained. Even the official rounding-up of a German spy ring, announced triumphantly in the Commons by the Home Secretary the day after war was declared, to shouts of 'Shoot them!' from assorted members, was not quite what it seemed. Twenty-one spies, or suspected spies, were said to have been arrested in various places all over the country on the authority of the head of counter-espionage, Vernon Kell. In fact it later transpired that the arrests of only fourteen agents said to be working in Britain had been authorized, and that the police were able to find just eight of them. Out of this eight, only one was ever brought to trial, presumably because of the lack of firm evidence for the rest.

Real spies were far outnumbered by those who existed as figments of people's imaginations. By mid September, in London alone, the police had received 9,000 reports from ordinary people of suspicious Germans. Ninety cases were investigated. Not one proved to have the slightest foundation. At the end of the war, it would be estimated that if one tenth of the men and women reported to the police had actually been enemy agents, Britain would have been overrun by at least 10,000 spies. But arrests remained few, and not a single act of genuine sabotage was ever reported: no telegraph wires were cut, no stash of arms or bombs was uncovered. That didn't stop people from making false reports. On the first day of war Scotland Yard was informed that a culvert near Aldershot and a railway bridge in Kent had been blown up by saboteurs. Both were found to be intact.

Spy fever was a malady which had assumed 'a virulent epidemic form', as Basil Thomson, head of the Criminal Investigation Department at New Scotland Yard, and the man responsible for the enforcement of the apparatus of military intelligence, later said. Every foreigner, or stranger with a foreign name or odd appearance or accent, was potentially a German agent. A perhaps not so novel national characteristic had suddenly emerged into the foreground: that of treating all foreigners with dark suspicion. Trades like hairdressing and baking, which contained dominant numbers of foreigners, and a preponderance of German immigrants, were especially suspect. So, too, was the occupation of waiting tables in restaurants and hotels. By 1914, for instance, Germans made up roughly 10 per cent of waiters and waitresses working in London restaurants. The *Daily Mail* advised its readers to 'Refuse to be served by an Austrian or German waiter', warning that 'If your waiter says he is Swiss, ask to see his passport'; while in October the *Spectator* pontificated that 'the work of a waiter, since it lends itself with such peculiar ease to the work of espionage, should not in wartime be practised by enemy aliens.'

A suspicious eye fell naturally enough on Germans living and working in England as household staff. Concerned about the outbreaks of violence against the 'enemy within' being reported in the autumn of 1914, John Riddey wrote home to his sister in Moreton-in-Marsh, inquiring about the welfare of their German governess: 'I hope no one will dare to attempt to duck Fraulein in the pond. I'd duck him in if I was big enough.' At 10 Downing Street, the Asquiths employed a German governess whose husband had been called back to Germany to fight. The governess had been with them for many years and was treated almost as one of the family. The police were at first intent on interviewing her. Only Margot Asquith's intervention with the Home Secretary, Reginald McKenna, on the governess's behalf spared her from being questioned. There were angry protests in the press when it emerged that both the Lord Chief Justice, Lord Reading, and the Secretary for the Colonies, Lewis Harcourt, employed German chauffeurs, and, furthermore, that these chauffeurs had been given naturalization certificates on the outbreak of war.

Men and women with German names offered easy targets. Many German shopkeepers, including naturalized citizens of several generations' standing, hurriedly anglicized the names displayed on their shopfronts. 'Deutsche Apotheke' quickly disappeared from German chemists' shops. Andrew Clark, the Great Leighs diarist, noted that, according to the provisioner Luckin Smith, thick smoked wurst was no longer known as 'German Sausage', but had been renamed 'Dunmow Sausage' after the neighbouring Essex market town. The composer Gustav von Holst, starting work on 'Venus' for his *Planets* suite, a sublime expression of the theme of peace, had tried to enlist, but been rejected because of his poor eyesight and neuritic right arm. None the less, at Thaxted, in north Essex, where he rented a cottage, 'Von Holst' was viewed with suspicion by local people and was reported to the local police as a German spy, though, as Holst himself said, 'the only German thing about me is my unspringing hair.' The police, not surprisingly, could find no evidence against him, and the villagers subsequently treated the composer with more respect, referring to him almost with affection as 'our Mr Von'. Suspicion also lighted on German names resurrected from the past. Gustav Hamel, the celebrity aviator, lost while flying his plane over the Channel in the spring, was confidently declared to be alive in Germany, advising on the construction of military aircraft for the government, even though his remains had been discovered on the French coast a month before the war began.

Stories that dachshunds, the short-legged, long-bodied dog breed, were stoned to death in the streets because of their German name are almost certainly apocryphal. However, the killing of homing pigeons, said to be used by spies to carry messages to the enemy, is well documented. An amendment to the Defence of the Realm Act had ruled that pigeon fanciers now required a permit to keep their birds. In September, when the initial phase of spy mania was at its peak, Basil Thomson reported that 'it was positively dangerous to be seen in conversation with a pigeon; it was not always safe to be seen in its vicinity. A foreigner walking in one of the [London] parks was actually arrested and sentenced to imprisonment because a pigeon was seen to fly from the place where he was standing and it was supposed that he had liberated it.' The press urged the public to shoot pigeons on sight. It took several prosecutions by the National Homing Union, which had cooperated with the government in introducing a system to register all native pigeons, to ensure the protection of the country's pigeon population.

Imaginary spies were said to signal at night to guide U-boats to attack British ships. In November, a naturalized German, who had a wireless installation and flashlight signalling equipment at his home in Thorpe Bay, Sunderland, was brought to trial. The case was dismissed after it was revealed that the equipment was 'not actually connected up and there was no evidence of it being used'. Basil Thomson recalled how signalling from a window in the Bayswater district of Central London 'was believed in some way to be conveyed to the commanders of German submarines in the North Sea'.

Tennis courts constructed from heavy concrete – particularly ones on high ground – were rumoured to be intended as gun emplacements for invading Germans. If Germany invaded, hidden howitzers, it was said, would be wheeled out, or raised from underground, to bombard British cities. In October 1914 police descended on a factory near Willesden Junction, in North-West London, and twenty foreign aliens of military age were marched out to jeers from the assembled crowd. Suspicion had attached to the firm, which had a branch in Leipzig, because of the robust floor of its single-storey concrete building. It was assumed that this might be used as a base to launch weapons, despite the protestations of innocence from its architect, who maintained that the solid foundation was necessary in case the building was made higher.

Secret visual codes were believed to be employed by spies posing as artists. At the beginning of October, the *Illustrated London News* published a double-page spread to demonstrate the way in which 'an apparently innocent drawing of a landscape made by a spy' could in fact contain 'a secret pictorial code known to the government in whose interest he was spying'. The magazine proceeded to explain that in this code 'a windmill, for example, would represent a lighthouse; a plantation of trees, a fort; a single farmhouse or cottage, a group of buildings; a group of houses, a town; a church, Admiralty offices or a Town Hall; double lines (ostensibly roads), railway tracks, and so on.' Gladys Dolby New, a student at Liverpool University, briefly fell victim to this powerful identification of artists with espionage. She and her art teacher were sketching near the Mersey Estuary when they were arrested by two soldiers. They were released only after Miss New's work had been dismissed as being of insufficient quality to aid the Germans.

For the police, and for soldiers on home duty, the excitement of spy scares relieved the monotony of an often tedious existence. But their enthusiasm could also get the better of them, making them overzealous in their guarding of vulnerable points such as railway bridges. John Riddey reported from the Deptford business where he worked that 'one of the fellows in the office' had been arrested while taking his dog for a walk at Blackheath. 'He was . . . stopped for a minute on a Railway Bridge when he was challenged by 2 soldiers & marched off between fixed bayonets to the Police Station.' Boy scouts, mobilized to provide auxiliary assistance on the outbreak of war, were no less keen. The composer Ralph Vaughan Williams used to tell a story of how the tune for *The Lark Ascending* suddenly came into his head as he was walking on the cliffs overlooking the Channel near Margate, where he was staying with his mother at the start of the war. He sat down to write the music in his notebook, but was interrupted by a young scout who told him that he was under arrest. 'Why?' asked Vaughan Williams. 'Maps,' replied the boy. 'Information for the enemy.' Vaughan Williams allowed himself to be escorted to the police station, where he was released with a caution.

The stopping of cars, and other forms of motor transport, in order to question and search their passengers was becoming a common occurrence. Fifteen-year-old Cecil Forester wrote in his diary on 28 August of his astonishment when the car in which his family was travelling was halted by a 'Policeman who thought we were German spies!!'

Earlier that month, Helen Thomas, Edward Thomas's wife, experienced something similar when she made the complicated journey by train and car from Petersfield to Ledbury to join her husband and Robert Frost on the first day of war. Accompanying her on the midnight moonlit drive across the Malvern Hills, with two of her children and their pet dog, was a Russian boy, Peter Mrosovski, who was spending his holidays with them. In the market square at Ledbury, where they'd stopped to obtain directions to the Frosts' isolated cottage, a policeman shone his lantern on them, and asked, 'Who are you and why are you travelling at this time of night?' His suspicions grew when he discovered that one of the occupants of the car was a foreigner and, furthermore, that their destination was a house belonging to other foreigners, the Frosts.

After stumbling over the spelling of 'Mrosovski', as he jotted their names down in his notebook, the policeman allowed them to complete their journey. However, a few days afterwards, a village policeman called at Little Iddens and informed the Thomases and Frosts that several anonymous letters had arrived at his station, suggesting that they were spies. The policeman was sure that the accusations were false, but declared that it was his duty to follow up any inquiries from the public.

Edward Thomas treated the episode as a joke. But Frost, characteristically, was consumed with rage, and said, 'If that policeman comes nosing about here again I shall shoot him.'

———

'I *know* I travelled in a bus with two German spies today,' Hallie Eustace Miles wrote in her diary on 31 October, 'and it was such an awful feeling, as if a dark shadow was present.' The air buzzed with rumours about suspicious aliens, odd-looking strangers – 'old women in trousers' were a particular source of concern to the local authorities at Southwold, in Suffolk – and of the successful capture and shooting of enemy agents. Everywhere, spy mania seemed to have taken hold of normally sane and rational people. Florence Schuster, who arrived back in Manchester in September 1914 after time abroad, was disturbed by the pervasive level of this obsessive behaviour, and thought that people had simply 'lost their heads'.

The temptation to report anything out of the ordinary – or anyone, for that matter, whom one disliked – to the authorities appeared overwhelming. The merest sniff of something foreign, of course, was immediately seized upon. 'We were rather suspicious about a man who sang some amusing patter-songs in broken English & Yiddish at Cowshott Camp,' wrote Beatrice Trefusis, who had been entertaining troops from Kitchener's New Army at the Oxfordshire training depot. 'So I wrote a note to Mr Bulstrode, the chaplain, & stated our fears – probably quite unfounded.' Sometimes these fears moved beyond straightforward espionage to alarm at a possible threat to human life. From Dover in Kent, Mabel Rudkin described a sentry, on duty at the local reservoir, firing at a stranger who was said to have emptied a bottle containing typhoid germs into the water tanks.

> On the following day, a notice was sent to every householder, directing that all drinking water should be boiled for at least two hours . . .
> I obediently boiled . . . but though many defied the order, ascribing the intruder and his bottle to the over-wrought imagination of the sentry, boilers and non-boilers fared equally well. No case of illness occurred which was traced to contaminated water.

Ada Reece had let her house at Sturry, not far from the Kent coast, in order to remain in London while she waited for her husband to be sent to France, but her tenants soon felt forced to vacate the property because of local people 'prowling round the house at night and generally watching their every movement'. In November, G. S. Stevens, from Exmouth, wrote to the Lord Lieutenant of Devon about his suspicions of a German family who had recently moved into his area. His letter offers a perfect illustration of the 'overwrought imagination' that was the most obvious symptom of spy fever:

> Herr Hengl and his family occupied a house in Morton Road . . . for several weeks and then took an unfurnished house in Phillipps Avenue

next to this house, where I am present, on a visit. Upon re-taking possession of the house in Morton Road, the owner found a saucepan hidden away in a cupboard which has evidently been used for other than domestic purposes. There also appears to have been a hole dug in the back garden . . . He has bought *new* furniture for the house, but, rather curiously *brought* a number of stuffed birds – very ordinary looking birds – is it possible they may be the receptacles of incriminating papers? Yesterday, at about 2 o'clock . . . I saw a carrier pigeon steadily flying over the roof of this house – apparently in a beeline for the mouth of the river. It disappeared from my view at once. I saw Herr Hengl pacing 7 paces along the right hand wall of his garden, his back about 5ft from the house, soon after his arrival. The policeman to whom I reported this thought he might be measuring for a clothes line!

Tales of spies being rounded up and shot were a common feature of ordinary people's observations about imaginary espionage, as if these provided a consoling resolution for some of these fears, and comfort for fevered imaginations. In the first week of the war Ada Reece was relieved to receive a letter from a friend 'telling of the precautions at Portsmouth and how 4 German spies have been shot there'. Frederick Oliver, manager of Debenham & Freebody, the department store, as well as a prominent Conservative polemicist, wrote to his brother in Canada, in September 1914, telling him of a German, a leading hairdresser at Aldershot for twenty years, who had been caught at the Aldershot waterworks with poison concealed in his shirt and 'put up against a wall and shot forthwith'. According to Oliver, 'some hundreds of spies have been shot at naval and military barracks since the opening of the war, though not a single one of the cases has been in the paper.'

None of these stories of spies being executed, summarily or otherwise, was true. Despite all the frenzied activity by the police, no spy apprehended in Britain faced a firing squad in the first three months of war, and remarkably few got as far as being brought to trial. The only significant arrest early on – though he was strikingly absent from Vernon Kell's list of those detained on the outbreak of war – was that of Karl Ernst. Born in Britain, Ernst was married to a German woman, the proprietor of a hairdresser's in the Caledonian Road, North London. On 12 November 1914 Ernst was convicted on a charge of espionage and sentenced to seven years' penal servitude for acting as a forwarding agent for letters sent from the office of Gustav Steinhauer, the Kaiser's master spy in Berlin, and for attempting to procure a naval officer as a German agent.

But mostly the individuals put on trial were small fry, like Franz Losel, a German photographer who had worked from a studio at Sheerness in north Kent for some years. Losel was arrested in August for placing his camera on a sea wall at eight o'clock at night, and accused of taking photographs at the Ravelin Battery which he sent back to Germany. Losel protested his innocence, and no firm evidence of his alleged crime was presented in court. After a short time in custody, he was deported. More pathetic was the case of an Englishman, eighteen-year-old Robert Arthur Blackburn, who was indicted at the Liverpool Assizes in October for 'communicating to another person information useful to an enemy'. Back in May, Blackburn had written to the German Embassy in London, offering his services as a spy. The information he obtained for master spy Leo Sirius of Berlin was acknowledged to be worthless, made up of local details taken from almanacs, and from replies to inquiries made by Blackburn at the Liverpool Chamber of Commerce. As part of his defence, Blackburn said that he was willing to join the British Army. He was informed that 'the Army did not want men like him' and sent for Borstal training.

At his trial, Blackburn admitted that he'd got his ideas about being a spy from books about German spies in Britain, an indication perhaps of just how influential the writings of that leading spy writer, William Le Queux, continued to be. Le Queux's fortunes had risen again with the outbreak of war, though he was fearful that the Germans were out to get him 'for rumbling their schemes' and involved himself in a dispute with the Metropolitan Police over his plea for special protection from enemy agents. His first wartime bestseller, in the autumn of 1914, was in the familiar Le Queux mould: a novel entitled simply *The German Spy*.

The absence of any high-profile arrest and trial of enemy spies in these early months did nothing to dampen the atmosphere of rising hysteria and contributed to the belief that elements within the government itself were guilty of being pro-German. Establishment figures with German backgrounds, like Sir Alfred Mond, the Liberal MP and managing director of his family's chemical company, provided easy targets for attack. Mond, with his guttural Teutonic accent, was libelled by R. T. Palmer, a box manufacturer from Leicester. Palmer had sent a letter to Mond calling him 'a German swine' and added that he hoped 'you are satisfied with the devastation and misery caused by your fellow hogs in Belgium and France.'

It didn't take long for a whispering campaign to start against certain members of the government. Prince Louis of Battenberg, the First Sea Lord, was a major casualty. His German origins, together with the catastrophic sinking of three British cruisers by enemy U-boats in the North Sea on 22 September, ensured that he was swiftly hounded from office at the end of October, amid rumours that he was being confined in the Tower 'as an alien enemy' while awaiting trial for treason. At about this time, General D. G. Johnson was informed by his wife that there was definitely a spy in the cabinet. She identified this mysterious individual as Lord Haldane, the Lord Chancellor, or Reginald McKenna, the Home Secretary. Admiral Beatty wrote to his wife, Ethel, recommending that both men 'should be locked up and removed from any responsible position'.

Haldane's German connections, his oft-quoted remark that Germany was his 'spiritual home', combined with his responsibility for pre-war army reforms to reduce expenditure and promote efficiency, made him the focus of violent press attacks. In response to an appeal in the *Daily Express*, 26,000 letters were addressed to Haldane at the House of Lords protesting against his disloyalty to the interests of the nation. These letters were forwarded to Haldane's home, where they were opened, and disposed of, by a kitchen maid. The letters page of the *Express* itself was overflowing with invective directed against the Lord Chancellor. One reader from Finsbury in London observed that 'After Lord Haldane wiped out some of our third battalions . . . &

the way in which he and his friend "the Master Hun" have scratched each other's backs . . . [i]t is high time for this supporter of Germany to give up his fat public office and go into retirement.'

Haldane offered Asquith his resignation, but for the time being the Prime Minister stuck by him. However, Haldane found himself threatened in the street with assault and commented later that he 'was on occasions in some danger of being shot at'.

At the Home Office, Reginald McKenna, once such a doughty antagonist of the suffragettes, was a further favoured object of attack in the right-wing press. He was accused of being far too lenient towards enemy aliens, and of not taking the spy scare seriously enough. 'The papers are all clamouring for more drastic steps to be taken as regards spies,' Ada Reece recorded in her diary, '& everyone is furious at the slack & suicidal methods of the Home Office.' Some thought McKenna was encouraged in what they saw as his pro-Germanism by his wife Pamela, with whom Asquith was known to enjoy the occasional flirtation. 'When a Ssssssssspy is reported to the Home Office nowadays – by which I mean the Home Office supplemented by its wife,' Edwin Montagu wrote mockingly to McKenna in September, 'it puts its nose to the clue, it silently, grimly, determinably ferrets and investigates, and criticises and then conclusively, undeniably, indisputably, infallibly, unfalteringly, unerringly, etc, etc, etc, proves that HE DOES NOT EXIST.'

The Royal Family, with its German blood and connections – and its name Saxe-Coburg-Gotha – was not above suspicion, especially after it emerged that one of George V's first cousins was serving in the German Army. Prince Albert of Schleswig-Holstein, son of Princess Christian, Queen Victoria's third daughter, had reached the rank of Lieutenant-Colonel in the 3rd Uhlans, part of the Prussian Army. The Kaiser himself had excused Albert – who was also his first cousin through the German Emperor's mother, Vicky – from taking part in military operations against the British, and Albert was to spend much of the war in Berlin on the staff of the Governor of the city. In November, however, and not without some justification, the Liberal MP William Young rose in the Commons to ask why, given Prince Albert's position in the German Army, the country was continuing to pay £6,000 a year for his upkeep through the civil list (just weeks before, the death in action at Ypres had been announced of Prince Maurice of Battenberg, a lieutenant in the King's Royal Rifles Corps; he was another of Queen Victoria's grandsons, the son of her youngest child, Princess Beatrice).

But a far worse furore ensued that month when the Archbishop of York, Cosmo Gordon Lang, objected in public to the excesses of anti-Germanism, and unwisely recalled a 'sacred memory' of the Kaiser kneeling beside Edward VII at the bier of his grandmother Queen Victoria in January 1901. These remarks produced an outcry, later described by Lang as 'a perfect hail of denunciation'. Hundreds of letters arrived condemning him and his 'utterances . . . concerning the greatest living enemy of the human race'. The response of Mary Ackroyd of Keighley, writing to the *Yorkshire Post* on 25 November, was representative of the tenor of these attacks. 'May I suggest that as a punitive and preventive measure, his Grace be interned in one of the concentration camps with aliens until the termination of the war?' Enduring this onslaught of critical scorn, Lang was reduced to a nervous wreck. The onset of alopecia, as a result, drastically altered Lang's youthful, dark-haired appearance. He suddenly turned, at the age of fifty, into an elderly-looking, balding man with white hair.

As far as spy fever was concerned, hysteria in Britain reached its height in October and November 1914. According to Michael MacDonagh, the *Times* journalist, this was because the public was experiencing the 'first bewildering shock of being at war'. But the hysteria also had its roots in more deep-seated fears. One was the realization, becoming clearer every day, that this was not going to be a short-lived war. The other was quite simply the recognition that Britain might not be assured of victory. The Fall of Antwerp to the Germans, in early October, was one enormous setback, accompanied by the foreboding produced by the absence of firm information as to how close the German Army was to Calais and the likelihood of its reaching Britain's Channel ports.

There were some attempts at humour to defuse the tension surrounding the alleged omnipresence of enemy spies. Towards the end of the year, Alfred Leete, the artist responsible for the finger-pointing recruitment poster of Lord Kitchener, started publishing his drawings of 'Schmidt the Spy' in the weekly journal *London Opinion*. Schmidt, a small, round, moustachioed German, arrives in England hidden in a crate of Dutch cheese. He adopts a variety of unconvincing disguises, and amusingly misconstrues everyday scenes of London life, sending misleading information back to his masters in Germany. So, the sight of a group of female Salvation Army members, playing their accordions in the street, is misinterpreted by Schmidt, in messages back to Berlin, as 'an army of women . . . armed with strange weapons' and possessing 'a peculiar war-cry of their own'; while a glimpse of a commissionaire standing on duty outside a picture palace is misunderstood by the ineffectual spy as being a sign that martial law has been imposed in England.

London's great theatrical hit of the end of 1914, opening at the Royalty Theatre on 10 December, was a play which poked fun at spy mania, while managing at the same time not to underestimate the actual threat posed by enemy espionage. *The Man Who Stayed at Home* by Lechmere Worrall and J. E. Harold Terry is set in a genteel East Coast boarding-house on a September day in 1914. The proprietress of the Wave Crest Hotel is a Mrs Sanderson, the widow of a German officer. She and her son Carl, who claims to work at the Admiralty, are in fact German spies passing on information about coastal positions, sending documents by carrier-pigeon, and making signals to outlying ships. The play's hero, and the man who scotches their dastardly plans, is Christopher Brent, an English detective. Brent has taken on the guise of a monocled, silly-ass type of young man, who has apparently failed to enlist and accepts a white feather from a young woman staying at the boarding-house at the beginning of Act One.

At the climax of the play, Brent prevents the Sandersons and their accomplices, who include Fritz, the waiter 'with a distinct German accent', from burning down the house as a signal to an outlying submarine. Instead Brent signals to English warships, which destroy the vessel. Among the play's characters is a German governess, who has served 'in a dozen of our most exclusive households'; she assists Mrs Sanderson by drawing a map of the harbour defences for her.

Other aspects of the play that would have immediately struck a chord with its original audience are the fireplace, which reveals an apparatus for the receipt and dispatch of wireless messages from under the grate, and the homing pigeons kept by Fritz, with essential maps tied to their feet.

The problem of monitoring and controlling the activities of Germans resident in Britain had been a pressing one since the beginning of the war. On 5 August the House of Commons passed the Aliens Restriction Act with little opposition (the simultaneous announcement of the arrest of the dubious list of twenty-one German spies may well have been intended to aid the passage of the Act). The Act restricted 'the movements of alien enemies from, to, and in the United Kingdom'. No alien, for instance, could now enter or leave Britain except through an approved port. All Germans and Austrians who remained in Britain after the outbreak of war had to register themselves, by 17 and 24 August respectively, at their nearest registration office, usually their local police station. Outside Tottenham Court Road Police Station in London, one day in early August, according to a report in the *Manchester Guardian*, stood a long queue of 'many quiet looking old ladies, probably teachers, young German girl students, tourists caught without money, barbers, stockbrokers, shipping clerks, waiters, bankers', together with 'some of the much less reputable occupations'.

Other piecemeal legislation took further steps against 'the enemy within'. An order of 20 August banned German-language publications that did not have the Home Secretary's permission; another of 9 September placed restrictions on the possession of communication equipment; a further order of 8 October forbade aliens from changing their names, again, unless they had Reginald McKenna's consent.

These new powers were transforming the role of state in the interests of national security. However, the most contentious of them for Asquith's government – because it clashed with cherished Liberal principles – as well as the most difficult to put into practice, was the policy of internment of enemy aliens. For the present there was no question of introducing universal enemy adult male internment. But both the police and army made forceful objections against the continuing presence of German and Austrian reservists in Britain, whom they considered to be a source of danger. The Home Office responded by issuing instructions for the arrest of 'those most likely to be dangerous'. By 13 August almost 2,000 enemy aliens had been interned. Five weeks later the figure had reached 11,000. The available space for internment was rapidly running out, and there were no longer enough soldiers in the country to act as guards.

The Home Office was responsible for internment policy, the War Office for its implementation. The first internees were held in a variety of buildings and makeshift huts, and on board nine transatlantic liners requisitioned by the Admiralty. London's Olympia, holding anywhere from 300 to 1,500 men, provided a clearing house, until December 1914, for prisoners before they were transferred to other camps. Frimley, in Surrey, and Newbury, in Berkshire, were among the camps established in the early months, the latter turning its race course into an internment centre, with prisoners being housed in horse boxes, deprived of heat and light. An old wagon-works in Lancaster was taken over by the War Office in September, and among the prisoners held there were boys as young as sixteen captured from fishing boats.

The arrival in Britain in August and September of several thousand German prisoners of war necessitated the establishment of POW camps. In contrast to internment centres, these were often visited by local people, curious to have a glimpse of the enemy. Beatrice Trefusis noted in her diary in October that people went in their hundreds to gaze at the German prisoners at the camp at Frith Hill, near Deepcut in Surrey, close to where she lived, 'as if they were animals at the zoo!' On a visit she watched 'one of them solemnly doing the goose step all by himself'.

Beatrice Trefusis was among the apparent majority of the general public who believed in 'interning *every* enemy alien'. At the outset of the war, Reginald McKenna had issued a press release on behalf of the Home Office, stating that 'The public may rest assured that a great majority of the Germans remaining in this country are peaceful and innocent persons from whom no danger is to be feared.' Almost predictably, however, 'Intern Them All' became a pervasive cry in the press and among the radical right in Parliament. While the *Daily Mail* called for stronger measures against enemy aliens, the magazine *John Bull* went even further, demanding the internment of every naturalized German and arguing against the policy of interning only men of military age because, after all, a spy could be seventy years old or female.

Even members of McKenna's own party privately criticized him for being too indulgent towards enemy aliens, and for his poor presentation of the case for limited internment. Lloyd George's ally, the press baron Sir George Riddell, commented that there was no doubt that McKenna 'hates the anti-German agitation. He is always talking of "fighting like gentlemen", of "not losing our heads", of "lack of evidence of German machinations" and of the "absence of danger" etc etc.' In the hope that it might strengthen McKenna's resolve, and make him less scared of the mob, Riddell gave the Home Secretary a copy of G. H. Lewes's biography of Robespierre.

The Prime Minister, though, was not among those in his party who was in favour of a more proactive stance towards internment. On two occasions in the autumn of 1914, Asquith visited internment camps, accompanied by Margot and McKenna, and was horrified by what he saw there. At one camp, he reported to Venetia Stanley, he had come across 'lots of cases which it was simply cruel & criminal to have treated as "interned" . . . I loathe the excesses of the spy-fever.'

There was a sudden shift in the government's policy on internment on 20 October, when McKenna ordered the arrest of every German and Austrian of military age. This was a reaction to the anti-German rioting that had taken place in Deptford, South-East London, between 17 and 19 October, and was as much a measure to protect ordinary German civilians from attack as an extension of the legislation to secure national interests. 'I hear there was an anti-German riot in Deptford,' the clerk John Riddey wrote to his mother after the first night's disturbance. 'Several German shops were raided & all the furniture, including beds & pianos were thrown into the street. I wish I had been there.'

There had been other instances of rioting against Germans in the early weeks of war. Isolated attacks against German shopkeepers and their property in the East End of London, in August, occurred at a time when feelings against Germany were running high, just after the declaration of war. The attacks also occurred as a result of provocation from the Germans involved. In Poplar, for instance, a German baker had allegedly hoisted an enemy flag. In another instance, two German bakers had made insulting remarks about the British and their troops, and had had their shop windows smashed.

A more serious disturbance, involving some 3,000 men, broke out in Peterborough across two days in the second week of August. Again the root cause was 'provocative language with reference to the present unhappy state of war between England and Germany' by a local pork butcher Frederick Frank, who had been born in Germany but had lived in the city for thirty years. On the Friday night, a crowd, mostly of young labourers and manual workers fuelled by alcohol, assembled outside his shop and hurled bricks and other missiles at the windows. The police were unable to control the crowd, and eventually the yeomanry was called out. They, too, encountered opposition, until a dozen mounted men sent people scattering in all directions. The following evening's unrest was worse. Frank had advertised the auction of his stock that afternoon, but those purchasing his goods found themselves stripped of their items. Youths climbed an electric standard and hung strings of sausages from the wires. By midnight a large number of people had gathered outside a local pub, where the publican, a Mr Guest, was said to have made remarks in support of the butcher. His windows were also smashed. A hose-pipe was then turned on the crowd as they attempted to rush the pub doors in a wild stampede.

A further outbreak of violence, this time at Keighley, West Yorkshire, at the end of August, targeted the German community, including a shopkeeper whose wife was alleged to have danced in the streets at the announcement of 2,000 British casualties. But here feelings were exacerbated by local economic conditions. A strike of moulders and engineers had been going on in Keighley since May, and at one point in the disturbances, which lasted for several days, an attack was made on the property of a factory owner.

The October riot in Deptford, however, was the most ferocious yet. It involved the largest number of people, as many as 5,000 or 6,000 during the disturbances in the high street on the evening of Monday, the 19th. Moreover, in contrast to the earlier riots, the Deptford crowd did not consist simply of intoxicated youths (though they undoubtedly played their part), but contained a broader cross-section of the town's men, women – and children, who kept the adults supplied with bricks to hurl at German and Austrian shops. At the height of the trouble, with furniture being thrown out of windows, the police summoned the army: 350 soldiers, armed with rifles, arrived and surrounded the shops to keep the crowd back.

In the days following, the more Liberal portions of the press blamed right-wing newspapers for inciting hatred against innocent enemy aliens. The *Daily Mail*, for its part, launched yet another salvo against 'the apathy of officialdom in dealing with the German and Austrian subjects in our midst'.

One catalyst for the rioting in Deptford may have been the arrival in the area, shortly before the disturbances began, of 800 Belgian refugees. According to a journalist on the *Daily News*, it was the sight of these people, and the evidence of their suffering, that ignited the spark 'which set on fire the ugly portion of the crowd'. Stories of German atrocities against Belgians were by now circulating widely, and it's hardly surprising to find English people taking retaliatory measures of their own against those they regarded as 'the enemy within'. It's also no coincidence that this major outbreak of rioting took place at a time when anxiety about the threat of German invasion of Britain, following the fall of Belgium, was at its height, and when fears of enemy espionage were also reaching their peak.

There were a few lone voices protesting against attacks on the German population of Britain. A reader of the *Liverpool Echo* wrote into the paper on 27 October:

> I am ashamed to see English people making violent attacks on individual people, who cannot defend themselves . . . Leave the German and Austrian spies in England to the police. Public action is only a hindrance. Surely we cannot fight brutality with brutality. We would make ourselves just as bad as those concerned.

A little earlier, during the first ten days of September, travelling through England, from Swindon to Newcastle-on-Tyne, Edward Thomas had noted the existence among the people he'd encountered of 'a strong, simple idea of a perfidious barbaric Germany'. Engaged upon a 1914 version of a vox pop, Thomas interviewed men and women about their opinion of the enemy. One man was in a state, with his 'nerves run down', because he thought he'd eaten a German sausage. Another bemoaned the fact that due to the ban on the import of German goods he could no longer buy an effective pair of nail-scissors. Some were more direct in their estimate of the threat posed by Germans present in their communities:

> I'd turn all the Germans out of England, same as they would turn us out.' 'I wouldn't; I would shoot the lot of them.' 'These nationalized [*sic*] Germans – you don't know what they are up to. Double-faced, they're all double-faced. They're savages, killing children and old men.

Given the heightened anxiety about spies, the arrest and high-profile public trial for espionage of Carl Hans Lody was a fortuitous development for the government, although Lody's impact on the public's conception of the German spy would turn out to be very different from what was initially expected. The *Daily Express* seized upon the 'grim fascination' of the 'life-and-death struggle which none of the spy trials during the past few years has possessed'; and reminded its readers that, if found guilty, Lody might be sentenced to be shot within twenty-four hours.

Born in 1877, in Nordhausen, near Lübeck, Carl Hans Lody had joined the First Naval Reserve in 1901, after a year in the German Navy. From there he had entered the merchant service, later finding employment as a tourist agent on the Hamburg–Amerika line, where he acted as a guide for Germans and Americans in London. Among the sites on his itinerary was the Tower of London.

In 1912 Lody married Louise Storz, an American of German descent, the daughter of a wealthy Omaha brewer, whom he had met on a tour of Germany and other parts of Europe. The marriage didn't last. But its dissolution did provide Lody with a degree of financial independence, when, in April 1914, his erstwhile father-in-law paid him $10,000 in compensation, suggesting that Lody may have been forced into a divorce. Later that spring Lody was contacted by the director of German Naval Intelligence, Fritz Prieger, who asked if he was prepared to work for him as an agent. Lody agreed, feeling 'honoured' by Prieger's trust in him. Initially he was deployed to report from southern France during times of international tension. Then, as the July crisis unfolded, Lody found himself reassigned to Britain. Posing as an American tourist, with a passport under the name Charles A. Inglis, Lody arrived in Newcastle by steamer from Norway on 27 August, and made his way to Edinburgh. He was to report on the disposition of the first British battle fleet and battle cruiser squadrons at Leith and Grangemouth, and instructed to remain in Britain 'until the first naval encounter had taken place between the two powers and gather information as regards the actual losses of the British fleet'.

Lody's first coded telegram, sent from the city's general post office on 30 August, to his contact in Stockholm, Adolf Burchard, read: 'Must cancel Johnson very ill last four days shall leave shortly.' This apparently meaningless message was intercepted by the British censorship authorities. Five days later a letter posted in Edinburgh to the same Stockholm address was also opened. This asked Burchard to communicate to Berlin 'that on Sept. 3rd great masses of Russian soldiers have passed through Edinburgh on their way to London and France . . . I went to the depot [station] and noticed trains passing through at high speed, blinds down.'

This, the familiar canard about Russians in Britain with snow on their boots, was one of only two of Lody's reports filed throughout mid September which military intelligence in London allowed to reach Berlin (where it caused understandable confusion among the German general staff). Other intercepted messages, signed 'Charles' or 'Nazi' (a Bavarian short form of 'Ignatz') and addressed to Georg Stammer of Berlin's Admiralty Intelligence Staff, contained less fantastic observations based on Lody's perambulations around Edinburgh's Carlton Hill, which allowed him a clear view of the bay as far as the Forth Bridge and the pier at Leith. 'In the North Sea as far as I can ascertain 22 small vessels have been sunk. Also a small cruiser is lying at Leith. And 4 armed cruisers and about 10 torpedo boats and 2 destroyers are lying at Grangemouth.'

In order to dispel suspicion, Lody associated himself with 'other' Americans, and generally stayed in his room at his lodgings in Drumsheugh Gardens until midday. In the middle of September he went to London for two days, reporting on the recruitment of the New Army, and getting into a conversation with a sailor from Harwich, who told him about the deployment of mines at the port.

But Lody was becoming more nervous, increasingly frightened to walk about the streets of Edinburgh and apprehensive about being caught. Prieger instructed another German agent working in Britain to contact Lody and provide him with a new cover address for his reports, but the contact arrived too late. 'I think it is absolutely necessary to disappear for some time because several people have approached me in a disagreeable manner', Lody wrote to Stammer in another intercepted letter. At the end of September, he decided 'to vanish for a few days'. He took the train to Liverpool, and from there boarded the S. S. *Munster*, bound for Dublin via Kingstown. He continued to write letters to Stockholm. In the dining-car of the train to Liverpool he had sat in a compartment adjoining that of the Irish Nationalist MP Willie Redmond (younger brother of John) and overheard a conversation about 'the probability of an invasion and of a bombardment of London chiefly by Zeppelins. All important buildings such as the Houses of Parliament, Bank of England, Library, etc. are accordingly protected by strong wire nets.'

However, like so many of Lody's other reports, this one fell into the hands of British intelligence, which, on 2 October, finally decided to make a move against the spy. A message was sent from the War Office to the Royal Irish Constabulary in Dublin. The 'Suspected German Agent believed to be passing in name of CHARLES INGLIS as American subject' was to be arrested 'and all documents seized minutest search necessary probably has code with him'.

Lody was traced to the Great Southern Hotel in Killarney by District Inspector Cheesman, who informed him that he was being detained as a suspect German agent under the provisions of the

Defence of the Realm Act. 'What is this: me a German agent?' Lody responded. 'Take care now; I am an American citizen.' A search of his room revealed a notebook with a list of cruisers which had been sunk in the North Sea, and the names and addresses of contacts in Berlin. A tailor's ticket sewn inside the breast pocket of a jacket with the words 'J. Steinberg, Berlin, R. C. H. Lody 8.5.14' at last provided the true identity of the prisoner, who was taken to London and placed in the Wellington Barracks in the Tower.

Captain Reginald Drake of MO 5 (g) had been in favour of a closed trial for Carl Hans Lody. But this idea was quickly replaced by plans for a public court martial, to take place at the Middlesex Guildhall, the new medieval-style Gothic building opposite Westminster Abbey, between 30 October and 2 November. A public trial, it was hoped, might deter other potential spies as well as convince the British people that the government was succeeding in tracking down genuine cases of enemy espionage.

On the first day Lody was marched into the oak-panelled courtroom between two soldiers carrying fixed bayonets to answer charges of war treason and attempting to convey information useful to an enemy. Appearing for the defence, George Elliott, K. C., appealed to a British sense of fair play. But the prosecuting counsel, Archibald Bodkin, who earlier in the year had appeared for the Crown in the Starchfield Murder Case, portrayed the prisoner as 'a dangerous man' and an 'alien enemy'.

However, in the course of the next few days, it became difficult for the onlookers in court to equate the mild-mannered, affable individual, sitting beneath a glass canopy covered in netting, with this description. To one reporter from the *Daily Mail*, Lody seemed more a typical clerk than a sinister spy. In this respect he certainly didn't resemble Karl Ernst, whose trial on espionage charges ran almost concurrently with Lody's, and who conformed much more closely to the public's image of a suspicious-looking agent.

Instead, Lody's testimony emphasized his patriotism, courage and sense of honour. When he was asked to give the name of Fritz Prieger, his German spymaster, he refused, even though there is no evidence that the Germans had expected him to conceal Prieger's identity, and despite the fact that Lody might have avoided capital punishment by doing so. 'I have pledged my word of honour not to name that name,' he told the court, with tears coming into his eyes. 'I was pressed for secret service, but not as a spy – oh, no. If that would have been mentioned to me at Berlin I surely would have refused. The word in the sentence, I do not think it goes together.' At that moment, Lody struggled to regain his composure. He turned to the judges to explain that after a month's imprisonment, his nerve had given way.

The climax in this presentation of Lody as man of honour came on 2 November with his counsel's summing up. Carl Hans Lody, according to George Elliott, was compelled by patriotic motives. He wasn't 'a miserable coward asking for forgiveness for his offence' but a man 'born in a land of which he was proud, whose history and traditions he cherishes'. His own grandfather had been a great soldier who had held a fortress against Napoleon. Lody 'was ready to offer himself on the altar of his country . . . Many a man would do for England what he did for Germany.'

He would die as an officer in the service of his fatherland, Lody wrote to his sister Hanna on the eve of his execution, not as a traitorous spy. This projection of Lody as a courageous, honourable man continued right up to his final minutes. As the procession escorting him to the firing squad formed up on the veranda in the Tower, Lody said to the Assistant Provost-Marshal, 'I suppose that you will not care to shake hands with a German spy?'

'No,' came the reply. 'But I will shake hands with a brave man.'

Bombardment

Wednesday, 16 December

8 a.m.

A small band of hearty gentlemen were bathing in the South Bay area of the seaside town of Scarborough. Suddenly they witnessed a terrifying sight emerging from the thick bank of fog that covered the north-east coastline. Ominously black in the grey light of morning, three battleships – the hulking German battle-cruisers *Derfflinger* and *Von der Tann*, and the triple-funnelled light cruiser *Kolberg* – were steaming steadily in the direction of the shore. The swimmers barely had time to register their approach before the gigantic naval guns of the warships, eventually positioning themselves within half a mile of the harbour, opened fire on the town. The sky, darkened by the dense smoke belching from their funnels, was suddenly turned dramatically red by spurts of flame. Thunderous broadsides of high explosive and shrapnel shells smashed into buildings, throwing up enormous piles of debris high into the air.

There was a brief lull in the bombardment as the Germans paused to reload their guns. This allowed the bathers just enough time to get to the shore, gather their belongings and seek refuge under the sea wall. From here they watched in horror as shell after shell, about 500 of varying calibres, burst over the town. People, still in bed, dressing or having breakfast rushed to find out what kind of freak thunderstorm was making all the noise and causing their windows to rattle so violently. Seeing the action out at sea, some in the confusion believed that 'it is our own Battleships practising.' Others were convinced that the hour of the great naval engagement between Britain and Germany had at last arrived.

The initial fusillade of shells landed on the War Signal Station

Two boys gaze at the shell damage to a Baptist church in Hartlepool, caused by the German naval bombardment of the East Coast, December 1914

on Castle Hill and blew it to pieces. The twelfth-century castle, a conspicuous landmark situated 300 feet up on a promontory separating Scarborough's North and South bays, was an obvious target. At several points, its ten-foot-thick walls were shattered 'as mere timber'. Shells crashed through the ruined keep and ploughed into the disused yeomanry barracks near by. Not far away, Phyllis Lunn, a pupil at High Cliff School, evacuated with her classmates to a cloakroom in the school basement, felt the whole building shake 'as if it were coming down about our ears'. Two 'of the wee girls' clung to her and asked, 'It isn't the Germans going to kill us?'

From the castle, the German ships moved to direct their fire along the heavily populated area of the town's South Bay. Thirty-five shells struck the yellow-brick Grand Hotel, overlooking the bay. Only the fact that the influx of Christmas guests had yet to arrive ensured that there weren't any casualties. On the steps outside a private hotel, the Granville, further along the Esplanade, Alice Duffield was among the first to be killed, fatally wounded by a shell which exploded almost on top of her. At Dunollie, a large house in Filey Road, in the South Cliff area, three shrapnel shells exploded above its front portico, instantly killing both the postman Albert Beal, as he attempted to deliver the early-morning mail, and the maid Margaret Briggs, whose body was discovered afterwards in the main hallway, her stomach cut clean open. At Wood End, Sir George Sitwell's home in The Crescent, the Sitwell family and servants had a narrow escape when a shell crashed through the front door. Despite her husband's entreaties, Lady Sitwell refused to alter her morning routine of reading the newspapers in bed in order to join the other members of the household, who were taking shelter in the cellar. The next day Ida Sitwell left Scarborough to see her son Osbert before he left for France with the Grenadier Guards, and presented him with a piece of shrapnel from the German attack for good luck.

Hotels, boarding houses, churches, chapels, schools, warehouses and workshops, as well as private residences, were hit. Instead of remaining indoors, many townspeople, panicked and frightened, dashed into the streets, where they were caught by flying glass, splinters of shrapnel and falling debris. At the post office in Aberdeen Walk, there were crowds of people desperate to withdraw their life savings before the Germans landed and looted the place. 'Streams of people moved out of the town along Scalby Road, Stepney Road and Seamer Road,' the *Scarborough Mercury* reported later. 'So hurried had been the flight in some instances that they trudged along in their stockinged feet.' Cars and taxi-cabs helped to ferry the elderly and infirm. G. B. Halliday remembered 'People making for the moors with bundles on their backs, some with wheelbarrows and prams'.

During the pandemonium one woman was observed carrying a Christmas cake to safety in a pillow slip. Even escaping to the countryside could not guarantee protection from attack. Shells were reported to have reached as far afield as the village of Cayton, to the south of the town, and Ayton, several miles to the west. The sound of 'frequent booming' could be heard at Malton, twenty miles away.

Some made their way to the railway station, even though shells were obviously being aimed at the railway and, according to Harold Hainsworth, a Bradford merchant staying at the Waverley Hotel, 'were not far from missing their mark'. Here they scrambled on to any available service, to Pickering, Hull, York and London. Finding no room in the third-class carriage on the 8.25 to Leeds, passengers entered first-class compartments, only to be removed by porters and other staff, in a piece of official petty mindedness, before the train was given the signal to leave.

Half an hour after the bombardment had started, the battleships steamed away in a northerly direction towards Whitby. A parting shot was fired at another of Scarborough's familiar landmarks, its lighthouse. Three days later it would be declared 'distinctly unsafe', and work would begin on dismantling the structure.

The Germans left behind eighteen dead, including women and children, and more than eighty injured, together with an atmosphere of panic, uproar and shock. The schoolgirl Phyllis Lunn recorded in her diary that 'it was all over at about twenty-five minutes to nine . . . We went upstairs to wash and pack . . . then we put on our coats and caps and waited in the Library singing "It's a long way to Tipperary". . . till the Heads were ready to walk with us on the way to York. It was no use trying to get into any train at that moment as the station was black with people fleeing, and we could get no carriages, the horses were mad with fear.'

Further up the coast, commencing at roughly the same time as the Scarborough attack, the shelling of the Hartlepools (Hartlepool and West Hartlepool) was under way. This time, three German warships, the *Seydlitz*, *Moltke* and *Blücher*, had approached the coastline, to be met by some resistance from British destroyers, *Doon*, *Waveney*, *Test* and *Moy*, out on a routine patrol. These, though, were quickly forced to withdraw after coming under heavy fire, and the bombardment had continued.

Unlike Scarborough, Hartlepool maintained its coastal defences. The Durham Royal Garrison Artillery, a Territorial unit, consisting of eleven officers and 155 other ranks, manned two defence batteries, 'Lighthouse' Battery, and 'Heugh' Battery. Situated within 150 yards of each other, on a promontory in the old town, they were armed with three aged six-inch guns. It was here that the first round of fire fell, killing a sentry and three other members of the Durham Light Infantry (including Private Theophilus Jones, later declared the first soldier to be killed on British soil during the Great War). The citizens of Hartlepool were accustomed to hearing the sound of artillery practice coming from the gun emplacements, and many initially assumed that this was the source of the early-morning disturbance. In fact shells were ripping through the residential districts, causing massive destruction, making a sound 'like wind against telegraph wires'. 'I never thought it was the Germans,' said George Jobling, speaking the following day at the inquest into the killings. 'I thought they were ours practising':

> I went to the door and saw the people running round. I turned into the house again. I was just going to get a drop of tea when all at once *smash* went the corner of the house. I was knocked to the other side. It took me a few minutes to recover. When I did so I went round to the door, and found three children among a lot of bricks, two of them being my son's children [Jobling's son, a stoker in the Royal Navy, was away on duty]. They had been killed by a shell which struck my house.

The cost in human life and damage to property was far more extensive than in the Scarborough attack. The final number of reported casualties was 118 killed (including several who died later from their injuries) and about 200 wounded. Of those who died, only twenty-three were killed in their homes; the rest were struck down in the streets as they attempted to reach the railway, police station, or simply to flee the town.

The sky was lit up by violent explosions, visible from many miles away, as three gasometers were struck at the Hartlepool Gas & Water Company. Ships in the harbour were damaged, and the railway station and goods yard were hit, while a train to Leeds narrowly avoided a shell attack as it steamed out of the station.

The bombardment lasted about fifty minutes, during which time around 1,500 shells landed in and around the town, many of which failed to explode and had to be salvaged later. The batteries fired 123 rounds in pursuit of the German ships as they disappeared into the heavy mist, killing and injuring members of their crews.

9.05 a.m.

Meanwhile, the battleships responsible for shelling Scarborough had made their way to Whitby, the tiny picturesque fishing port further along the East Coast. A guard stationed on the East Cliff saw a ship he didn't recognize and ran a message up his flagpole: 'What ship is that?' The *Derfflinger* responded to his inquiry by firing a salvo of shells. A fragment from one of these tore through the head of Coastguard Boatman Frederick Randall, who had risen from his breakfast table and run outside to get a better look at the ships in the bay. He was killed outright.

The raid continued for just eleven minutes, causing three deaths and heavy damage to the houses in the old town beneath the East Cliff, where the shells 'made holes in the ground large enough to have buried a horse in'. With the sound of explosions echoing all around, Mrs Griffin, of 52 The Cragg, went into labour, giving birth to a ten-pound boy. 'Poor little fellow,' she told a reporter from the *Whitby Gazette* the next day, proudly handing him the baby. 'Shot and Shell they already call him about here, but he knows nothing about it.'

A gaping hole was blown in the walls of the west doorway of St Hilda's Abbey, Whitby's most historic landmark, dating back to the eleventh century. After 'delivering their devastating message', the ships 'suddenly turned to the east and disappeared in the mist, as silently as they had come'.

As the morning wore on, rumour and hearsay about the nature of the raids spread across the country. Every train into Leeds, Hull and

Bradford seemed to be transporting a fresh stream of refugees from the raided towns. They presented a pitiable sight, some dressed in nightclothes, often with little beyond what they stood up in. But many were full of 'thrilling narratives' of the dangers they'd experienced, encouraging some of those listening to purchase day excursion tickets to see the devastation for themselves, and pick up a piece of shrapnel as a souvenir. Fifty miles inland, at the market town of Knaresborough, stories of bombardment were met with incredulity, but these doubting Thomases were silenced at midday when a telegram verifying the news was posted in a shop window. Already, at lunchtime in West Hartlepool, one of the ravaged towns, a bale of pale blue silk, shredded to ribbons after a piece of shrapnel had pierced the chest of drawers in which it was lying, had been placed in one of the main street's shops to symbolize the suffering of the Hartlepools, and expedite the sale of war saving stamps.

Restrictions imposed by the censor meant that the local press on the East Coast was unable to publish details of the morning's events until the following day. Far away in London, Ada Reece noticed placards at lunchtime on the day of the raids, announcing the news that 'the Germans are shelling the Yorkshire coast towns.' She wondered whether this might be 'the grand naval battle we have expected' and confessed that 'Even now one does not realize it enough to feel personal alarm.'

Any sense of detachment experienced by inhabitants in the south was quickly to evaporate in the course of the next few days, as a combination of powerful eyewitness accounts and shocking photographs, tracing the path of the recent destruction, brought England's civilian population face to face with the realities of war.

———

The East Coast raids of 16 December 1914 were far from unexpected. The navy lacked the capacity to defend the 600 miles or so of Britain's extended eastern coastline. As it faced Continental Europe, this offered an easy and irresistible target for enemy assault, as well as a speedy exit route for an escaping German fleet. Six weeks earlier, in the early morning of 3 November, four German cruisers, including the *Seydlitz*, subsequently involved in the Scarborough attack, had crossed the Channel to bombard an East Coast town for the first time.

They fired on Great Yarmouth in East Anglia for a quarter of an hour from a distance of ten miles, to avoid the risk of collision with mines, so that all the shells fell short, some falling into the water, others reaching only as far as the beach. A sense of nervous excitement prevailed among the residents of Yarmouth and neighbouring Lowestoft. Many felt emboldened to walk down to the water's edge to observe the huge columns of water thrown up by the explosions. According to one newspaper report, the 'arc cut in the sky by the swift shell could be easily seen and the air was shaken by detonations'. The Territorials were called out, and three submarines gave chase as the German ships made their departure, one of them sunk by a mine as it attempted to leave the harbour. But the town itself survived unscathed, and there were few signs of panic.

There was, however, some recognition in the national and local press of the strong likelihood that the Germans would try again, that a future raid on another East Coast town could prove more costly, or even that an enemy invasion might be in prospect. At the end of November, Katherine Alexander, the precocious nine-year-old daughter of a Worcestershire doctor, recorded in her diary the news of one false alarm that a neighbour had given her: 'that there was an hourly expectation of Germans landing, that lots of our troops were being sent to the East coast in motor cars, and [that] some of the civil population are leaving to go further inland'. Already aware that wartime rumours should not necessarily be taken at face value, she added, 'It is very exciting if it is true.'

In fact, the Royal Navy's sinking of several German cruisers off the Falkland Islands on 8 December, a humiliating defeat for Germany's High Command and a severe setback for German naval morale, ensured that the enemy would seek swift reprisals and effectively sealed the fate of England's coastal towns. By 14 December the Admiralty in London, basing its conclusion on reports from Navy Intelligence, was certain that an attack was imminent. On the afternoon of the 15th, it was able to report that 'There is a good probability of German battle-cruisers, cruisers, and destroyers being off our coast tomorrow at daybreak.' What the Admiralty was unable to throw any light on was where exactly this projected attack might take place.

In the immediate aftermath of the East Coast raids, there were indignant protests from official representatives, and members of the populations of the shelled towns, about the Royal Navy's failure to protect them from bombardment. In defence of naval strategy, *The Times* felt forced to remind its readers that the safeguarding of England was not the primary objective of the navy in wartime. 'The purpose of the Royal Navy,' it insisted, 'is to engage and destroy the ships of the enemy . . . Neither raids nor even invasion will deter our fleet from the aim for which it was created, and for which it keeps the seas.' Raising once more the possibility that the Germans might actually land forces on the vulnerable eastern coastline, the newspaper declared that 'the duty of repelling invasion, should it be attempted' rested not with the Navy, but 'upon the manhood of the nation'.

In the early months of war, fears of German invasion weighed heavily in the imaginations of English men and women. The pre-war stories of Erskine Childers and William Le Queux had given them some notion of what to expect. The spectre of Belgium added a frightening dose of reality. Reminders of Germany's murderous assaults on Belgian life and property were never far away, constantly evoked in propaganda, newspaper reports and pictures, and by the stark presence on British streets and in British homes of Belgian refugees. 'At the back of the mind of everyone,' Arnold Bennett wrote as early as 10 August, 'is a demi-semi fear lest the Germans should after all by some *coup*, contrive an invasion.'

The apprehension, as the German Army advanced along the Channel coast in the autumn of 1914, that Britain might soon share Belgium's fate, and that a German invasion was imminent, became almost palpable in certain parts of the country. 'Will Invasion be Tried?' *The Times* asked in mid October. The paper warned that 'We must expect to be attacked at home, and must not rest under any comforting illusions that we shall not be assailed', and argued that such an attack had no serious objective other than 'to land an expedition in England for the purposes of compelling us to sign a disastrous peace'.

From Malvern College, where he was a pupil, the young C. S. Lewis mildly rebuked his father for giving credence to invasion scares, which he pronounced as being about as believable as stories of Russian troops travelling through Britain with snow on their boots. It was hardly surprising, though, in the panic of the moment during the East Coast raids on 16 December, that the bombardment was widely perceived as a preliminary to the landing of an invasion force. 'Run for your lives, the Germans have landed,' shouted a soldier, running down a street in the centre of Hartlepool, at the height of the action. On his way to school that morning at Ferryhill, in County Durham, Leslie Craig, who could hear the reports of the guns 'like distant thunder', was informed that fourteen miles away the citizens of Hartlepool were already surrendering to German soldiers. Similarly, at the North Yorkshire town of Malton, twenty miles inland from Scarborough, the *Leeds Mercury* reported that 'rumours were speedily circulated to the effect that the much talked about invasion by the Germans had at last taken place.'

The government had accepted that a German invasion of England launched from Calais was at least feasible, though, after a meeting of the Committee of Imperial Defence (CID) on 7 October, Asquith noted that everyone present had agreed 'that nothing of the kind was likely to occur at the present'. This, the Prime Minister went on to say, was just as well, as the country had rarely been so ill-prepared to defend itself. Most Regular troops were in France as part of the British Expeditionary Force, and stocks of guns and ammunition were running low.

Nevertheless, it was clearly essential that the population should receive some sort of preparation in the event of an invasion taking place, however hypothetical such an eventuality seemed. As Maurice Hankey, Secretary of the CID, admitted to the Archbishop of Canterbury, 'the contingency is not so remote that it can be safely ignored', though he personally thought that a raid, in order to instil panic, rather than an invasion, was more probable. The prime targets for a German landing, in order of likelihood, were believed to be the East Coast, especially the areas of Yarmouth and Cromer; the Essex coastline, in particular Southend-on-Sea and Harwich; the mouth of the River Tyne; and, last of all, the Kent coastline.

In early November, a government memorandum, 'Preparations by civil authorities for action in the event of a hostile landing', was sent out for the guidance of Local Emergency Committees. The main task of these committees, and of the Parish Committees further down the chain of command, was to instruct the civilian population 'so that their conduct might not interfere with, and might be assistance to, the military authorities'. Most importantly of all, the population was to be encouraged to stay in their own homes, and not attempt to flee in the event of an invasion, as a stampede of fugitives would be a threat to the movement of British troops and their artillery. The coastline was to be held from entrenched positions, and in some areas farmers were requested 'to spare men for three days . . . in public service of digging trenches', an operation that, it was envisaged, would require some 40,000 participants.

Instructions were also provided about the necessary measures to be taken to obstruct the enemy's advance in the face of an invasion. A six-point guide outlined the proposed course of action: all means of transportation and communication, as well as livestock and food supplies, were either to be removed or destroyed. The strict lighting regulations after 11 p.m., already enforced in certain big cities, were now extended to provincial towns, and made to apply on every day of the week. A greengrocer, in Chelmsford, a town regarded as being of particular significance because of its proximity to the Marconi wireless works, found himself serving seven days in prison when he refused to lower the lights in his shop not long before Christmas.

By far the most contentious area of preparation for invasion revolved around the question of civil defence, and whether ordinary people should be allowed to carry weapons or wear uniforms. At the beginning of the war, H. G. Wells, himself a resident of Essex, had called for the formation of a home defence reserve, to include both men above the age of statutory military service and those below it. Wells's opponents were quick to point out that Belgian *francs-tireurs*, who had been killed in acts of armed resistance against the Germans, had signally failed to halt their country's invasion. Wells's response was to argue forcefully that 'Many men, and not a few women, will turn out to shoot Germans. There will be no preventing them after

the Belgian stories . . . They will get shot, and their houses will be
burnt according to the established German rules and methods . . . so
they may just as well turn out in the first place, and get some shooting as consolation in advance for their inevitable troubles.' Wells did
not succeed in winning his case. Civilians were forbidden from offering armed resistance to invaders in all circumstances.

The last thing the government wanted to do was to increase the
existing high level of alarm in parts of the country. But, for all its
precautionary measures, it couldn't vanquish the nightmare vision of
German troops overrunning coastal areas, committing atrocities
against innocent British civilians and carrying out the destruction of
their property. In Canterbury, close to one of the suspected target
areas, Randall Davidson, its Archbishop, offered counsel and advice
to parishioners who were terrified, as he informed Asquith, 'about
the possibility of an invasion or raid in this particular bit of Kent'. His
senior clergy were also expressing concern. At the beginning of
December the Bishop of St Edmundsbury and Ipswich, near the Suffolk coastline, wrote to Davidson seeking his advice about burying
communion plate and parish registers to protect them from German
invaders, in what must have seemed strangely like a throwback to the
medieval church's secreting of valuables from Viking marauders in
the ninth and tenth centuries. Davidson sensibly urged the Bishop to
send valuables to London, adding that 'I emphatically do not believe
in the policy of burying articles of value.'

Private citizens, as well as national institutions, were by now making their own arrangements for the protection of their possessions.
Rudyard Kipling, whose examination of the evidence for the Belgian atrocities had made him keenly aware of what Germany might
have in store for a subjugated Britain, had already sent his manuscripts and household valuables into hiding. Sydney Cockerell,
Director of the Fitzwilliam Museum in Cambridge, believed that the
city would be 'the first objective of the enemy in the unlikely event
of a successful landing in force'. On 11 December he gathered together
'watches and certain ivories, enamels, coins, gems and manuscripts'
and had them transported to a place of safety.

Five days later, the raids on the East Coast towns, falling short of a full-scale invasion, confirmed to many that the worst might be yet to come. Amid all the shock and outrage at the enemy attack, several northern newspapers published scare stories, with imaginary but convincing and closely detailed plans of an approaching invasion, in which the German Army would land on the East Coast and march across the West Riding into Lancashire, demolishing all the mills and businesses as they went, and making millions of people homeless and destitute.

—

The atmosphere in Scarborough, the Hartlepools and Whitby, in the days immediately following the raids, was sombre, as the official inquests into the casualties opened, and the first funerals of those killed in the attacks began to take place. In West Hartlepool the Deputy Coroner opened the proceedings by reminding those present that 'They now had some idea what the Belgians and the French had suffered by invasion. He mentioned this . . . because he thought it might bring it home to their minds what the war really meant.'

The extent of the suffering of the East Coast communities was reinforced by the testimony of witnesses: bodies riddled by shells, or so mutilated that they were unrecognizable; victims minus arms or legs, their limbs smashed to pulp. Nineteen-year-old Freyda Wainright was discovered in the mortuary by her stepfather. She had lost an arm, and part of her head had been blown off. Time and again the shocking suddenness and unpredictability of death impressed themselves on the inquests. William Caws of 57 Grosvenor Street, West Hartlepool, related how he and his wife, daughter and son were in their back sitting-room eating breakfast when a shell burst through the ceiling and instantly killed his daughter, Dorothy, sitting by the fire.

The remarkable range of the German ships' firepower was demonstrated. Shells had possessed the capacity to reach several blocks behind Scarborough's seafront, along the length, for example, of Prospect Road, where Emily Merryweather, proprietor of the general store, was mortally wounded by shrapnel from a shell just as she was ushering friends to the shelter of the cellar. They also, on more than one occasion, travelled with lightning speed through the interiors of several houses before crashing to earth. One shell entered a house on Scarborough's Esplanade, passed straight through it and a garden wall, and smashed into a house across the street at 1 Belvedere Road, killing the maid Emily Crosby as it did so. It then continued on its way, ploughing into the house next door before landing in the back garden.

The tragic fate of the Bennett family of 2 Wykeham Street, Scarborough, was much remarked upon. At breakfast time that day there had been seven people in the house: Mr Bennett and his wife, Johanna; their children, Christopher (aged twenty-five) and Albert (aged twenty-two); their grandchildren, George (aged nine) and John (aged five); and their servant Mrs Edmond. When the house took a direct hit, four members of the family were killed, while the others had to be treated for injuries and shock. Christopher Bennett, who survived, fell through the bedroom floor into the kitchen, where he found his brother Albert in one corner, and his mother, who'd lost a hand, and the children in the other. 'We moved mother into the yard with little Jack and little George,' he recalled, 'but it was too late . . . Mother was gone by the time we got her into the yard. I carried little George into the next house, but he died as I put him down.' The other boy, John, together with Christopher's brother, Albert, died that afternoon.

The danger of escaping a house in the middle of a raid, to flee to safety in the country, was illustrated in Hartlepool by the experience of the Dixon family of William Street. They were hurrying down a road when a shell exploded in front of them. Fourteen-year-old George, eight-year-old Margaret and seven-year-old Albert were all killed immediately. Their mother, blown to the ground by the explosion, lost one of her legs in the blast but still clutched her baby John close to her. Although barely conscious, she begged her surviving son, twelve-year-old Joseph, to carry his wounded three-year-old brother Billy to safety. Joseph and Billy collapsed outside Trinity Church, were found by two soldiers, and taken to hospital, where Joseph later had seventeen pieces of shrapnel removed from his legs.

The jury at Scarborough's inquest had tried to insist on a verdict of 'Wilful Murder' against the Germans until it was explained to them by the Coroner that this was impossible. Instead the much less emotive 'death by fire from enemy vessels' was recorded in every case.

Newspapers across Britain printed the coroners' reports, eyewitness accounts and human-interest stories of the attacks at enormous length. As a consequence *The Times* had sold out by 9.15 on the morning of 17 December. More popular titles gave over several of their pages to a wealth of photographic journalism: pictures of the victims and of the crowds attending their funerals; of people, their faces still registering shock, standing outside devastated homes; and of the damage to public and private property, estimated at several hundred thousand pounds, including buildings with gaping holes blown right through them. Police Constable Harry Hunter and his cape was one of the most popular images published in the press. Wet from Hunter's night patrol, the cape had been hung out to dry on railings in the grounds of Scarborough Castle minutes before the bombardment began. On returning to retrieve it, Hunter found that the cape had been shredded to ribbons by the shrapnel that had scarred the Castle walls.

Reading 'the seasoned narratives of the eyewitnesses', Harold Cousins reacted with a degree of cynicism: 'Most of the casualties,' he commented in his diary, 'seem to have been caused by people coming out into the streets to see the fun.' Ethel Bilsborough, by contrast, was roused to indignation by the barbarism of the 'Hun'. 'Over 100 lives were lost – or massacred,' she wrote. 'It is horrible to think that such things can take place in these enlightened days, but then the Germans are proving every day that they have no sense of right or justice, morality, or honour.' The association with the death and destruction wrought by the Germans in Belgium was clear, and made clearer still in Ethel Bilsborough's diary by two pictures clipped from newspapers with the label: 'House in Scarborough where dead babies were found after the bombardment'.

The connection between Scarborough's dead babies, and reports of atrocities against young children committed by the invading Germans in Belgium earlier that autumn, was cemented by a widely reported remark made by Winston Churchill as First Lord of the Admiralty on 20 December.

In an open letter to the Mayor of Scarborough, Churchill, who had been 'sick with disappointment' that thick fog had allowed the German ships to escape back to port, extended his sympathy on behalf of the navy 'for the loss that Scarborough has sustained'. His concluding sentence, branding the German Navy as the 'baby killers of Scarborough', was a striking, though controversial, bit of propaganda. Asquith summed up the phrase as 'rather banal; a lot of cheapish rhetoric & an undertone of angry snarl!' Margot Asquith was rather less forgiving: 'the one thing in war times that no one can stomach is rhetoric – a LOT of words & high words . . . are quite out of place now.'

Churchill's well publicized sympathy for Scarborough caused understandable resentment in the Hartlepools, which had suffered so much more heavily in the 16 December raids. At the same time, his remarks unfortunately also appeared to suggest that the Hartlepools were a lawful wartime target for German attack, in accordance with international law established by the Ninth Hague Convention of 1907, because they were occupied by land forces and formed part of the coastal defences. In that case, the *Northern Daily Mail* commented testily, 'we have surely a right to ask that if the Hartlepools are to be treated as a fortified place the defences should be more adequate to the work which is expected of them.'

With fears of invasion again running high, a battalion of Territorials, known as the Leeds Rifles, had been rushed into Scarborough to defend the town and assist in keeping order. Scarborough's hopes of entertaining a ghoulish Christmas tourist trade, after the arrival in the first days following the attacks of hundreds of sightseers, intent on viewing the damage, were short lived. Within two weeks it was reported that as many as 6,000 people had left the town. Sylvia Pankhurst visited Scarborough on Christmas Eve. She found the people 'weary and dishevelled', and the big amusement palaces 'scarred and battered by shell-fire', and fled quickly back to London: 'Scarborough was too sad for me.'

All the same, Scarborough found itself the focus of a new kind of celebrity. Within forty-eight hours of the bombardment, recruiting posters exhorting men to enlist and 'Avenge Scarborough!' and 'the murder of innocent women and children' began to appear on billboards across the country (the most popular image, taken from a painting by Edith Kemp-Welch, showed a sword-bearing Britannia rousing men to enlist, with Scarborough in flames in the background). Later a set of commemorative medals was struck, in various alloys, one the size of a sixpence, the other of a half-crown. In the run-up to the first Christmas of the war, reported Katherine Mansfield, the East Coast raids seemed to be the only topic of conversation. On 23 December *Punch*'s editor, Owen Seaman, summed up the national mood by turning a defiant face to the enemy:

> Come where you will – the seas are wide;
> And choose your Day – they're all alike;
> You'll find us ready where we ride
> In calm or storm and wait to strike;
> But – if of shame your shameless Huns
> Can yet retrieve some casual traces –
> Please fight our men and ships and guns
> Not women-folk and watering places.

Preaching at St Mary's, Scarborough, on the Saturday after the bombardment, the Archbishop of York, Cosmo Gordon Lang, who was still atoning for his sympathetic remarks about the Kaiser, interpreted 'the cruel onslaught' on the East Coast as 'a fresh vindication of the righteousness of our cause'. It had brought with it, he continued, 'a quick, vivid sense of the dread realities of war, in order that they should prepare us to steel our hearts for the inevitable sacrifices which a great war demands'.

Lang was not alone in believing that the raids might give new unity and purpose to Britain's conduct of the war. Alan Morton, serving in France with the Royal Field Artillery, wrote to his fiancée Iris Holt that he hoped the bombardment would 'wake people up a bit' to the reality of war. However, the widespread assumption that the raids would have a beneficial effect on recruiting proved wide of the mark. *The Times* was confident that 'the agricultural worker labourer of the East Riding and the industrial worker of the North Riding have had the horrors of the war brought to their doors and recruiting is certain to be accelerated as a result.' A poem by Jessie Pope, the well-known patriotic tub-thumper, portrayed 'Young Brown', untouched by war 'up to date', who is spurred on to enlist by thoughts of Scarborough, 'The happy haunt of summer revels,/Bombarded!'

> Those Yorkshire Women lying dead!
> The news grew blurred – he tried to skim it,
> Then rose, 'This is'; he calmly said,
> 'The Limit!'

But the anticipated rush to the recruiting stations did not materialize. Across Yorkshire, as the *Leeds Mercury* reported on 19 December, that week's raid did not appear 'to have had the slightest effect, and recruiting was, if anything, below the previous Friday's figures'. Many men were said to be 'holding back until after Christmastide', and there was the suggestion that some had decided to stay at home and protect their families from possible future attacks rather than volunteer for service overseas.

What the fate of the East Coast towns undoubtedly did achieve was a new sense of soldier and civilian fighting together against a common enemy, who now stood revealed in his true colours as an embodiment of pure evil. England had been bloodied by a Germany that had failed to observe any distinction between legitimate military targets and the massacre of innocent women and children. It confirmed more than ever that the future of civilization itself depended on an early and decisive victory against the warped values of German 'Kultur'.

Eleanor Acland, wife of Liberal MP Sir Francis Acland, manifested this new sense of purpose in her diary on 19 December. The bombardment, she wrote, had arrived 'just when we are getting rather bored with the other reasons for fighting, just to remind us that the reason for going on is that we have begun; just to show us once again what the inward gist of Potsdam is . . . The repetition of a good cry soon gets monotonous, & we want to have our blood stirred by something that really pricks.'

Not with a Bang but a Whimper

'These are sad days,' Charlotte Despard wrote in the third week of November. 'We hear all sorts of miseries and the war does not seem to move. Germans and allies still face one another, with little advantage from day to day. *When* is this awful war to end?' This was a question that Despard, an eminent feminist, socialist and pacifist, might well have addressed to her younger brother, the commander-in-chief of the British Expeditionary Force, Sir John French, to whom she remained devoted, even though his views on the war remained diametrically opposed to hers.

In the weeks immediately preceding Christmas, Hallie Eustace Miles felt the shadows deepening as she watched the casualty lists lengthen. 'We are losing friend after friend,' she wrote despairingly in her diary. One of her relatives in the Household Brigade had just been home on leave, and had recounted his experience of trench warfare. 'Such a horrible time, he says it was! The worst part of all was hearing the cries and groans of the wounded and dying, and not being able to leave the trenches to help them.' Kate Courtney thought it likely, on the basis of reports she had received from officers returning from the Front, that the war would be over by the spring of 1915, as 'the men don't and can't stand the strain of the awful trench fighting on either side any longer.'

News of the bombardment of the East Coast increased the pervasive sense of gloom hanging over the country as it entered the first winter of the war. For some it was all too much. One London man became so depressed by the lack of positive news that he took out an action for damages against his father for having caused his existence, and for having thereby brought 'distress and dismay upon him'. His lawyers argued, on a sound legal principle, that if a man does another man an injury which the victim cannot prevent, and to which he did not give his consent, he must indemnify him. Before the end of the year, however, reason prevailed, and the action was withdrawn.

A mock-up picture on the front page of the *Daily Express*, depicting a Zeppelin hovering menacingly over the Houses of Parliament, December 1914

A dramatic turn in the weather made its contribution to the nation's low spirits. That autumn had been an unusually mild and dry one. In Great Leighs, in Essex, Andrew Clark had noted the 'exceptional mildness of the season' and recorded that even at the beginning of November it was still unnecessary to light fires to warm the church. A drought had persisted over much of England from mid September to the last week of October, but by the end of that month heavy rains were beginning to lash the country. This change was heralded by the storm-force gales and heavy seas that pounded the north-east and east English coasts. On 30 October these weather conditions were partly responsible for the tragic sinking of the hospital ship H.M.H.S. *Rohilla* on rocks off Whitby. The *Rohilla*, equipped with two operating theatres and transporting 229 passengers – crew, doctors and nurses – was on its way from Leith to Dunkirk. The wartime blackout meant that there were no navigation lights, and in the early-morning darkness, and buffeted by a raging storm, the ship rammed at full speed a shelf of rock running out from the base of the East Cliff.

The *Rohilla* had foundered only 600 yards from the shore, but the treacherous weather – overpowering winds and waves rising as high as twenty feet – left the ship inaccessible to the rescue services. The five women on board were the first to be saved. One of them, stewardess Mary Roberts, had survived the sinking of the *Titanic* two and a half years earlier. She later maintained that her experience on the *Rohilla* had been even worse. As they waited to be rescued, the men on board faced the terrifying choice of whether to stay on the wrecked ship or to take their chances swimming to shore in the rough sea. Fifty men spent over two days on the *Rohilla* as a succession of six lifeboats attempted to reach them. Of the 229 who had set sail from Leith, 145 survived. Bodies were washed ashore, but many found their grave only at sea.

Rain was almost relentless throughout England in December. There were only six days without measurable rainfall, making it the wettest December for nearly forty years. At the end of the month, rain and strong south-westerly gales battered a large part of southern England, damaging buildings and causing fatalities in London, Kent and Essex.

Some amateur meteorologists put about the theory that the heavy rainfall was a consequence of the number of gunpowder particles entering the atmosphere after being exploded on the Continent. The quagmires that Kitchener's new recruits were wading about in at their training camps were certainly a good preparation for the liquid mud they would shortly face on the Western Front. 'In some of the Salisbury Plain camps,' reported Christopher Addison, Parliamentary Secretary at the Board of Education, 'the Tommies are slithering about in a sea of mud from six to eighteen inches deep'. The breakdown in the weather was also delaying the construction of military encampments. At Shoreham, men were still sleeping in tents as their huts were not ready. The roads were a churned-up mess, and in order to reach their sleeping quarters the trainees had 'to flounder ankle-deep' through mud 'as gingerly as an acrobat treads a tight-rope'.

Meanwhile, grimly but irrelevantly – though continuing on a watery theme – a classic serial murder case was reaching its climax. George Joseph Smith (a bigamist using the aliases Oliver Charles

James, Henry Williams and John Lloyd, among others) had already murdered two wives, drowning them in their baths after ensuring that he had gained possession of their money or their life insurance. At Bath (a grisly coincidence), on 17 December 1914, Smith, posing as John Lloyd, married again, this time to Margaret Lofty, a clergyman's daughter. She would be his final victim. The same day the newly-weds travelled to London and took rooms at a boarding-house at Bismarck Road (later renamed Waterlow Road), just off Highgate Hill. The next afternoon, Margaret visited a solicitor's office and made a will in her husband's favour. That evening at their lodgings, Margaret took a bath. The landlady heard splashing from the bathroom, then the noise of someone putting wet hands or arms on the side of the bath. Finally, there was the sound of a sigh.

A few minutes later the mournful strains of 'Nearer my God to Thee', said to have been played on the *Titanic* as the ship went down, could be heard coming from the harmonium in the couple's sitting-room.

Edward Thomas had returned home in September after his journey around England, gathering people's impressions of the war for several commissioned articles. He wasn't sorry to be back in Hampshire, as he'd felt as if he 'were rather the grub in the apple', talking to men and women who had 'as little to do with the pen as the sword'. But he was once more in a state of uncertainty about his future. The sight everywhere on his travels of raw young recruits queuing up to volunteer had turned his mind to thoughts of enlisting. He might join the Territorials, he told his friend Jesse Berridge, only he couldn't leave his family to be kept by other people 'till I know I can't do it myself'. Alternatively, it might be a good time for him to stake out a new life in America, though again he wasn't prepared to leave his wife and younger children behind in order to do so. As he continued to waver over what to do, he made two visits to Gloucestershire that autumn to see Robert Frost and his family, who had moved from Little Iddens and were staying with the Abercrombies in their cottage at Ryton. Thomas's friendship with Frost had intensified on long walks that summer, overflowing with conversation. However, Frost was now himself too unwell and out of sorts to help rescue Thomas from his indecision.

While Thomas waited for 'some really strong impulse one way', his future remained as unresolved as ever. Passing through London in November, he went so far as to collect enlistment papers from the offices of the Parliamentary Recruiting Committee, but then hesitated to fill them in. Some friends expressed surprise that he should even think of joining up. After all, they told him, he had a family to consider, and although his age – he would be thirty-seven in March – brought him within the current age limit for recruitment, there were plenty of younger men who could take his place for the time being.

So what pulled Edward Thomas in the direction of enlisting? He didn't pretend to feel 'warlike', though he may well have feared being shamed as a coward. Undoubtedly he wished to exert some control over his future while he still could. Otherwise he might find himself being 'pitchforked' into the army, if and when a system of compulsion was introduced. He wondered whether it was too late in life to escape from 'the mess of journalism', which, more than ever, was denying him an adequate living. But perhaps he also looked upon a soldier's existence as one way of combating the depression and despair that had sometimes threatened to overwhelm him in recent years.

Motivating him above all was the renewed sense of his love of England, which war had instilled in him, and a new-found desire to protect it. Previously, he admitted in an article for the *Nation* in November, he had loved England 'foolishly, aesthetically, like a slave, not having realized that it was not mine unless I was willing and prepared to die rather than leave it as Belgian women and old men and children had left their country'.

Something, he continued, had to be done before he could 'look again composedly' at the English landscape. However, his final decision to join the British Army was still more than eight months away when, on 3 December, he experienced a moment of epiphany that gave him the 'strong impulse' he had looked for. It was to transform Edward Thomas not into a soldier but into the poet that many in his immediate circle had been convinced for years was his true creative destiny.

Drawing closely on impressions recorded in the field notebooks he always carried with him – like the one containing his description of the station stop at Adlestrop back in June – he reworked the prose that had so often appeared to stray over into verse. From 3 to 7 December, Thomas wrote 'Up in the Wind', 'November', 'March', 'Old Man' and 'The Sign-Post', a poem that dramatizes the poet's own inability to choose which path to take. 'I am in it and no mistake,' he wrote to Frost, expressing his new sense of liberation. 'I find myself engrossed and conscious of a possible perfection as I never was in prose.'

A heightened sense of place would come to dominate his poetry, as Edward Thomas discovered the core of his patriotism in his observation of England and Englishness. In the first days of the New Year, his decision about enlisting was again delayed when he fell and severely sprained his ankle. Confined to bed for a week, he continued to produce poetry. Finely attuned as ever to changes in the climate, one of these poems commemorated an end to so many water-logged days: 'After Rain'.

Edward Thomas had looked on almost enviously as Rupert Brooke, his younger contemporary, had secured a commission, in late September, in the Royal Naval Division. Brooke had appeared to accomplish this, using his elevated connections as high up as Winston Churchill himself, with none of the vacillation that characterized Thomas's attitude to taking an active part in the war. In reality, though, Brooke had initially been frustrated by his absence of firm employment. He had half-heartedly pursued a job as a war correspondent. When this failed he had resolved to find some special mission for himself that would utilize his intelligence, and help him to avoid becoming 'a mere part of a machine'.

As often before, Brooke's inner turmoil was reflected in his relationships with women. His affair with Cathleen Nesbitt, the young actress who had captured his attention shortly before he embarked on his travels in North America and the South Seas, was cooling. Publicly, he lavished sentiment on her: she was the best thing in his life, he worshipped and adored her. Privately, he retained nagging doubts that anything more lasting and mature could be created from this basis. And he had begun to turn his attentions elsewhere. With Lady Eileen Wellesley, daughter of the Duke of Wellington, Brooke enjoyed an uncomplicated dalliance. Potentially more involving, not least because he seems to have failed to recognize the signs of her developing infatuation, was a friendship with the Prime Minister's daughter, Violet Asquith.

But war offered Rupert Brooke the chance of a clean break. It was an opportunity to distance himself from the chaotic, messy love affairs of the recent past, and to draw a line under the bitter attacks he had been making, with a worrying ferocity and paranoia, on his former Bloomsbury friends and allies. The certainties of military life were a way out of all this confusion and uncertainty. He felt so happy, he was to tell Cathleen Nesbitt a little later, 'in this new safety and brightness'.

In the first week of October, Brooke, as a member of the Royal Naval Division (along with Asquith's son Arthur, known as 'Oc'), was present at the siege of Antwerp. The Belgian Army was already in retreat by the time the RND arrived. But every day that the Flemish city, now little more than a flaming ruin, could hold out offered more time for the defence and strengthening of the English Channel ports against possible German invasion. For a brief time Brooke witnessed the true horror of war at first hand, contradicting posterity's belittling accusation that the impetus behind his war poetry derived from nothing more than a naive patriotism experienced at one remove. During its twenty-five-mile retreat from the Front, Brooke's Brigade, bedraggled and shell-shocked, was witness 'to one of the greatest crimes of history'. Lit by 'hills and spires of flame', they saw thousands of Belgian refugees in flight, two unending lines of old men, 'mostly weeping', and of 'women with hard drawn faces'. Belgium had become a country, Brooke commented angrily, 'where three civilians have been killed to every one soldier . . . Has ever a nation been treated like that? And how can such a stain be wiped out?'

Back in England, Brooke moved to naval barracks at Chatham. At the beginning of November, he joined the Royal Naval Division's Hood Battalion and was sent to a training camp at Blandford, in

Dorset. Here he slept in a wooden hut with seven other officers, went on regular route marches and battled against the deteriorating weather. 'My God, this mud!' he exclaimed.

He had started work on the five war sonnets, later published under the title *1914 and Other Poems*, that were to bring him immortality. The first in the sequence – though the second in order of composition – is misleadingly called 'Peace', though it celebrates the personal and moral regeneration brought about by the war:

> To turn, as swimmers into cleanness leaping,
> Glad from a world grown old and cold and weary,
> Leave the sick hearts that honour could not move,
> And half-men, and their dirty songs and dreary,
> And all the little emptiness of love!

Full of the time-honoured language of war, to the point of verbal flatulence, Brooke's sonnets speak of 'Honour, Glory', 'Sacrifice', 'Heroism' – and a near mystical idea of 'England'. No wonder they would soon serve as a bugle call to Englishmen who had yet to put on the mantle of patriotism and enlist. For Brooke, time was running out. On the day before Christmas Eve 1914, he scribbled a single line in his field-training notebook. It was the opening of his fifth and final sonnet: 'If I should die, think only this of me.' Four months later, Rupert Brooke himself would join the ranks of the dead.

It was a patriotic duty to celebrate Christmas as far as possible in the usual way. Various newspapers took this line, and it appeared to win widespread acceptance. Unlike the Parisians during the Franco-Prussian War of 1870, there would be no boycott of the Christmas tree because of its German origins. The display of patriotism would be evident in the sending of Union Jack greetings cards, and in the replacement of conventional decorations with strings of the brightly coloured flags representing all the Allied nations: Great Britain, France, Russia, Belgium and Japan (which had formally declared war against Germany on 23 August).

The traditional Christmas dinner promised to be only slightly more expensive than in peacetime, with turkey priced at 1*s*.2*d*. a pound, compared with 11*d.* a pound a year earlier (one thoughtful innovation for harassed housewives, from Selfridges in London, was a prepared and part-cooked Christmas meal, ready for reheating and available to order by telephone). Stores in big cities were generally crowded in the run-up to the festive season. The London housewife Ada Reece remarked that this was 'a change from a short time ago when nothing seemed doing except at the wool counters', and some shops had notices outside 'inviting customers to walk through even if they did not wish to buy, to encourage the assistants'. In the capital, Macleod Yearsley observed that 'the streets and shops were full, but less so than usual, and the crowds were well sprinkled with khaki.' Michael MacDonagh, on the other hand, who noted in passing that khaki uniforms obliterated the differences in class that were so apparent in civilian attire, thought the streets of the West End of London were 'as thronged' as he had ever seen them at Christmas. 'In the suburbs the butchers' shops were bulging with beef and mutton; the poulterers' with geese and turkeys; the grocers' with wine, spirits and beer; the fruiterers' with apples and oranges. Yes, supplies were abundant; prices seemed only a little in advance of those of last year.'

To MacDonagh, it was, 'in most respects', the same old Christmas. The biggest surprise was that the season of goodwill had withstood the shock 'of the greatest war in the world's history'. There were, of course, 'Puritanically minded people' who thought it wrong 'to be jolly "when there is a war on"'. Mary Drew, Gladstone's daughter, was among them. Writing to a friend from Hawarden, her family home, she railed against the celebrations. 'I could not bear the buns and balls and bands and mince pies and Christmas cards and turkeys. Chester was filled with motors and gay, light-hearted people the week before Christmas Day – laughing, talking, shopping, shops crowded. They don't realise a bit yet.'

Katherine Mansfield was spending part of the holiday with D. H. Lawrence and his wife, Frieda. Frieda's position, as a German, was 'a little delicate', Mansfield wrote with decided understatement, but Frieda was contentedly making marzipan to go on the cake, and talking cheerfully about her cousins Otto and Franz – who were 'sure to be killed in this war – *if* not dead already'. London's Christmas, Mansfield

thought, was something of a farce, as everything had been given over
to the military, with the shop windows in Oxford Street filled with
'khaki and wool and pots of vaseline and marching socks'. Wherever
she went, women seemed to be knitting: girls in shops, women on
buses and tubes. 'I can't help wondering what the results are like.'

Many shops were placarded with signs carrying the words 'Gifts
for Our Men at the Front', and leading department stores had baskets
on display into which shoppers could drop presents for wounded
soldiers. 'Two receivers of gifts are specially catered for,' *The Times*
reported, 'the khaki hero and the child.' Among popular presents for
the former were 'tinder lighters with their natty little plaited rope
and striker', which had 'found their way into the trenches', and
'waterproof squares for trench seats'. 'There is very little of the brand
of Christmas present which usually appears at this season,' the report
continued, 'tawdry, made for show, and of no use once the season is
past. Such gifts were, one suspects, originally imported from Germany.' Children's toys that reflected the war – nurses' uniforms for
girls, and toy soldiers and weapons for boys – sold out quickly. The
Jason, the so-called 'Santa Claus' ship, had docked at Plymouth at the
end of November. It carried a cargo of five million individual gifts
from the children of the United States for the children 'of the bel-
ligerents of Europe' who had been made orphans through the war or
who had fathers at the Front.

Christmas mail for troops threatened at one point to overwhelm
the postal system: 250,000 parcels had been sent to the forces by
12 December, and a further 200,000 the following week. Parcels of
up to seven pounds in weight were permitted; among the prohibited
items were perishable articles, bottles and pudding basins. George V
and Queen Mary dispatched 700,000 Christmas cards to every soldier
and sailor on active service in Flanders, France and the North Sea.

The campaign launched in October by Princess Mary, the King's
seventeen-year-old daughter, to send 'a gift from the nation' to all
serving men at the Front and at sea, had raised over £150,000 by
Christmas. The money was spent on an embossed brass box, based on
a design by architects Adshead & Ramsey. The surface of the lid
depicted the profile of the Princess, and a cartouche at the top con-

tained the words 'IMPERIUM BRITANNICUM', with a sword and scabbard on either side. The contents of the boxes varied. For smokers there was a pipe, an ounce of tobacco, a packet of cigarettes and a tinder lighter; for non-smokers, a packet of acid tablets and a khaki writing case. Both types of brass box were accompanied by a Christmas card and a picture of the Princess. The wounded, those in hospital or on convalescent leave, as well as the widows or parents of those who had been killed, were also entitled to the gift.

Blackout restrictions lent a sombre mood to streets filled with busy shoppers. Advertisements in shop windows for mourning clothes, or 'Roll of Honour' mementos, including enlargements of photographs of 'The Fallen' to 'life size', were reminders that many would be spending their first Christmas in the absence of their loved ones. Fears of another German raid, following the East Coast bombardment, had led to the last-minute cancellation of leave for soldiers training in the British Isles to enable them to take part in home defence. But thousands of Kitchener's recruits had been granted leave for which they received free railway passes. 'Bring a soldier pal home with you' or 'Invite a friendless soldier or two to your Christmas dinner' were among the festive hints appearing in newspapers, along with the perhaps by now less welcome suggestion to 'Make sure that the Belgians are not forgotten either.' At Earls Court, 3,000 Belgians would be given Christmas dinner and a Christmas tree, and at Alexandra Palace in North London, 2,500 more were entertained in similar circumstances.

The centenary of the Treaty of Ghent, signed between Britain and the United States in 1814, fell on Christmas Eve. However, the official celebrations, planned earlier in the year, of one hundred years of unbroken peace between the two great English-speaking nations, were now frustrated by the war in Europe. In the first days after Christmas, news began to filter through from the trenches of a more unexpected incidence of peace. Although it had been anticipated in sections of the press, the Christmas truce – a series of unofficial cease-fires between German and British soldiers along more than two thirds of the British-held sector on the Western Front – took many people by surprise, not least the soldiers themselves. 'Just you think,' Oswald

Tilley of the London Rifle Brigade wrote home excitedly to his parents, 'that while you were eating turkey etc., I was talking and shaking hands with the very men I had been trying to kill a few hours before!! It was astounding!'

'The Power of Peace in the Time of War' proclaimed one post-Christmas headline. However, for parts of the civilian front this sudden outburst of seasonal goodwill to all Germans struck a discordant note, coming so soon after events in Scarborough, Hartlepool and Whitby had confirmed the enemy in the guise of pure evil. 'We do not hate the Germans as they hate us,' one churchman had observed less than a week after the bombardment, 'but I should think that within the last few days we have been nearer to it than we ever were before.'

In her diary that December, Ada Reece took stock of how her life had changed in the course of five months of war. She was delighted that war had brought an end to the tiresome Victorian custom of 'At Homes', when women of the upper and middle classes received each other on a preordained weekday afternoon. Furthermore, she was relieved that she hadn't been forced to reduce the size of her household, as some of her friends had done, out of reasons of wartime economy. At their home, a sizeable villa in Addison Gardens, West Kensington, the Reeces employed three maids and a cook. In October the local servants' registry, through which they obtained their staff, had issued a general circular addressed to domestic employees. It advised them 'to assist cheerfully in household economies, now that any waste may be a crime against the country, to keep their places if they can, to undertake cheerfully any extra work that may be asked of them, even to take lower wages'. It was couched in just the right tone, Mrs Reece noted approvingly, and likely to be all the more effective as it was written 'from the servants' point of view'.

She remained uneasy about her elder son Harold's situation. Her husband Dick was convinced that conscription wasn't far off, and that Harold, a Cambridge medical student, 'had better not be among those who are made to go'. He was therefore reversing his opposition to Harold's applying for a commission. As for Dick himself, serving as medical officer to a battery of the Honourable Artillery Company, Ada knew how much he wanted to see active service, but she worried that, at fifty-two, he was too old, and she was terrified of his health breaking down. 'But he loves his soldiering and his heart is with his battery.' The strain of repeated farewells, after several false alarms had made it appear certain that he was about to leave for France, was beginning to tell on them all. 'It is so tiring to behave quite nicely & be so much more cheerful than you feel,' Ada confided to her diary after yet another cancellation of Dick's promised embarkation in mid October. 'Now comes the anti-climax, uncertainty, all to do over again.'

One great transformation that Ada Reece observed in herself was the new-found power she assumed during her husband's absences from home. She was so accustomed 'to defer every decision to him' that she feared the responsibility of being 'left in charge and all trusted in my hands'. Would she be able to make 'wise decisions' for her children? She instantly recognized the contrast with her pre-war life whenever Dick returned to Addison Gardens 'and a bit of his old hectoring manner came out', straining 'the wonderful harmony a little'. The bank had given her permission to draw on Dick's account, but this turned out to be 'an empty honour' when his bank book arrived revealing merely an overdraft of £13.

The family's Christmas had been on a smaller scale than usual. 'We have sent no cards this year and received comparatively few,' Ada noted, 'and our presents have been of a "useful" sort. Of course . . . the servants have not gone short, but all our Christmas luxuries have been in smaller quantities and some have been forgone.' Dick had got Christmas leave and arrived home on 21 December. But he was suddenly recalled on the 23rd, amidst reports that the German fleet 'had at last put to sea with transports and landing boats' and would be off the Norfolk coast by the following morning.

This proved to be another false alarm, but the air was 'full of rumours of coming invasion [and] Zeppelin raids on London'. Ada's mother came to stay on Christmas Eve and told her 'a rather thrilling account' of a letter she had received from an acquaintance whose wife was in Germany. This had included the warning 'For God's sake keep out of London on Christmas Day.' Ada's mother was 'very nervous' and infected her daughter with sufficient anxiety 'to make me sleep with my small jewellery & ready money in a neat parcel under my pillow'. On Christmas morning, having suffered no ill-effects, Ada walked with her children through the thick fog to church. Later, the younger children put on an 'entertainment', a drama in two scenes, and danced to the gramophone and pianola.

Dick returned on 27 December, and the family paid visits to the West End theatre where they saw, on successive nights, *Charley's Aunt*; David Garrick's *The Country Girl*, adapted from Wycherley's original, starring Gertie Millar, the pixie-like actress with the chirrupy voice; and a revival of *Where the Rainbow Ends*. This last, a play for children by Clifford Mills and John Ramsey, with music by Roger Quilter, originally had been staged three years earlier, at the height of the Anglo-German naval armaments race. It already seemed like a relic from a more innocent age. Two boys, with their sisters, set out on a magic carpet, accompanied by a genie, on their journey 'to the land where the rainbow ends'. St George of England is their protector, and the Dragon King their enemy. They wear the uniform of British naval cadets, and the play's underlying message is that Britain needs its great navy.

In Chelsea, Georgina Lee, a solicitor's wife, had spent an anxious holiday worrying that the Germans might be about to send England 'a Christmas greeting'. On the morning of the 25th, she had awoken to find foggy conditions, and the thought had immediately entered her head: 'just the weather for an air-raid'.

The Boxing Day newspapers contained at least a partial fulfilment of the news that Ada Reece and Georgina Lee had been dreading. These papers reported that on Christmas Eve a German biplane had dropped a bomb into a garden in Dover, causing an explosion but no casualties, and that on Christmas Day itself another enemy biplane had appeared over Sheerness heading in the direction of London. It had got as far as Erith, an outlying south-eastern district of the city, where it had been pursued back down the Thames by three British planes before being lost in fog over Essex.

Headed 'A Santa Claus Surprise that Failed', the *Graphic*'s report commented that if 'the much vaunted air-raiding of England' was to consist of nothing more than this pathetic whimper rather than a resounding bang, 'there is not much occasion for alarm.' However, despite the bravado, there was none the less recognition of the fact that a momentous event had just taken place: the first aerial bombardment of Great Britain.

Three weeks earlier, a mock-up picture on the front of the *Daily Express* had conjured up many people's worst nightmare. It showed a Zeppelin airship hovering menacingly over the Houses of Parliament. A fortnight before Christmas, the *Express* had printed a report about an English lady, Miss Kirby. She had recently returned from Germany where she claimed to have heard high-ranking officials 'talking of a Zeppelin raid on England with a hundred airships, capable of firing projectiles from the sides, top or bottom'. The paper created further alarm by telling its readers that Count Ferdinand von Zeppelin himself, who had completed the first successful trial run of one of his airships fourteen years earlier, had 'promised the Kaiser to make an aerial raid on England, and especially on London before the end of the year'.

Fear of Zeppelin attacks on Britain had been on a steep rise since the onset of war, resulting in a large number of false sightings. On the night of 5 September, the Hendon impresario Claude Grahame-White, now a flight commander in the Royal Naval Air Service, carried out the first night patrol over London, searching for a non-existent Zeppelin over the Essex coast. Another celebrated pre-war aviator, B. C. Hucks, flew over the Lake District in a Blériot monoplane to dispel the rumour that a Zeppelin was operating from a clandestine base near Grasmere.

Churchill's Admiralty, employing its own Royal Naval Air Service, with assistance, where available, from the Royal Flying Corps, was responsible for the defence of London and other large undefended towns. In October, Churchill admitted to the cabinet that arrangements against potential aerial attack were not yet 'in a satisfactory state'. 'Loss and injury,' he told them, 'followed by much public outcry, will probably be incurred in the near future.' Steps had been taken to position a captive observation balloon, which could operate in fog or low cloud, at Hendon for the sighting of Zeppelins. Considerable study was also made of the extent to which Zeppelins might gain assistance from ground illuminations. On a foggy September night, Wing Commander Maitland and Flight Lieutenant Lock had flown over London in their airship *Beta* to see whether Zeppelins might be able to locate targets in such weather conditions. Their results were inconclusive. They got lost shortly after take-off and managed to regain their bearings when the airship came low enough to make out the illuminated sign of Golders Green Underground Station.

The only advice Scotland Yard had to offer the general public, 'if a German airman comes to London', was to remain indoors and take refuge in the basement, 'if you have one'. Determined to be prepared in the event of a Christmas Zeppelin attack, aircraft were on standby at various inland and coastal aerodromes. But, unknown to the British authorities, Germany still lacked the resources to launch an immediate bombardment by airship, and December's attacks came instead from small floatplanes of the German Navy's first seaplane squadron.

An attack, on 21 December, was barely noticed. At lunchtime that day, a Friedrichshafen FF-29 floatplane appeared off Dover and dropped two bombs in the sea near Admiralty Pier. On the morning of Christmas Eve, however, much of the town was startled by the muffled roar of an explosion, which sent many rushing to the seafront. Minutes before, observers had spotted a pale-brown coloured seaplane approaching from the sea at about 5,000 feet.

The first enemy bomb on British soil fell at 10.45 a.m., forming a crater of about ten feet wide and five feet deep in a garden at the back of Church Villas, belonging to Thomas A. Terson, an auctioneer and valuer, who lived in Taswell Street. The bomb had evidently been intended for Dover Castle, but had fallen less than a mile short. James Banks, a gardener in the adjoining rectory garden, was up a tree cutting evergreens for Christmas decorations. He saw a blinding flash and heard a deafening explosion. The tree was struck and he fell to the ground unhurt. The windows of Mr Terson's greenhouse, and those of other houses in the neighbourhood, were smashed, while the cabbages growing in his garden were blown away to some distance. Small, sharp zig-zag pieces from the bomb case cut off the lighter branches from the trees. The airman made for the market square and then turned seawards, followed by two Bristols from Eastchurch, which gave unsuccessful chase across the Channel.

Mabel Rudkin, who lived a few streets away in Harold Terrace, was just putting the filling into her mince pies when she heard a loud crash. She continued with her baking until, twenty minutes later, her husband Erasmus rushed into the house and announced dramatically that 'the Germans have come!' Mrs Rudkin, taking a tighter hold of her rolling pin, imagined for a moment that 'Myriads of ferocious, looting Teutons' were 'parading the once-peaceful streets of Dover', until her husband corrected her and the 'marauding host' was reduced to 'one, perhaps two' airmen. Outside in the streets, Dovorians were scrambling for fragments of the shrapnel, and offering shillings and half-crowns for small scraps (a specimen was later mounted and sent to the King).

The German sortie during Christmas Day was more audacious. This time a Friedrichshafen, piloted by Oberleutnant-zur-See Stephan Prondzynski, flew north of the Isle of Grain, then turned westwards and proceeded up the Thames. It was intercepted over Erith by Second Lieutenant Chidson and Corporal Martin in their Vickers Gunbus. This fired several bursts from its machine-gun as the German plane reached Purfleet and Tilbury, crossed the river and unloaded two bombs into a field near the railway station at Cliffe. The enemy again escaped, though German sources later admitted that the Friedrichshafen's floats and fuselage had been damaged by machine-gun fire. The next day Prondzynski was awarded an Iron Cross for his escapade.

With three aeroplane raids in under a week, people began to suspect that 1915 would provide a great many more, to say nothing of the likelihood of the first Zeppelin attacks. Georgina Lee issued her household with strict instructions about what to do if they heard explosions. They were to seize eiderdowns, rugs and coats and head for the basement. 'Our house,' she explained in her diary, 'is well adapted for a Zeppelin raid, as the basement has two exits, back and front to the outside, street and garden, so there is little fear of being trapped underground, even if the house did partly collapse.'

Georgina Lee was leaving London for the New Year, entrusting her nine-month-old son Harry to the care of his nanny. 'I wonder if it will strike you as strange that I leave you alone in London with the bare chance of a raid,' she wrote in her diary, addressing her thoughts to Harry and imagining that he would one day read his mother's account of her experiences in the Great War. 'It is typical of the prevailing state of mind over here. Nobody alters their plans for the chance of a raid; we all face it quite calmly and in a spirit of fatalists. What is to be, will be.'

'You will see that they have been dropping bombs on the coast of Kent,' Asquith wrote to Venetia Stanley on Boxing Day. The Prime Minister and his family had been staying on the Kent coastline, at Walmer Castle, lent him by the Lord Warden of the Cinque Ports as a weekend retreat, and Asquith thought that they ought to make 'quite a good target'.

Venetia was preparing to take up a post as an auxiliary nurse at the Royal London Hospital in Whitechapel. Her plans perturbed Asquith, who worried that a life on the wards would leave her with little time to continue her role as his confidante. At midnight, on the penultimate day of the year, he wrote to Venetia, looking back on 1914 as 'in the fullest sense what the Ancients used to call "annus mirabilis"'. From 'the world-wide point of view', it was impossible to exaggerate the difference that this one year had made 'in values & the things that matter'. But in terms of their personal relationship, 1914 had also represented a decisive turning point:

> Looking back, I can hardly remember a day out of the 365 when I have not either written to you, or seen you, or often done both. And there have been very few when you have not either seen or written to me. We have interchanged everything – the greatest & the smallest; never has there been between man & woman fuller & franker confidence: & whatever may be the case with you, rarely, if ever, has a man gained or owed so much.

Asquith's need for Venetia had reached a new intensity. If she failed him, as he sometimes warned her, it might precipitate his complete collapse. 'Will you be the same in 1915?', he asked, little realizing that the end of their special relationship was already in sight. The deaths in Flanders and France of so many of the young men she had grown up with had altered Venetia's attitude to marriage, and when her erstwhile suitor, Edwin Montagu, asked her again to marry him, she encouraged his courtship. The news of Venetia's engagement to Montagu would shatter Asquith's personal and political equilibrium, coming just at the point when public criticism of his government's handling of the war had risen to a destructive crescendo.

'The lull is finished,' the *Daily Mirror* announced in its report on the end of the Christmas truce on the Western Front, and the prospects for the New Year. 'The absurdity and tragedy renew themselves.' Eighty thousand British men had already sacrificed their lives in the fighting. In a few months' time, the first ranks of Kitchener's new armies would arrive at the Front, and 'once more', the *Mirror* continued, 'we who watch will have to mourn many of our finest men.'

The year 1914 was fading out in the grip of a grim, new certainty, as illusions about a short-lived war were replaced by the widely held conviction of a long-drawn-out struggle for victory. 'One does not meet many people who think that the War is soon going to be over,' Randall Davidson, the Archbishop of Canterbury, had observed in mid December. 'There were many such in the early weeks, and I still meet such a person now and then, but they are rare.'

Still, it was only human to put one's trust in the hope that 1915 might see an end of the conflict. In Lichfield, as the church bells rang out and the colliery sirens hooted, in the eerily darkened celebrations that proclaimed the advent of a wartime New Year, the brewer William Pead made an entry in his diary. He was certain 'that many troubles and difficulties will have to be overcome . . . and that many calamities will happen to us'. But he hoped none the less that England, 'with God's help', would 'withstand our enemies and bring this war to a successful issue before this New Year is ended'.

At that same moment, in the village of Halton in Cheshire, Evie

Davies was writing a letter to her husband Will, serving out in France. She had not seen him for the past four months, and had only recently discovered that she was pregnant with their third child. Looking back on a year that had brought some tumultuous changes to their lives, she admitted, 'I little knew what was coming. Now I am utterly in the dark about what to expect.'

Perhaps above all else, England in 1914 had shown that nothing about the future could be taken for granted.

Background Information about England in 1914

Unless otherwise stated, the figures provided are for England only.

Population

34 million approximately (2012 comparison: 50 million approximately)
Only 21.9 per cent of the population of England and Wales lived in
rural areas
Females per males: 1.068 approximately

Population of major conurbations

- Greater London: 7,256 million
- South-East Lancashire: 2,328 million
- West Midlands: 1,634 million
- West Yorkshire: 1,590 million
- Merseyside: 1,157 million
- Tyneside: 761,000

Life expectancy

51.50 (male); 55.35 (female)
In Britain in 1913, 262 people died aged 90 and over; centenarians
numbered 26 (2010 comparison: 12,640 centenarians in Britain)

Marriage rates

294,000 marriages in 1914

52.9 males marrying per 1,000 unmarried males; 44.3 females marrying per 1,000 unmarried females

856 divorces and nullity decrees in 1914 (a sharp rise since the beginning of the century)

Home ownership

10 per cent of homes in Britain belonged to owner-occupiers (property ownership remained a precondition of the eligibility to vote until 1918)

In 1913, the acute shortage of housing in Britain was estimated at between 100,000 and 120,000 homes

Transport

- 132,000 private cars in Britain in 1914
- 124,000 motorcycles
- 51,000 buses, taxis and coaches
- 13,000 trams on 2,500 miles of electrified tramway
- 20,038,000 miles of railway

A 1913 traffic census of London revealed that only 6 per cent of passenger vehicles were horse-drawn. By 1914 many of the old horse omnibuses from London streets were being used to convey children to school in rural areas. Motor appliances were expected to replace the last of the grey horses of the London Fire Brigade within three years. However, 88 per cent of goods traffic in London remained horse-drawn

Religious observance

Adult membership of faith bodies (Anglican communicants, members of Free Churches and sects, and Roman Catholic and non-Christian communities) in Britain in 1914 comprised 27 per cent of the adult population

At Easter 1914 there were 2,226,000 communicants in the Church of England (stronger attendance than in the middle years of the nineteenth century)

Wealth and poverty

2.5 per cent of Britain's population held two thirds of the country's wealth

Lowest figure on which income tax was assessed: £160 per annum

13,850 people in Britain earned annual incomes of over £5,000; 47,000 with annual incomes of over £2,000

- Chancellor of the Exchequer's salary: £5,000 per annum
- Member of Parliament's salary: £400 per annum
- Average income for salaried class: £340 per annum
- Average wage for industrial male worker: £75 per annum
- Average income for living-in maid: £10–£12 per annum
- An old-age pensioner was paid from 1s. to 5s. a week depending on circumstances

In 1913, Maud Pember Reeves (*Round About a Pound a Week*) concluded that there were 2 million men, 8 million people in all including dependants, who existed on less than 25s. a week

Prices

In 1914, the average British family, reckoned by the Board of Trade as equivalent to 3.84 males in calorific requirements, spent about 23s. a week on food. This diet included:

7lb of meat at about 6*d.* to 8*d.* a pound
1lb of bacon at 1*s.*
6 x 4lb loaves at 5*d.* each
9–10 pints of milk at 2*d.* a pint
10 eggs at 1*d.* each

- Price of *The Times*: 1*d.* (reduced from 2*d.* in March 1914)
- Standard price of a novel: 6*s.*
- Price of a standard off-the-peg men's suit: 37*s.*
- Price of a woman's corset: 21*s.*9*d.*
- Cost of a two-seater car: £350–£550

State of the major political parties in Britain

(Based on the results of the December 1910 General Election, the last to be held before the War)
Every adult male householder had a parliamentary vote (therefore about 8 million adult males in Britain possessed the franchise)

- Liberal (led by H. H. Asquith): 272 seats
- Conservative (led by Andrew Bonar Law): 271 seats
- Labour (led by Ramsay MacDonald): 42 seats
- Irish Parliamentary (led by John Redmond): 74 seats

H. H. Asquith's Liberal Administration governed with the support of John Redmond's Irish Parliamentary Party

The British Army

In January 1914, the Regular Army numbered fewer than 250,000 men scattered throughout the world.

- Army Reserve: 150,000
- Special Reserve: 63,000
- Territorial Force: 63,000

Expenditure on the army: less than £29 million per annum (compared with £51.5 million spent per annum on the navy)

Bibliographical Essay

Abbreviations

BL – British Library, London
Bodleian – Bodleian Library, Oxford
IWM – Imperial War Museum, London
Lambeth – Lambeth Palace Library, London
Liddle – Liddle Collection, University of Leeds
NA – National Archives, Kew

General

The following national newspapers, magazines and periodicals have been essential in reconstructing England in 1914, along with the provincial and foreign titles mentioned in the text. Where there is no specific reference, it may be assumed that my source is a newspaper report:

Aeroplane, Bystander, Country Life, Daily Chronicle, Daily Express, Daily Graphic, Daily Herald, Daily Mail, Daily Mirror, Daily Sketch, Daily Telegraph, Economist, Evening News, Financial Times, Flight, Graphic, Illustrated London News, Lloyd's Weekly Newspaper, London Budget, Manchester Guardian, Morning Post, Nation, New Statesman, News of the World, Nineteenth Century and After, Pall Mall Gazette, The Passing Show, Play Pictorial, Punch, Spectator, Sphere, The Suffragette, Sunday Times, The Times, Votes for Women, Westminster Gazette

The volumes of *Hansard* for 1914 give official reports of parliamentary debates.
The *Annual Register* for 1914 offers a chronology for the year.
The *Oxford Dictionary of National Biography* (2004–) has been a vital resource.

General histories of the period which have provided valuable guidance:

R. C. K. Ensor, *England 1870–1914* (1936)
Edgar Feuchtwanger, *Democracy and Empire: Britain 1865–1914* (1985)
G. R. Searle, *A New England? Peace and War 1886–1918* (2004)
Richard Shannon, *The Crisis of Imperialism 1865–1915* (1974)

John Stevenson, *British Society 1914–1945* (1984)

James Cameron's *1914* (1959) offers a more impressionistic picture

Preface

The original photograph of the river cruise belongs to George and Margaret Chapman. George Chapman's father, Herbert Chapman, a delivery man for the Curzon Laundry, who happily survived the war, is in the front row, leaning on the rail, with a flower in his button hole. He served in the British Army in Palestine, 1915–19.

The background to the writing of Philip Larkin's 'MCMXIV' can be found in *The Complete Poems of Philip Larkin*, edited with an introduction and commentary by Archie Burnett (2012).

Henry James's letter to Edward Emerson, dated 4 August 1914, is from *Henry James: A Life in Letters*, edited by Philip Horne (1999).

Further information about John Joyce is contained in my article 'The Name of the Game', *Guardian*, 25 March 2006.

Prologue: Welcoming 1914

All the information about the seeing in of 1914 comes from contemporary newspaper reports, with the addition of the account of London's New Year in Geoffrey Marcus, *Before the Lights Went Out* (1965).

For the British Museum's acceptance of Scott's journals and Sir Frederic Kenyon's remarks, see the excellent introduction and editorial material in Max Jones's edition, *Journals: Captain Scott's Last Expedition* (2005). Herbert Ponting's photographs of Scott's expedition were on display at the Fine Art Gallery in London's New Bond Street in early 1914. Ponting also gave one hundred lectures about Scott to audiences amounting to 120,000 at the Philharmonic Hall in London between January and March 1914. On 12 May 1914, Ponting gave a similar lecture at Buckingham Palace in the presence of the King.

In July 1914 John Mitford attempted to sue the editor of *Sporting Life* for making allegations about the breakdown of his marriage.

One: January to April

Murder on the 4.14 from Chalk Farm

The major sources for Willie Starchfield's murder are the files of correspondence and witness depositions collected by the Metropolitan Police as they investigated the crime: NA/ MEPO 3/237B (1914–21), NA/ MEPO 3/1832 and NA/ CRIM 1/145.

The National Archives also hold the records of the Stephen Titus case, from 1912, in which John Starchfield helped to secure Titus's arrest and was wounded in the process: NA/ CRIM 1/135/2.

The proceedings of John Jasper's 'Trial' are published in *The Trial of John Jasper, Lay Precentor of Cloisterham Cathedral in the County of Kent, for the Murder of Edwin Drood, Engineer. Heard by Mr Justice Gilbert Keith Chesterton, sitting with a Special Jury, in the King's Hall, Covent Garden, W. C., on Wednesday, the 7th January, 1914* (1914).

Details of Spilsbury's examination of the dead boy are recorded in his 'Notes on Autopsies', a set of index cards at the Wellcome Library in London, PPSPI/A/2.

Chief-Inspector W. C. Gough's career is outlined in his autobiography, *From Kew Observatory to Scotland Yard* [n.d.], while the rise of the Victorian and Edwardian detective is considered by Haia Shpayer-Makov in *The Ascent of the Detective: Police Sleuths in Victorian and Edwardian England* (2011).

Details of common lodging-houses of the period may be found in Tom Crook, 'Accommodating the outcast. Common lodging houses and the limits of urban governance in Victorian and Edwardian London', *Urban History* (2008), and also in Kate Macdonald's 2011 online article 'The Use of London Lodgings in Middlebrow Fiction 1900–1930s' in *Literary London: Interdisciplinary Studies in the Representation of London*: http://www.literarylondon.org/london-journal/march2011/macdonald. html.

Two narrative accounts of the Starchfield murder are interesting, though their value is limited by the fact that the police papers on the case had still to be released at the time they were written. The fullest narrative to date, based on press reports, was provided by Winifred Duke in a collection about unsolved crimes, entitled *The Stroke of Murder* (1937). *The Railway Murders*, edited by Jonathan Goodman (1984), has a chapter on Willie Starchfield, and additionally contains an account of the 1864 train murder of Thomas Briggs.

A Prime Minister in Love

The main source here, and at other points throughout this book, is the magnificent edition of Asquith's letters to Venetia Stanley: H. H. Asquith, *Letters to Venetia Stanley*, selected and edited by Michael and Eleanor Brock (1982). The Brocks' superb introductions and notes provide an illuminating commentary on this extraordinary correspondence.

For the other side to the love triangle, see Naomi B. Levine, *Politics, Religion and Love: The Story of H. H. Asquith, Venetia Stanley and Edwin Montagu, Based on the Life and Letters of Edwin Samuel Montagu* (1991).

Those inclined to believe that Asquith's relationship with Venetia Stanley was a sexual one will find their suspicions reignited by Bobbie Neate's *Conspiracy of Secrets* (2012), which alleges that her stepfather, the Formula One racing manager Louis T.

Stanley, was the illegitimate son of Asquith and Venetia. There is currently no way of proving – or disproving – these claims.

On Asquith, see Roy Jenkins, *Asquith* (1964), and Stephen Koss, *Asquith* (1976). Further details of the Asquiths' family life are revealed in *Lantern Slides. The Diaries and Letters of Violet Bonham Carter 1904–1914*, edited by Mark Bonham Carter and Mark Pottle (1996). Margot Asquith's diary is at Bodleian. The oral testimony about Margot's declaration about the boredom of having Venetia at the Wharf 'all the time' comes from the novelist Anthony Powell's *Journals 1982–1986* (1995).

Three books have contributed greatly to my understanding of the Curragh crisis and the background to Home Rule in 1914: James Fergusson, *The Curragh Incident* (1964), A. T. Q. Stewart, *The Ulster Crisis* (1967), and Patricia Jalland's important study of *The Liberals and Ireland* (1980).

The Slashing of the Rokeby Venus

The National Gallery's dossier on Velázquez's *Rokeby Venus* (NG2057) contains reports and correspondence about the incident, as well as Emery Walker's photographic negative of the damaged painting (2067/2). The gallery forbids reproduction of the original negative lest it provoke latter-day iconoclasts into action. The National Portrait Gallery's Heinz Archive and Library preserves the 'Minutes and Papers of the Board of Trustees Meetings 1914' (NPG2/22) with details of the suffragette damage to paintings in the NPG's collection.

Mary Richardson's autobiography of her years as a suffragette, *Laugh a Defiance* (1953), is subjected to critical scrutiny by Hilda Kean in 'Some Problems of Constructing and Reconstructing a Suffragette's Life: Mary Richardson, Suffragette, Socialist and Fascist', *Women's History Review*, 7 (1998), and in the same author's 'A Study of Mary Richardson, Suffragette, Socialist and Fascist' in *Seeing through Suffrage: New Themes and Directions in the Study of British Suffrage History*, edited by C. Eustance and J. Ryan (1999). For further details of Richardson's life, see the article on her in Elizabeth Crawford, *The Women's Suffrage Movement: A Reference Guide 1866–1928* (2001).

Richardson herself can be heard talking about her experiences as a militant suffragette, including her attack upon the painting, in an interview with Sorrel Bentinck, originally broadcast on the BBC Home Service on 23 April 1961. At the time, Bentinck was an eighteen-year-old secretarial trainee who recorded the interview on a portable tape recorder at Richardson's one-room flat in Hastings, little more than six months before Richardson's death. It can now be heard via the BBC's online archive at: http://www.bbc.co.uk/archive/suffragettes/8321.shtml.

Background information on Velázquez and the *Rokeby Venus* may be found in Andreas Prater's *Venus at Her Mirror: Velázquez and the Art of Nude Painting* (2002) and José López-Rey's *Velázquez: Catalogue raisonné* (1999). Christiana Herringham's role in securing the purchase of the painting for the National Gallery is examined by Mary Lago in *Christiana Herringham and the Edwardian Art Scene* (1995).

Annabel Jackson's letter to the Keeper of the Wallace Collection is from the Women's Suffrage Collection at the University of Glasgow (MS MacColl 31). Vera Brittain's diary entry is published in *Chronicle of Youth: Vera Brittain's War Diary 1913–1917*, edited by Alan Bishop with Terry Smart (1981). Henry James's comments on the fate of his portrait by Sargent are taken from Leon Edel, *Henry James: A Life* (1987).

For a useful analysis of suffragette attacks on works of art in 1914, see Rowena Fowler, 'Why Did Suffragettes Attack Works of Art?', *Journal of Women's History*, 2 (1991), which draws in turn on A. E. Metcalfe, *Woman's Effort: A Chronicle of British Women's Fifty Years' Struggle for Citizenship 1865–1914* (1917), for its appendix, listing the pictures attacked. A more general perspective is presented by Suzanna MacLeod in 'Civil Disobedience and Political Agitation: The Art Museum as a Site of Protest in the Early Twentieth Century', *Museum and Society*, 5 (2006). The chapter on 'The Damaged Venus' in Lynda Nead's *The Female Nude. Art, Obscenity and Sexuality* (1992) treats Richardson's attack in the context of 1914's attitudes to the female nude.

Two invaluable articles chart the lives of suffragettes and the destructiveness of their acts of militancy: Brian Harrison, 'The Act of Militancy: Violence and the Suffragettes 1904–1914' in *Peaceable Kingdom. Stability and Change in Modern Britain*, edited by Michael Bentley and John Stevenson (1982), and June Purvis, '"Deeds not Words": The Daily Life of Militant Suffragettes in Edwardian Britain', *Women's Studies International Forum*, 18 (1995). See also Harrison's biographical portraits of suffragettes and suffragists, *Prudent Revolutionaries: Portraits of British Feminists between the Wars* (1987).

A copy of Mary Richardson's *Tortured Women: What Forcible Feeding Means – A Prisoner's Testimony* is in the collection of the Museum of London (50.82/601). J. F. Geddes, 'Culpable Complicity: The Medical Profession and the Forcible Feeding of Suffragettes 1909–1914', *Women's History Review*, 17 (2008), considers the failure of the medical profession to condemn the practice of forcible feeding.

E. S. [Sylvia] Pankhurst, *The Suffragette Movement: An Intimate Account of Persons and Ideals* (1931), is the standard account of the impact of suffragette bombings, arson and other attacks. It has been challenged in a stimulating article by C. J. Bearman, 'An Examination of Suffragette Violence', *English Historical Review*, 120 (2005).

Pupil Power

Records concerning the Burston School and the strike are held in the school file: NA/ED 21/12712B. Documents about the strike held at the Norfolk Record Office include the minutes of the Norfolk Education Committee (C/ED 16/6) and the Norfolk County Council's file on the strike (C/ED 36/5). Norfolk Record

Office Information Leaflet 65, 'The Burston School Strike', gives details of the main county records.

Tom Higdon's *The Burston Rebellion* (1917, reprinted 1984) is a narrative of the development of the strike by one of its major protagonists. In 1974, sixty years after the schoolchildren processed around the village in support of their teachers, Bertram Edwards published his seminal study *The Burston School Strike*, based on original reports and documents, and on oral testimony from surviving participants. Edwards's book may be supplemented by the chapter 'The Burston Rebellion: 1914' in Willem van der Eyken and Barry Turner, *Adventures in Education* (1969), Betka Zamoyska's account, *The Burston Rebellion* (1985), published to accompany a BBC TV drama of the same name, and the pamphlet *The Burston Strike School* [n.d.], published by the school's trustees. 'Pupil Power, 1914: The Burston School Strike', *Listener*, 1 August 1974, is a transcript of a BBC TV *Yesterday's Witness* programme about the strike, including an interview with Violet Potter, the strikers' ringleader.

Details of Miss Outram's 'sex teaching' at Dronfield Elementary School are at NA/ED 50/185. Frank Mort, *Dangerous Sexualities: Medico-Moral Politics in England since 1830* (1987), includes a discussion of the case.

On school strikes more generally, see Stephen Humphries, *Hooligans or Rebels? An Oral History of Working-Class Childhood and Youth 1889–1939* (1981), and William Baker, 'Explaining the outbreak and dynamics of the 1911 school strike wave in Britain', *Reflecting Education*, 6 (2010). On the state and education, S. J. Curtis and M. E. A. Boultwood, *An Introductory History of English Education since 1800* (1966), and A. Morton, *Education and the State*, are both helpful. Robert Lee, *Rural Society and the Anglican Clergy 1815–1914: Encountering and Managing the Poor* (2006), places the Burston strike in the context of the relationship between Church and rural society.

Today it is possible to visit the Burston strike school, opened in 1917, which continued to function until the beginning of the Second World War. Tom Higdon died in August 1939, and the school closed a few months later. Kitty, who lived until 1946, was unable to carry on alone, and her remaining eleven pupils were transferred to the county school. The strike school sits in the middle of Burston, just behind the church, on Church Green. Four trustees manage the school and have developed it as a museum, visitor centre, educational archive and village amenity. An annual rally on the first Sunday in September takes place each year to commemorate the first rally in 1914. For details, see http://burstonstrikeschool.wordpress.com/.

Not Bloody Likely

The outstanding modern edition of Shaw's *Pygmalion: A Romance in Five Acts* is published in the New Mermaids series by Methuen Drama (2008). It is edited by L. W. Conolly, whose lengthy introduction has proved invaluable in retelling the story of the first English production of the play.

BL Add. MS 50629, G. B. Shaw Papers: Series II, Vol. XXXVII, is a performing copy of the play, published by Constable as a rough proof in 1913, on to which Shaw has written his rehearsal notes and changes to the text, and arranged his blocking for the actors.

BL Add. MS 66056F, Lord Chamberlain's Plays, contains G. S. Street's letter, dated 23 February 1914, recommending a licence for *Pygmalion*.

Biographical information about Shaw, Mrs Pat and Tree has been derived from: *Bernard Shaw: Collected Letters. Volume 3: 1911–1925*, edited by Dan H. Laurence (1985); *Bernard Shaw and Mrs Patrick Campbell: Their Correspondence*, edited by Alan Dent (1952); Margot Peters, *Bernard Shaw and the Actresses* (1980); Michael Holroyd, *Bernard Shaw. 1898–1918: The Pursuit of Power* (1989); Madeleine Bingham, *The Great Lover: The Life and Art of Herbert Beerbohm Tree* (1978).

Richard Huggett's *The Truth about 'Pygmalion'* (1969) is a diverting account of events leading up to the play's opening night. Bernard F. Dukore, 'The Director as Interpreter: Shaw's Pygmalion', *Shaw*, 3 (1983), provides some illuminating insights into Shaw's direction of the first English production. Peter Conolly-Smith, 'Shades of Local Color: *Pygmalion* and Its Translation and Reception in Central Europe, 1913–1914', *Shaw*, 29 (2009), considers the play's first performance in Vienna. *George Bernard Shaw's Pygmalion*, edited by Harold Bloom (1988), is a helpful collection of critical essays about the play. The chapter 'Dressing Mrs Pat' in *Theatre and Fashion: Oscar Wilde to the Suffragettes* by Joel H. Kaplan and Sheila Stowell (1995) is a fascinating look at the design of Eliza's costumes for the His Majesty's production.

The first time I experienced *Pygmalion* on stage was as a schoolboy in 1974, when I saw a performance of John Dexter's production, starring Diana Rigg as Eliza and Alec McCowen as Higgins. Among the other memorable productions I have seen since then is Peter Hall's 2008 version at the Old Vic, with Michelle Dockery and Tim Pigott-Smith. The 1938 film, directed by Anthony Asquith, starring Wendy Hiller and Leslie Howard, whatever Shaw's reservations about the casting of Howard as Higgins, remains irresistible.

Two: May to August

Honeymoon in the Sky

1914 issues of the *Aeroplane* and *Flight*, two British magazines devoted to aircraft and aviation, were essential in reconstructing the course of flying for the year. Gustav Hamel's *Flying: Some Practical Experiences*, co-written with C. C. Turner (1914), conjures up the experience of flying at this time.

A picture of pioneering developments is provided by R. Dallas Brett, *History of British Aviation 1908–1914* (1934); Harald Penrose, *British Aviation. The Pioneer Years*

1903–1914 (1967); Christopher Chant, *Aviation: An Illustrated History* (1983); and Hugh Driver, *The Birth of Military Aviation: Britain 1903–1914* (1997).

Graham Wallace, *Claude Grahame-White: A Biography* (1960), charts the life and career of one of the most successful early aviators and aircraft manufacturers, including his establishment of the London Aerodrome at Hendon. Clive R. Smith, *Flying at Hendon: A Pictorial Record* (1974), contains many rare photographs. Andrew Horrall, *Popular Culture in London c. 1890–1918: The Transformation of Entertainment* (2001), looks at aviation as a spectator sport during this period. The letters of John Riddey are at Liddle. On the popular fiction prophesying war in the skies, see Michael Paris, *Winged Warfare: The Literature and Theory of Aerial Warfare in Britain 1859–1917* (1992).

On Robert Blackburn, see the entry by Humphrey Wynn in the *Dictionary of Business Biography*; and A. J. Jackson, *Blackburn Aircraft since 1909* (1968). Winston Churchill's flying exploits are described by Randolph Churchill in *Winston S. Churchill: Young Statesman 1901–1914* (1967).

The Royal Air Force Museum, situated today on the historic site of Hendon's London Aerodrome, includes not only examples of early aircraft, but also a small exhibition illustrating the history of Grahame-White's pre-war centre for British aviation.

Premonitions

For my description of the relative quiescence of international affairs in the spring of 1914, I am indebted to Samuel R. Williamson Jr's chapter 'The Origins of the War' in *The Oxford Illustrated History of the First World War*, edited by Hew Strachan (1998). For Sir Arthur Nicolson's remark and its context, see Harold Nicolson's biography of his father, *Sir Arthur Nicolson* (1930). On the subject of Anglo-German antagonism, Paul Kennedy, *The Rise of the Anglo-German Antagonism* (1980), and the relevant chapters of Lawrence James's *Rise and Fall of the British Empire* (1994) are useful.

The motion in the Wiltshire village of Downton about the likelihood of war with Germany is taken from Edward Green, *Downton and the First World War* (2002). I. F. Clarke, *Voices Prophesying War 1763–1984* (1966), remains the standard work on prophetic writing about the next war. On Le Queux, see D. A. T. Stafford, 'Conspiracy and Xenophobia: The popular spy novels of William Le Queux 1893–1914', *Europa*, 4 (1981), and David French, 'Spy Fever in Britain 1900–1915', *Historical Journal*, 21 (1978). Details of the case of Frederick Adolphus Gould are at NA/ CRIM 1/145/2.

Anglo-German ties are examined in *Wilhelmine Germany and Edwardian Britain: Essays on Cultural Affinity*, edited by Dominik Geppert and Robert Gerwarth (2008). Particularly helpful were the contributions by David Blackbourn, '"As dependent on each other as man and wife": Cultural Contacts and Transfers between Wilhelmine

Germany and Edwardian Britain'; Thomas Weber, 'Our friend "the enemy": German Students in Britain, British Students in Germany'; Sven Oliver Müller, ' "A musical clash of civilisations"? Musical Transfers and Rivalries between Britain and Germany around 1900'; and Marc Schalenberg, ' "Only connect": Personal and Cultural Entanglements between Britain and Germany in E. M. Forster's *Howards End*. Peter Firchow's essay 'Germany and Germanic Mythology in E. M. Forster's *Howards End*', *Comparative Literature*, 33 (1981) also has interesting things to say about Forster's idea of 'a rainbow bridge'. On Germans in Britain in 1914, see Panikos Panayi, *The Enemy in Our Midst: Germans in Britain during the First World War* (1991). The significance of Oxford University's 1914 Encaenia is pointed out by J. M. Winter in 'Oxford and the First World War' in *The History of the University of Oxford. Volume VIII: The Twentieth Century*, edited by Brian Harrison (1994).

Samuel Hynes's *A War Imagined. The First World War and English Culture* (1990) offers a stimulating discussion of 'preliminary skirmishes' in a war to come.

Thomas Hardy's attitude to Anglo-German antagonism, and the naval arms race, is outlined in *The Life and Work of Thomas Hardy by Thomas Hardy*, edited by Michael Millgate (1985). The chapter on 'Hardy's Apocalypse' in J. O. Bailey, *The Poetry of Thomas Hardy* (1970), describes the growing pessimism about war in Hardy's poetry. I have benefited from Rodger L. Tarr's analysis of 'Channel Firing' in his article 'Hardy's "Channel Firing" ', *Explicator*, 36 (1978).

Michael Short's *Gustav Holst: The Man and His Music* (1990) provides a sympathetic portrait of the composer, as does Imogen Holst's portrait of her father, *Gustav Holst: A Biography* (1938; second edition 1969). On Holst's astrological influences, including the role of Alan Leo, see Raymond Head, 'Holst: Astrology and Modernism in The Planets', *Tempo*, 187 (1993), and Patrick Curry, *A Confusion of Prophets: Victorian and Edwardian Astrology* (1992). The outstanding critical guide to *The Planets* is Richard Greene's *Holst: The Planets* (1995). See also Daniel Jaffé, 'A Journey through the Planets', *BBC Music Magazine* (June 2012) and the section on Holst in Rob Young, *Electric Eden: Unearthing Britain's Visionary Music* (2010).

Two recordings of 'Mars' are especially recommended: Simon Rattle's with the Philharmonia (1987) and Colin Davis's live recording with the London Symphony Orchestra from 2003. The second-hand piano that Holst bought for £12 can be seen, along with other memorabilia associated with the composer, at the Holst Birthplace Museum in Cheltenham.

David Bomberg's *The Mud Bath* hangs today in the Tate Gallery in London. Essential reading for understanding Bomberg's life and work is Richard Cork's *David Bomberg* (1987). The exhibition catalogue *Vorticism and Its Allies* (Hayward Gallery, London, 27 March–2 June 1974), with an introduction by Cork and reproductions from the first issue of *Blast*, explains the movement's place in the art world in 1914. *London, Modernism and 1914*, edited by Michael J. K. Walsh (2010), is a collection of illuminating essays, including Walsh's 'Introduction: Avant-garde and

Avant-guerre' and Sarah MacDougall's '"Something is happening there": Early British Modernism, the Great War and the "Whitechapel Boys"'.

Adlestrop

Yes. I remember Adlestrop –
The name, because one afternoon
Of heat the express-train drew up there
Unwontedly. It was late June.

The steam hissed. Someone cleared his throat.
No one left and no one came
On the bare platform. What I saw
Was Adlestrop – only the name

And willows, willow-herb, and grass,
And meadowsweet, and haycocks dry,
No whit less still and lonely fair
Than the high cloudlets in the sky.

And for that minute a blackbird sang
Close by, and round him, mistier,
Farther and farther, all the birds
Of Oxfordshire and Gloucestershire.

A manuscript draft of Edward Thomas's 'Adlestrop', written on 15 January 1915, is at BL Add. MS 44990. The field notebook entry in which Thomas recorded his train's stop at Adlestrop on 24 June 1914 is reproduced in the notes to *Edward Thomas, The Collected Poems and War Diary 1917*, edited by R. George Thomas with an introduction by Peter Sacks (2004).

Adlestrop Revisited: An Anthology Inspired by Edward Thomas's Poem, compiled and edited by Anne Harvey (1999), is an interesting guide to the creation of 'Adlestrop' and its influence, as well as offering testimony to the lasting affection in which the poem is held. Ultimately Harvey's researches reveal the extent of Thomas's poetic licence: that the poem conflated impressions from different stops along the Great Western Railway line from London to Oxford, Worcester and Malvern, and that Thomas's train on 24 June did not stop 'unwontedly' at Adlestrop. Edna Longley's commentary on the poem in her *The Annotated Collected Poems: Edward Thomas* (2008) is detailed and acute. Adlestrop Station was finally closed on 3 January 1966, a victim of Dr Beeching's cuts.

There is no collected edition of all Thomas's extant letters. However, a *Selected Letters*, edited by R. George Thomas (1995), is available, together with *Letters from Edward Thomas to Gordon Bottomley*, edited by R. George Thomas (1968), and *Elected*

Friends. Robert Frost and Edward Thomas to One Another, edited by Matthew Spencer (2003).

Biographical works about Edward Thomas include R. G. Thomas's *Edward Thomas: A Portrait* (1985), Eleanor Farjeon's *Edward Thomas: The Four Last Years* (1958), as well as Helen Thomas's autobiographical works, said to have been written as a form of therapy to lift her from depression after the poet's death: *As It Was* (1926) and *World without End* (1931), reprinted in one volume as *Under Storm's Wing* in 1988 (this latter volume also includes further reminiscences by Helen and her daughter Myfanwy, as well as reprinting six letters from Frost to Thomas). Thomas's own autobiographical writings are collected in the recent edition *Prose Writings: A Selected Edition. Volume 1: Autobiographies*, edited by Guy Cuthbertson (2011).

Matthew Hollis's *Now All Roads Lead to France: The Last Years of Edward Thomas* (2011) is a sensitive and moving treatment of the forces that combined to make Thomas a poet, though in many ways the most valuable biographical and critical study of Thomas remains William Cooke's *Edward Thomas: A Critical Biography* (1970). Jean Moorcroft Wilson is in the process of writing a new biography of Thomas. Her article, 'The sere and the ember', *The Times Literary Supplement*, 31 August 2012, provides decisive evidence that Edward Thomas's first poem, discovered in his notebooks in the Berg Collection at New York Public Library, was written in September 1913, a month before he met Robert Frost in the restaurant in St Martin's Lane.

Jacek Wiśniewski, *Edward Thomas: A Mirror of England* (2009), and Keith Clark, *The Muse Colony: Rupert Brooke, Edward Thomas, Robert Frost and Friends – Dymock, 1914* (1992), are two other books that I've found helpful. A useful summary of 1914's weather is given by John Kington in *Climate and Weather* (2010).

For Rupert Brooke in 1914, see *The Letters of Rupert Brooke*, edited by Geoffrey Keynes (1968), and Nigel Jones, *Rupert Brooke: Life, Death and Myth* (1999), which goes a long way towards replacing Christopher Hassall's more timid *Rupert Brooke: A Biography* (1964).

Summer Mayhem

George Pike's Buckingham Palace break-in has all but disappeared from the accounts of the period. It has been reconstructed from contemporary newspaper reports, e.g., *Morning Post*, 8 June 1914.

In addition to newspaper reports, information about the suffragettes' deputation to Buckingham Palace may be found in E. S. [Sylvia] Pankhurst, *The Suffragette Movement: An Intimate Account of Persons and Ideals* (1931), June Purvis, *Emmeline Pankhurst: A Biography* (2002), and Martin Pugh, *The Pankhursts* (2001).

Carrie Kipling's remarks about the Blomfield incident are taken from the copies, made by C. E. Carrington, of extracts from her diaries at the University of Sussex Special Collections, Book 3, 1914–1918, ff. 11 1/11. See also Kirsty McLeod, *The Last*

Summer (1983). The Peace Ball is described in Maud Warrender, *My First Sixty Years* (1933). Lord Selborne's observations about Blomfield and his account of his meeting with George V are taken from his letters to his wife Maud, at Bodleian MS Selborne 1012. Philip Snowdon's comment at the Birmingham meeting is quoted by C. J. Bearman in 'An Examination of Suffragette Violence', *English Historical Review*, 120 (2005).

On Sarajevo, David Stevenson, *1914–1918: The History of the First World War* (2005), gives an excellent account of the assassination and its fallout. Martin Gilbert's *The First World War* (1994) is a valuable introduction to Sarajevo and the ensuing crisis. D. C. Watt, 'The British Reactions to the Assassination at Sarajevo', *European Studies Review*, 3 (1971), is an interesting study of the development of British opinion of the murder through the press. H. Wickham Steed's recollections of the impact of the event at *The Times* are contained in his *Through Thirty Years 1892–1922* (1924). George Cecil's letter to his mother, Violet, requesting that she buy a print of the murdered Archduke, is at Bodleian Violet Milner Papers 27. Edith Sellers's article, 'The Murdered Archduke', was published in the August 1914 issue of *Nineteenth Century and After*. Edmund Gosse's account, 'What I Saw and Heard: July–August 1914' (revised and completed 16 October 1914), is at BL Ashley 5738.

The Earl of Crawford's letters and diaries have been published as *The Crawford Papers. The Journals of David Lindsay, twenty-seventh Earl of Crawford and tenth Earl of Balcarres, 1871–1940, during the years 1892 to 1940*, edited by John Vincent (1984). Count Harry Kessler's diaries, *Journey to the Abyss: The Diaries of Count Harry Kessler 1880–1918*, are edited and translated by Laird M. Easton (2011). Winston Churchill's words are from *The World Crisis 1911–1914* (1923).

Recoiling from the Abyss

Sir Edward Grey's personal and political life in 1914 is well covered by Keith Robbins, *Sir Edward Grey: A Biography of Lord Grey of Fallodon* (1971), supplemented by G. M. Trevelyan's respectful *Grey of Fallodon* (1937). Grey's contented existence at Itchen Abbas is the subject of *The Cottage Book. The Undiscovered Country Diary of an Edwardian Statesman: Sir Edward Grey*, edited and introduced by Michael Waterhouse (1999). This country diary was originally privately printed in 1909, after Dorothy Grey's death, for a small group of friends as testimony to the happiness they had enjoyed together at their Hampshire retreat. *Capital of Happiness: Lord Grey of Fallodon and the Charm of Birds*, selected and introduced by Jan Karpinski (1984), considers Grey's ornithological enthusiasm against the background of his life at Itchen Abbas.

On the Foreign Office in 1914, see Zara S. Steiner, *The Foreign Office and Foreign Policy 1898–1914* (1969). On Grey's foreign policy, *British Foreign Policy under Sir*

Edward Grey, edited by F. H. Hinsley (1977), is an outstanding collection of essays. Douglas Hurd's chapter on Grey in *Choose Your Weapons: The British Foreign Secretary – 200 Years of Argument, Success and Failure* (2010) provides a helpful introduction from the vantage point of a later incumbent of the office of Foreign Secretary.

Unravelling the complex reasons behind Europe's decision to go to war in August 1914 is the subject of *Decisions for War 1914*, edited by Keith Wilson (1995). I found the essays 'Germany' by John C. G. Röhl and 'Britain' by Keith Wilson especially helpful. Britain's position is also examined in Keith Robbins, 'Britain in the Summer of 1914' in *Politicians, Diplomacy and War in Modern British History* (1994). A more popular study of the fateful lead-up to war is George Malcolm Thomson's *The Twelve Days: 24 July to 4 August 1914* (1964). Prince Lichnowsky's ignorance of Berlin's plans is excused in his autobiography, *Heading for the Abyss: Reminiscences* (1928). Herbert Samuel's comment is quoted in Cameron Hazlehurst, *Politicians at War, July to May 1915: A Prologue to the Triumph of Lloyd George* (1971), an invaluable study based on a wide range of archival sources.

Geoffrey Marcus, *Before the Lamps Went Out* (1965), contains a useful survey of press reaction to the developing European Crisis, while Patrick Esposito's 'Public Opinion and the Outbreak of the First World War: Germany, Austria-Hungary, and the War in the Newspapers of Northern England', unpublished M.St. thesis, Oxford 1996, offers a more unusual, less metropolitan perspective on the subject.

Katherine Isherwood's remarks are quoted in Christopher Isherwood's *Kathleen and Frank* (1971); Dorothy Holman's diary is at the Devon Record Office and is quoted in Catriona Pennell, *A Kingdom United: Popular Responses to the Outbreak of the First World War in Britain and Ireland* (2012). The diary of Kate, Lady Courtney of Penwith, *Extracts from a Diary during the War*, was privately printed in 1927; there is a copy at Liddle.

Mary Coules's diary is at IWM. Hallie Eustace Miles published her diary as *Untold Tales of War-Time London: A Personal Diary* (1930). The diaries of Bessie Rayne and Clement Webb are at Bodleian. Georgina Lee's diary has been published as *Home Fires Burning: The Great War Diaries of Georgina Lee*, edited by Gavin Roynon (2006).

Wilfrid Scawen Blunt's conviction of an imminent declaration of neutrality is from *My Diaries: Being a Personal Narrative of Events 1888–1914*, Volume 2 (1920). The Archbishop of Canterbury's letter to the Kaiser's Chief Chaplain is from *Randall Davidson, Archbishop of Canterbury* by G. K. A. Bell (1935).

On the reaction of Anglican clergy to the possibility of war, see Adrian Gregory, *The Last Great War: British Society and the First World War* (2008).

S. C. Joad's recollections of two Midlands meetings on 2 August are at Liddle. Edmund Gosse's account of the Trafalgar Square rally is from his 'What I Saw and Heard, July–August 1914': BL Ashley 5738.

Bank Holiday

Mabel Rudkin's description of Bank Holidays is taken from her book *Inside Dover 1914–1918: A Woman's Impressions* (1933). Agnes Smithson's recollections are at Liddle.

Ethel Beatty's observations about London on 3 August are from *The Beatty Papers. Volume I: 1902–1918 – Selections from the Private and Official Correspondence of Admiral of the Fleet Earl Beatty*, edited by Bryan Ranft (1989).

On cinema in 1914, see *The Big Show: British Cinema Culture in the Great War 1914–1918* by Michael Hammond (2006).

Christopher Addison's remarks about Grey's speech are from the first volume of his *Four and a Half Years: A Personal Diary from June 1914 to January 1919* (1934). Arnold Rowntree's note to his wife is included in *The Letters of Arnold Stephenson Rowntree to Mary Katherine Rowntree 1910–1918* (2002). Beatrice Webb's view of Grey's speech is from her diary: *The Diary of Beatrice Webb. Volume III: 'The Power to Alter Things'*, edited by Norman MacKenzie and Jeanne MacKenzie (1984). George V's diary entry for 3 August is quoted in Catriona Pennell, *A Kingdom United: Popular Responses to the Outbreak of the First World War in Britain and Ireland* (2012).

Grey's famous remark about 'The lamps are going out . . .' first appeared in Grey (with J. A. Spender), *Twenty-five Years 1892–1916* (1925).

Ada Reece's extraordinary diary is at Liddle. Ada Eleanor Reece, née Perkins, was born in 1867. She died in 1968, having kept a diary, largely uninterrupted, throughout the twentieth century up to the decade of her death. In 1894 she married Dr Richard James Reece (1862–1924), an epidemiologist and sanitarian, and later a senior medical officer at the Ministry of Health. They had two sons and two daughters. See the obituary of Richard Reece in the *British Medical Journal*, 3 May 1924.

The issuing of paper money is dealt with by Thomas Johnston in *The Financiers and the Nation* (1934).

On the general question of 'war enthusiasm' in August 1914, and the revisionist argument that the mood of excitement of the British public has been exaggerated, see Adrian Gregory, *The Last Great War: British Society and the First World War* (2008), and Gregory's earlier article, 'British "War Enthusiasm" in 1914: A Reassessment' in *Evidence, History and the Great War: Historians and the Impact of 1914–1918*, edited by Gail Braybon (2003). See also Hartmut Pogge von Strandmann, 'The Mood in Britain in 1914' in *The Legacies of Two World Wars: European Societies in the Twentieth Century*, edited by Lothar Kettenacker and Torsten Riotte (2011).

Irene Cooper Willis's memories are from her *England's Holy War: A Study of English Liberal Idealism during the Great War* (1920). Reverend James Mackay's recollections are at IWM, those of R. W. M. Gibbs at Bodleian.

The resolution of the villagers of Holmfirth in favour of Britain's neutrality is from Cyril Pearce, *Comrades in Conscience: The Story of an English Community's Opposition to the Great War* (2001).

Details of the first Glastonbury Festival are derived from *Rutland Boughton and the Glastonbury Festivals* by Michael Hurd (1993).

Three: August to December

Two recent books, which challenge common assumptions about reactions to the outbreak of war in Britain, and to the war's early phases, have been especially helpful. They are Adrian Gregory, *The Last Great War: British Society and the First World War* (2008), and Catriona Pennell, *A Kingdom United: Popular Responses to the Outbreak of the First World War in Britain and Ireland* (2012).

Among older works, Arthur Marwick's *The Deluge: British Society and the First World War* (1965) is still valuable, while Trevor Wilson, *The Myriad Faces of War: Britain and the Great War 1914–1918* (1986), remains the standard work on the British experience of the war. In a lighter vein, E. S. Turner's *Dear Old Blighty* (1980) is an engaging study of Britain's First World War home front.

I am also indebted to Kit Good's unpublished Ph.D. thesis, 'England goes to war 1914–1915', University of Liverpool (2002), for a number of references in provincial newspapers to food and anti-German riots, Belgian refugees and the spy scare.

A Different World

John Galsworthy's diary is quoted in H. V. Marrot, *Life and Letters of John Galsworthy* (1935). David Robson's comments are at IWM; Elsie Stephens's are quoted in Stuart Dalley, 'The Response in Cornwall to the Outbreak of the First World War', *Cornish Studies*, 11 (2003); Mrs A. Purbrook's are at IWM.

Dorothy Holman's diary is at the Devon Record Office and is quoted in Catriona Pennell, *A Kingdom United: Popular Responses to the Outbreak of the First World War in Britain and Ireland* (2012). The reactions of Mary Lees's cook are at IWM; Beatrice McCann's postman's efforts to get the news to her are recorded at Liddle. Irene Rankin's recollections are also at Liddle, as are those of Lucian Hunt and A. D. Gardner. William Johnson's account of his ignorance of war on his return from holiday is contained in his papers at IWM.

Frederick Robinson's diary is at IWM. On railways in the early part of the war, see Adrian Gregory, 'Railway stations: gateways and termini' in *Capital Cities at War: Paris, London, Berlin 1914–1919. Volume 2: A Cultural History*, edited by Jay Winter and Jean-Louis Robert (2007). James Mackay's observations of departing soldiers are at IWM.

Beatrice Trefusis's diaries are at Liddle. William Pead's are at IWM. On the army's requisition of horses, see John Singleton, 'Britain's Military Use of Horses',

Past and Present, 139 (1993). The story of Freda Hewlett's pony is recounted in the *Daily Mail*, 11 February 2012.

Will Eaves's report of the trenches is quoted in Catriona Pennell, *A Kingdom United* (2012). Gladys Cruickshank's description is at Bodleian.

John Burns on the London blackout is from his diary at BL Add. MSS 46332. W. W. Collins's letter to his brother is at Liddle. Michael MacDonagh's diary was published as *In London during the Great War* (1935).

John Galsworthy's description of the beauty of 1914's Indian Summer is contained in his short story 'Told by the Schoolmaster', reprinted in *The Penguin Book of First World War Stories*, edited by Barbara Korte and Ann-Marie Einhaus (2007). Robert Bridges's remarks are from *The Selected Letters of Robert Bridges: With the Correspondence of Robert Bridges and Lionel Muirhead*, edited by Donald E. Stanford (1982–4), Katherine Mansfield's from *The Collected Letters of Katherine Mansfield. Volume 1: 1903–1917*, edited by Vincent O'Sullivan and Margaret Scott (1984).

On war posters in general, see Philip Dutton, 'Moving Images? The Parliamentary Recruiting Committee's Poster Campaign', *Imperial War Museum Review*, 4 (1989). On the early rush to the colours, see Peter Simkins, *Kitchener's Army: The Raising of the New Armies 1914–1916* (1988).

Frederick Oliver's letter to his brother is from *The Anvil of War: Letters between F. S. Oliver and His Brother (William Edgar Oliver) 1914–1918*, edited by Stephen Gwynn (1936).

The diaries of the Kensington woman, remarking on food hoarding, and that of Miss G. West are at IWM.

Winifred Towers's diary is at IWM.

For my description of Wells's and West's relationship, I have found much of interest in Gordon Ray's *H. G. Wells and Rebecca West* (1974). Wells's letters for 1914 are to be found in *The Correspondence of H. G. Wells. Volume 2: 1904–1918*, edited by David C. Smith (1998). Other biographical works I have drawn on are Norman and Jeanne MacKenzie, *Time Traveller: The Life of H. G. Wells* (1973); Anthony West, *H. G. Wells: Aspects of a Life* (1984); David C. Smith, *H. G. Wells: Desperately Mortal* (1986); and Michael Sherborne, *H. G. Wells: Another Kind of Life* (2010).

Wells's *Mr Britling Sees It Through* (1916) is now among his lesser known works of fiction. However, when it was published in 1916, it revived Wells's flagging reputation and quickly became a bestseller, going through thirteen reprintings in Britain within four months of publication. The novel is a thinly veiled piece of autobiography – for instance, its attractive and clever sisters, Cecily and Letty, are portraits of Rebecca West (whose real name was Cecily) and her sister Letitia – and an attempt to chart Wells's own shifting attitudes towards the war. For anyone interested in England in 1914, *Mr Britling Sees It Through* is highly recommended.

It is possible to read *The War That Will End War* online at http://archive.org/stream/warthatwillendwa00welluoft#page/no/mode/2up.

On the entertainment world's war effort, see Samuel Hynes's *A War Imagined: The First World War and English Culture* (1990). See also L. J. Collins, *Theatre at War 1914–1918* (1998).

D. G. Wright, 'The Great War, Government Propaganda and English Men of Letters 1914–1916', *Literature and History*, 7 (1978), is an invaluable study of writers' responses to the war.

Lionel Gibbs's letter to George Bell is at Lambeth, as is the text of Randall Davidson's sermon. The letter from Major D. G. Johnson's wife is among the Johnson Papers at Liddle.

Ada McGuire's letter to her sister is at IWM. Rudyard Kipling's to his publisher is from *The Letters of Rudyard Kipling*, Volume 4, edited by Thomas Pinney (1999).

On the Belgian Refugee Depot in London at Earls Court, see the report in the *British Nursing Journal*, 23 October 1914.

Archbishop Cosmo Gordon Lang's letter to Lord Robert Cecil about the length of the war is at BL Add. MSS 51154. Vera Brittain's letter is from *Letters from a Lost Generation: First World War Letters of Vera Brittain and Four Friends*, edited by Alan Bishop and Mark Bostridge (1998). Irma McLeod's remarks are at Liddle. Walter Hines Page's comment is quoted in Caroline E. Playne, *Society at War 1914– 1916* (1931).

All the King's Men

The major work on white feather recruitment, which has been invaluable here, is Nicoletta F. Gullace, *The Blood of Our Sons: Men, Women and the Renegotiation of British Citizenship during the Great War* (2003). See also Gullace's earlier article, 'White Feathers and Wounded Men: Female Patriotism and the Memory of the Great War', *Journal of British Studies*, 36 (1997).

Charles Penrose Fitzgerald's belief in the need for conscription is stated in his *From Sail to Steam* (1916). Macleod Yearsley's unpublished memoir is at IWM.

Iris Holt's letter is at Liddle. Compton Mackenzie's view of women handing out white feathers is contained in his *My Life and Times: Octave Four 1907–1915* (1964).

A copy of Frank Pettingell's musical monologue is at IWM. Details of the Devon men involved in white feather campaigns are from Bonnie J. White, 'Volunteerism and Early Recruitment Efforts in Devonshire, August 1914–December 1915', *Historical Journal*, 52 (2009).

The seminal work on recruitment in 1914, which provides an essential guide, is Peter Simkins, *Kitchener's Army: The Raising of the New Armies 1914–1916* (1988).

James Brady's recollections of the news from Mons, and Alexander Thompson's letter, are at IWM. Andrew Buxton's letter is from *Andrew R. Buxton: The Rifle Brigade – A Memoir*, edited by Edward S. Woods (1918).

Jimmy Carpenter's experiences of enlistment and training are from 'Jimmy Carpenter's War Diary. Part One', edited by Peter Mealyer and Colin Hague, *Stand To!*, 72 (2005).

On the general background to farm workers' responses to recruitment, see Nicholas Mansfield, *English Farmworkers and Local Patriotism 1900–1930* (2001). Cornwall's poor recruitment record is examined in Stuart Dalley, 'The Response in Cornwall to the Outbreak of the First World War', *Cornish Studies*, 11 (2003), Devon's in Bonnie J. White, 'Volunteerism and Early Recruitment Efforts in Devonshire, August 1914–December 1915', *Historical Journal*, 52 (2009). John Hartigan's article, 'Volunteering in the First World War: The Birmingham Experience, August 1914–May 1915', *Midland History*, 24 (1999), usefully employs evidence from Birmingham to show the impact of a variety of factors – the economy, the pals' movement, propaganda and other psychological pressures – on volunteering. David Silbey's *The British Working Class and Enthusiasm for War 1914–1916* (2005) is an ambitious, though not always convincing, attempt to explain working-class motivation in 1914 for joining up.

The letter to J. E. B. Gray is at IWM. *Leeds Pals* by Laurie Milner (revised edition 1998) provides a detailed account of one community's recruiting drive.

Edward Thomas's essays 'Tipperary' and 'It's a Long, Long Way', noting the reactions around the country of ordinary people to the war, are reprinted in *The Last Sheaf* (1928).

I was alerted to Arnold Bennett's story 'The White Feather: A Sketch of English Recruiting' by George Simmers's blog on his website 'Great War Fiction': http://greatwarfiction.wordpress.com/.

Bruce Baily's remarks are from a letter to his father at IWM; Edward Robinson's are quoted in Laurie Milner's *Leeds Pals*.

Mrs Tully's written comment at the top of her son Linster's letter is at Liddle. William Orchard's letter is at IWM.

Dim Fading Hope

The final lines from the last stanza of Rudyard Kipling's 'The Children' are from *Rudyard Kipling's Verse: Definitive Edition* (1940).

The discovery of the grave is described in *'Fifteen Rounds a Minute': The Grenadiers at War, August to December 1914. Edited from the Diaries and Letters of Major 'Ma' Jeffreys and Others* by J. M. Craster (1976).

Letters and diaries relating to George Cecil are from the Violet Milner Papers at Bodleian. Biographical information about George and his parents is to be found in Hugh and Mirabel Cecil, *Imperial Marriage: An Edwardian War and Peace* (2002), and in Kenneth Rose, *The Later Cecils* (1975).

The Wounded and Missing Enquiry Bureau is the subject of Eric F. Schneider's article 'The British Red Cross Wounded and Missing Enquiry Bureau: A Case of Truth-Telling in the Great War', *War in History*, 4 (1997).

On the aristocracy's rush to war, see Gerald Gliddon, *The Aristocracy and the Great War* (2002).

Lord Hugh Cecil's letter to the Archbishop of Canterbury is at Lambeth. Mary Drew's remarks about the casualty list are contained in *Mary Gladstone (Mrs Drew): Her Diaries and Letters*, edited by Lucy Masterman (1930). R. D. Blumenfeld's diary is quoted in R. D. Blumenfeld, *All in a Lifetime* (1931).

On Binyon's 'For the Fallen', see John Hatcher, *Laurence Binyon: Poet, Scholar of East and West* (1995). The dating of Binyon's poem has never been established precisely, and I differ from Hatcher in suggesting that 'For the Fallen' may reflect the publication of the first casualty lists following the retreat from Mons.

The story of John Kipling's war is told by Tonie and Valmai Holt in *My Boy Jack: The Search for Kipling's Only Son* (1998). Kipling's attitude to the war and to his son's enlistment is discussed by David Bradshaw in 'Kipling and War', *The Cambridge Companion to Rudyard Kipling*, edited by Howard J. Booth (2011).

Kipling's efforts to uncover the truth about George Cecil's death are related in *The Letters of Rudyard Kipling*, Volume 4, edited by Thomas Pinney (1999).

Pat Jalland has written a moving and illuminating chapter about Violet Cecil's search for her missing son, and about the way in which Violet was able to offer consolation to the families of working-class soldiers who had served with George, in her *Death in War and Peace: A History of Loss and Grief in England 1914–1970* (2010).

A Country Parish in Wartime

Olive May Taylor's recollections are at IWM. Bessie Rayne's diary is at Bodleian. Miss E. Barkworth's diary is discussed by Adrian Gregory, *The Last Great War: British Society and the First World War* (2008). Frederick Robinson's diary is at IWM.

Andrew Clark's diary is at Bodleian MSS Eng. hist. e. 88–177c. It runs from August 1914 to December 1919, and was presented to the library between 1915 and 1920. Clark died in 1922.

Selections from the diary were published as *Echoes of the Great War: the Diary of the Reverend Andrew Clark 1914–1919*, edited by James Munson (1985). I am heavily indebted to Munson's excellent introduction, which draws in part on the memories of surviving Great Leighs villagers who had lived through the war, for much of my background information about Clark and Great Leighs. Regrettably, this selection has fallen out of print and deserves to be republished.

Trevor Wilson, *The Myriad Faces of War: Britain and the Great War 1914–1918* (1986), includes an interesting chapter about the diary.

On the Tritton family, see J. H. Tritton, *Tritton: The Place and the Family* (1907). For J. H. Tritton's address to the Institute of Bankers, see *Journal of the Institute of Bankers*, November 1886.

Andrew Clark's 'English Words in War-Time' for 1914 are at Bodleian MSS Eng. misc. c. 265–7. Lynda Mugglestone, 'Andrew Clark, the *OED* and the Language of the First World War' in *Current Issues in Late Modern English*, edited by Ingrid Tieken-Boon van Ostade and Wim Van Der Wurff (2009), assesses the significance of the project.

A Spy in Every Stranger

For accounts of Carl Hans Lody's execution, see Sidney Felstead, *German Spies at Bay: Being an Actual Record of the German Espionage in Great Britain during the Years 1914–1918, Compiled from Official Sources* (1920), and Leonard Sellers, *Shot in the Tower: The Story of the Spies Executed in the Tower of London during the First World War* (2009). The record of Lody's death sentence is at NA/WO 71/1236. Nigel Jones, *Tower: An Epic History of the Tower of London* (2011), provides further details of the location of the place of execution.

On the official rounding-up of spies, see Christopher Andrew, *Secret Service: The Making of the British Intelligence Community* (1986), and two articles by N. P. Hiley which counter Andrews's assertions about the success of British operations against German espionage: 'The Failure of British Counter-Espionage against Germany 1907–1914', *Historical Journal*, 28 (1985) and 'Counter Espionage and Security in Great Britain during the First World War', *English Historical Review*, 400 (1986).

On real spies versus those existing in people's imaginations, see David French, 'Spy Fever in Britain 1900–1915', *Historical Journal*, 21 (1978). Basil Thomson's observations about spy mania are from his *Queer People* (1922).

On secret visual codes, see James Fox, ' "Traitor painters": artists and espionage in the First World War 1914–18', *British Art Journal*, 9 (2009). Gladys Dolby New's recollections are at Liddle.

Ralph Vaughan Williams's experience is described by Ursula Vaughan Williams, *R. V. W.: A Biography of Ralph Vaughan Williams* (1964). Cecil Forester's diary is at Liddle.

Florence Schuster's remarks are from her diary at Liddle. G. S. Stevens's letter to the Lord Lieutenant of Devon is from the Devon Record Office, and is quoted in Catriona Pennell, *A Kingdom United: Popular Responses to the Outbreak of the First World War in Britain and Ireland* (2012).

On Karl Ernst's trial, see Robert Jackson, *Case for the Prosecution. A Biography of Sir Archibald Bodkin, Director of Public Prosecutions 1920–1930* (1962).

General D. G. Johnson's papers are at Liddle. For the attacks on Lord Haldane, see Richard Burdon Haldane, *An Autobiography* (1929). On Reginald McKenna's attitude to spy mania and internment, see Martin Farr, *Reginald McKenna: Financier among Statesmen 1863–1916* (2008). The impact of the attacks on Cosmo Gordon Lang for his pro-German remarks are described in J. G. Lockhart, *Cosmo Gordon Lang* (1949).

Cartoons by Alfred Leete of 'Schmidt the Spy' were published in book form in 1916 as *Schmidt the Spy and His Messages to Berlin*. In the same year, a film of the incompetent spy's misadventures, starring Lewis Sydney, was released in Britain.

Panikos Panayi, *The Enemy in Our Midst: Germans in Britain during the First World War* (1991), is a significant work which deals with legislation against 'the enemy within', including the policy of internment, and also analyses the causes of the anti-German riots in the autumn of 1914.

The life, arrest and trial of Carl Hans Lody is dealt with by Thomas Boghardt in *Spies of the Kaiser: German Covert Operations in Great Britain during the First World War* (2004), and by James Morton in *Spies of the First World War* (2010). See also the account of Lody's trial in Robert Jackson, *Case for the Prosecution. A Biography of Sir Archibald Bodkin, Director of Public Prosecutions 1920–1930* (1962). Originals and transcripts of Lody's incriminating telegrams and letters are at NA/WO 71/1236 and NA/HO 144/3324.

Bombardment

Official papers relating to the attacks on the East Coast include: NA/AIR 1/604/16/15/235 (details of casualties); NA/BT 102/27 (estimated figures of casualties and damage to property, compiled in 1920–22 by the Board of Trade's Reparation Claims Department); NA/CAB 45/262–4 (material on the raids on Scarborough and Hartlepool in the papers relating to the Official History of Naval Operations); NA/WO 32/5261–2 contains reports on the German bombardment of the coastal towns.

Mark Marsay, *Bombardment! The Day the East Coast Bled* (1999), is the fullest and most authoritative account of the events of 16 December 1914, containing many photographs and first-hand accounts of the attacks, including local newspaper reports and the testimony given at the inquests, as well as an index to the names of the victims. Marsay's work may be supplemented by F. Miller, *The Hartlepools and the Great War* (1920), J. M. Ward, *Dawn Raid: Bombardment of the Hartlepools, Wednesday, December 16th, 1914* (1989), and David Mould, *Remember Scarborough 1914* (1978).

Two fictional accounts of the bombardment of Scarborough are still worth reading. In *The Crowded Street* (1922), Winifred Holtby draws on her schoolgirl memories of the attack, as a pupil at Queen Margaret's School, Scarborough, to portray the shelling of the town as a defining moment in the life of her put-upon heroine, Muriel Hammond. In Osbert Sitwell's *Before the Bombardment* (1926), the German attack signals an abrupt ending to the security of the golden Edwardian age: 'death darted at her from the sea, and Mrs Waddington, and her bedroom with her, was pulverized, fading with a swift, raucous whistling and crashing into the murky air.'

Phyllis Lunn's account is at Liddle.

For an account of the attack on Great Yarmouth, see Richard van Emden and Steve Humphries, *All Quiet on the Home Front: An Oral History of Life in Britain during the First World War* (2003).

Katherine Alexander's diary is at Liddle. Arnold Bennett's remark is from *The Journals of Arnold Bennett. Volume 2: 1911–1921*, edited by Newman Flower (1932). C. S. Lewis's letter to his father is from his *Collected Letters. Volume 1: Family Letters 1905–1931* (2000). Leslie Craig's recollections are at Liddle.

Maurice Hankey's letter to the Archbishop of Canterbury, together with a copy of 'Preparations by civil authorities for action in the event of a hostile landing', can be found at Lambeth. Randall Davidson's letters to Asquith and to the Bishop of St Edmundsbury and Ipswich are also at Lambeth.

Sydney Cockerell's diary is at BL Add. MSS 52651.

Harold Cousins's diary and Ethel Bilsborough's are at IWM.

On the reaction nationally to the bombardment of the East Coast towns, see Troy R. E. Paddock, *A Call to Arms: Propaganda, Public Opinion and Newspapers in the Great War* (2004). Sylvia Pankhurst's observations are from her book *The Home Front: A Mirror to Life in England during the First World War* (1932). Edith Kemp-Welch's painting is displayed today in Scarborough Town Hall.

Alan Morton's letter to Iris Holt is at Liddle. Eleanor Acland's diary is quoted by Cameron Hazlehurst in *Politicians at War, July 1914 to May 1915: A Prologue to the Triumph of Lloyd George* (1971).

Not with a Bang but a Whimper

Charlotte Despard's diary is at the Public Record Office of Northern Ireland, and is quoted in Catriona Pennell, *A Kingdom United: Popular Responses to the Outbreak of the First World War in Britain and Ireland* (2012). Adam Hochschild's *To End All Wars: A Story of Protest and Patriotism in the First World War* (2011) includes a portrait of Despard's relationship with her younger brother, Sir John French.

The story of the depressed London man is told in James Cameron's *1914* (1959). The sinking of the *Rohilla* is the subject of Ken Wilson, *Wreck of the Rohilla* (1981), and Colin Brittain's *Into the Maelstrom: The Wreck of the H.M.H.S. Rohilla* (2002). There is British Pathé newsreel footage of the rescue of survivors from the *Rohilla* at http://www.britishpathe.com/video/hospital-ship-rohilla-aka-rescue-of-survivors-from.

The Magnificent Spilsbury and the Case of the Brides in the Bath by Jane Robins (2010) is a modern examination of this famous serial murder case.

Edward Thomas's essay 'England', which originally appeared in the *Nation*, was reprinted in the collection *The Last Sheaf* (1928).

Oswald Tilley's letter to his parents is quoted in Malcolm Brown and Shirley Seaton, *Christmas Truce: The Western Front, December 1914* (revised edition 1994), an excellent account of the unofficial peace.

On the German air threat to Britain, see Joseph Morris, *The German Air Raids on Great Britain 1914–1918* (1925), and Christopher Cole and E. F. Cheesman, *The Air Defence of Britain 1914–1918* (1984).

On the bombing of Dover, see Michael George and Christine George, *Dover and Folkestone during the Great War* (2008).

Randall Davidson's remark is at Lambeth. Evie Davies's letter to her husband is at IWM.

Background Information about England in 1914

Sources used include A. L. Bowley and A. R. Burnett-Hurst, *Livelihood and Poverty* (1915); A. L. Bowley, *Prices and Wages in the United Kingdom 1914–1920* (1921); *Census of England and Wales 1911. General Report* (1917); B. R. Mitchell, *British Historical Statistics* (1988); Maud Pember Reeves, *Round About a Pound a Week* (1913).

Acknowledgements

I am very grateful to the staff of libraries and archives responsible for conserving and providing access to the primary collections that make this kind of book possible: the British Library (especially the Newspaper Library during its last months at Colindale); the Bodleian Library, Oxford; the Imperial War Museum; Lambeth Palace Library; the Liddle Collection at the University of Leeds; the Museum of London; the National Archives at Kew; the National Gallery Archive; and the Heinz Archive at the National Portrait Gallery. I have also benefited enormously from the efficiency and professionalism of staff at the London Library.

I acknowledge my debts to the following individuals who made invaluable contributions to my research: Sorrel Bentinck, for describing her meeting, in 1961, with the suffragette Mary Richardson; Nikki Braunton; Hugh Cecil; George and Margaret Chapman, for generously providing me with a copy of their photograph of the Curzon Laundry's Bank Holiday outing in August 1914; Beverley Cook; Alan Crookham; Patrick Esposito, for going to great lengths to obtain a copy of his Master of Studies thesis for me; Rachel Foss at the British Library, for allowing me early access to the recently purchased Rupert Brooke–Cathleen Nesbitt correspondence; Kit Good, for permitting me to quote from various contemporary newspaper reports contained in his unpublished Ph.D. thesis; Chris Green, for giving me a conducted tour of Her Majesty's Theatre, and for allowing me to tread the boards where the first English production of Shaw's *Pygmalion* took place; Colin Harris, Superintendent of the Special Collections, and Helen Langley, Curator of Modern Political Papers, at the Bodleian; John Kington, of the Climatic Research Unit at the University of East Anglia, for advising me about England's weather in 1914; June Purvis, for answering enquiries about the suffragette movement in the months leading up to the war.

Friends have given me ideas and references, or offered practical or moral support. I would like to single out the following: Timothy J. Catlin, Daniel De Luca, Antonia Fraser (for jolly lunches), Lyndall and Siamon Gordon, Liz Hartford, David Horspool, Margaret and Alastair Howatson, Ghislaine and Nicholas Kenyon, Harry Mount, Pamela Norris and John Senter, Peter Parker, Claire Tomalin, Patricia Williams (for putting me up in Oxford while I worked at the Bodleian), Shirley Williams, Rebecca Williams, and Frances Wilson. Claire Harman has listened patiently to me talking about this book. I am extremely grateful for all the reassurance she has given me, and for her sage advice. Robin Baird-Smith, without whom nothing would be possible, or even worthwhile, sustained me throughout the final period of writing when illness – and building works – threatened progress.

Quotations from Margot Asquith's diaries are reproduced by kind permission of Christopher Oborn, the copyright holder, and the Bodleian Library. Quotations from Michael and Eleanor Brock's edition of *Letters to Venetia Stanley* (1982) are included by permission of Oxford University Press. James Munson has very kindly given me permission to reproduce two photographs from *Echoes of the Great War* (1985), his selections from the diary of the Reverend Andrew Clark, a memorable book, which first alerted me to the diary's existence. Every effort has been made to contact copyright holders, and the author and publisher would welcome information allowing them to rectify any sins of omission or commission.

Two books representing a significant revisionist break in the historiography of Britain's experience of the early months of war have given me valuable guidance, and I recommend them to readers who may wish to go deeper into the subject: *The Last Great War: British Society and the First World War* by Adrian Gregory (2008) and *A Kingdom United: Popular Responses to the Outbreak of the First World War in Britain and Ireland* by Catriona Pennell (2012).

At Viking Penguin, I have been extremely fortunate in my editor, Eleo Gordon, whose contribution and commitment to *The Fateful Year* have never flagged. She and I have been wonderfully supported by the inestimable Jillian Taylor. I am grateful, too, to Keith Taylor, Jenny Fry, Venetia Butterfield, Amelia Fairney, Ben Brusey, Robin Lord (an early reader) and Nicola Evans. Donna Poppy has been an outstanding copyeditor, saving me from several egregious errors. Dave Cradduck was responsible for the excellent index. Jonathan Chadwick designed the beautiful cover. My thanks to my agents, Simon Trewin at WME, and Georgina Gordon-Smith and Ariella Feiner at United Agents.

A very dear friend of mine died while I was in the midst of writing this book. His bravery and fortitude in battling a long and serious illness were no less remarkable than the courage displayed by the best of the generation of 1914. I leave a record of his name and lifespan here:

Christopher Honey
MCMLIX–MMXII

Index

Page numbers in *italic* indicate illustrations in the text. These are also listed, along with the inset plates, after the Contents.

MARK BOSTRIDGE won the Gladstone Memorial Prize at Oxford University. His first book, *Vera Brittain: A Life*, was shortlisted for the Whitbread Biography Prize, the NCR Non-Fiction Award, and the Fawcett Prize. His books also include the bestselling *Letters from a Lost Generation*; *Lives for Sale*, a collection of biographers' tales; *Because You Died*, a selection of Vera Brittain's First World War poetry and prose; and *Florence Nightingale: The Woman and Her Legend*, which was awarded the Elizabeth Longford Prize for Historical Biography, and named as a *Wall Street Journal* Best Book of 2008. He is currently consultant on the forthcoming feature film of Vera Brittain's *Testament of Youth*.